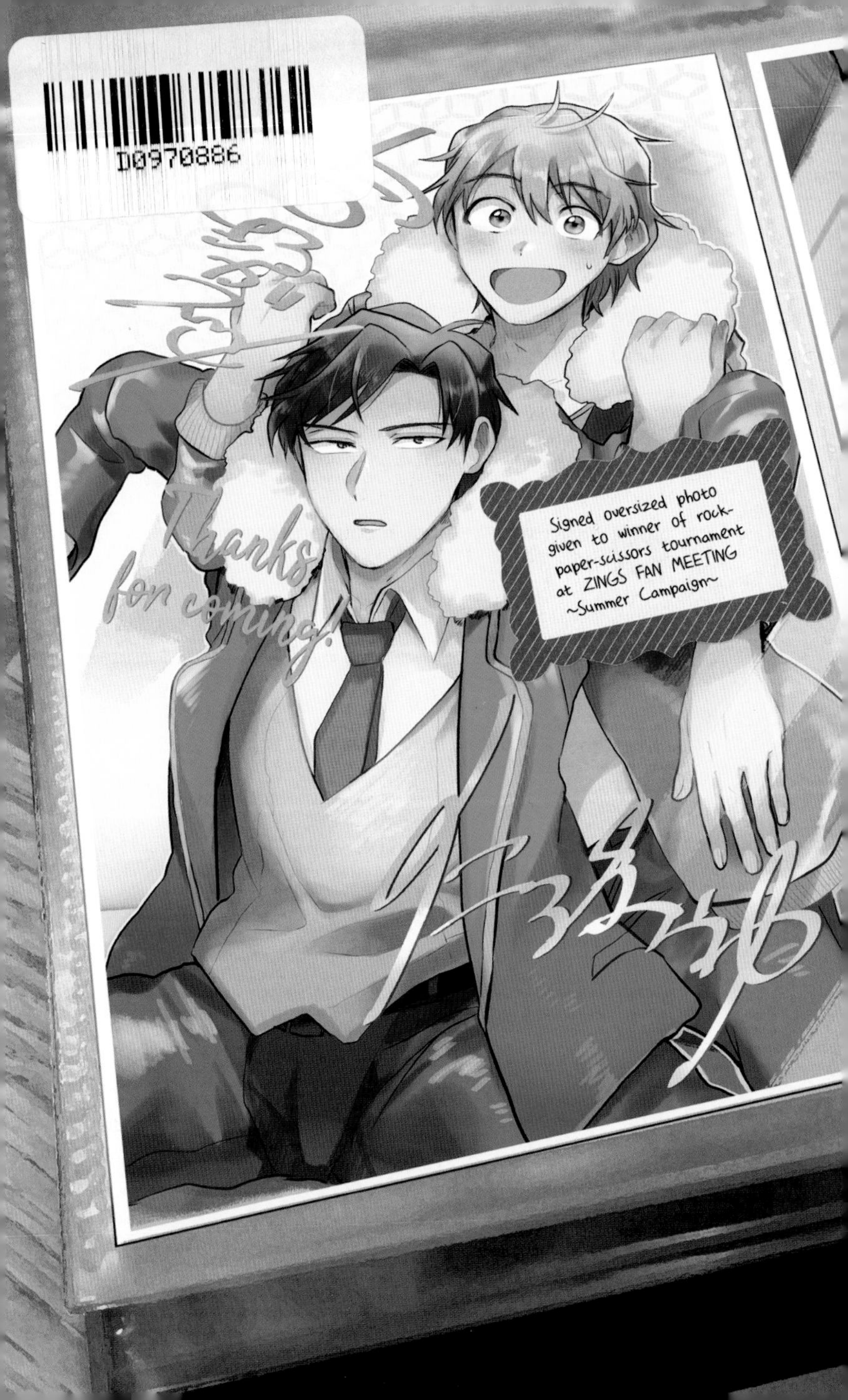
Thanks for coming!
Signed oversized photo given to winner of rock-paper-scissors tournament at ZINGS FAN MEETING ~Summer Campaign~

the flow

ving   Followers
         42

PHANTOM OF THE IDOL ☆ CONTENTS BOT
<<<-----SET 1---P.005---->>>

summer campaigner
Behold, comrades… Niyodo-kun is singing and dancing…

PHANTOM OF THE IDOL ☆ CONTENTS BOT
<<<-----SET 2---P.044---->>>

aya reborn
new zings song. dance video. im dying. watching it in emergency
stairwell at work. 30 times and counting #ZINGS

☆ 9

PHANTOM OF THE IDOL ☆ CONTENTS BOT
<<<-----SET 3---P.069---->>>

yumiko@winter campaign prep
Niyodo's all over the place lately. ¥1,000,000 says he's dead-eyed at
today's new release.

Q 4   ☆ 6

PHANTOM OF THE IDOL ☆ CONTENTS BOT
<<<-----SET 4---P.093---->>>

Kazuki Yoshino@See you at the mini concert!
Can you believe Yu-kun suggested we hang out?!
It's a first for ZINGS!!
We had cake. Surprising but a great time!

Q 24   ☆ 27

PHANTOM OF THE IDOL ☆ CONTENTS BOT
<<<-----SET 5---P.119---->>>

waaako
RT@kasenziki [PLEASE SHARE] I want everyone to know how great
my bias is #justlookatmybias

Q 64   ☆ 2

PHANTOM OF THE IDOL ☆ CONTENTS BOT
<<<-----SET 6---P.145---->>>

Yuya Niyodo's ladeh
according to the event reports Hottie Farm was crazy?!?!
should have gone even if it cost me my job

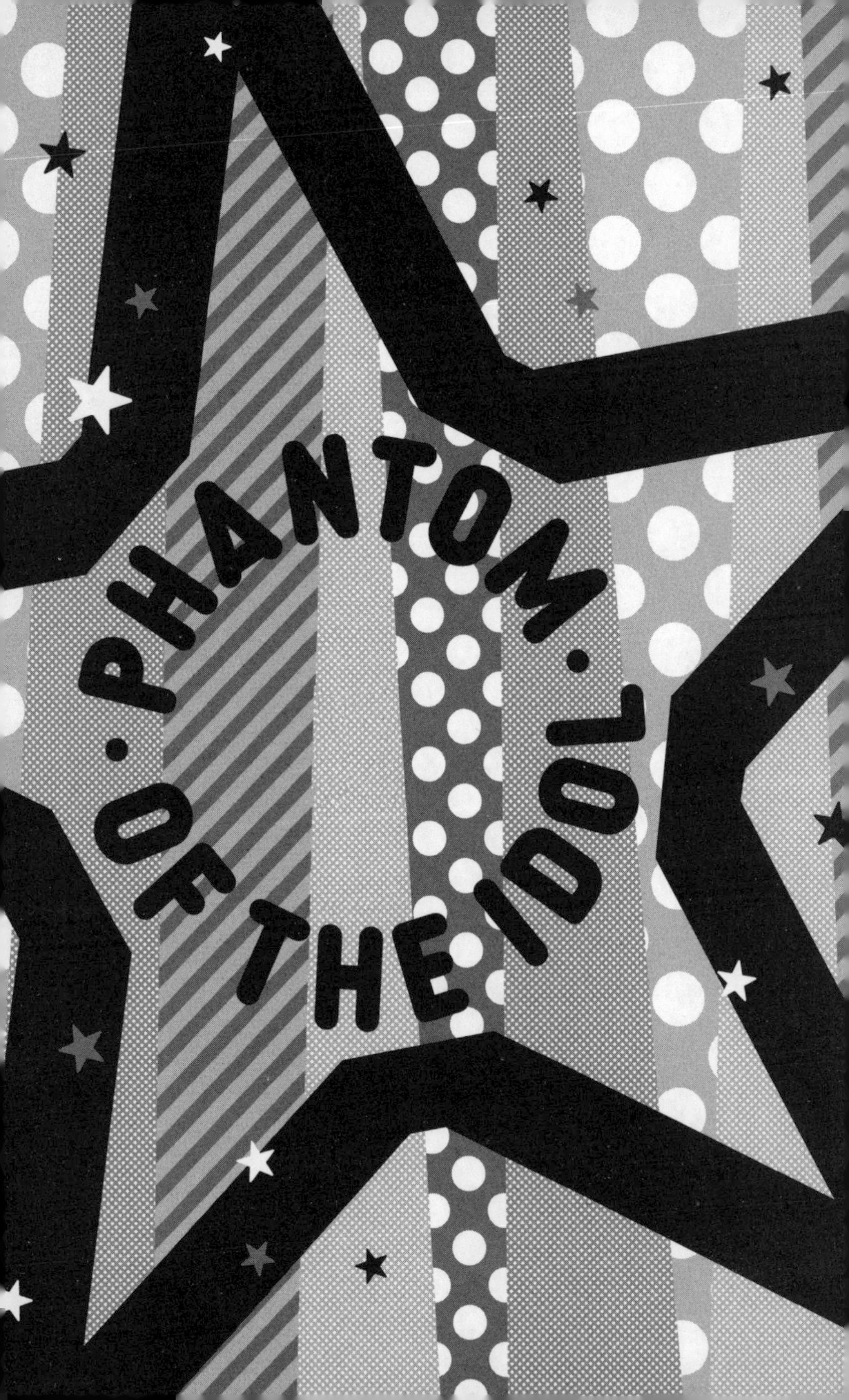
·PHANTOM·OF THE IDOL

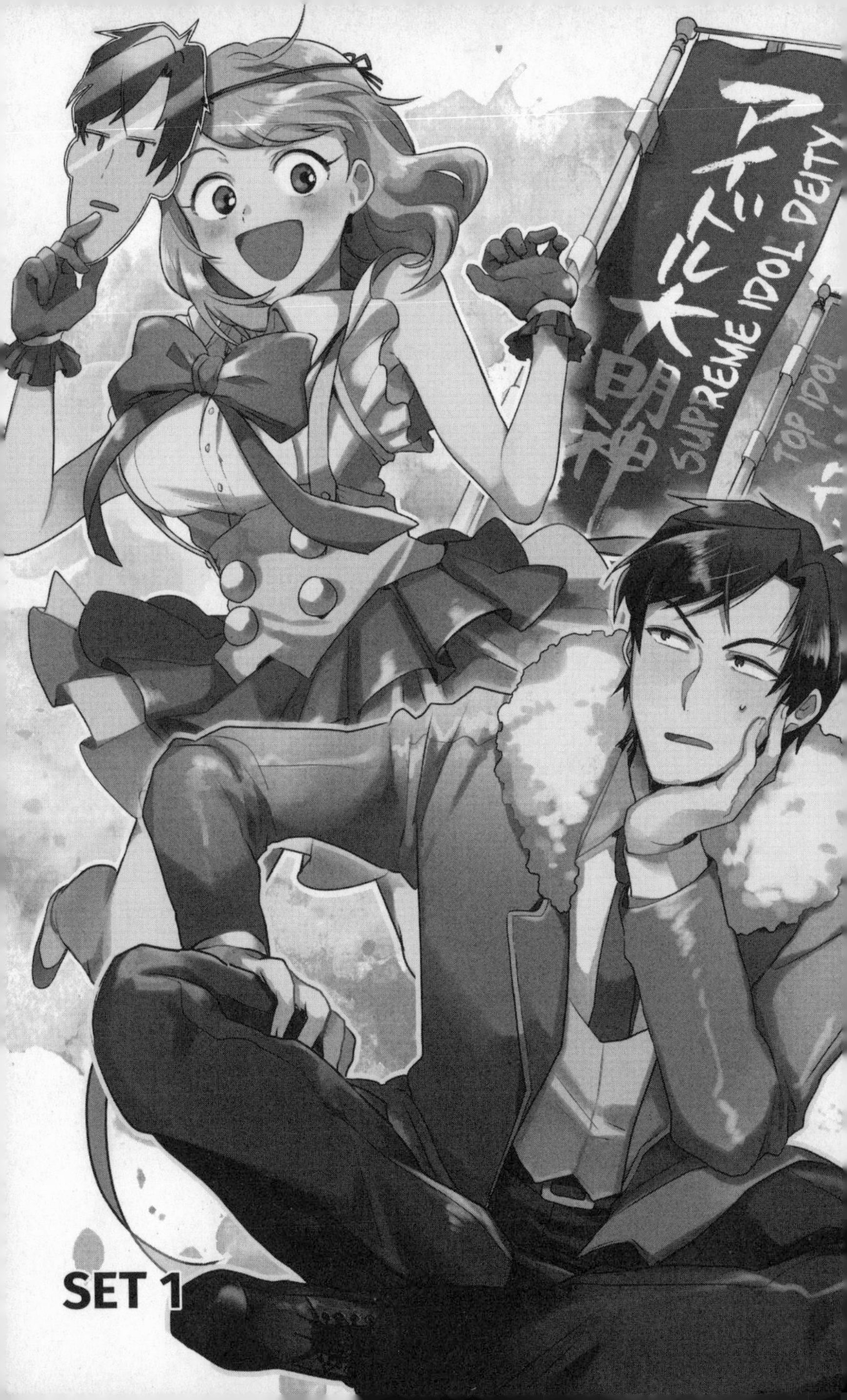
アイドル大明神
SUPREME IDOL DEITY
TOP IDOL

SET 1

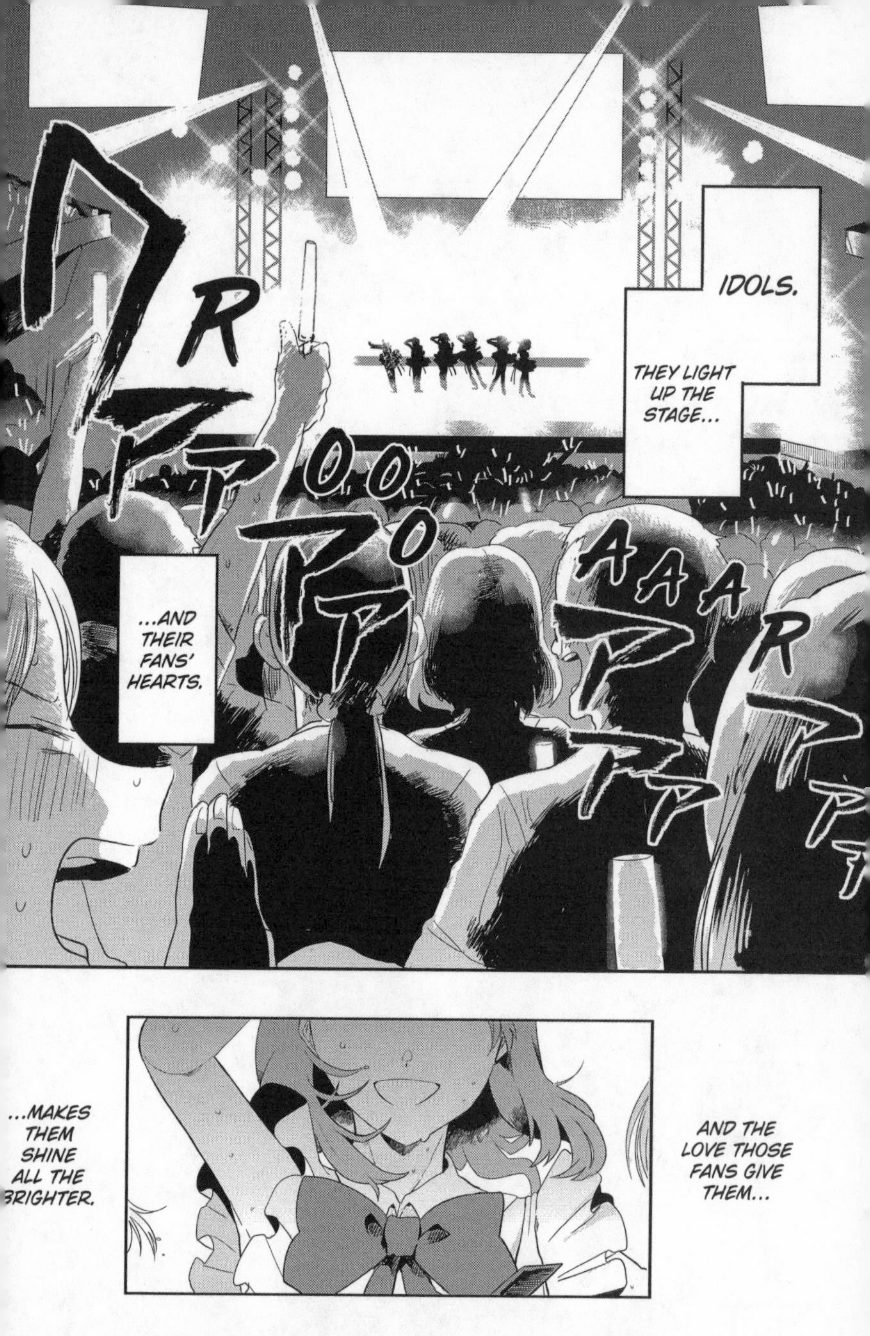
IDOLS.
THEY LIGHT UP THE STAGE...
...AND THEIR FANS' HEARTS.
AAAR
ROOO
AND THE LOVE THOSE FANS GIVE THEM...
...MAKES THEM SHINE ALL THE BRIGHTER.

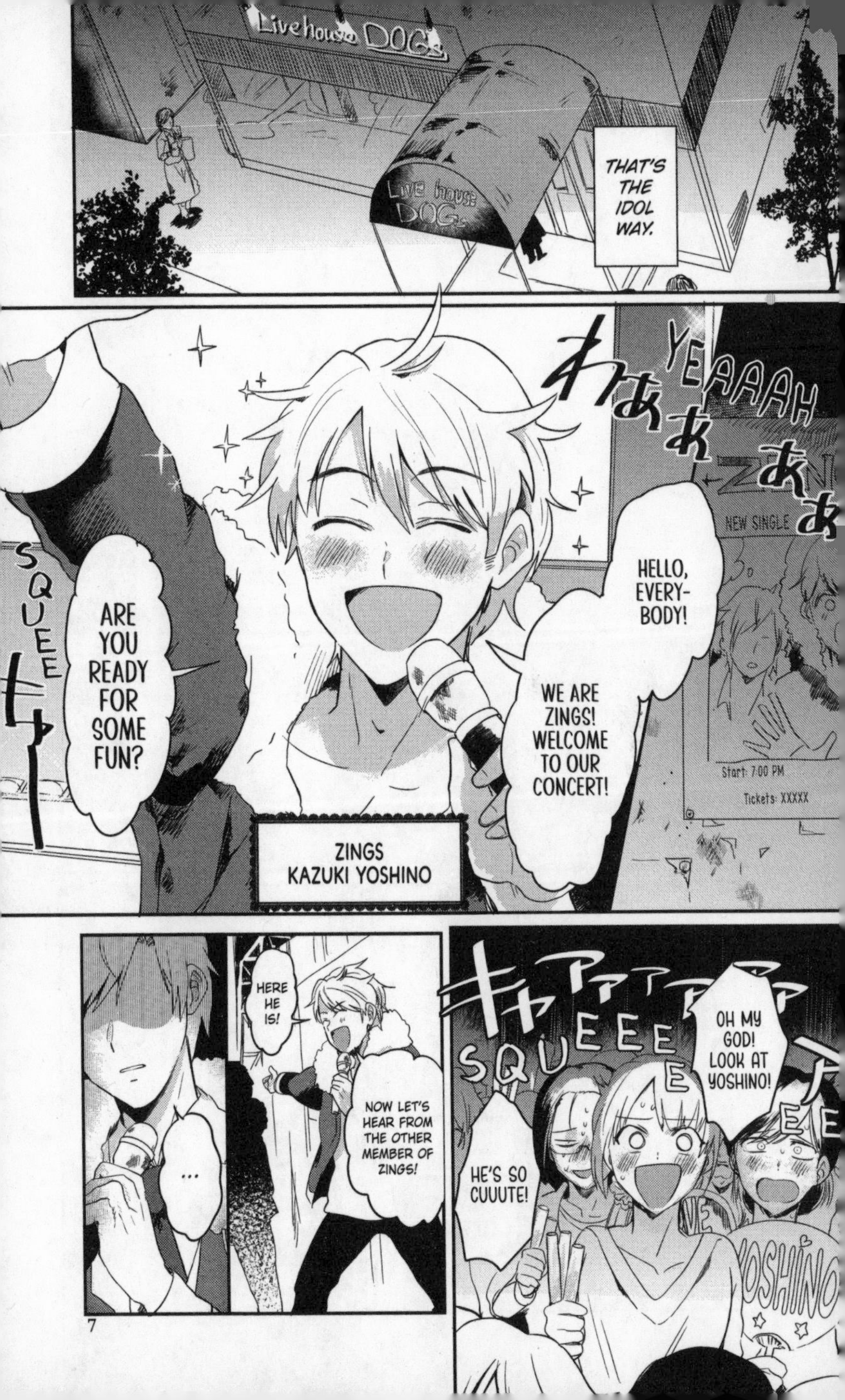
Livehouse DOGs
Live house DOGs
THAT'S THE IDOL WAY.
わあああああ
YEAAAAH
NEW SINGLE
Start: 7:00 PM
Tickets: XXXXX
HELLO, EVERY-BODY!
WE ARE ZINGS! WELCOME TO OUR CONCERT!
ZINGS KAZUKI YOSHINO
ARE YOU READY FOR SOME FUN?
キャー
SQUEEE
キャアアアアアア
SQUEEEEE
OH MY GOD! LOOK AT YOSHINO!
EE
HE'S SO CUUUTE!
YOSHINO
HERE HE IS!
NOW LET'S HEAR FROM THE OTHER MEMBER OF ZINGS!
...

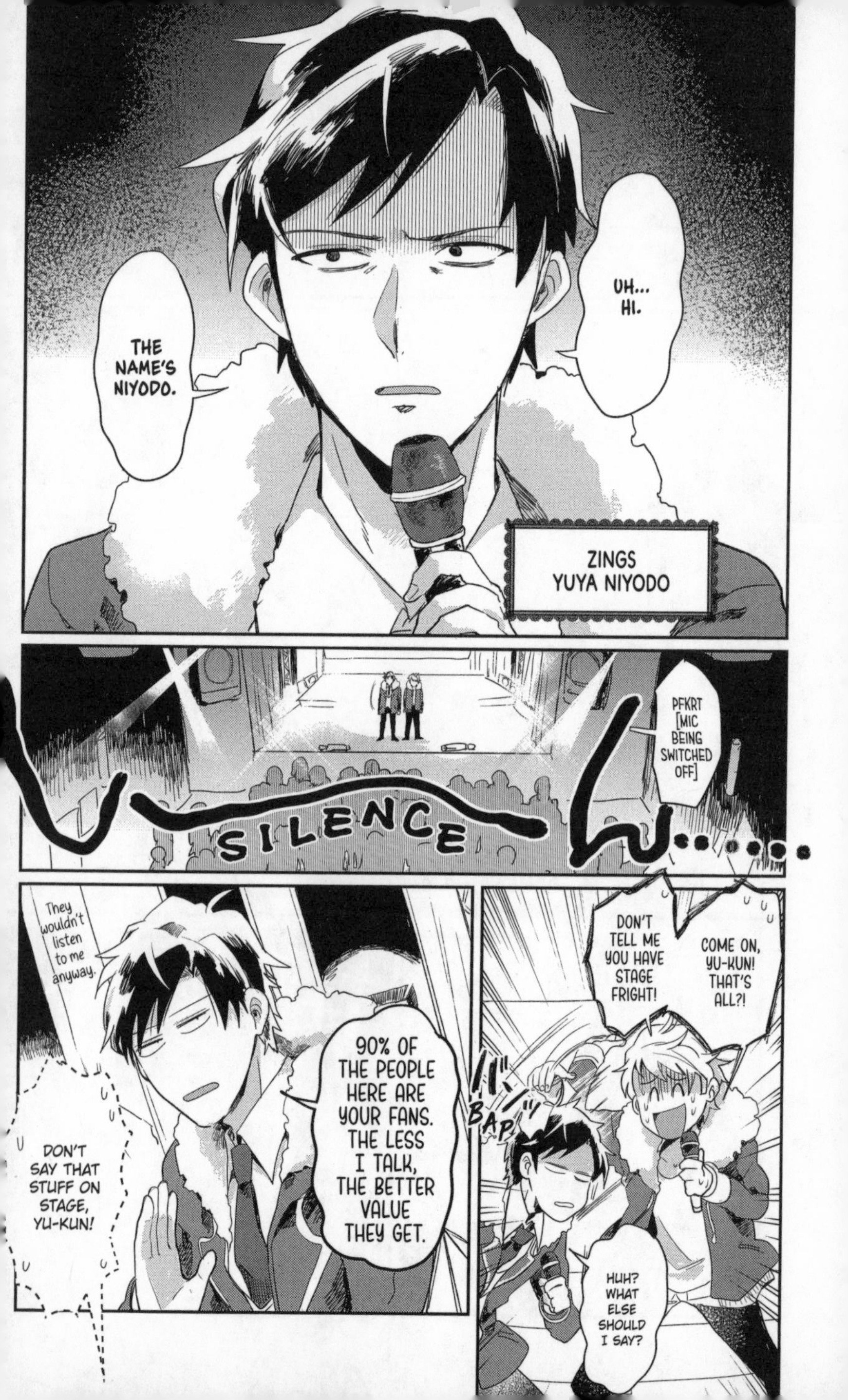
UH... HI.
THE NAME'S NIYODO.
ZINGS YUYA NIYODO
PFKRT [MIC BEING SWITCHED OFF]
SILENCE
COME ON, YU-KUN! THAT'S ALL?!
DON'T TELL ME YOU HAVE STAGE FRIGHT!
BAP
HUH? WHAT ELSE SHOULD I SAY?
They wouldn't listen to me anyway.
90% OF THE PEOPLE HERE ARE YOUR FANS. THE LESS I TALK, THE BETTER VALUE THEY GET.
DON'T SAY THAT STUFF ON STAGE, YU-KUN!

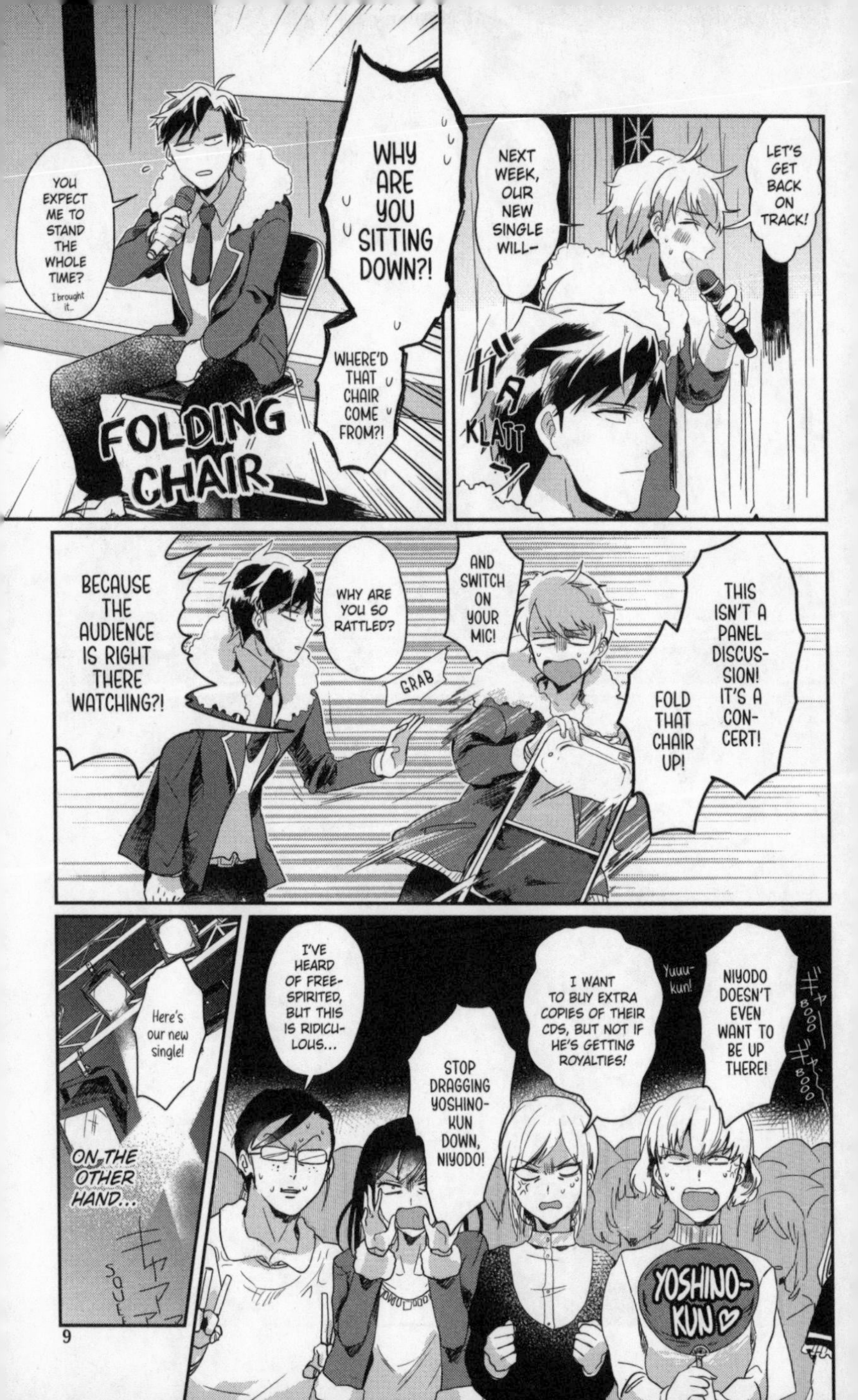
LET'S GET BACK ON TRACK!
NEXT WEEK, OUR NEW SINGLE WILL-
KLATT
WHY ARE YOU SITTING DOWN?!
YOU EXPECT ME TO STAND THE WHOLE TIME?
I brought it...
WHERE'D THAT CHAIR COME FROM?!
FOLDING CHAIR
THIS ISN'T A PANEL DISCUS-SION! IT'S A CON-CERT!
FOLD THAT CHAIR UP!
AND SWITCH ON YOUR MIC!
WHY ARE YOU SO RATTLED?
GRAB
BECAUSE THE AUDIENCE IS RIGHT THERE WATCHING?!
NIYODO DOESN'T EVEN WANT TO BE UP THERE!
BOOO
BOOO
Yuuu-kun!
I WANT TO BUY EXTRA COPIES OF THEIR CDS, BUT NOT IF HE'S GETTING ROYALTIES!
STOP DRAGGING YOSHINO-KUN DOWN, NIYODO!
I'VE HEARD OF FREE-SPIRITED, BUT THIS IS RIDICU-LOUS...
YOSHINO-KUN ♡
Here's our new single!
ON THE OTHER HAND...
SQUEAL

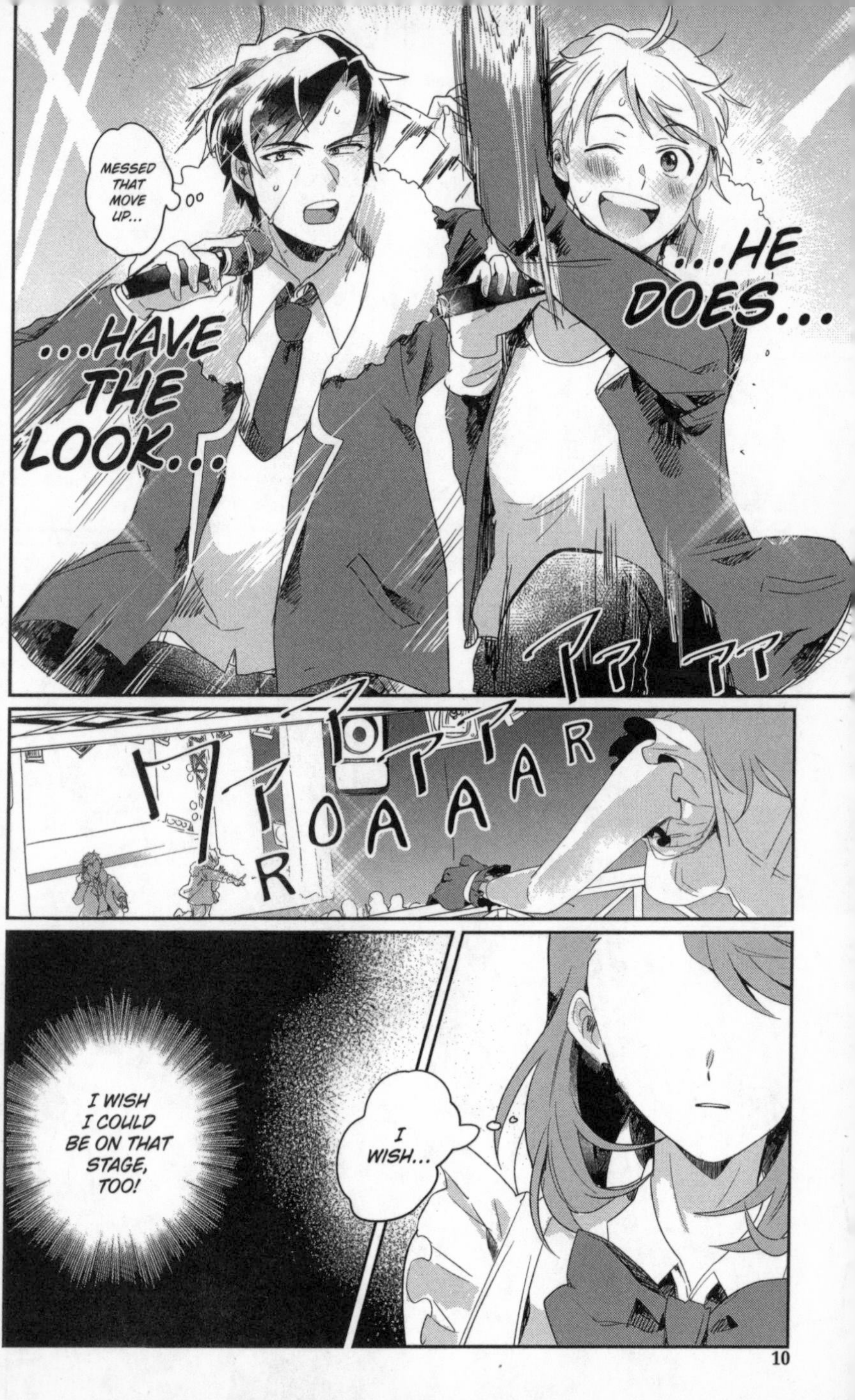
...HE DOES...
...HAVE THE LOOK...
MESSED THAT MOVE UP...
ROAAAR
I WISH...
I WISH I COULD BE ON THAT STAGE, TOO!

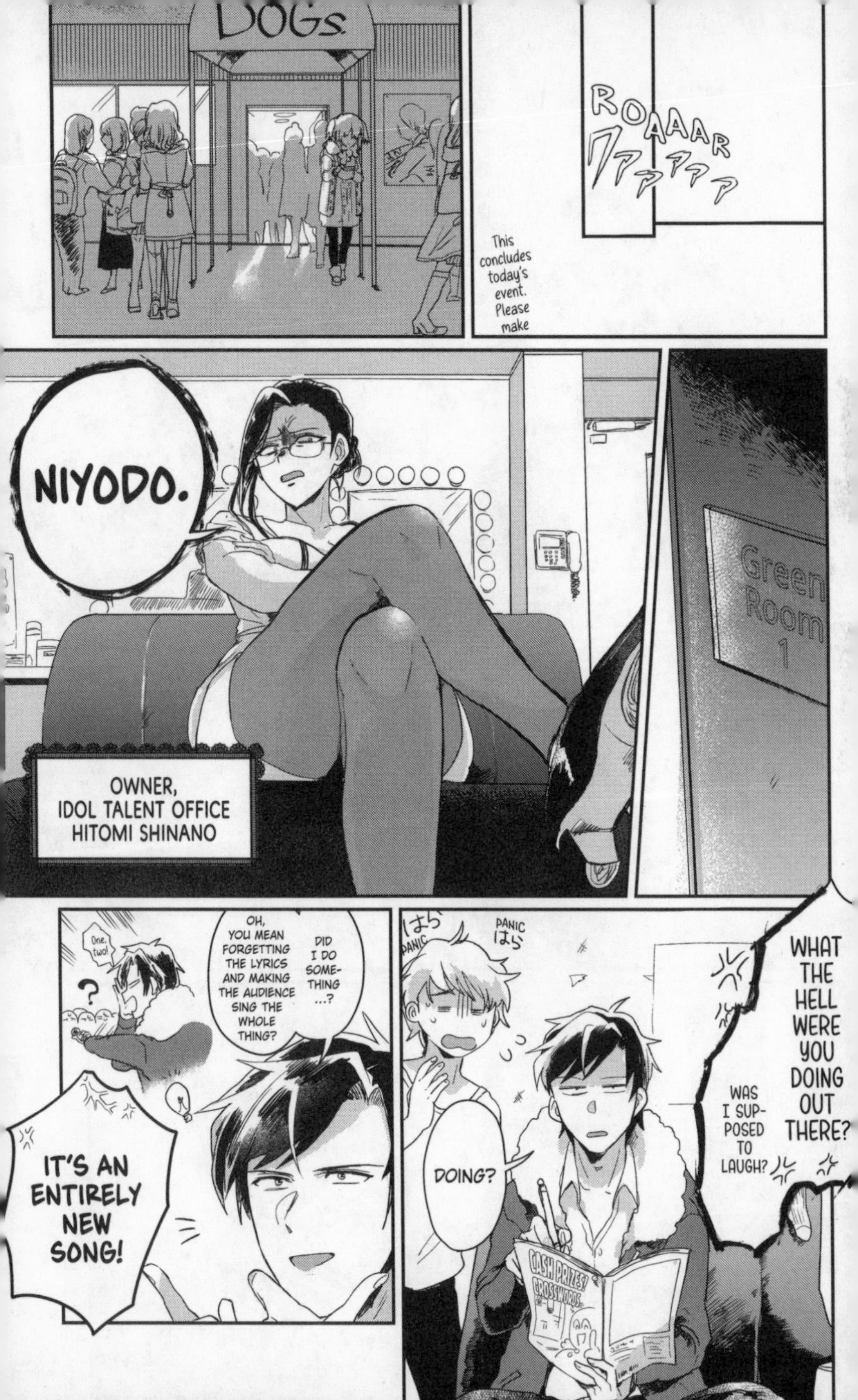
ROAAAR
ワァァァァァ
This concludes today's event. Please make
DOGs.
Green Room 1
NIYODO.
OWNER, IDOL TALENT OFFICE HITOMI SHINANO
WHAT THE HELL WERE YOU DOING OUT THERE?
PANIC はら
はら PANIC
DOING?
WAS I SUP-POSED TO LAUGH?
CASH PRIZES? CROSSWORDS
DID I DO SOME-THING ...?
OH, YOU MEAN FORGETTING THE LYRICS AND MAKING THE AUDIENCE SING THE WHOLE THING?
One, two!
IT'S AN ENTIRELY NEW SONG!

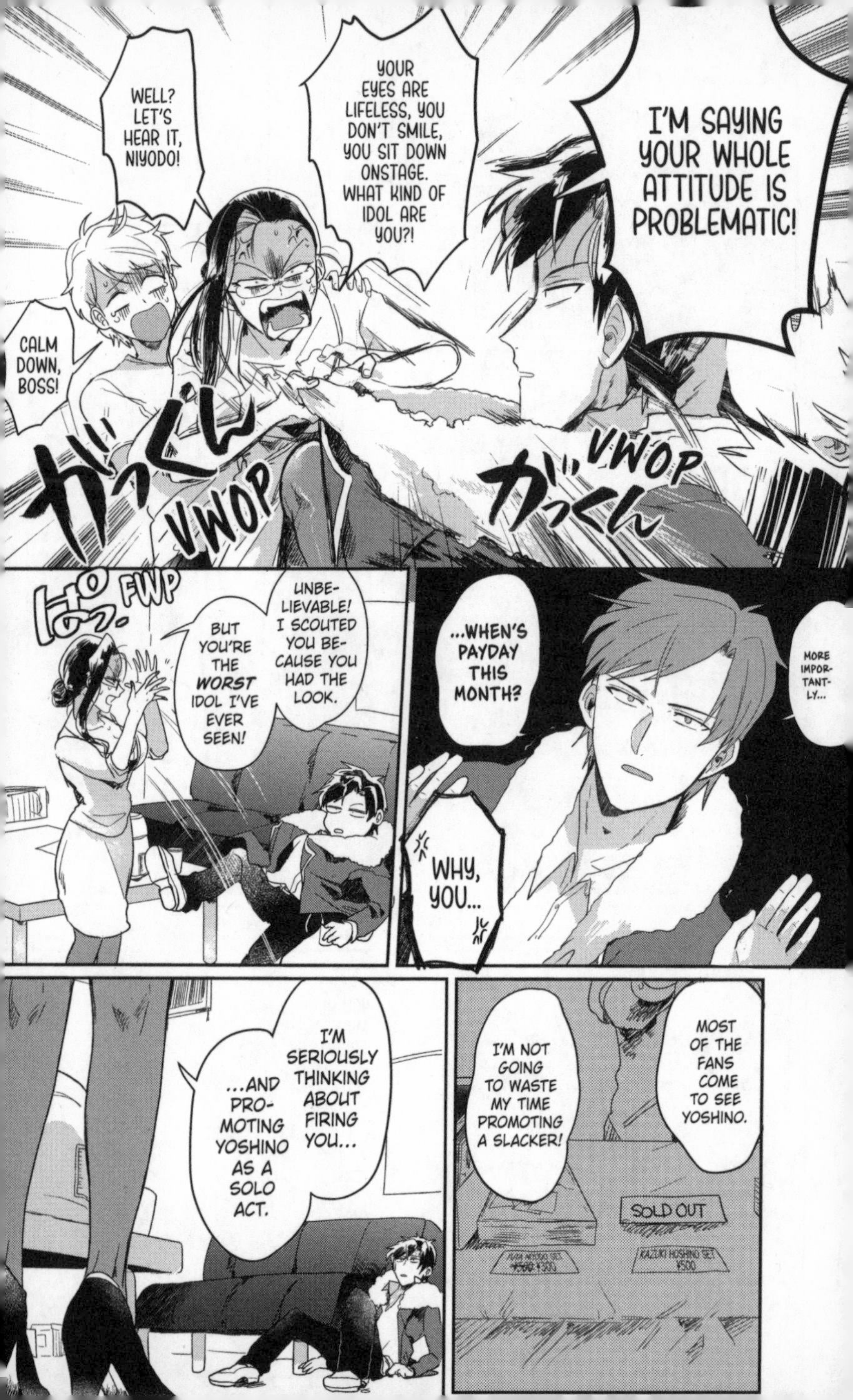
I'M SAYING YOUR WHOLE ATTITUDE IS PROBLEMATIC!
YOUR EYES ARE LIFELESS, YOU DON'T SMILE, YOU SIT DOWN ONSTAGE. WHAT KIND OF IDOL ARE YOU?!
WELL? LET'S HEAR IT, NIYODO!
CALM DOWN, BOSS!
がっくん VWOP
がっくん VWOP
MORE IMPORTANTLY...
...WHEN'S PAYDAY THIS MONTH?
WHY, YOU...
はっ FWP
UNBELIEVABLE! I SCOUTED YOU BECAUSE YOU HAD THE LOOK.
BUT YOU'RE THE WORST IDOL I'VE EVER SEEN!
MOST OF THE FANS COME TO SEE YOSHINO.
I'M NOT GOING TO WASTE MY TIME PROMOTING A SLACKER!
SOLD OUT
KAZUKI HOSHINO SET ¥500
I'M SERIOUSLY THINKING ABOUT FIRING YOU...
...AND PROMOTING YOSHINO AS A SOLO ACT.

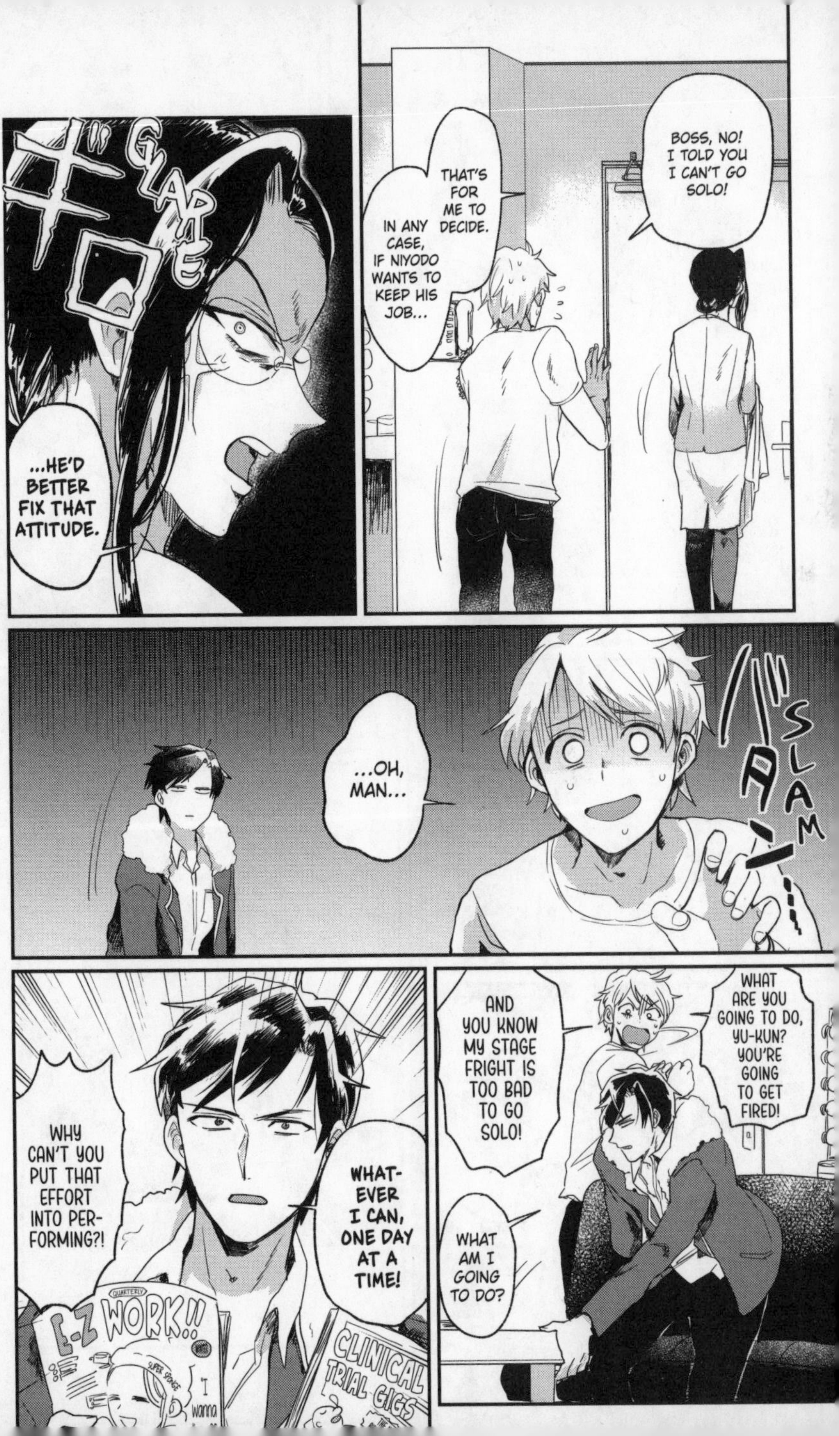
BOSS, NO! I TOLD YOU I CAN'T GO SOLO!
THAT'S FOR ME TO DECIDE.
IN ANY CASE, IF NIYODO WANTS TO KEEP HIS JOB...
GLARE
...HE'D BETTER FIX THAT ATTITUDE.
SLAM
...OH, MAN...
WHAT ARE YOU GOING TO DO, YU-KUN? YOU'RE GOING TO GET FIRED!
AND YOU KNOW MY STAGE FRIGHT IS TOO BAD TO GO SOLO!
WHAT AM I GOING TO DO?
WHAT-EVER I CAN, ONE DAY AT A TIME!
WHY CAN'T YOU PUT THAT EFFORT INTO PER-FORMING?!
QUARTERLY
E-Z WORK!!
SUPER SPONGE
I wanna
CLINICAL TRIAL GIGS

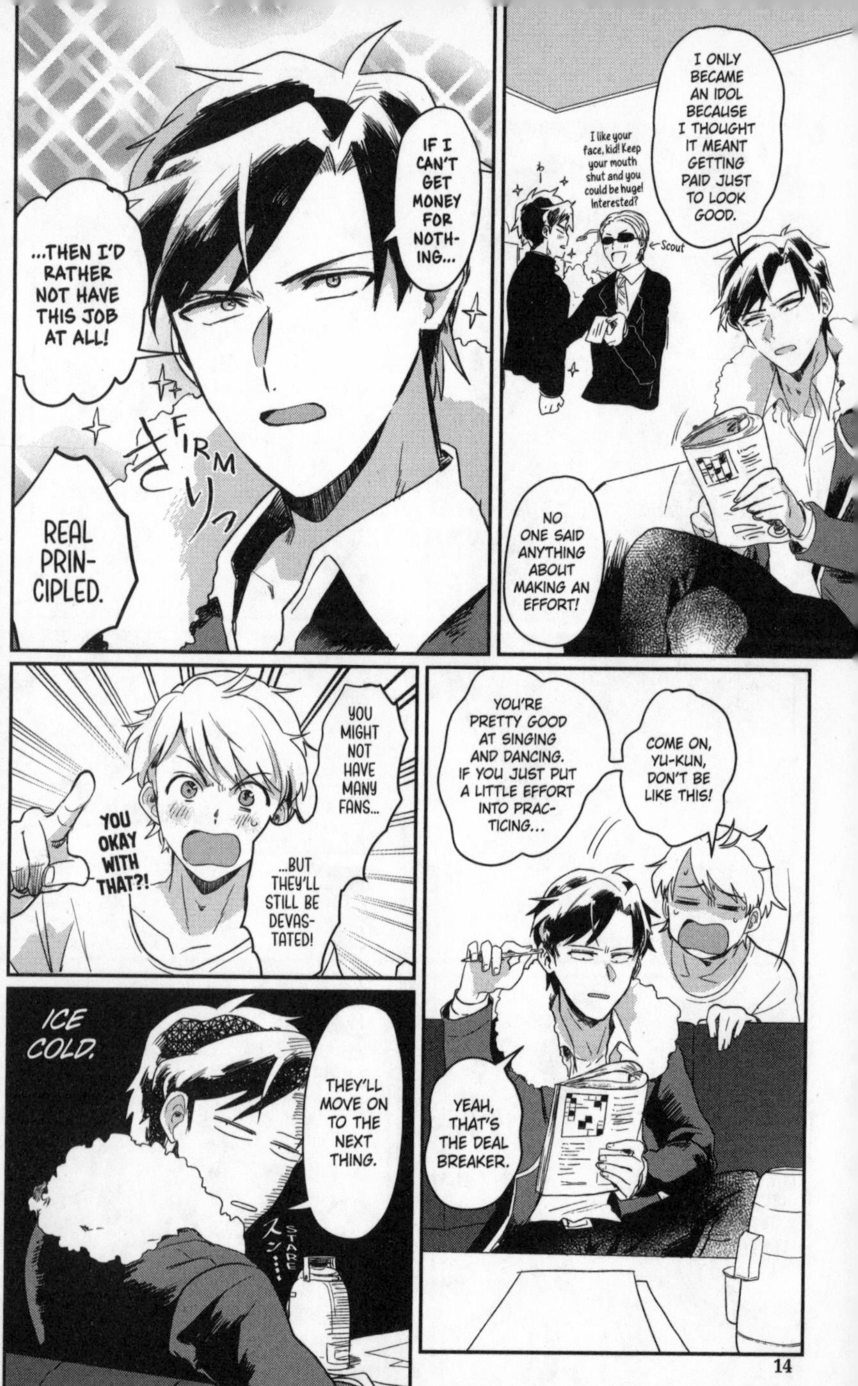
I ONLY BECAME AN IDOL BECAUSE I THOUGHT IT MEANT GETTING PAID JUST TO LOOK GOOD.
I like your face, kid! Keep your mouth shut and you could be huge! Interested?
Scout
NO ONE SAID ANYTHING ABOUT MAKING AN EFFORT!
IF I CAN'T GET MONEY FOR NOTHING...
...THEN I'D RATHER NOT HAVE THIS JOB AT ALL!
FIRM
REAL PRINCIPLED.
COME ON, YU-KUN, DON'T BE LIKE THIS!
YOU'RE PRETTY GOOD AT SINGING AND DANCING. IF YOU JUST PUT A LITTLE EFFORT INTO PRACTICING...
YEAH, THAT'S THE DEAL BREAKER.
YOU MIGHT NOT HAVE MANY FANS...
...BUT THEY'LL STILL BE DEVASTATED!
YOU OKAY WITH THAT?!
ICE COLD.
THEY'LL MOVE ON TO THE NEXT THING.
STARE

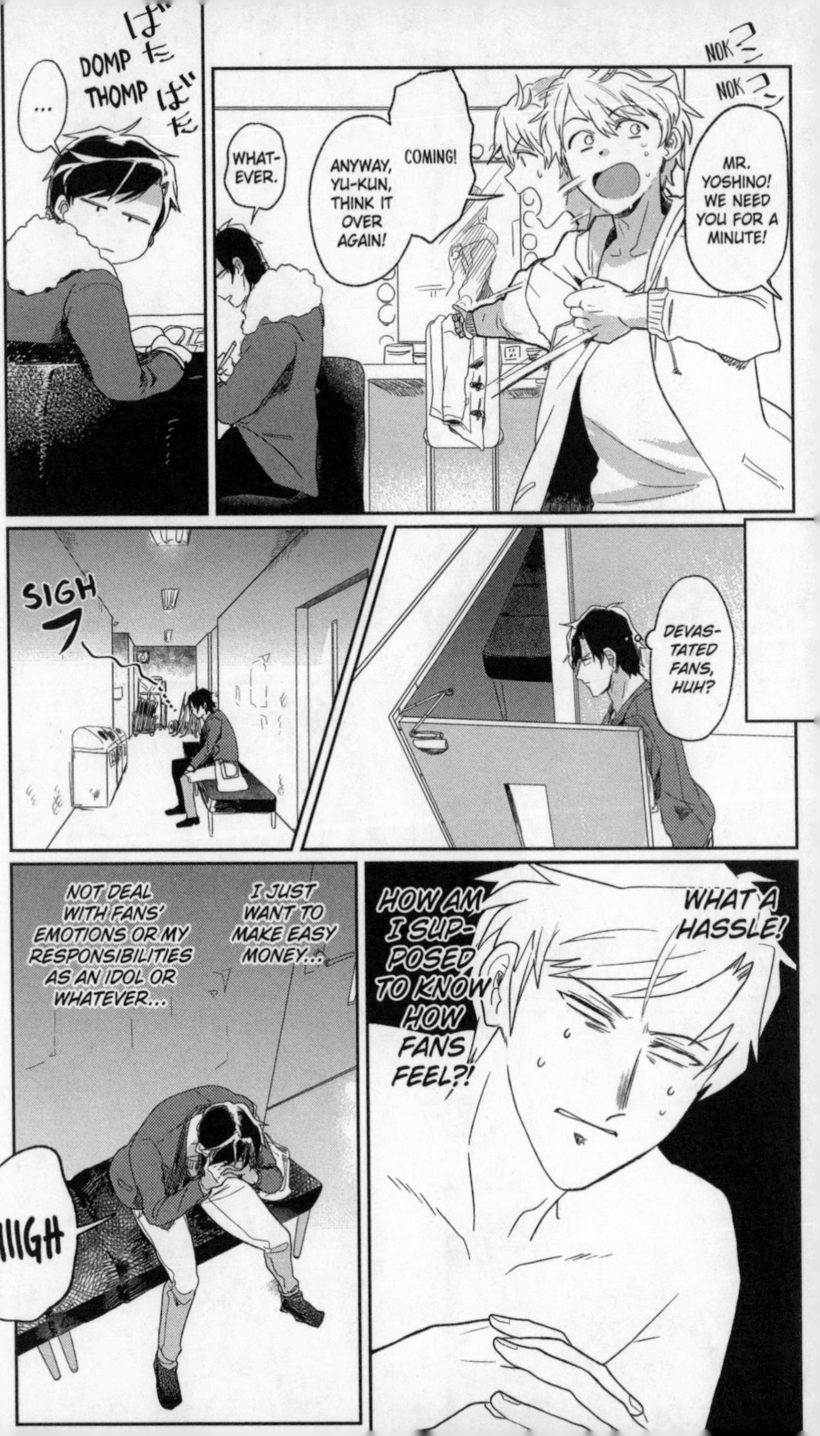
NOK NOK
MR. YOSHINO! WE NEED YOU FOR A MINUTE!
COMING!
ANYWAY, YU-KUN, THINK IT OVER AGAIN!
WHATEVER.
ばたばた
DOMP THOMP
...
DEVASTATED FANS, HUH?
SIGH
WHAT A HASSLE!
HOW AM I SUPPOSED TO KNOW HOW FANS FEEL?!
I JUST WANT TO MAKE EASY MONEY...
NOT DEAL WITH FANS' EMOTIONS OR MY RESPONSIBILITIES AS AN IDOL OR WHATEVER...
SIIIGH

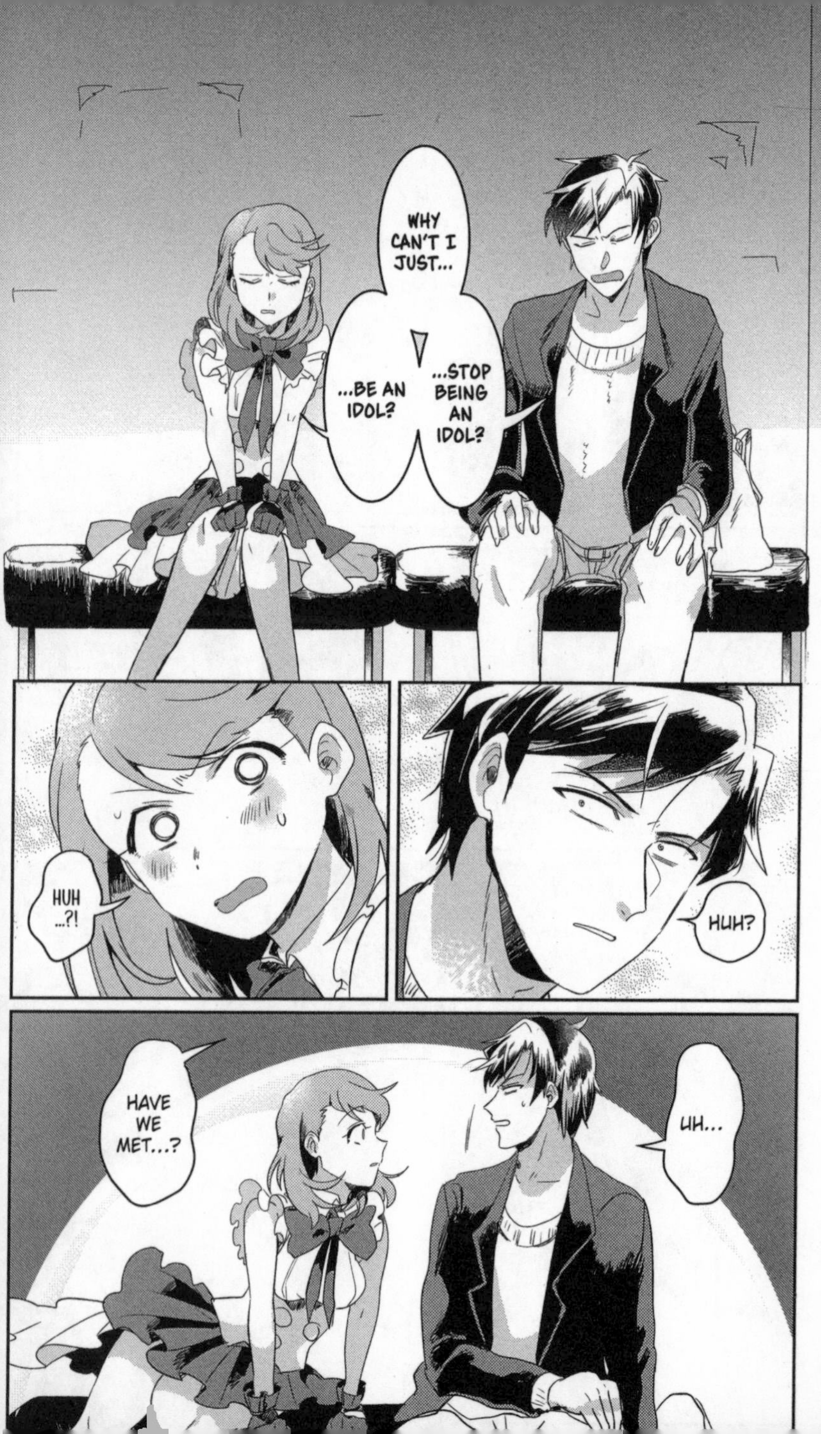
WHY CAN'T I JUST...
...STOP BEING AN IDOL?
...BE AN IDOL?
HUH?
HUH ...?!
UH...
HAVE WE MET...?

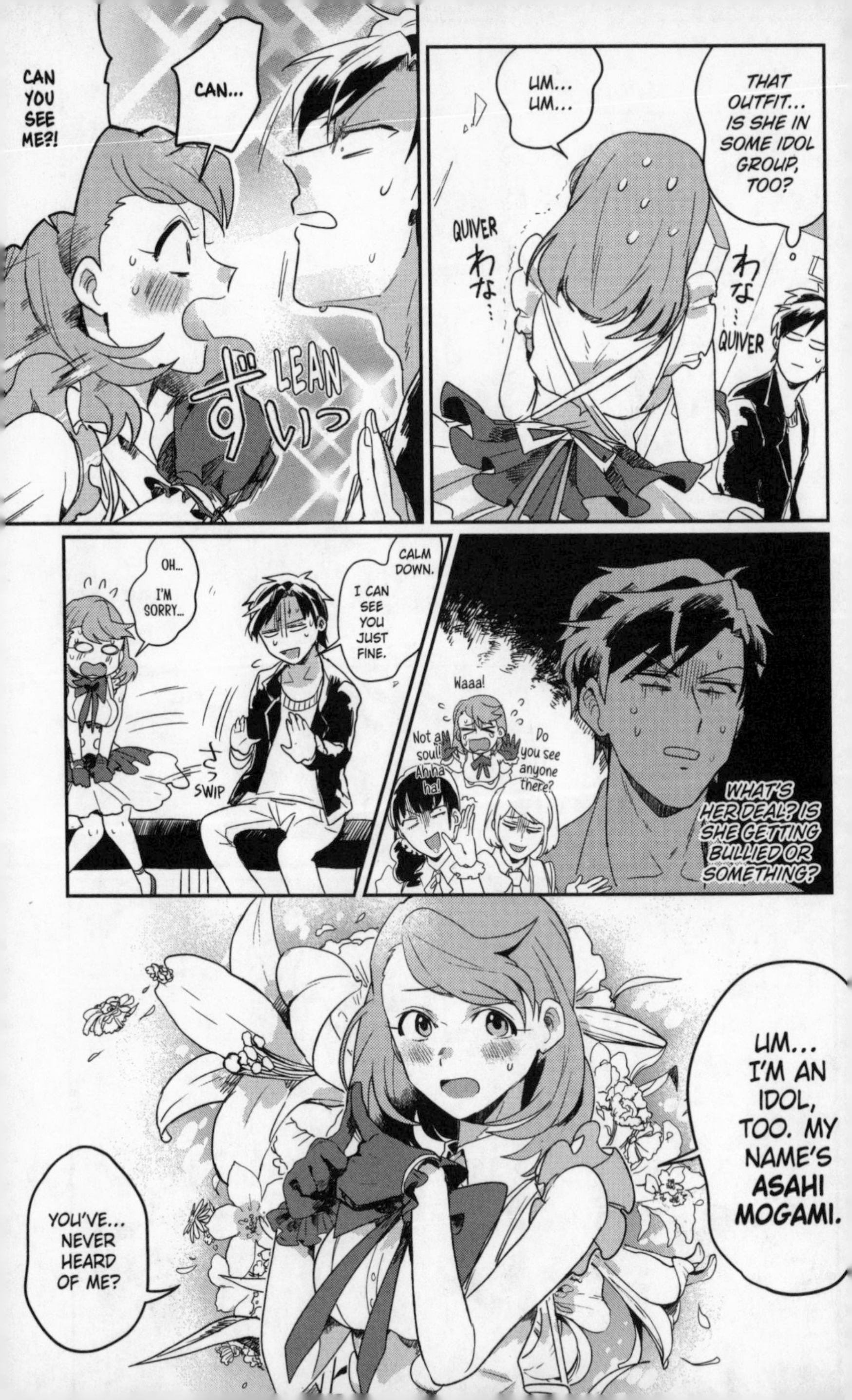
THAT OUTFIT... IS SHE IN SOME IDOL GROUP, TOO?
UM... UM...
わな... QUIVER
QUIVER わな...
CAN...
CAN YOU SEE ME?!
LEAN すいっ
Waaa!
Do you see anyone there?
Not a soul! Ah ha ha!
WHAT'S HER DEAL? IS SHE GETTING BULLIED OR SOMETHING?
CALM DOWN. I CAN SEE YOU JUST FINE.
OH... I'M SORRY...
さっ SWIP
UM... I'M AN IDOL, TOO. MY NAME'S ASAHI MOGAMI.
YOU'VE... NEVER HEARD OF ME?

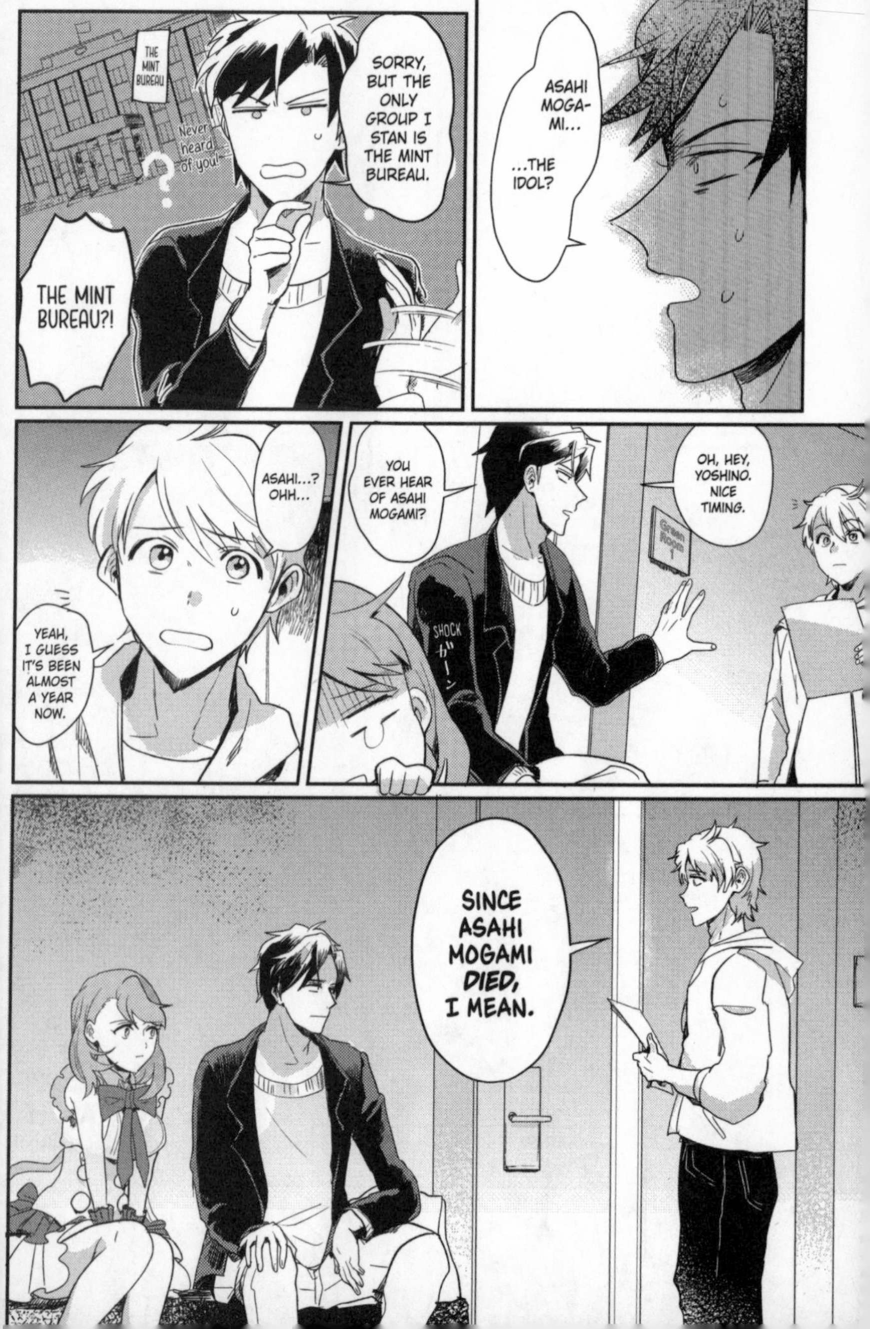
ASAHI MOGAMI…
…THE IDOL?
SORRY, BUT THE ONLY GROUP I STAN IS THE MINT BUREAU.
THE MINT BUREAU
Never heard of you!
THE MINT BUREAU?!
OH, HEY, YOSHINO. NICE TIMING.
Green Room 1
YOU EVER HEAR OF ASAHI MOGAMI?
SHOCK
ガーン
ASAHI…? OHH…
YEAH, I GUESS IT'S BEEN ALMOST A YEAR NOW.
SINCE ASAHI MOGAMI *DIED*, I MEAN.

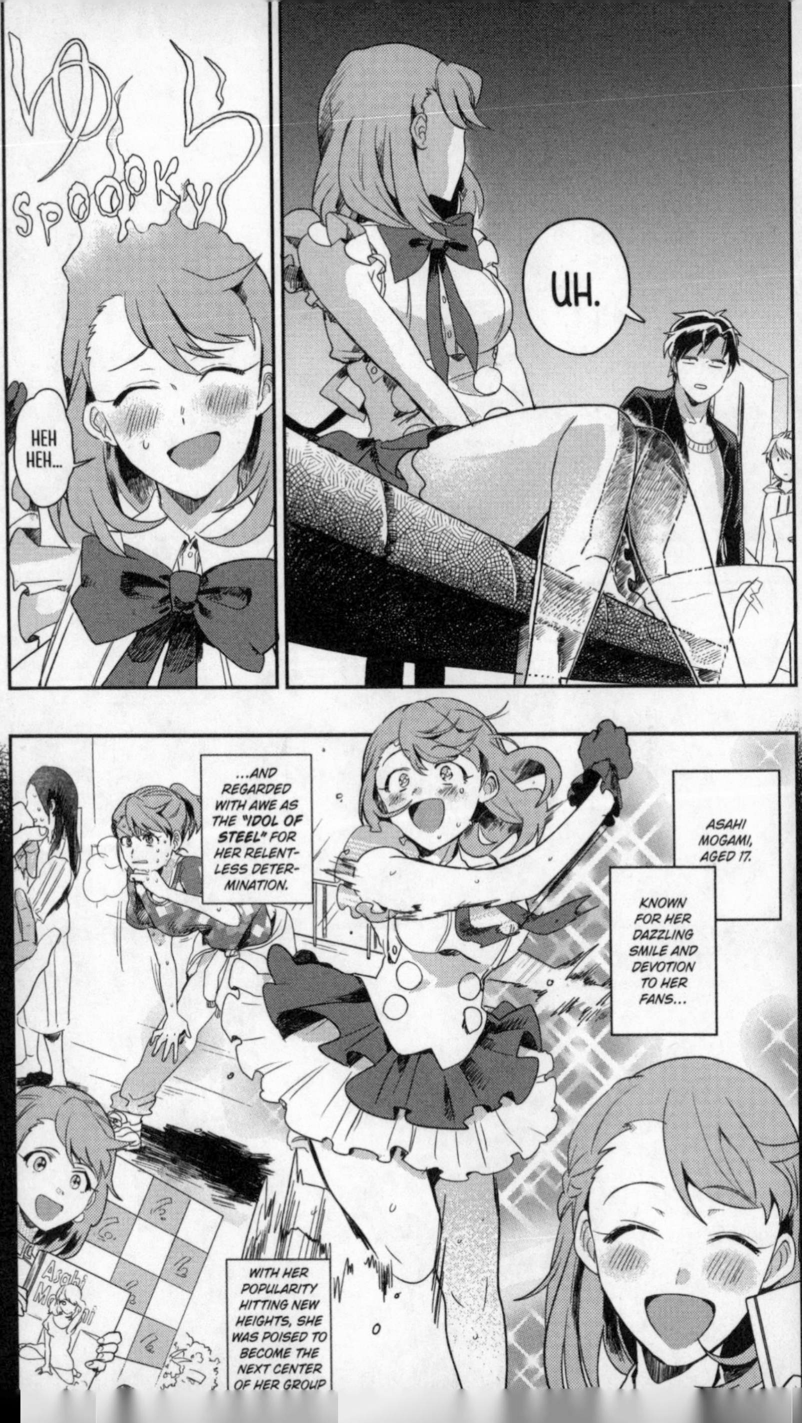
UH.
SPOOKY
HEH HEH...
ASAHI MOGAMI, AGED 17.
KNOWN FOR HER DAZZLING SMILE AND DEVOTION TO HER FANS...
...AND REGARDED WITH AWE AS THE "IDOL OF STEEL" FOR HER RELENTLESS DETERMINATION.
WITH HER POPULARITY HITTING NEW HEIGHTS, SHE WAS POISED TO BECOME THE NEXT CENTER OF HER GROUP
Asahi Mogami

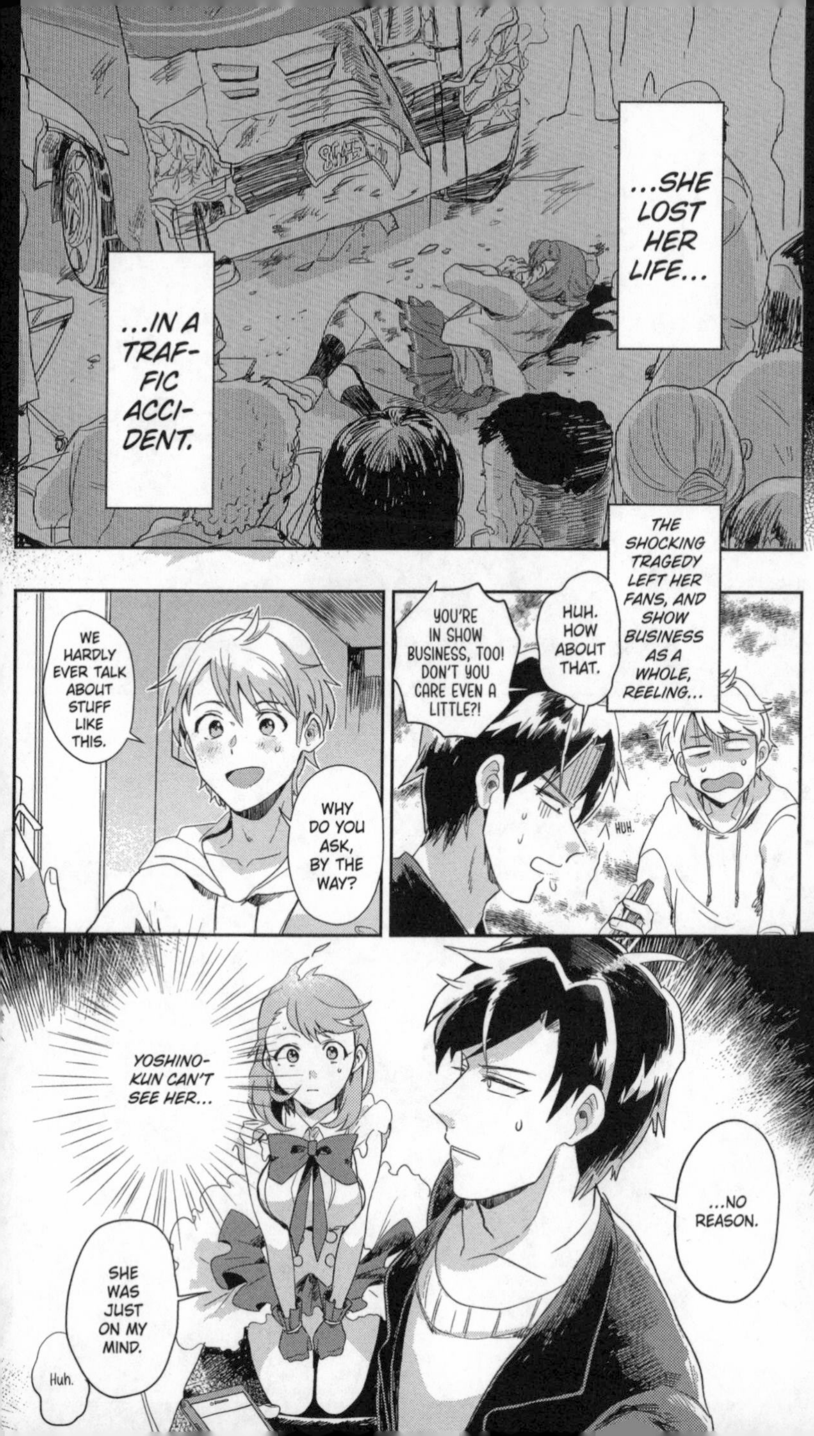

...SHE LOST HER LIFE...
...IN A TRAF-FIC ACCI-DENT.
THE SHOCKING TRAGEDY LEFT HER FANS, AND SHOW BUSINESS AS A WHOLE, REELING...
HUH. HOW ABOUT THAT.
YOU'RE IN SHOW BUSINESS, TOO! DON'T YOU CARE EVEN A LITTLE?!
HUH.
WE HARDLY EVER TALK ABOUT STUFF LIKE THIS.
WHY DO YOU ASK, BY THE WAY?
...NO REASON.
YOSHINO-KUN CAN'T SEE HER...
SHE WAS JUST ON MY MIND.
Huh.

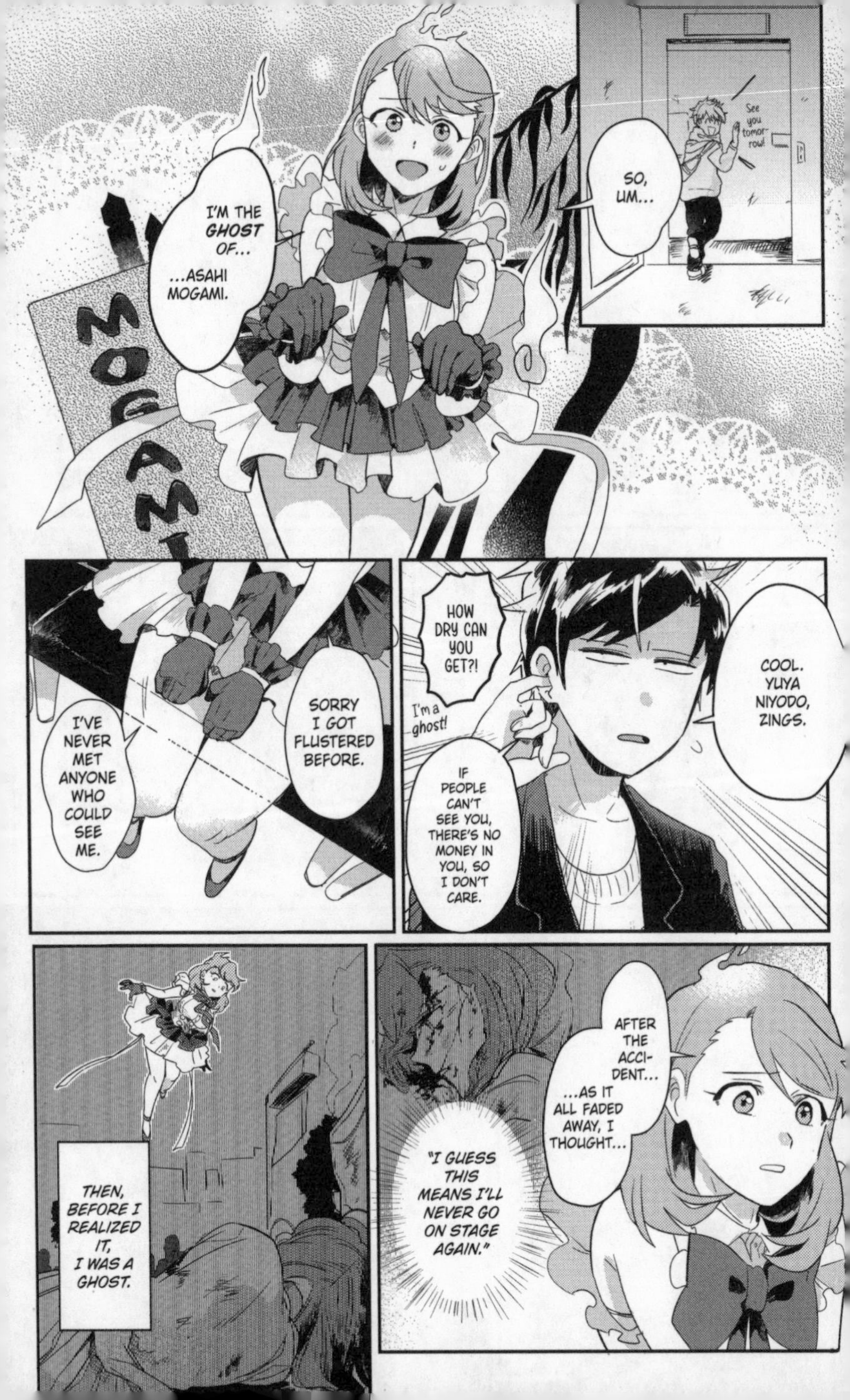

See you tomor-row!
SO, UM...
I'M THE GHOST OF...
...ASAHI MOGAMI.
MOGAMI
COOL. YUYA NIYODO, ZINGS.
HOW DRY CAN YOU GET?!
I'm a ghost!
IF PEOPLE CAN'T SEE YOU, THERE'S NO MONEY IN YOU, SO I DON'T CARE.
SORRY I GOT FLUSTERED BEFORE.
I'VE NEVER MET ANYONE WHO COULD SEE ME.
AFTER THE ACCI-DENT...
...AS IT ALL FADED AWAY, I THOUGHT...
"I GUESS THIS MEANS I'LL NEVER GO ON STAGE AGAIN."
THEN, BEFORE I REALIZED IT, I WAS A GHOST.

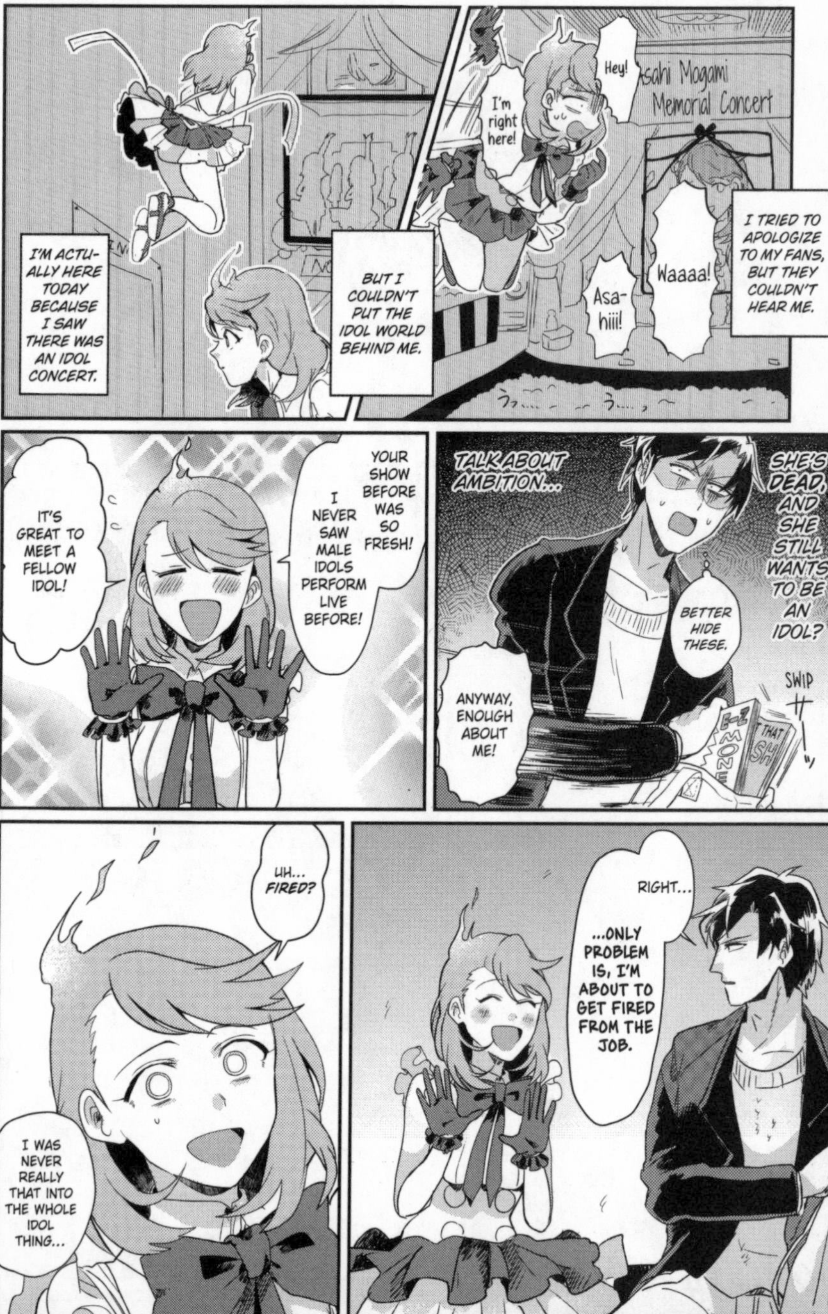
sahi Mogami Memorial Concert
Hey!
I'm right here!
I TRIED TO APOLOGIZE TO MY FANS, BUT THEY COULDN'T HEAR ME.
Waaaa!
Asa-hiii!
BUT I COULDN'T PUT THE IDOL WORLD BEHIND ME.
I'M ACTUALLY HERE TODAY BECAUSE I SAW THERE WAS AN IDOL CONCERT.
SHE'S DEAD, AND SHE STILL WANTS TO BE AN IDOL?
TALK ABOUT AMBITION...
BETTER HIDE THESE.
SWIP
ANYWAY, ENOUGH ABOUT ME!
YOUR SHOW BEFORE WAS SO FRESH!
I NEVER SAW MALE IDOLS PERFORM LIVE BEFORE!
IT'S GREAT TO MEET A FELLOW IDOL!
RIGHT...
...ONLY PROBLEM IS, I'M ABOUT TO GET FIRED FROM THE JOB.
UH... FIRED?
I WAS NEVER REALLY THAT INTO THE WHOLE IDOL THING...

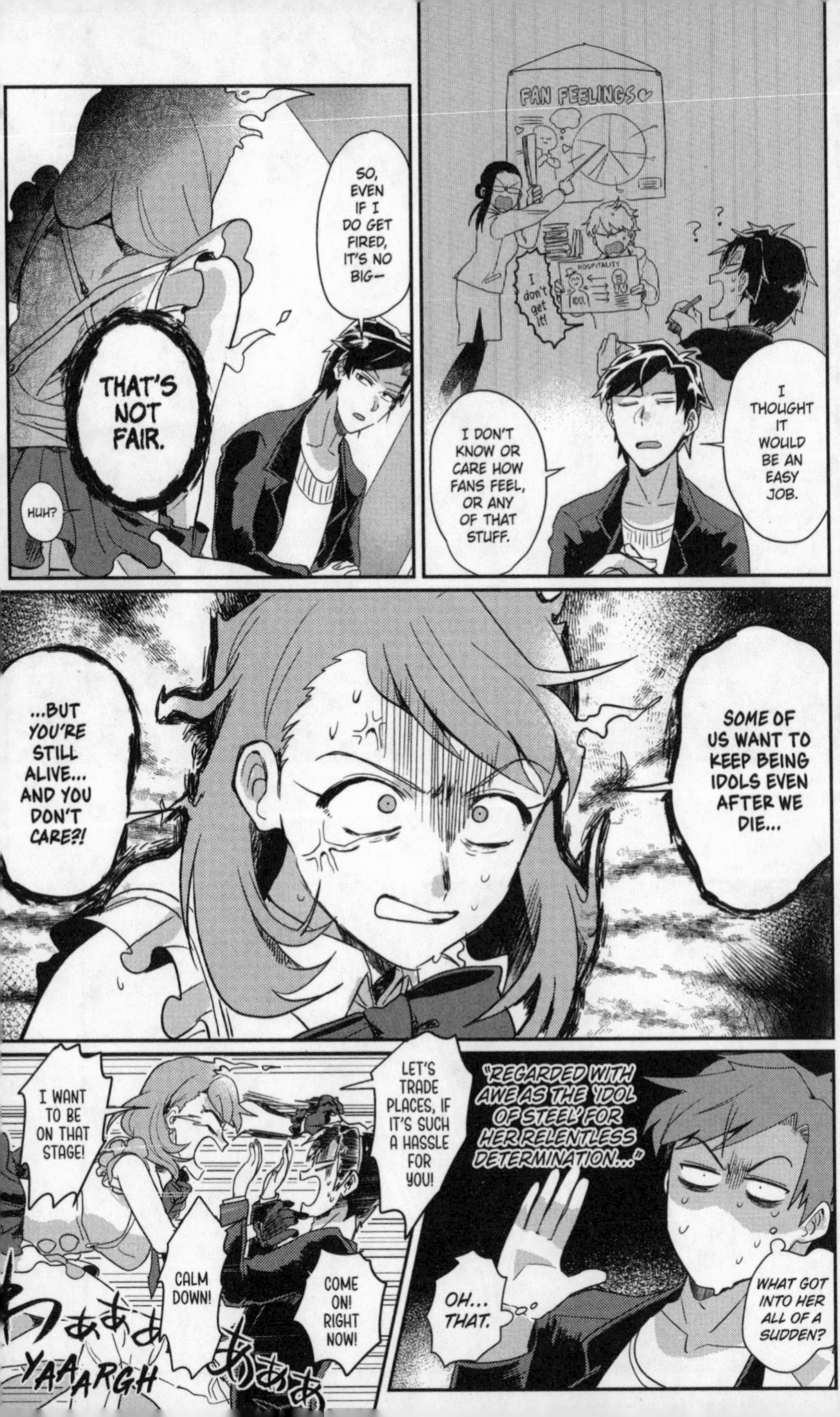
FAN FEELINGS
HOSPITALITY
IDOL
I don't get it!
?
?
I THOUGHT IT WOULD BE AN EASY JOB.
I DON'T KNOW OR CARE HOW FANS FEEL, OR ANY OF THAT STUFF.
SO, EVEN IF I DO GET FIRED, IT'S NO BIG—
THAT'S NOT FAIR.
HUH?
SOME OF US WANT TO KEEP BEING IDOLS EVEN AFTER WE DIE...
...BUT YOU'RE STILL ALIVE... AND YOU DON'T CARE?!
"REGARDED WITH AWE AS THE 'IDOL OF STEEL' FOR HER RELENTLESS DETERMINATION..."
WHAT GOT INTO HER ALL OF A SUDDEN?
OH... THAT.
LET'S TRADE PLACES, IF IT'S SUCH A HASSLE FOR YOU!
I WANT TO BE ON THAT STAGE!
COME ON! RIGHT NOW!
CALM DOWN!
あぁぁ
わぁぁぁ
YAAARGH

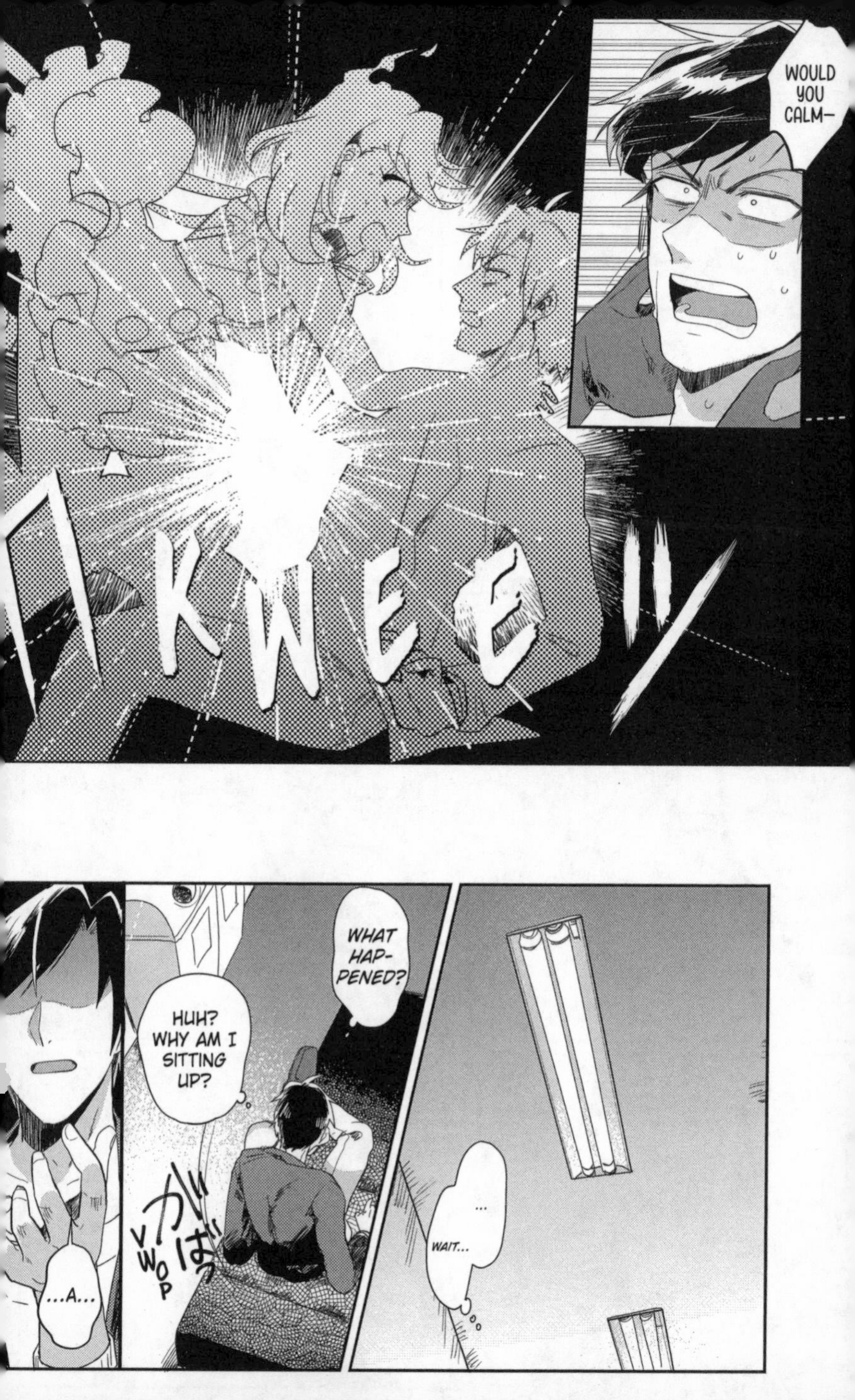
WOULD YOU CALM—
KWEE
...
WAIT...
WHAT HAP-PENED?
HUH? WHY AM I SITTING UP?
VWOP
...A...

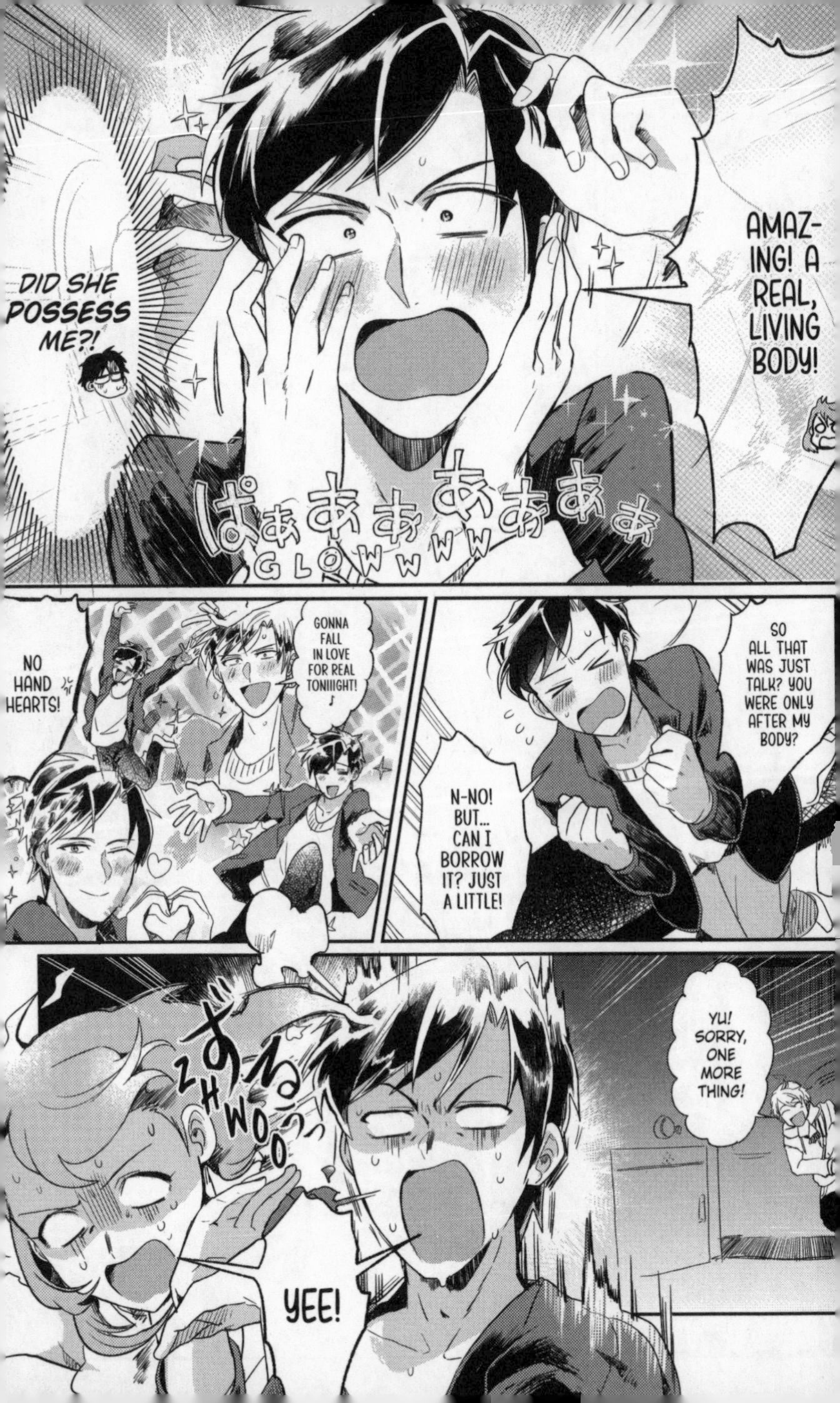
AMAZ-ING! A REAL, LIVING BODY!
ぱぁあああああぁ
GLOWWWW
DID SHE POSSESS ME?!
SO ALL THAT WAS JUST TALK? YOU WERE ONLY AFTER MY BODY?
N-NO! BUT... CAN I BORROW IT? JUST A LITTLE!
GONNA FALL IN LOVE FOR REAL TONIIIGHT! ♪
NO HAND HEARTS!
YU! SORRY, ONE MORE THING!
ずぉ
ZHWOO
YEE!

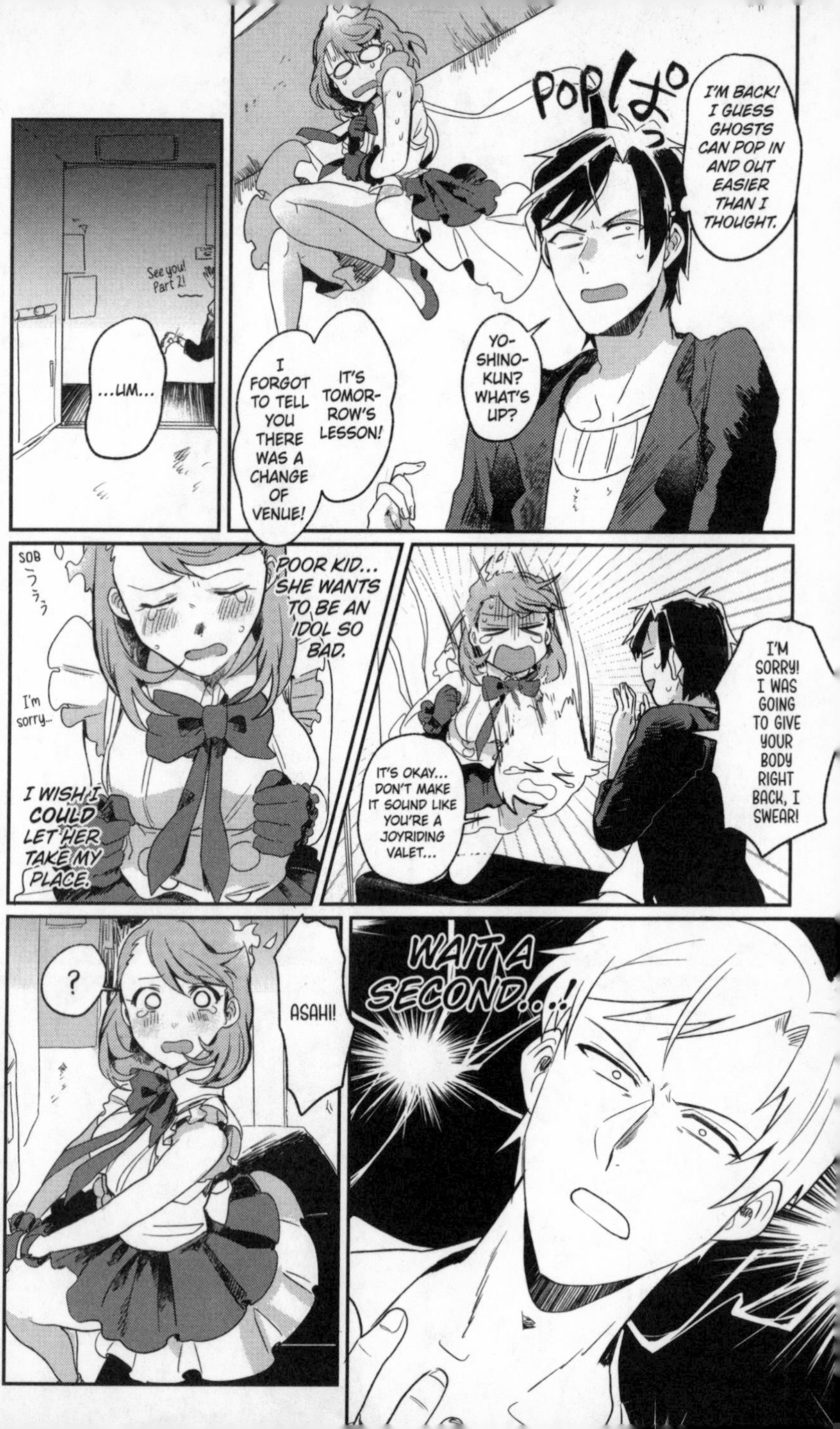
POP ぱっ
I'M BACK! I GUESS GHOSTS CAN POP IN AND OUT EASIER THAN I THOUGHT.
YO-SHINO-KUN? WHAT'S UP?
IT'S TOMOR-ROW'S LESSON!
I FORGOT TO TELL YOU THERE WAS A CHANGE OF VENUE!
See you! Part 2!
...UM...
I'M SORRY! I WAS GOING TO GIVE YOUR BODY RIGHT BACK, I SWEAR!
IT'S OKAY... DON'T MAKE IT SOUND LIKE YOU'RE A JOYRIDING VALET...
SOB
POOR KID... SHE WANTS TO BE AN IDOL SO BAD.
I'm sorry...
I WISH I COULD LET HER TAKE MY PLACE.
WAIT A SECOND...!
ASAHI!
?

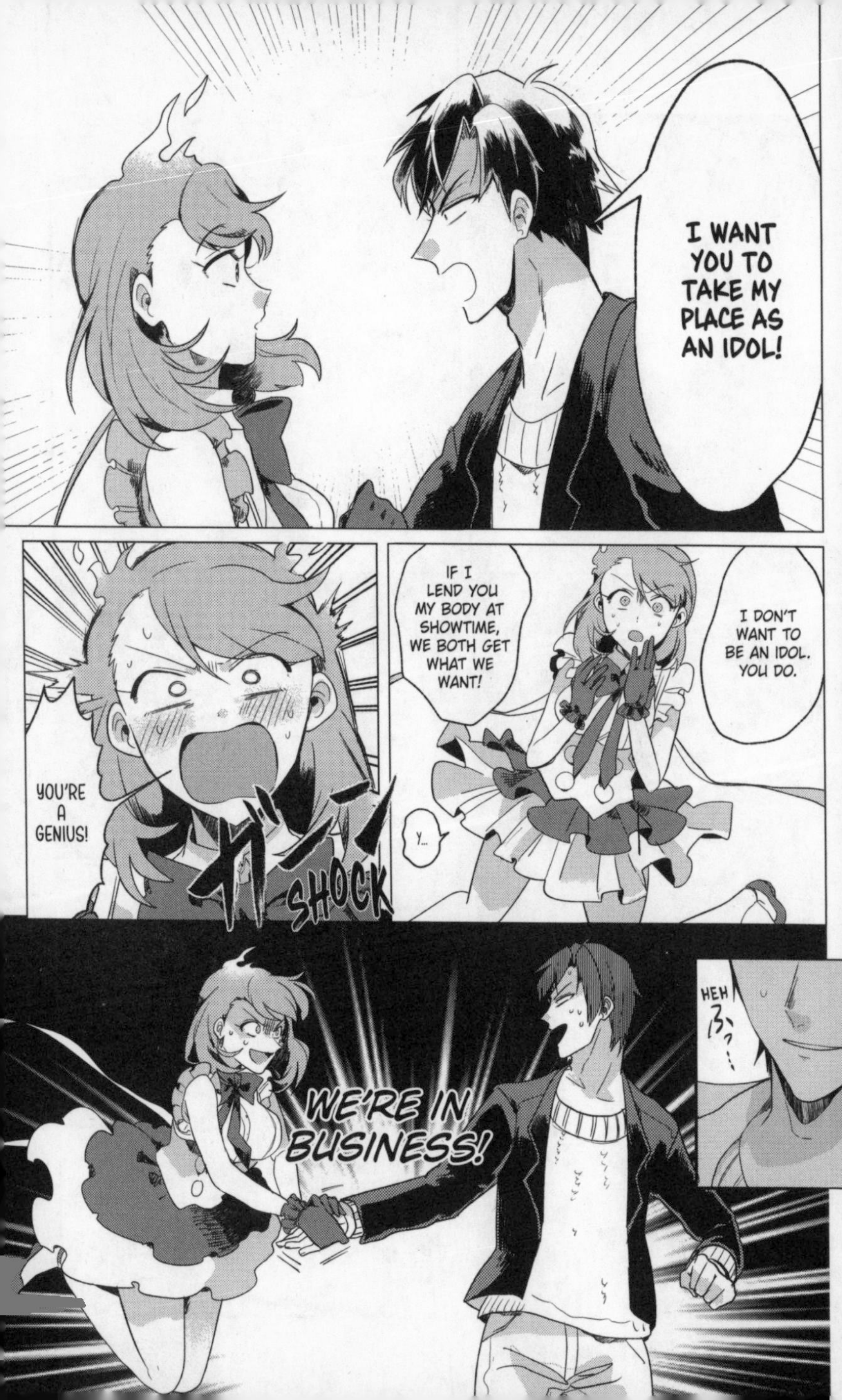
I WANT YOU TO TAKE MY PLACE AS AN IDOL!
I DON'T WANT TO BE AN IDOL. YOU DO.
IF I LEND YOU MY BODY AT SHOWTIME, WE BOTH GET WHAT WE WANT!
Y...
YOU'RE A GENIUS!
SHOCK
HEH
WE'RE IN BUSINESS!

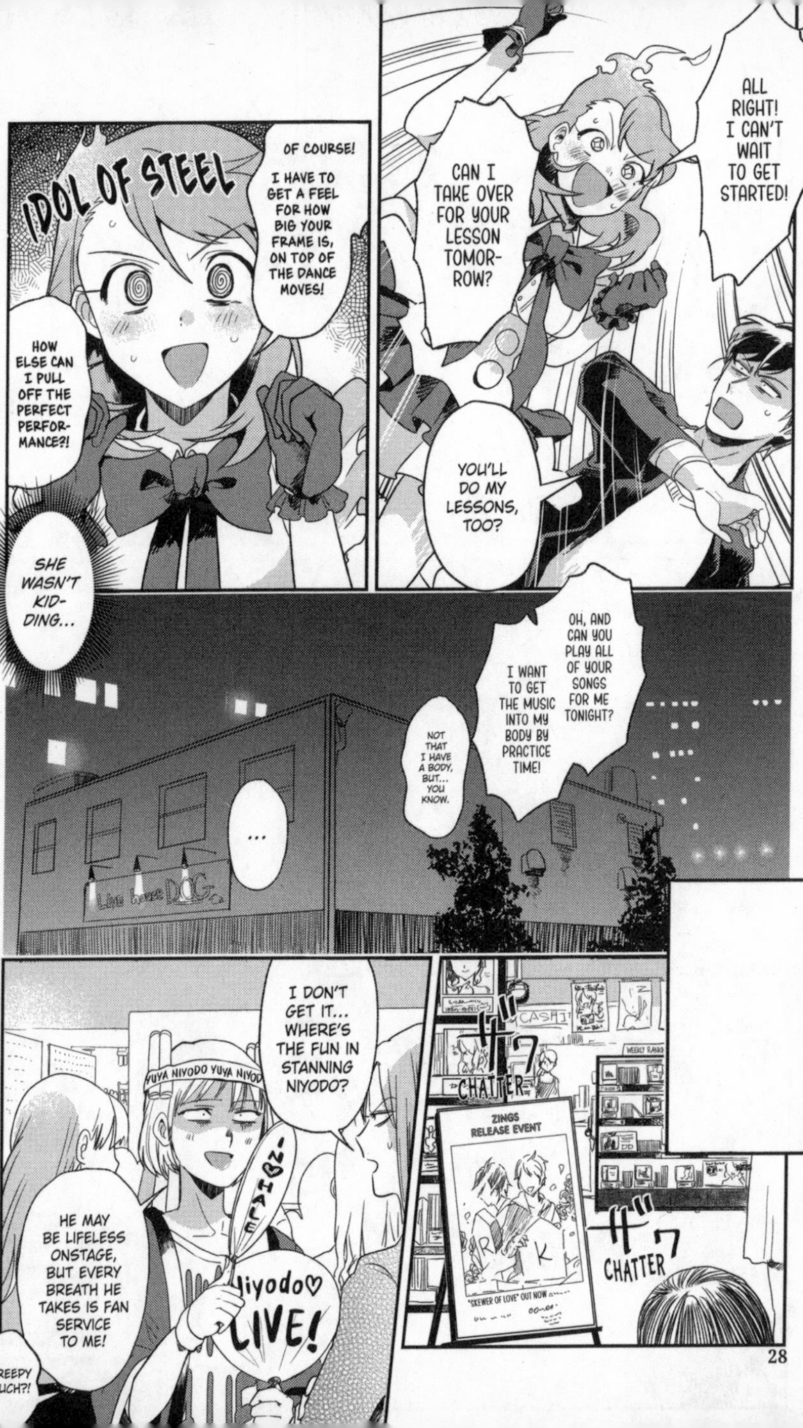
ALL RIGHT! I CAN'T WAIT TO GET STARTED!
CAN I TAKE OVER FOR YOUR LESSON TOMOR-ROW?
YOU'LL DO MY LESSONS, TOO?
IDOL OF STEEL
OF COURSE!
I HAVE TO GET A FEEL FOR HOW BIG YOUR FRAME IS, ON TOP OF THE DANCE MOVES!
HOW ELSE CAN I PULL OFF THE PERFECT PERFOR-MANCE?!
SHE WASN'T KID-DING...
OH, AND CAN YOU PLAY ALL OF YOUR SONGS FOR ME TONIGHT?
I WANT TO GET THE MUSIC INTO MY BODY BY PRACTICE TIME!
NOT THAT I HAVE A BODY, BUT... YOU KNOW.
...
CHATTER
ZINGS RELEASE EVENT
"SKEWER OF LOVE" OUT NOW
CHATTER
I DON'T GET IT... WHERE'S THE FUN IN STANNING NIYODO?
YUYA NIYODO YUYA NIYODO
INHALE
HE MAY BE LIFELESS ONSTAGE, BUT EVERY BREATH HE TAKES IS FAN SERVICE TO ME!
liyodo♡ LIVE!
CREEPY MUCH?!

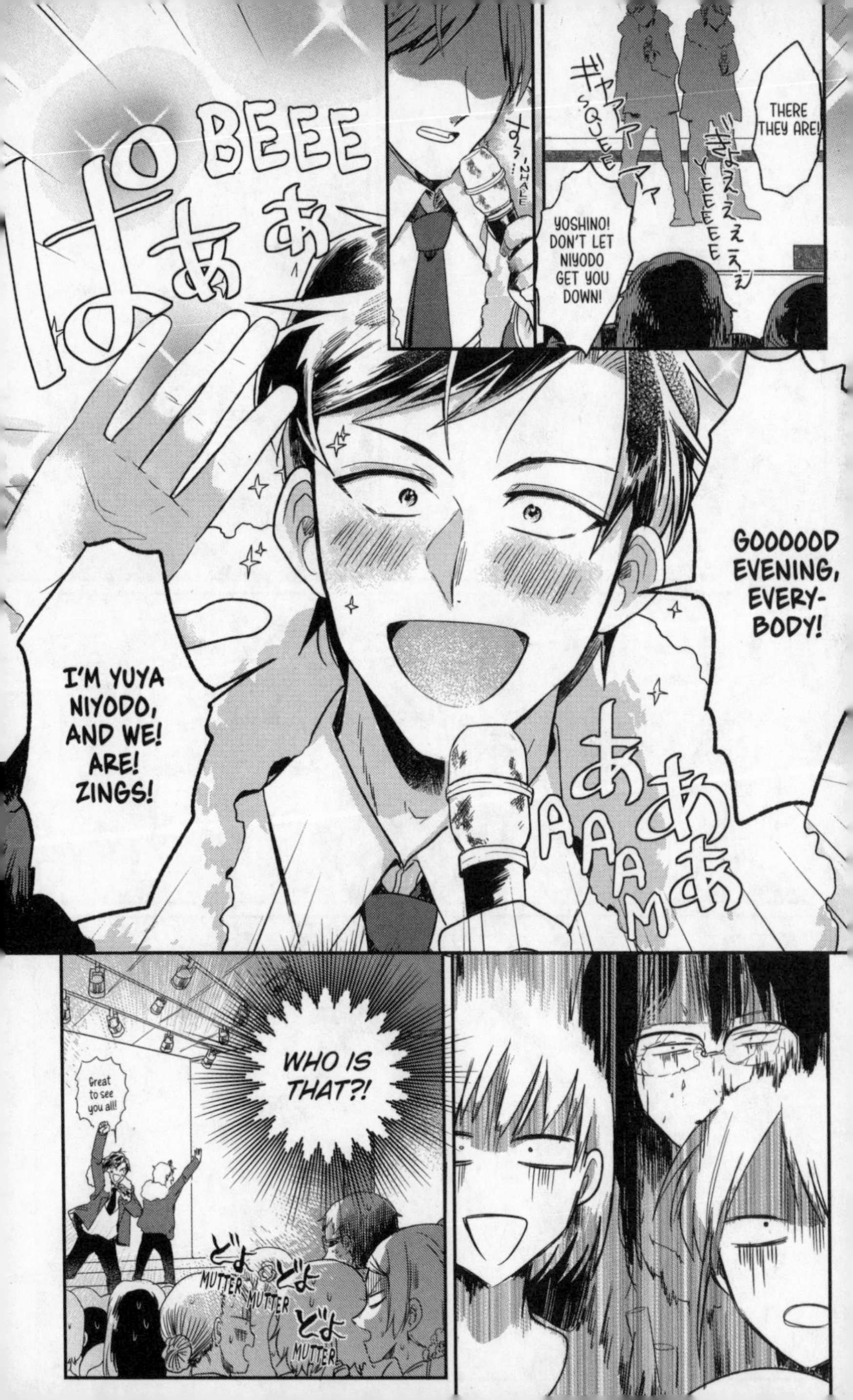

THERE THEY ARE!
YOSHINO! DON'T LET NIYODO GET YOU DOWN!
ぎょええええええ
YEEEEEE
ギャアアアア
SQUEEE
すぅ…
INHALE
ぱぁあ
BEEE
GOOOOOD EVENING, EVERY-BODY!
I'M YUYA NIYODO, AND WE! ARE! ZINGS!
あああ
AAAM
WHO IS THAT?!
Great to see you all!
どよ
MUTTER
どよ
MUTTER
どよ
MUTTER

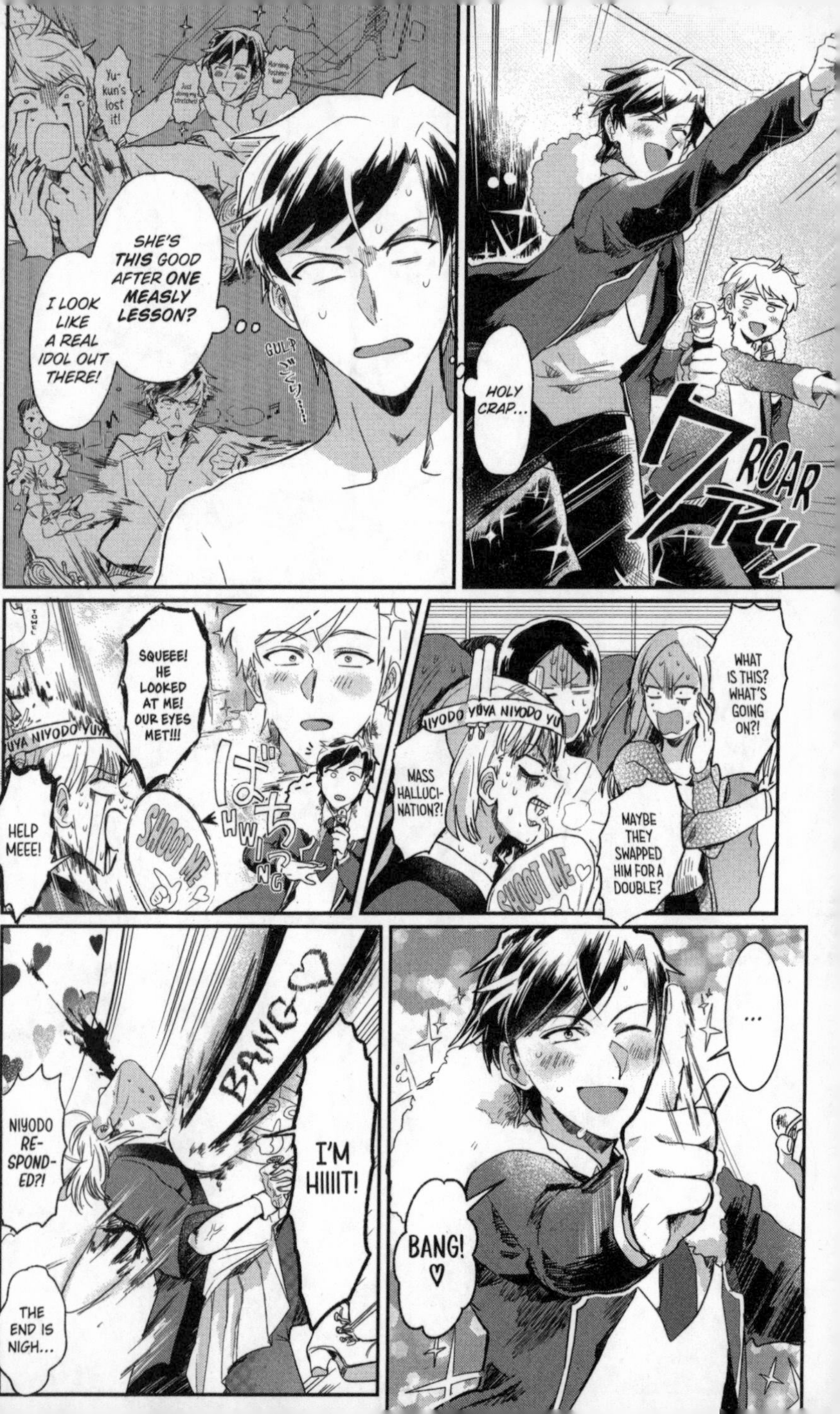
HOLY CRAP...
ROAR
Just doing my stretches!
Yu-kun's lost it!
SHE'S THIS GOOD AFTER ONE MEASLY LESSON?
GULP
I LOOK LIKE A REAL IDOL OUT THERE!
WHAT IS THIS? WHAT'S GOING ON?!
MAYBE THEY SWAPPED HIM FOR A DOUBLE?
MASS HALLUCINATION?!
NIYODO YUYA NIYODO YU
SHOOT ME
SQUEEE! HE LOOKED AT ME! OUR EYES MET!!!
HWING
HELP MEEE!
YUYA NIYODO YUYA
SHOOT ME
...
BANG! ♡
BANG ♡
I'M HIIIIT!
NIYODO RE-SPOND-ED?!
THE END IS NIGH...

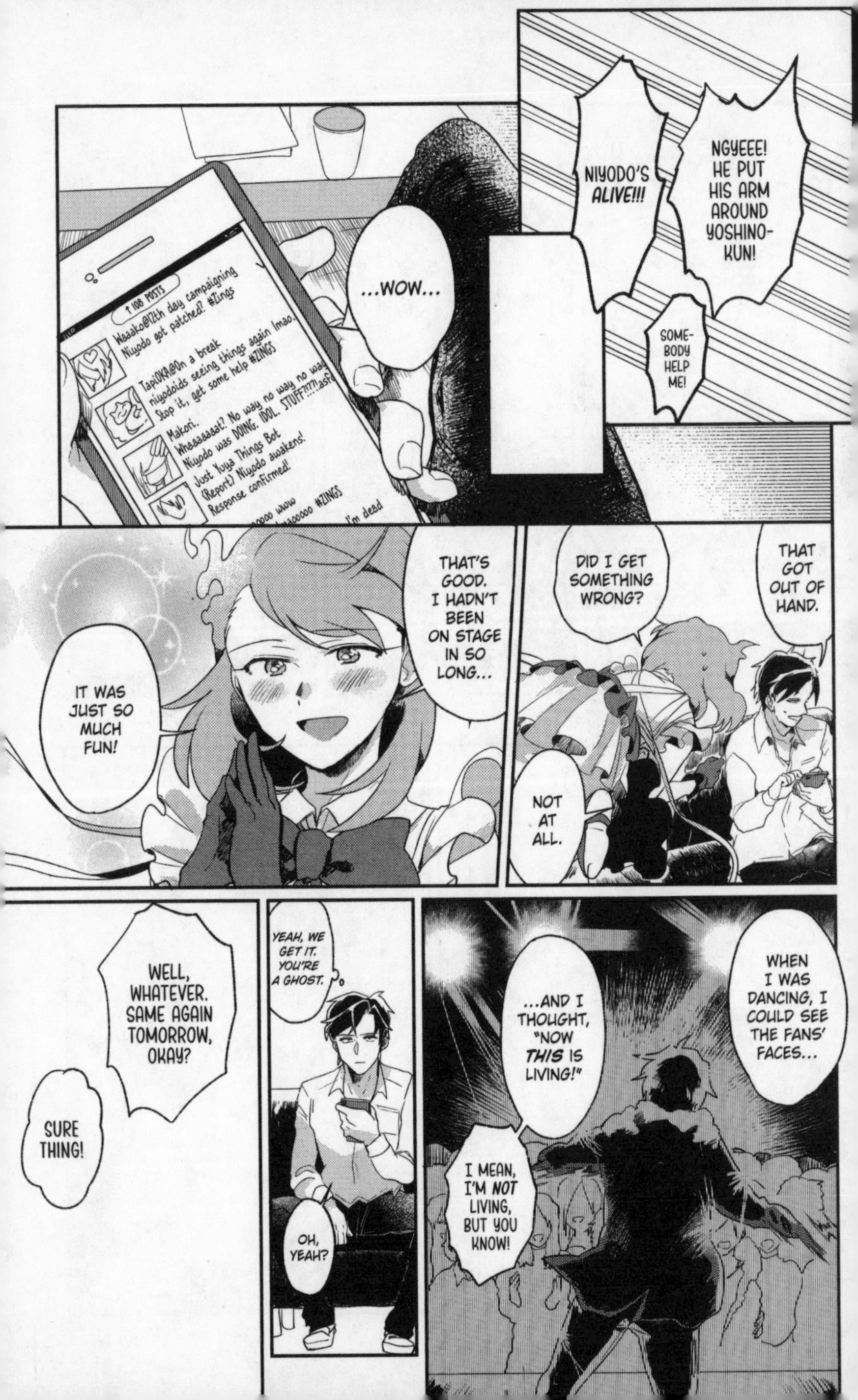
NGYEEE! HE PUT HIS ARM AROUND YOSHINO-KUN!
NIYODO'S *ALIVE!!!*
SOME-BODY HELP ME!
↑108 POSTS
Waaako@12th day campaigning
Niyodo got patched? #Zings
TapiOKA@On a break
niyodoids seeing things again lmao.
Stop it, get some help #ZINGS
Makori.
Whaaaaaaat?! No way no way no way
Niyodo was DOING. IDOL. STUFF?!?!?!
Just Yuya Things Bot
(Report) Niyodo awakens!
Response confirmed!
...WOW...
THAT GOT OUT OF HAND.
DID I GET SOMETHING WRONG?
NOT AT ALL.
THAT'S GOOD. I HADN'T BEEN ON STAGE IN SO LONG...
IT WAS JUST SO MUCH FUN!
WHEN I WAS DANCING, I COULD SEE THE FANS' FACES...
...AND I THOUGHT, "NOW *THIS* IS LIVING!"
I MEAN, I'M *NOT* LIVING, BUT YOU KNOW!
YEAH, WE GET IT. YOU'RE A GHOST.
OH, YEAH?
WELL, WHATEVER. SAME AGAIN TOMORROW, OKAY?
SURE THING!

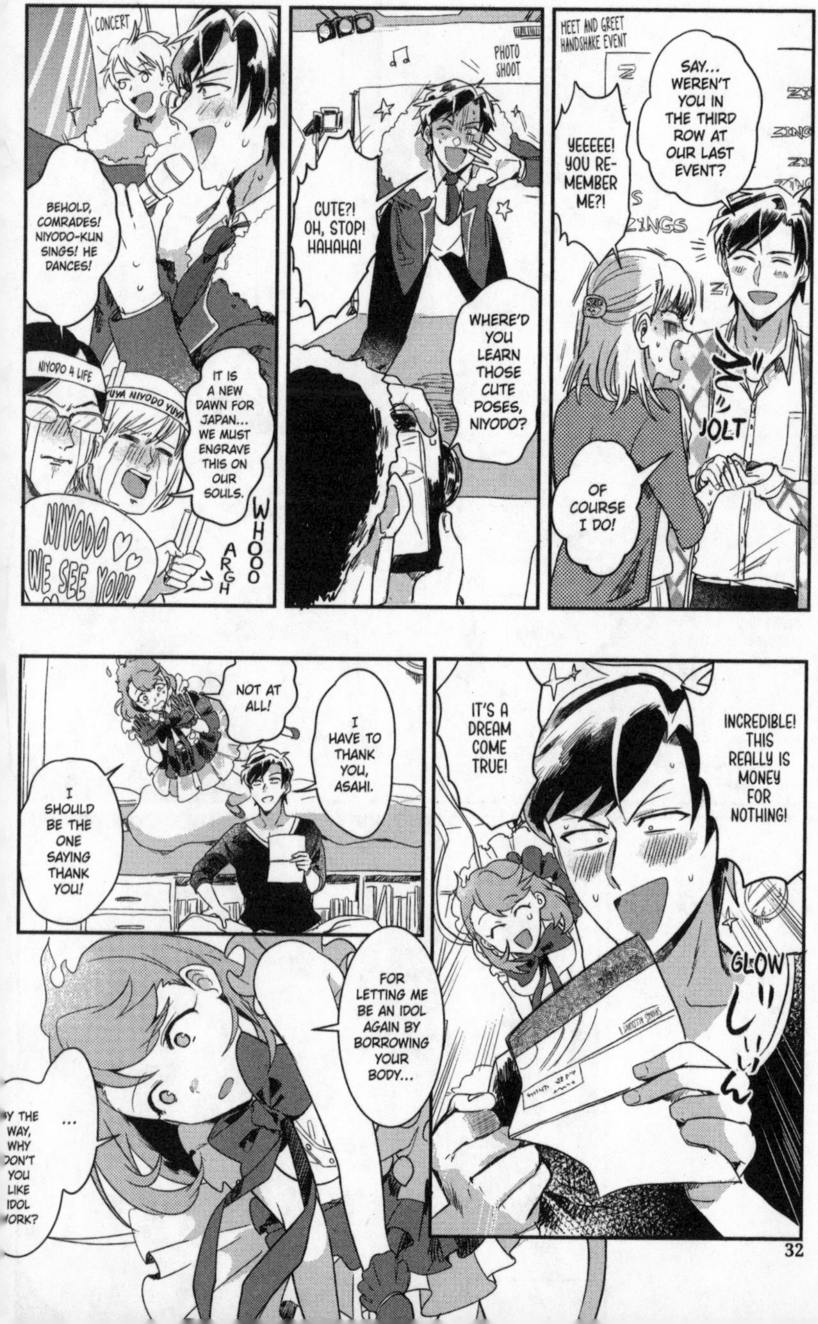
MEET AND GREET HANDSHAKE EVENT
SAY... WEREN'T YOU IN THE THIRD ROW AT OUR LAST EVENT?
YEEEEE! YOU RE-MEMBER ME?!
ZINGS
JOLT
OF COURSE I DO!
PHOTO SHOOT
CUTE?! OH, STOP! HAHAHA!
WHERE'D YOU LEARN THOSE CUTE POSES, NIYODO?
CONCERT
BEHOLD, COMRADES! NIYODO-KUN SINGS! HE DANCES!
NIYODO 4 LIFE
YUYA NIYODO YUYA
IT IS A NEW DAWN FOR JAPAN... WE MUST ENGRAVE THIS ON OUR SOULS.
WHOOO
ARGH
NIYODO ♡ WE SEE YOU!
INCREDIBLE! THIS REALLY IS MONEY FOR NOTHING!
IT'S A DREAM COME TRUE!
GLOW
I HAVE TO THANK YOU, ASAHI.
NOT AT ALL!
I SHOULD BE THE ONE SAYING THANK YOU!
FOR LETTING ME BE AN IDOL AGAIN BY BORROWING YOUR BODY...
...
Y THE WAY, WHY ON'T YOU LIKE IDOL ORK?

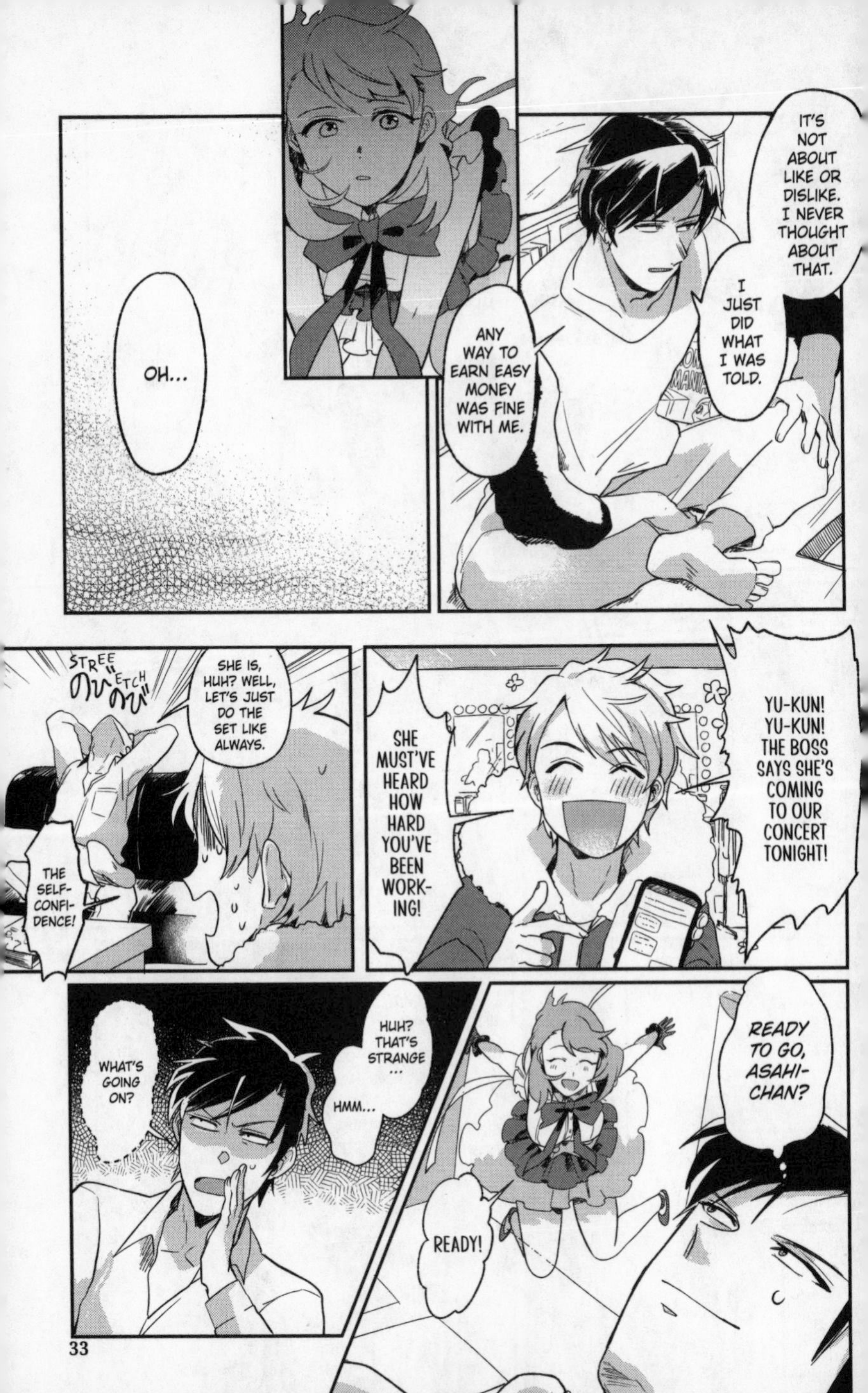
IT'S NOT ABOUT LIKE OR DISLIKE. I NEVER THOUGHT ABOUT THAT.
I JUST DID WHAT I WAS TOLD.
ANY WAY TO EARN EASY MONEY WAS FINE WITH ME.
OH...
YU-KUN! YU-KUN! THE BOSS SAYS SHE'S COMING TO OUR CONCERT TONIGHT!
SHE MUST'VE HEARD HOW HARD YOU'VE BEEN WORK-ING!
SHE IS, HUH? WELL, LET'S JUST DO THE SET LIKE ALWAYS.
STREEETCH
のびのび
THE SELF-CONFI-DENCE!
READY TO GO, ASAHI-CHAN?
READY!
HUH? THAT'S STRANGE...
HMM...
WHAT'S GOING ON?

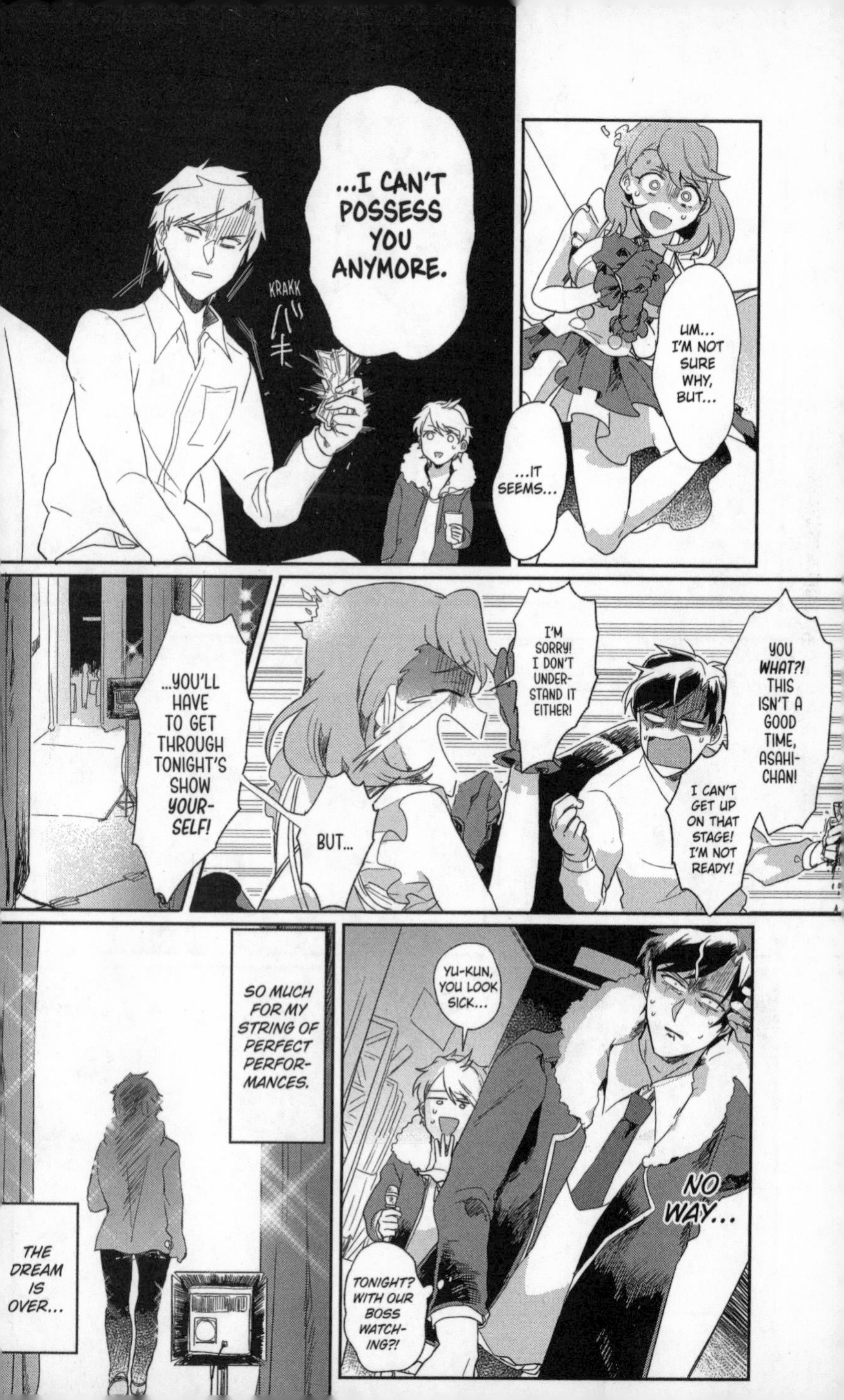
UM... I'M NOT SURE WHY, BUT...
...IT SEEMS...
...I CAN'T POSSESS YOU ANYMORE.
KRAKK
YOU WHAT?! THIS ISN'T A GOOD TIME, ASAHI-CHAN!
I CAN'T GET UP ON THAT STAGE! I'M NOT READY!
I'M SORRY! I DON'T UNDERSTAND IT EITHER!
BUT...
...YOU'LL HAVE TO GET THROUGH TONIGHT'S SHOW YOURSELF!
YU-KUN, YOU LOOK SICK...
NO WAY...
TONIGHT? WITH OUR BOSS WATCHING?!
SO MUCH FOR MY STRING OF PERFECT PERFORMANCES.
THE DREAM IS OVER...

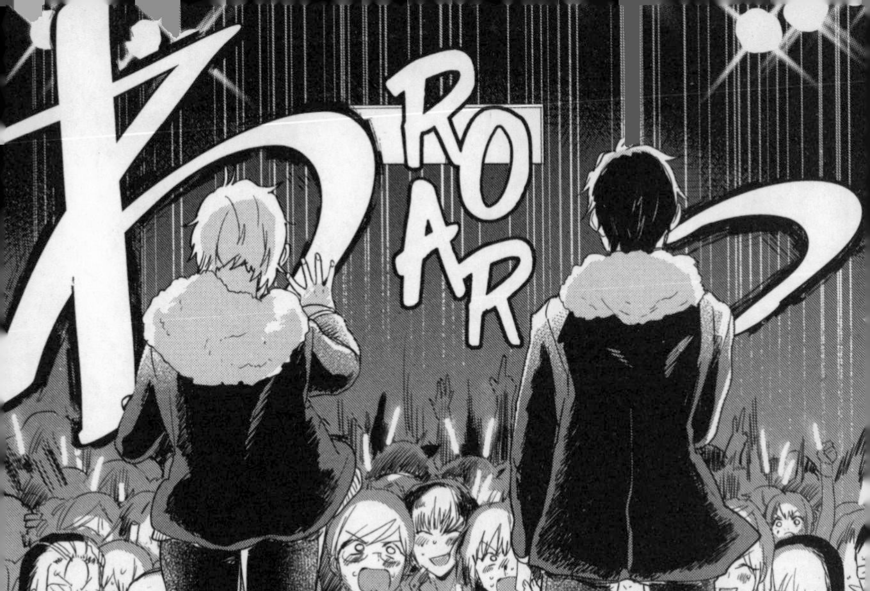
ROAR
YOSHINO
LOVE
NIYO
YU
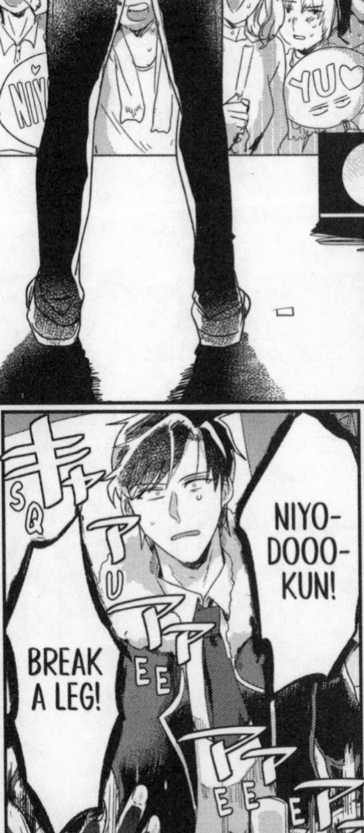
NIYO-DOOOO-KUN!
BREAK A LEG!
SQUEEEEP
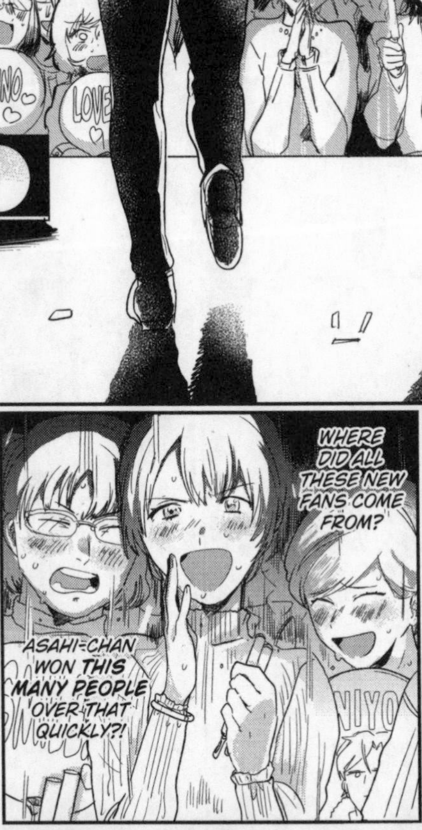
WHERE DID ALL THESE NEW FANS COME FROM?
ASAHI-CHAN WON THIS MANY PEOPLE OVER THAT QUICKLY?!
NIYO

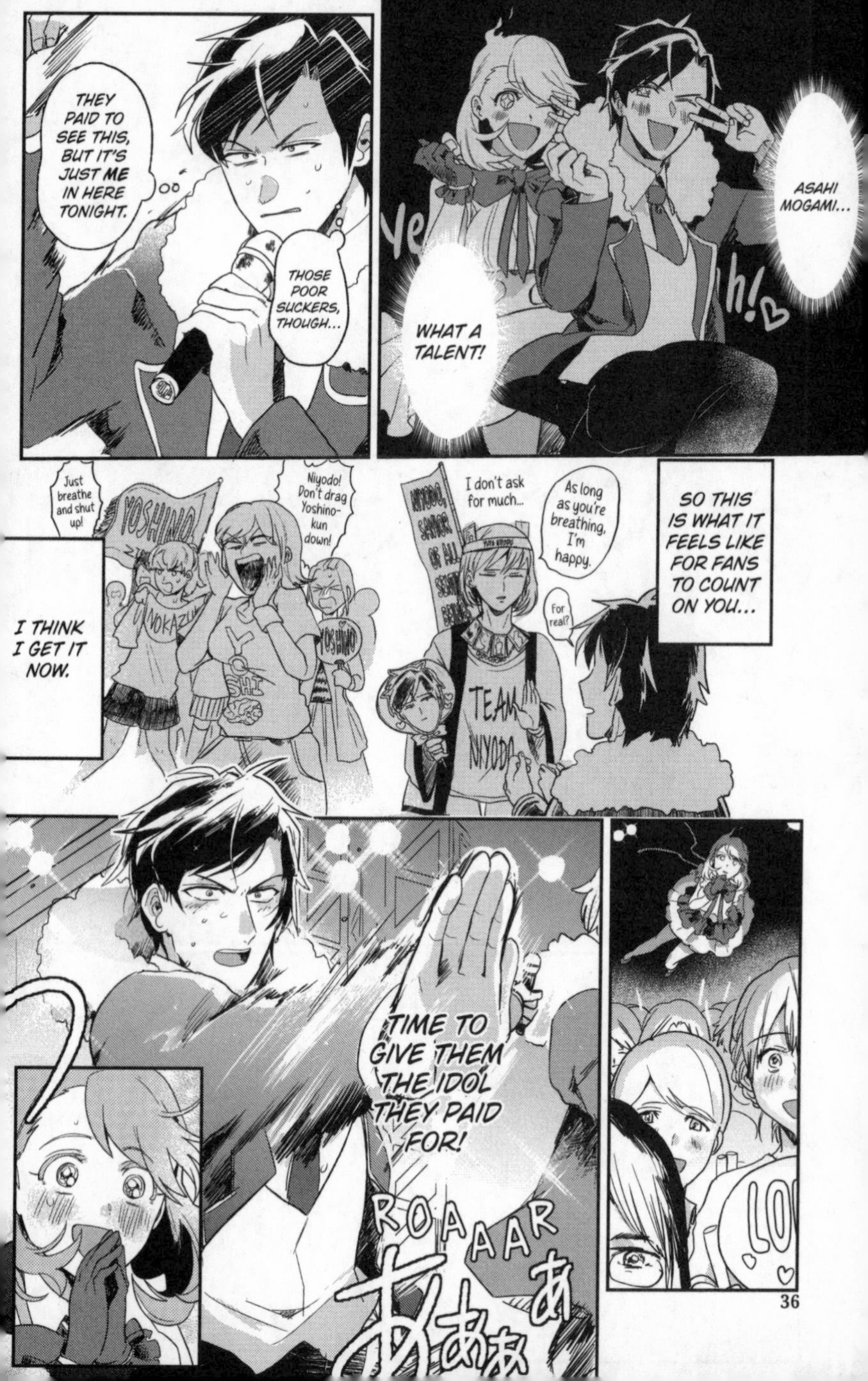

ASAHI MOGAMI...
WHAT A TALENT!
THEY PAID TO SEE THIS, BUT IT'S JUST ME IN HERE TONIGHT.
THOSE POOR SUCKERS, THOUGH...
SO THIS IS WHAT IT FEELS LIKE FOR FANS TO COUNT ON YOU...
As long as you're breathing, I'm happy.
For real?
I don't ask for much...
TEAM NIYODO
Niyodo! Don't drag Yoshino-kun down!
YOSHINO
Just breathe and shut up!
I THINK I GET IT NOW.
TIME TO GIVE THEM THE IDOL THEY PAID FOR!
ROAAAR

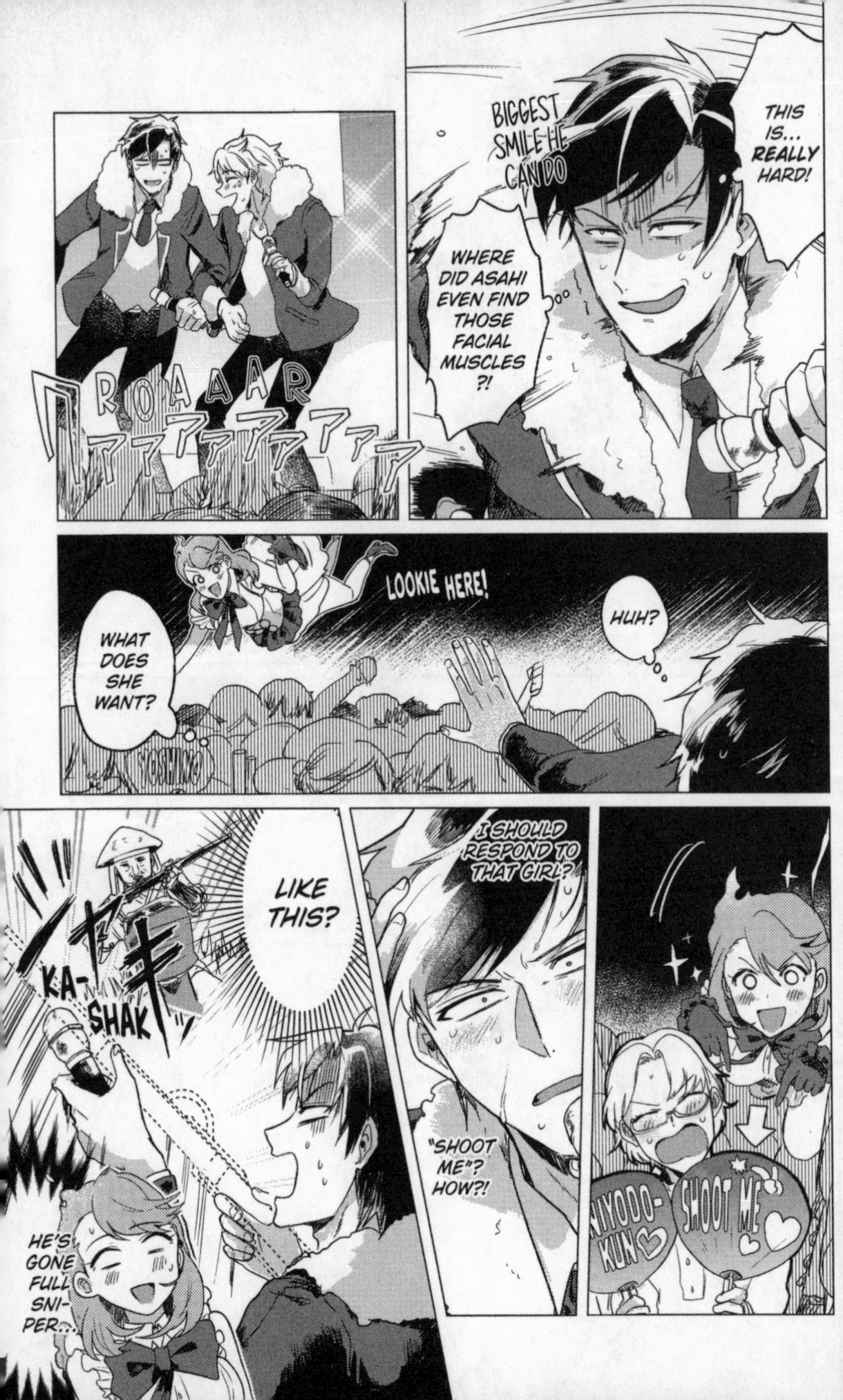
THIS IS... REALLY HARD!
BIGGEST SMILE HE CAN DO
WHERE DID ASAHI EVEN FIND THOSE FACIAL MUSCLES?!
ROAAAR
HUH?
LOOKIE HERE!
WHAT DOES SHE WANT?
NIYODO-KUN
SHOOT ME
I SHOULD RESPOND TO THAT GIRL?
"SHOOT ME"? HOW?!
LIKE THIS?
KA-SHAK
HE'S GONE FULL SNI-PER...

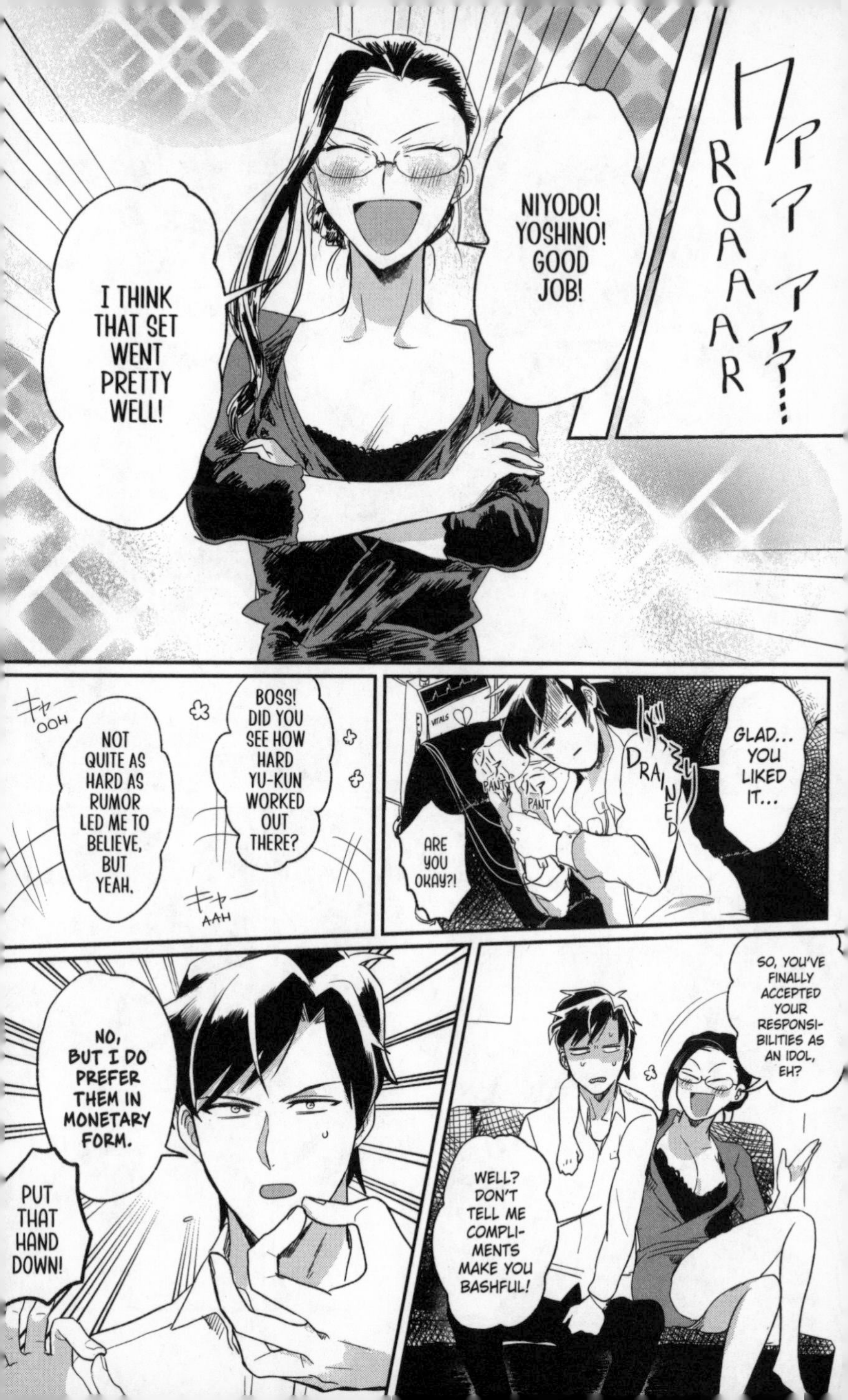
ROAAAR
NIYODO! YOSHINO! GOOD JOB!
I THINK THAT SET WENT PRETTY WELL!
GLAD... YOU LIKED IT...
DRAINED
PANT
PANT
ARE YOU OKAY?!
BOSS! DID YOU SEE HOW HARD YU-KUN WORKED OUT THERE?
OOH
NOT QUITE AS HARD AS RUMOR LED ME TO BELIEVE, BUT YEAH.
AAH
SO, YOU'VE FINALLY ACCEPTED YOUR RESPONSI-BILITIES AS AN IDOL, EH?
WELL? DON'T TELL ME COMPLI-MENTS MAKE YOU BASHFUL!
NO, BUT I DO PREFER THEM IN MONETARY FORM.
PUT THAT HAND DOWN!

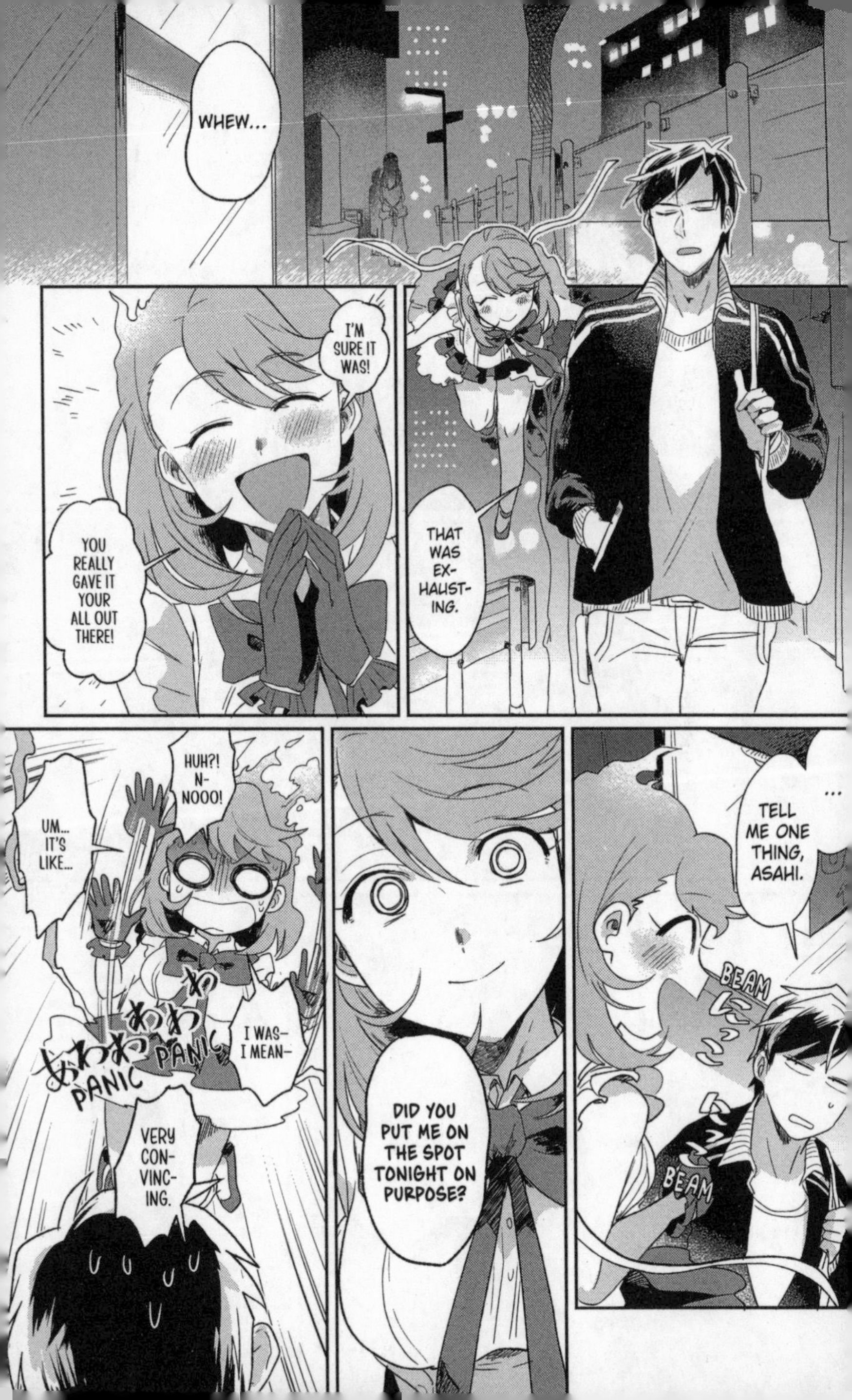
WHEW...
THAT WAS EX-HAUST-ING.
I'M SURE IT WAS!
YOU REALLY GAVE IT YOUR ALL OUT THERE!
...
TELL ME ONE THING, ASAHI.
BEAM
BEAM
DID YOU PUT ME ON THE SPOT TONIGHT ON PURPOSE?
HUH?! N-NOOO!
UM... IT'S LIKE...
I WAS- I MEAN-
PANIC
PANIC
VERY CON-VINC-ING.

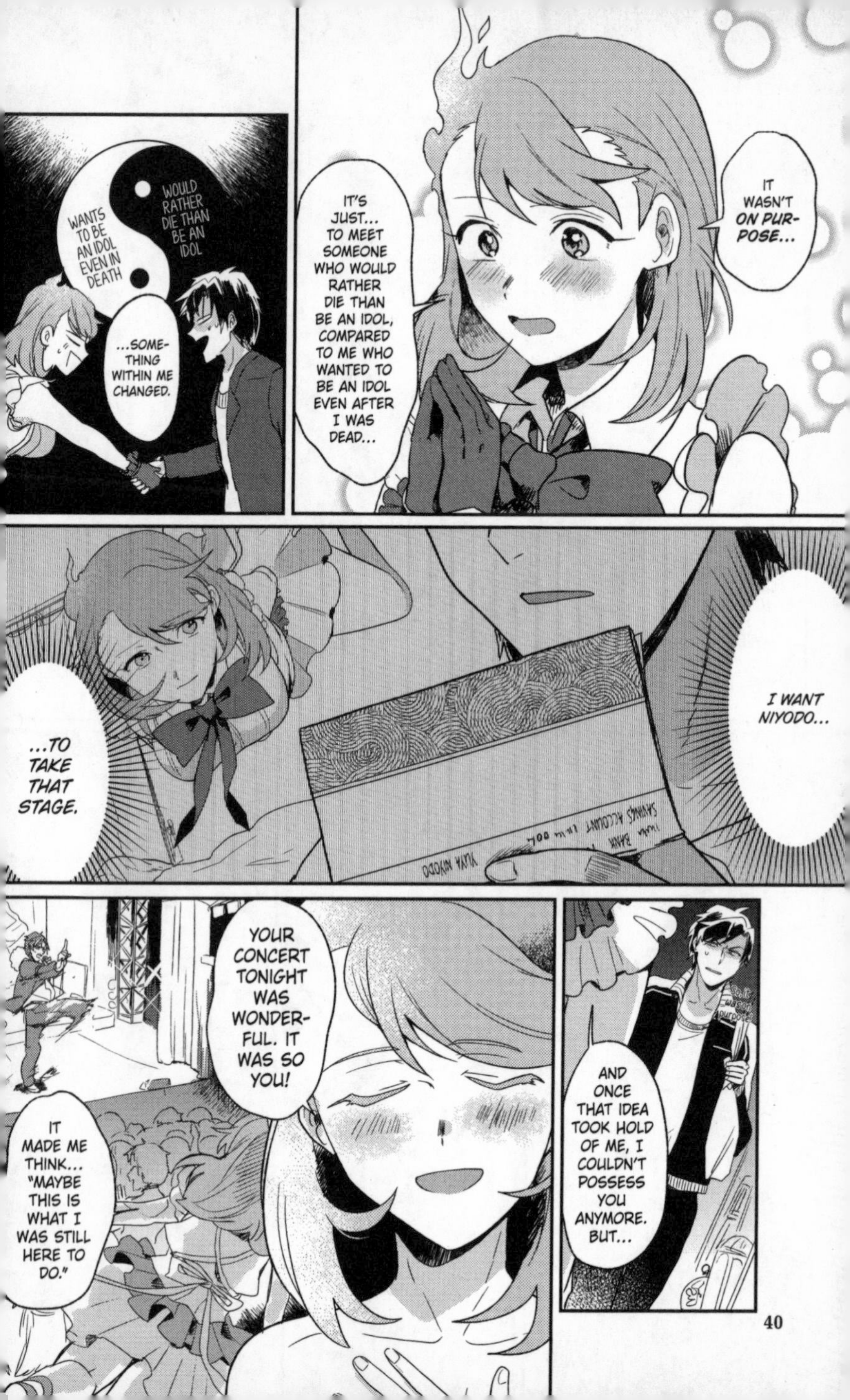
IT WASN'T *ON PURPOSE*...
IT'S JUST... TO MEET SOMEONE WHO WOULD RATHER DIE THAN BE AN IDOL, COMPARED TO ME WHO WANTED TO BE AN IDOL EVEN AFTER I WAS DEAD...
WOULD RATHER DIE THAN BE AN IDOL
WANTS TO BE AN IDOL EVEN IN DEATH
...SOMETHING WITHIN ME CHANGED.
I WANT NIYODO...
...TO TAKE THAT STAGE.
AND ONCE THAT IDEA TOOK HOLD OF ME, I COULDN'T POSSESS YOU ANYMORE. BUT...
YOUR CONCERT TONIGHT WAS WONDERFUL. IT WAS SO YOU!
IT MADE ME THINK... "MAYBE THIS IS WHAT I WAS STILL HERE TO DO."

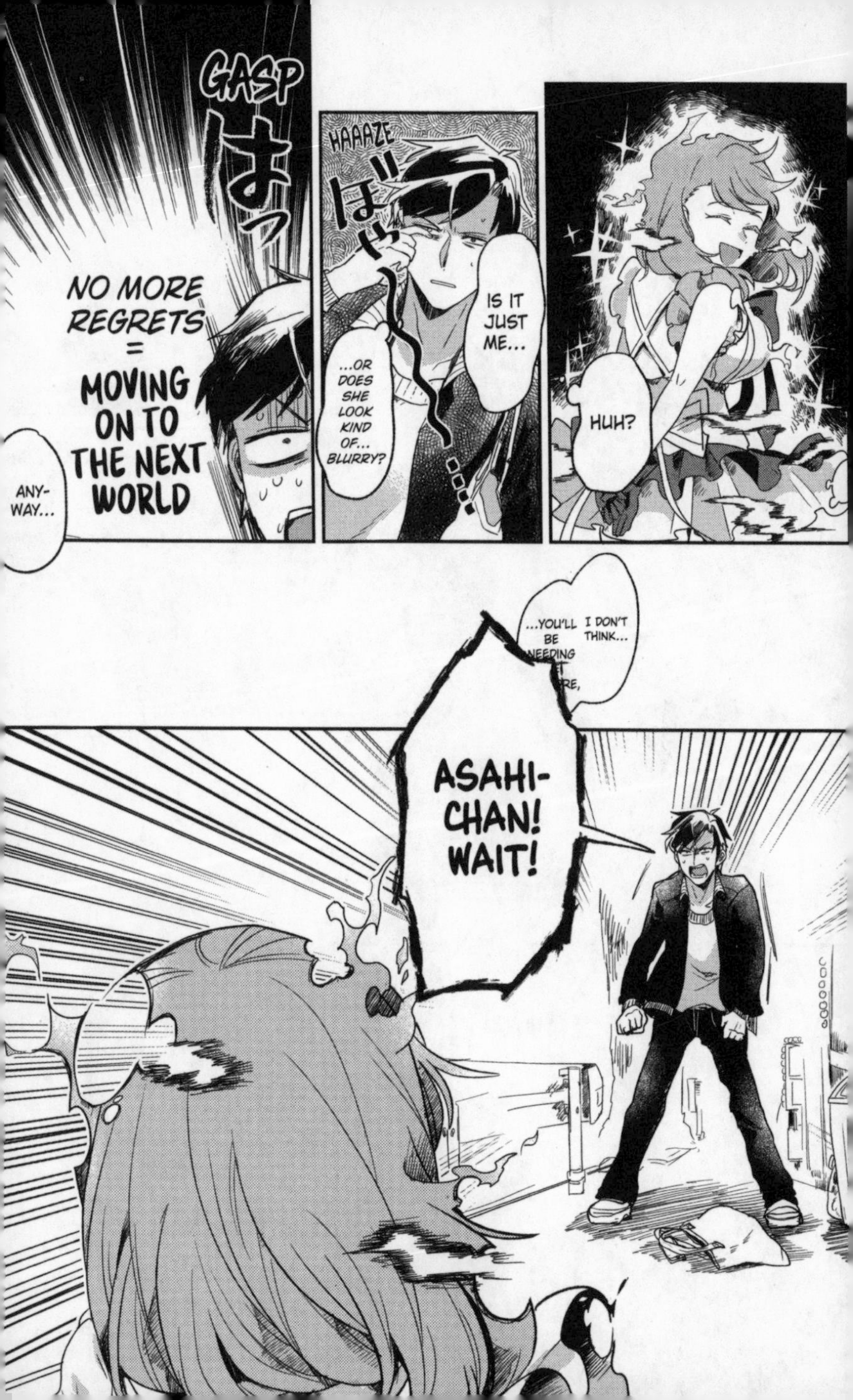
HUH?
IS IT JUST ME...
...OR DOES SHE LOOK KIND OF... BLURRY?
HAAAZE
ぼやぁ
......
GASP
はっ
NO MORE REGRETS = MOVING ON TO THE NEXT WORLD
ANY-WAY...
I DON'T THINK... ...YOU'LL BE NEEDING
ASAHI-CHAN! WAIT!

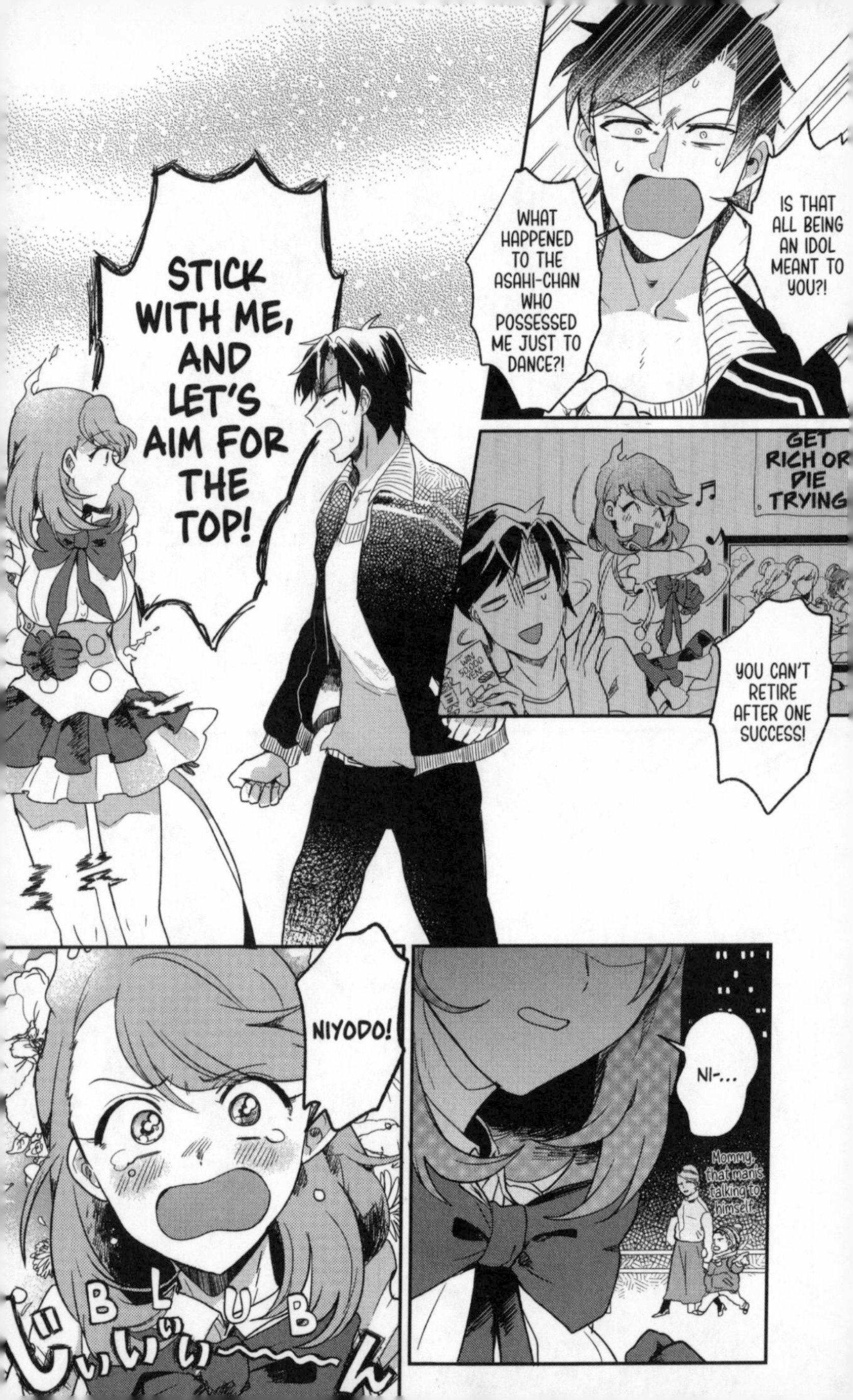
IS THAT ALL BEING AN IDOL MEANT TO YOU?!
WHAT HAPPENED TO THE ASAHI-CHAN WHO POSSESSED ME JUST TO DANCE?!
GET RICH OR DIE TRYING
YOU CAN'T RETIRE AFTER ONE SUCCESS!
STICK WITH ME, AND LET'S AIM FOR THE TOP!
NI-...
Mommy, that man's talking to himself.
NIYODO!
BLUB
じいいい〜〜ん

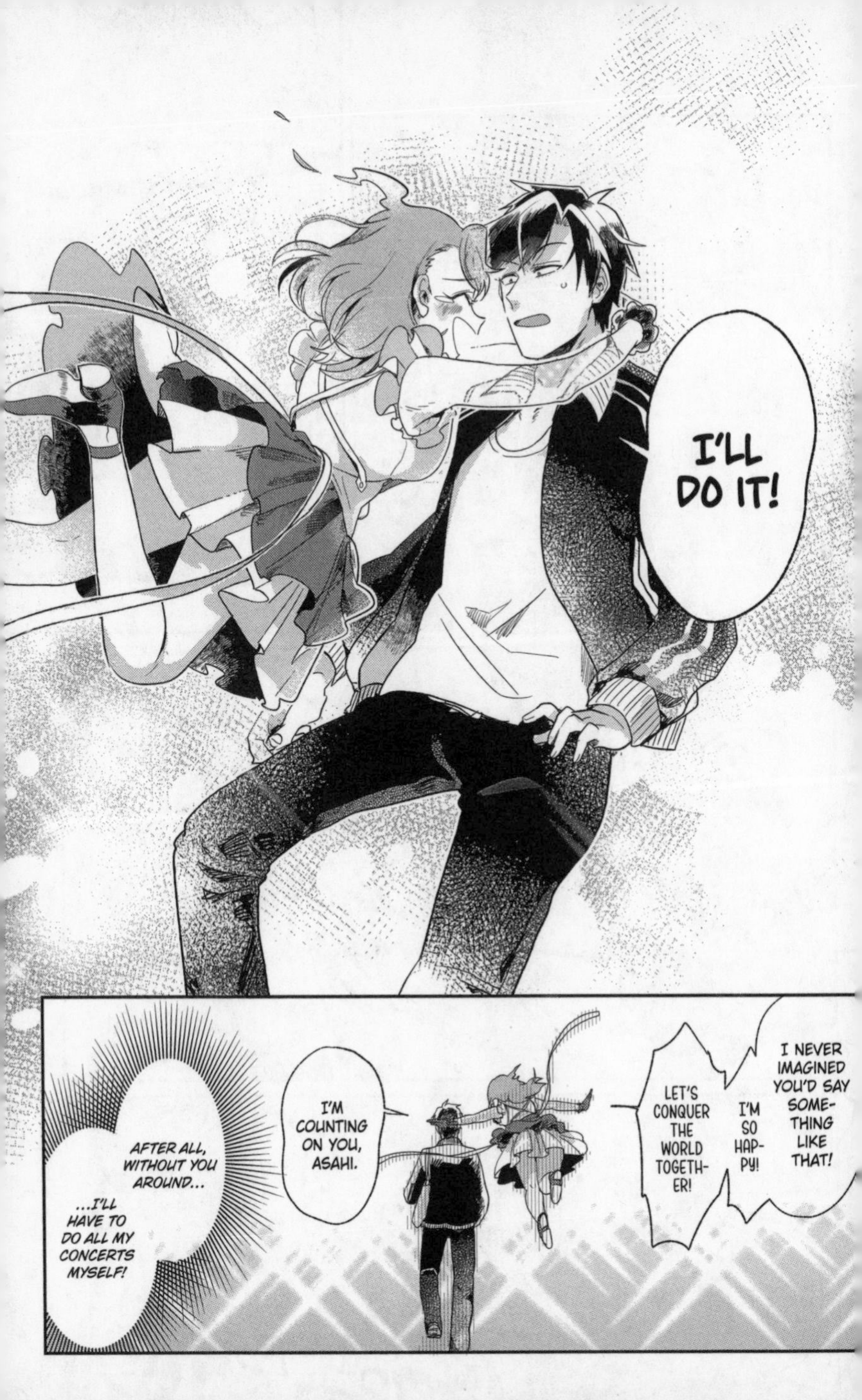
I'LL DO IT!
I NEVER IMAGINED YOU'D SAY SOME-THING LIKE THAT!
I'M SO HAP-PY!
LET'S CONQUER THE WORLD TOGETH-ER!
I'M COUNTING ON YOU, ASAHI.
AFTER ALL, WITHOUT YOU AROUND...
...I'LL HAVE TO DO ALL MY CONCERTS MYSELF!

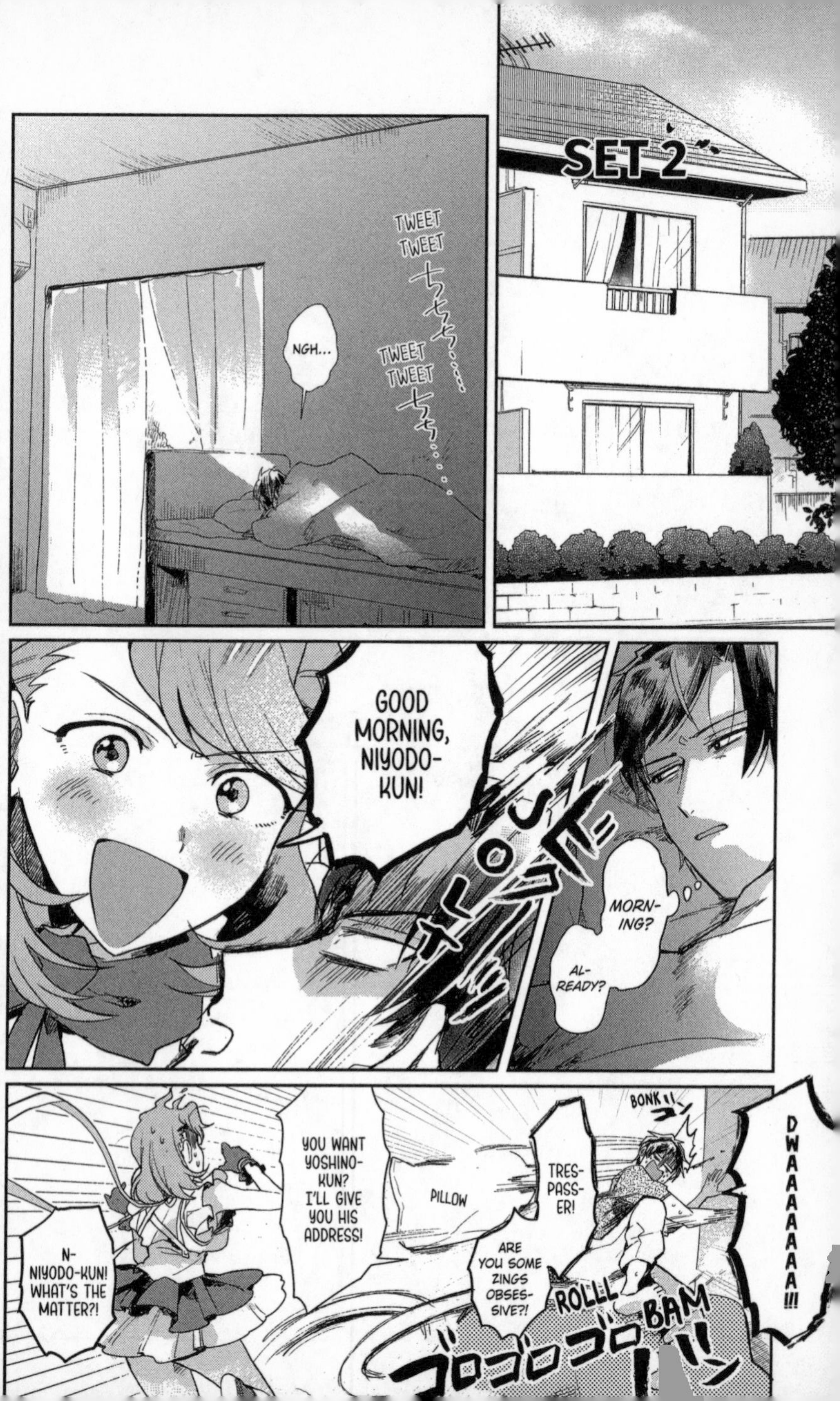
SET 2
TWEET TWEET
ちちち……
TWEET TWEET
ちち……
NGH...
MORN-ING?
AL-READY?
GOOD MORNING, NIYODO-KUN!
DWAAAAAAAA!!!
BONK!!
TRES-PASS-ER!
ARE YOU SOME ZINGS OBSES-SIVE?!
PILLOW
YOU WANT YOSHINO-KUN? I'LL GIVE YOU HIS ADDRESS!
BAM
ROLL
ゴロゴロゴロ
バン
N-NIYODO-KUN! WHAT'S THE MATTER?!

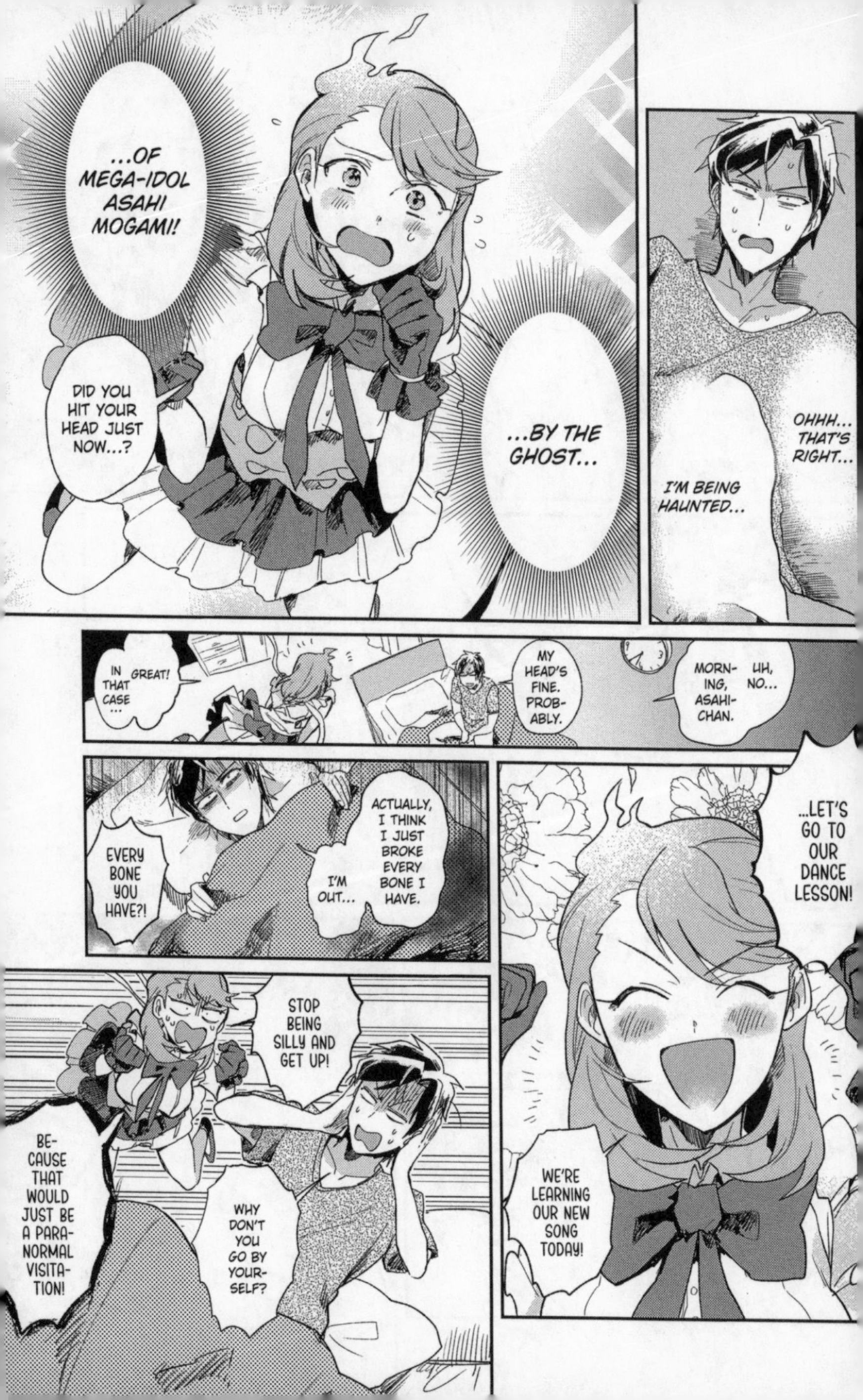
OHHH... THAT'S RIGHT...
I'M BEING HAUNTED...
...BY THE GHOST...
...OF MEGA-IDOL ASAHI MOGAMI!
DID YOU HIT YOUR HEAD JUST NOW...?
UH, NO...
MORNING, ASAHI-CHAN.
MY HEAD'S FINE. PROBABLY.
GREAT!
IN THAT CASE...
...LET'S GO TO OUR DANCE LESSON!
WE'RE LEARNING OUR NEW SONG TODAY!
ACTUALLY, I THINK I JUST BROKE EVERY BONE I HAVE.
I'M OUT...
EVERY BONE YOU HAVE?!
STOP BEING SILLY AND GET UP!
WHY DON'T YOU GO BY YOURSELF?
BECAUSE THAT WOULD JUST BE A PARANORMAL VISITATION!

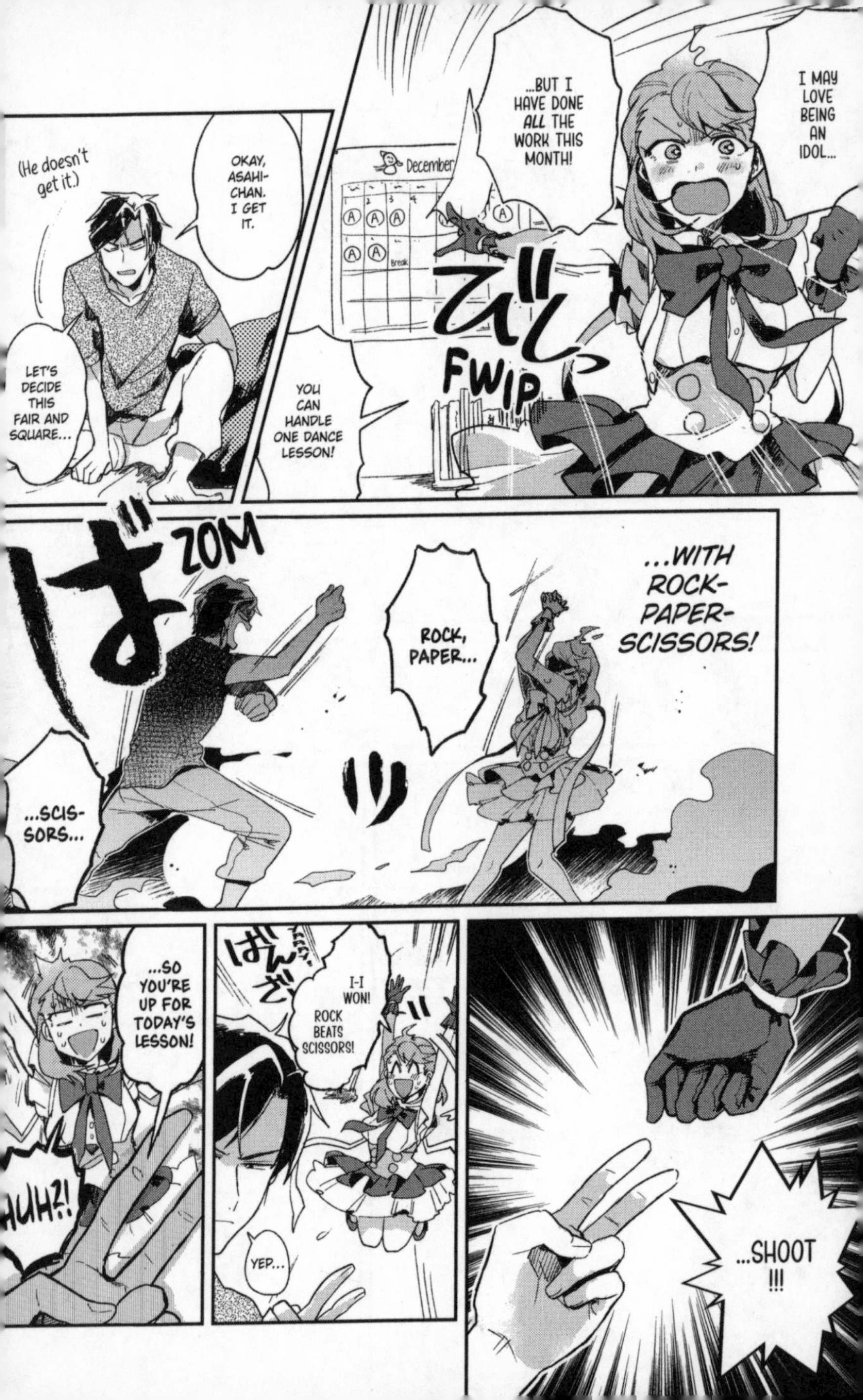
I MAY LOVE BEING AN IDOL...
...BUT I HAVE DONE ALL THE WORK THIS MONTH!
December
Break
びしっ
FWIP
YOU CAN HANDLE ONE DANCE LESSON!
OKAY, ASAHI-CHAN. I GET IT.
(He doesn't get it.)
LET'S DECIDE THIS FAIR AND SQUARE...
...WITH ROCK-PAPER-SCISSORS!
ROCK, PAPER...
ZOM
...SCIS-SORS...
...SHOOT !!!
I-I WON! ROCK BEATS SCISSORS!
YEP...
...SO YOU'RE UP FOR TODAY'S LESSON!
HUH?!

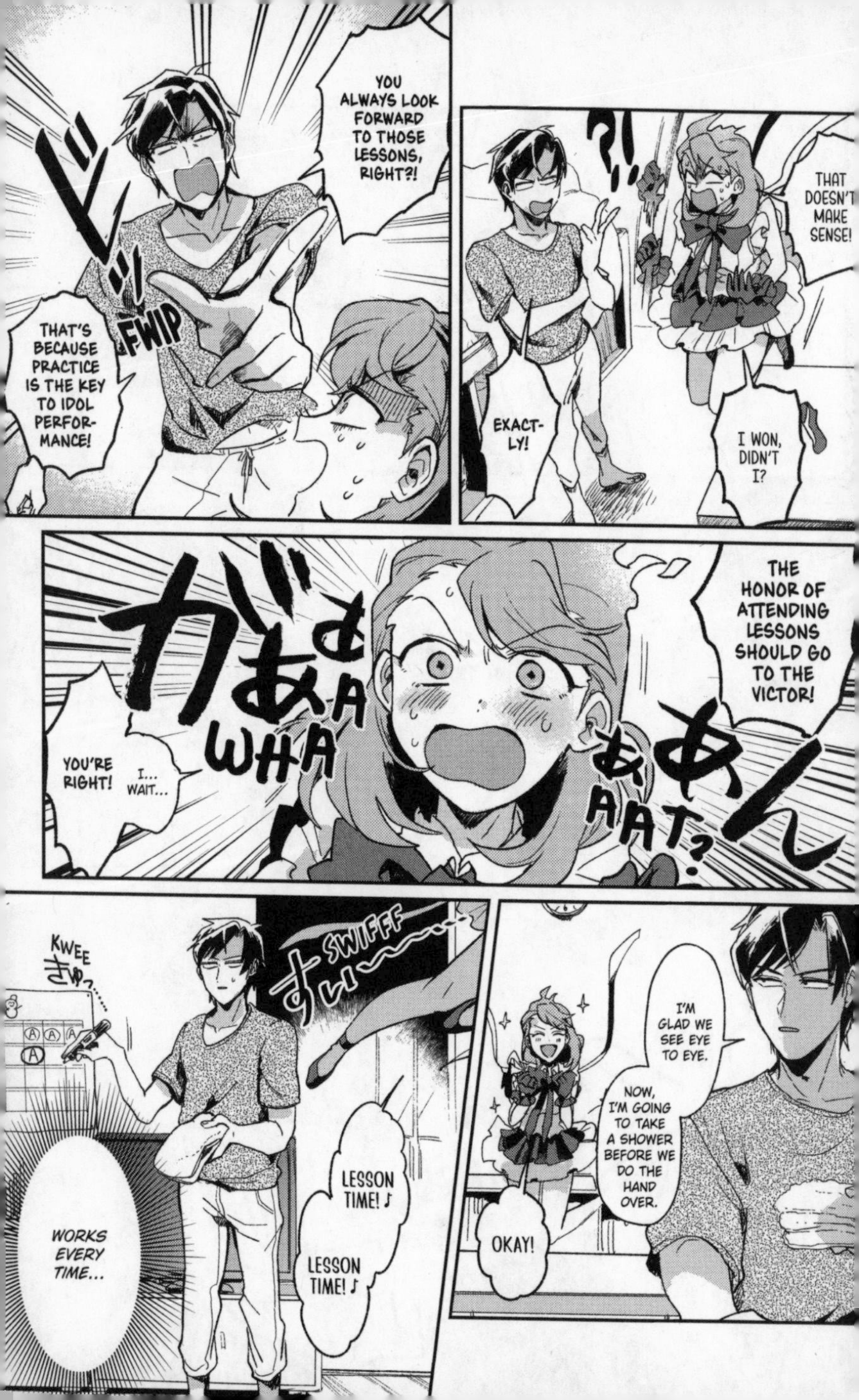
THAT DOESN'T MAKE SENSE!
I WON, DIDN'T I?
EXACTLY!
YOU ALWAYS LOOK FORWARD TO THOSE LESSONS, RIGHT?!
FWIP
THAT'S BECAUSE PRACTICE IS THE KEY TO IDOL PERFORMANCE!
THE HONOR OF ATTENDING LESSONS SHOULD GO TO THE VICTOR!
WHAAAT?
YOU'RE RIGHT!
I... WAIT...
I'M GLAD WE SEE EYE TO EYE.
NOW, I'M GOING TO TAKE A SHOWER BEFORE WE DO THE HAND OVER.
OKAY!
SWIFFF
LESSON TIME! ♪
LESSON TIME! ♪
KWEE
WORKS EVERY TIME...

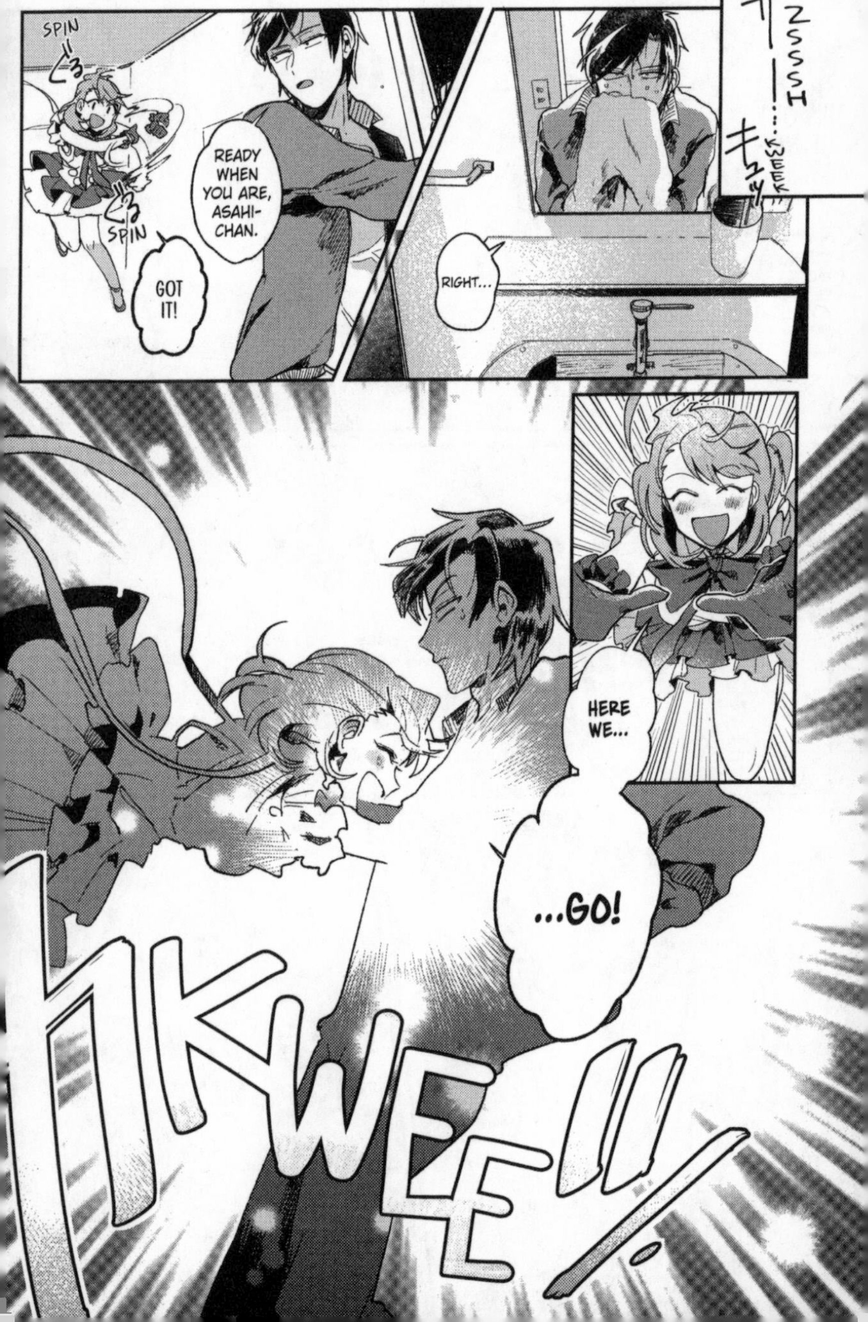
ZSSSSH
KWEEK
RIGHT...
READY WHEN YOU ARE, ASAHI-CHAN.
GOT IT!
SPIN
SPIN
HERE WE...
...GO!
KWEE!!

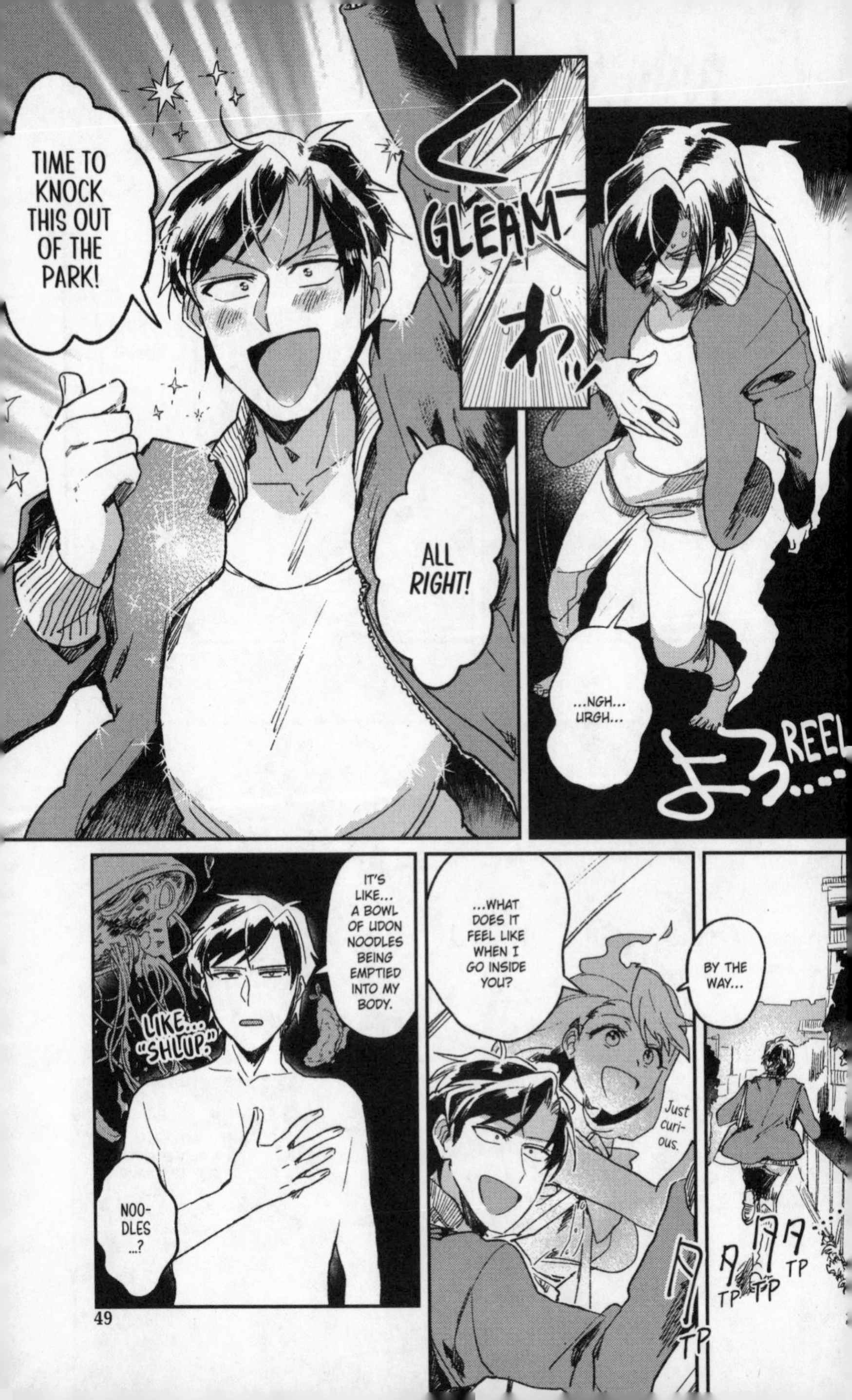
...NGH... URGH...
REEL...
GLEAM
TIME TO KNOCK THIS OUT OF THE PARK!
ALL RIGHT!
BY THE WAY...
TP TP TP TP TP
...WHAT DOES IT FEEL LIKE WHEN I GO INSIDE YOU?
Just curious.
IT'S LIKE... A BOWL OF UDON NOODLES BEING EMPTIED INTO MY BODY.
LIKE... "SHLUP."
NOODLES ...?

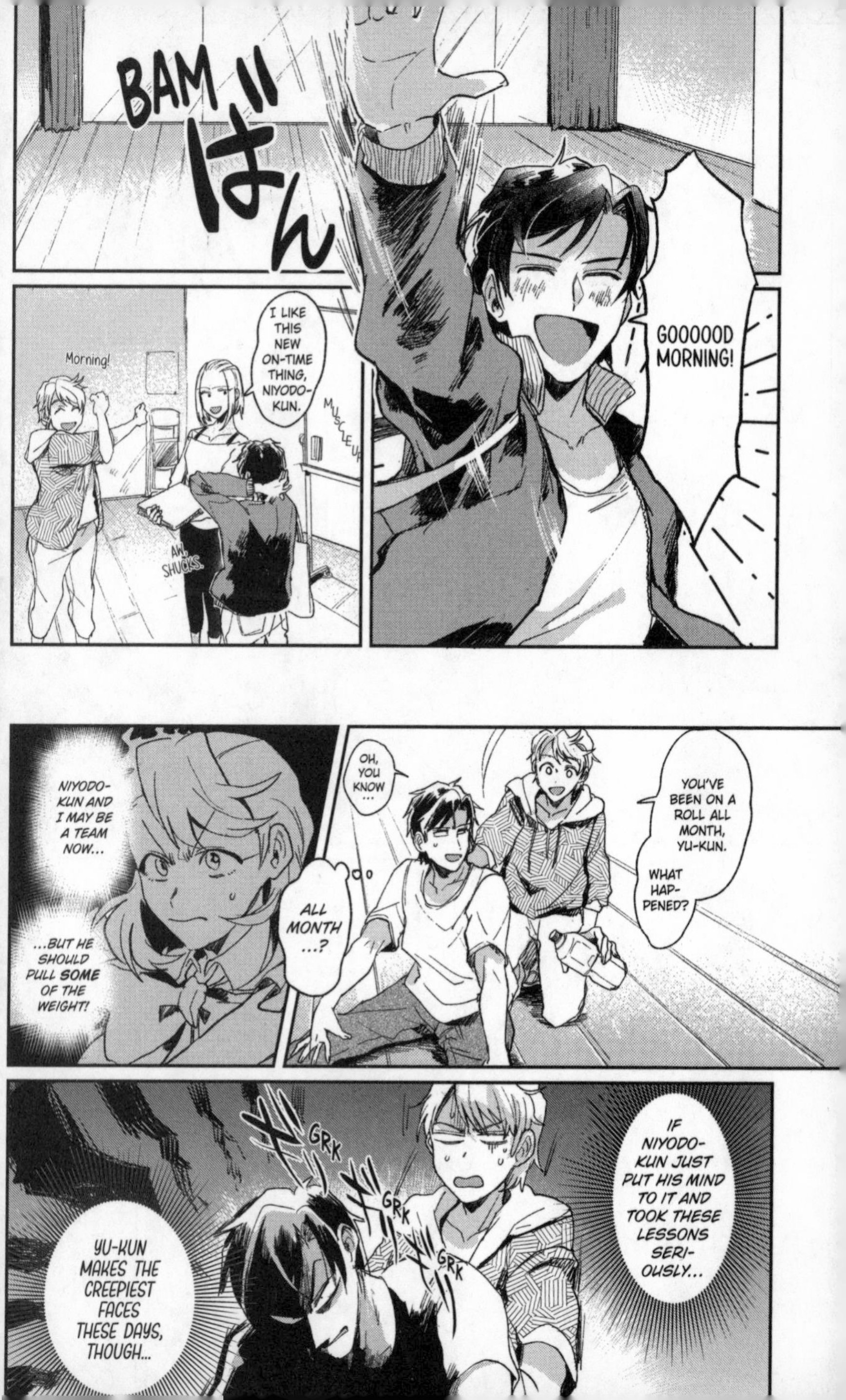

BAM
ばん
GOOOOOD MORNING!
I LIKE THIS NEW ON-TIME THING, NIYODO-KUN.
MUSCLE UP
Morning!
AW, SHUCKS.
YOU'VE BEEN ON A ROLL ALL MONTH, YU-KUN.
WHAT HAPPENED?
OH, YOU KNOW...
ALL MONTH...?
NIYODO-KUN AND I MAY BE A TEAM NOW...
...BUT HE SHOULD PULL SOME OF THE WEIGHT!
IF NIYODO-KUN JUST PUT HIS MIND TO IT AND TOOK THESE LESSONS SERIOUSLY...
GRK
GRK
GRK
YU-KUN MAKES THE CREEPIEST FACES THESE DAYS, THOUGH...

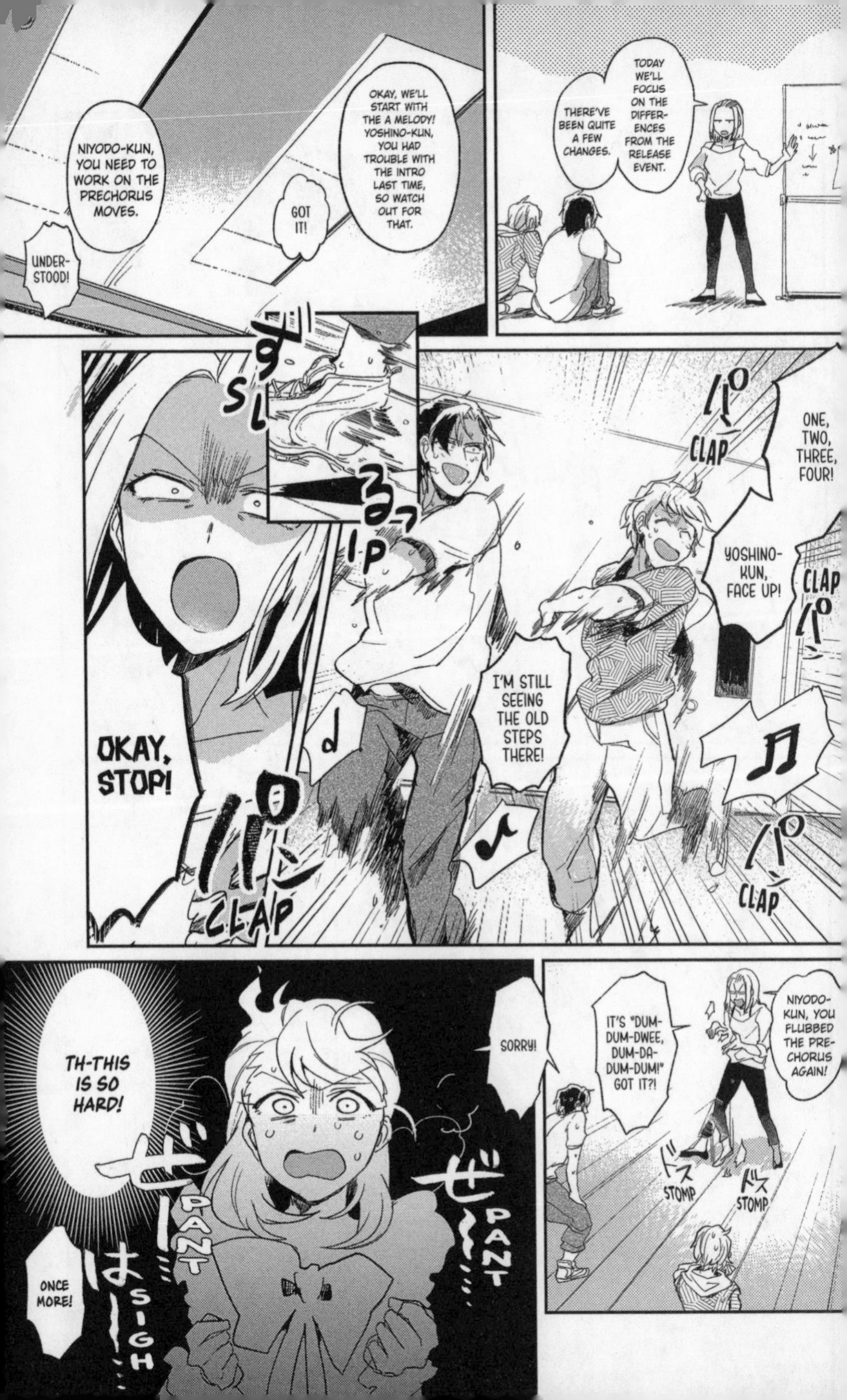
TODAY WE'LL FOCUS ON THE DIFFERENCES FROM THE RELEASE EVENT.
THERE'VE BEEN QUITE A FEW CHANGES.
OKAY, WE'LL START WITH THE A MELODY! YOSHINO-KUN, YOU HAD TROUBLE WITH THE INTRO LAST TIME, SO WATCH OUT FOR THAT.
GOT IT!
NIYODO-KUN, YOU NEED TO WORK ON THE PRECHORUS MOVES.
UNDERSTOOD!
パ
CLAP
ONE, TWO, THREE, FOUR!
YOSHINO-KUN, FACE UP!
CLAP
パ
パ
CLAP
I'M STILL SEEING THE OLD STEPS THERE!
パン
CLAP
OKAY, STOP!
ずるっ
SLIP
NIYODO-KUN, YOU FLUBBED THE PRECHORUS AGAIN!
IT'S "DUM-DUM-DWEE, DUM-DA-DUM-DUM!" GOT IT?!
ドス
STOMP
ドス
STOMP
SORRY!
TH-THIS IS SO HARD!
ぜ〜
PANT
ぜー
PANT
はー
SIGH
ONCE MORE!

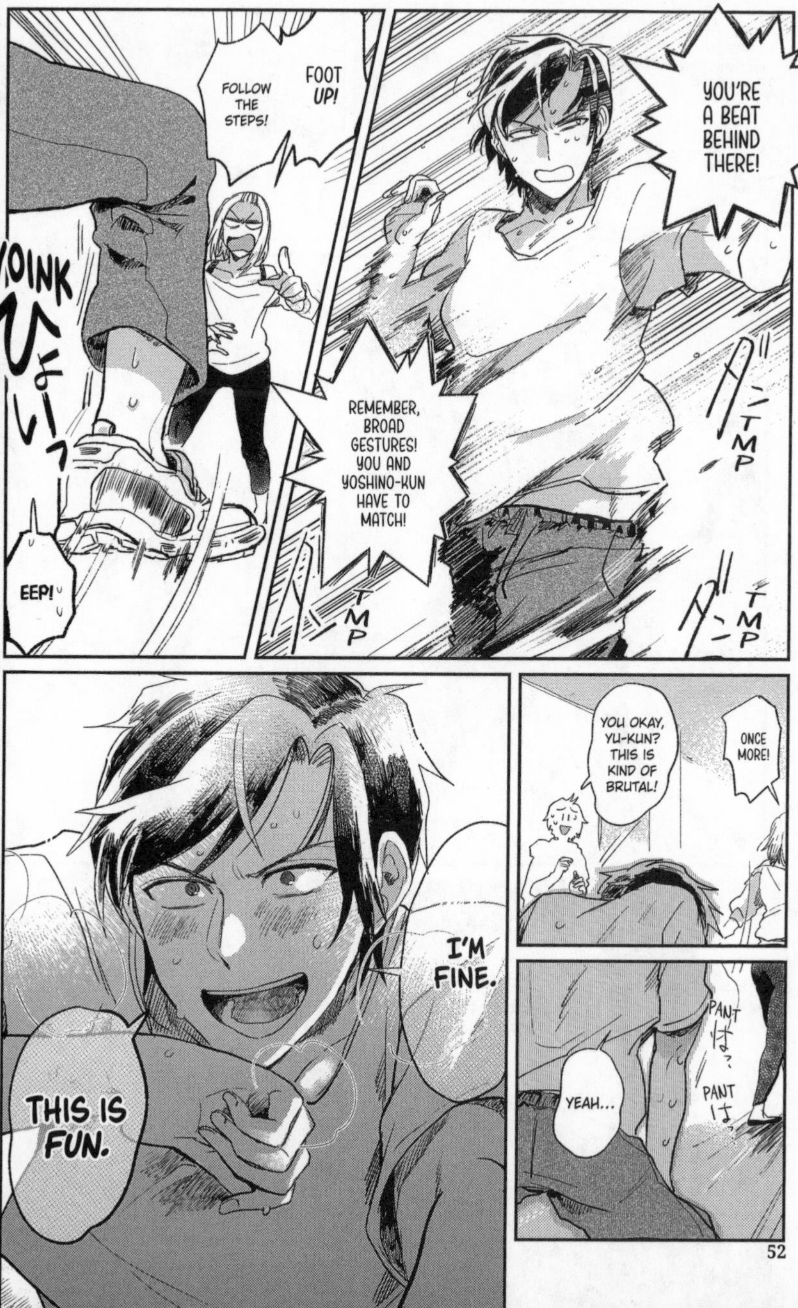

YOU'RE A BEAT BEHIND THERE!
TMP
REMEMBER, BROAD GESTURES! YOU AND YOSHINO-KUN HAVE TO MATCH!
TMP
TMP
FOOT UP!
FOLLOW THE STEPS!
YOINK
ひょいっ
EEP!
ONCE MORE!
YOU OKAY, YU-KUN? THIS IS KIND OF BRUTAL!
PANT
はっ
PANT
はっ
YEAH...
I'M FINE.
THIS IS FUN.

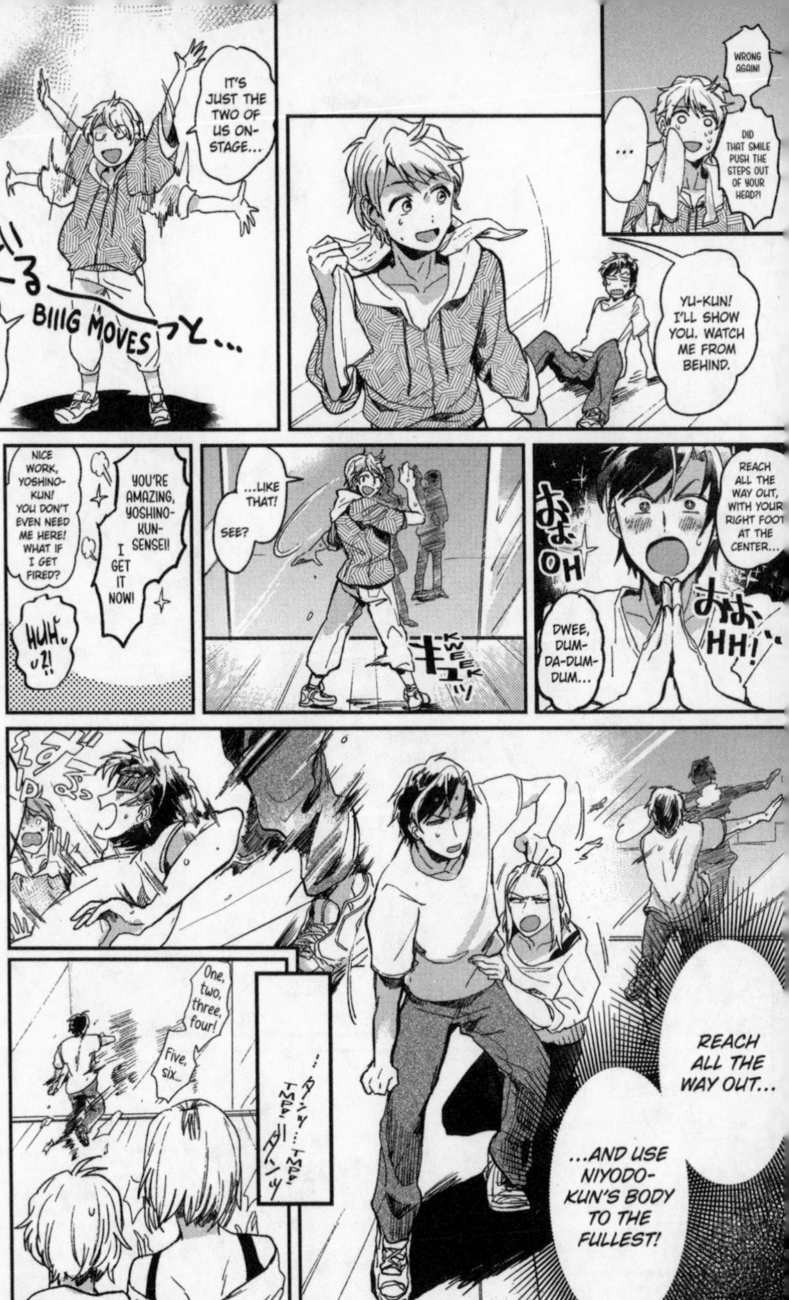
WRONG AGAIN!
...
DID THAT SMILE PUSH THE STEPS OUT OF YOUR HEAD?!
YU-KUN! I'LL SHOW YOU. WATCH ME FROM BEHIND.
IT'S JUST THE TWO OF US ON-STAGE...
BIIIG MOVES
...SO WE EACH HAVE TO FILL HALF THE SPACE!
REACH ALL THE WAY OUT, WITH YOUR RIGHT FOOT AT THE CENTER...
OH
HH!
DWEE, DUM-DA-DUM-DUM...
...LIKE THAT!
SEE?
KWEEK
YOU'RE AMAZING, YOSHINO-KUN-SENSEI!
I GET IT NOW!
NICE WORK, YOSHINO-KUN! YOU DON'T EVEN NEED ME HERE! WHAT IF I GET FIRED?
HUH?!
REACH ALL THE WAY OUT...
...AND USE NIYODO-KUN'S BODY TO THE FULLEST!
TMP! TMP! TMP!
One, two, three, four!
Five, six...

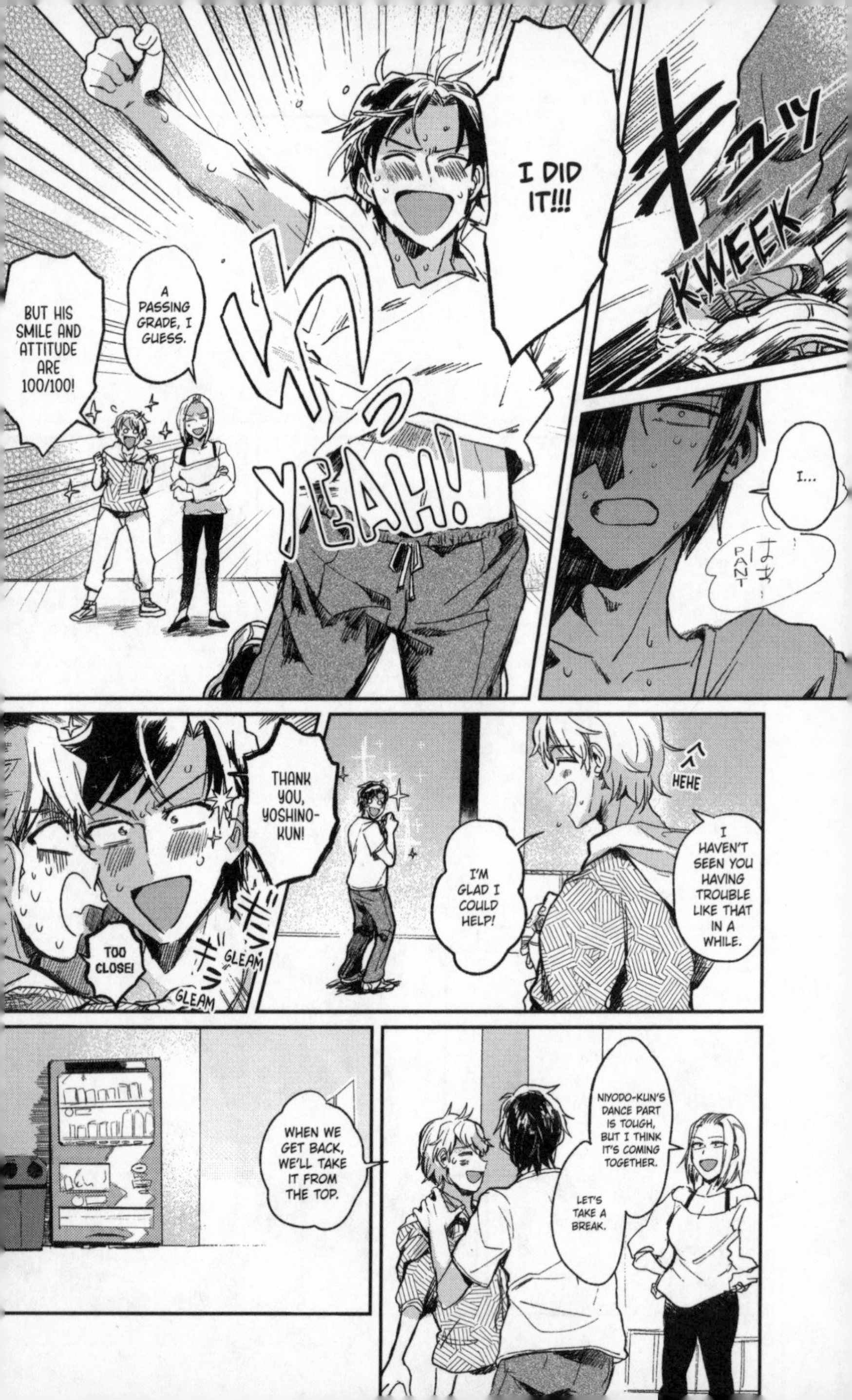
キュッ
KWEEK
I...
はぁ
PANT
I DID IT!!!
YEAH!
A PASSING GRADE, I GUESS.
BUT HIS SMILE AND ATTITUDE ARE 100/100!
HEHE
I HAVEN'T SEEN YOU HAVING TROUBLE LIKE THAT IN A WHILE.
I'M GLAD I COULD HELP!
THANK YOU, YOSHINO-KUN!
GLEAM
GLEAM
TOO CLOSE!
NIYODO-KUN'S DANCE PART IS TOUGH, BUT I THINK IT'S COMING TOGETHER.
LET'S TAKE A BREAK.
WHEN WE GET BACK, WE'LL TAKE IT FROM THE TOP.

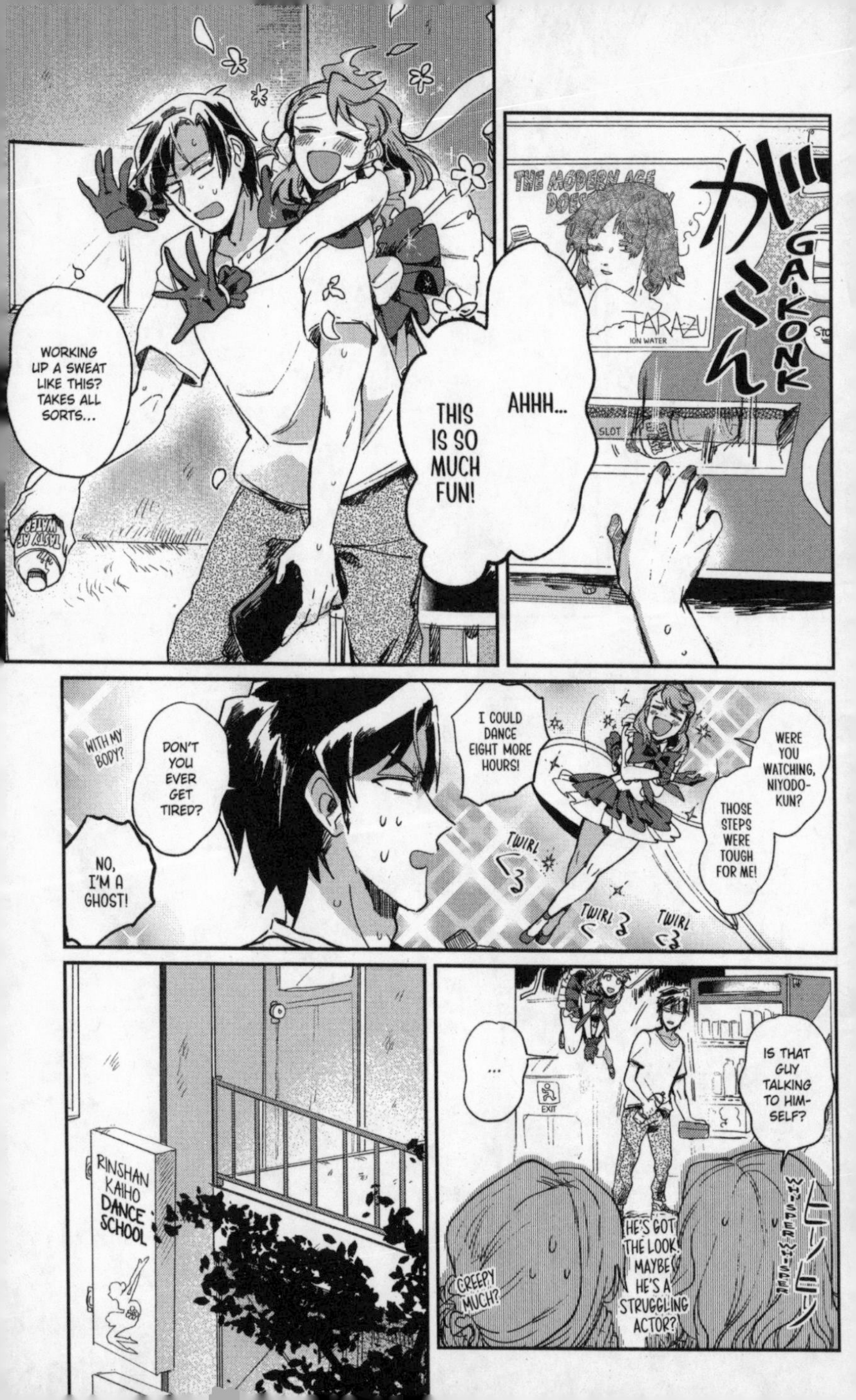
がこん
GA-KONK
THE MODERN AGE DOES
TARAZU
ION WATER
SLOT
AHHH...
THIS IS SO MUCH FUN!
WORKING UP A SWEAT LIKE THIS? TAKES ALL SORTS...
TASTY AE WATER
WERE YOU WATCHING, NIYODO-KUN?
THOSE STEPS WERE TOUGH FOR ME!
I COULD DANCE EIGHT MORE HOURS!
TWIRL
TWIRL
TWIRL
DON'T YOU EVER GET TIRED?
WITH MY BODY?
NO, I'M A GHOST!
IS THAT GUY TALKING TO HIMSELF?
...
EXIT
WHISPER WHISPER
HE'S GOT THE LOOK. MAYBE HE'S A STRUGGLING ACTOR?
CREEPY MUCH?
RINSHAN KAIHO DANCE SCHOOL

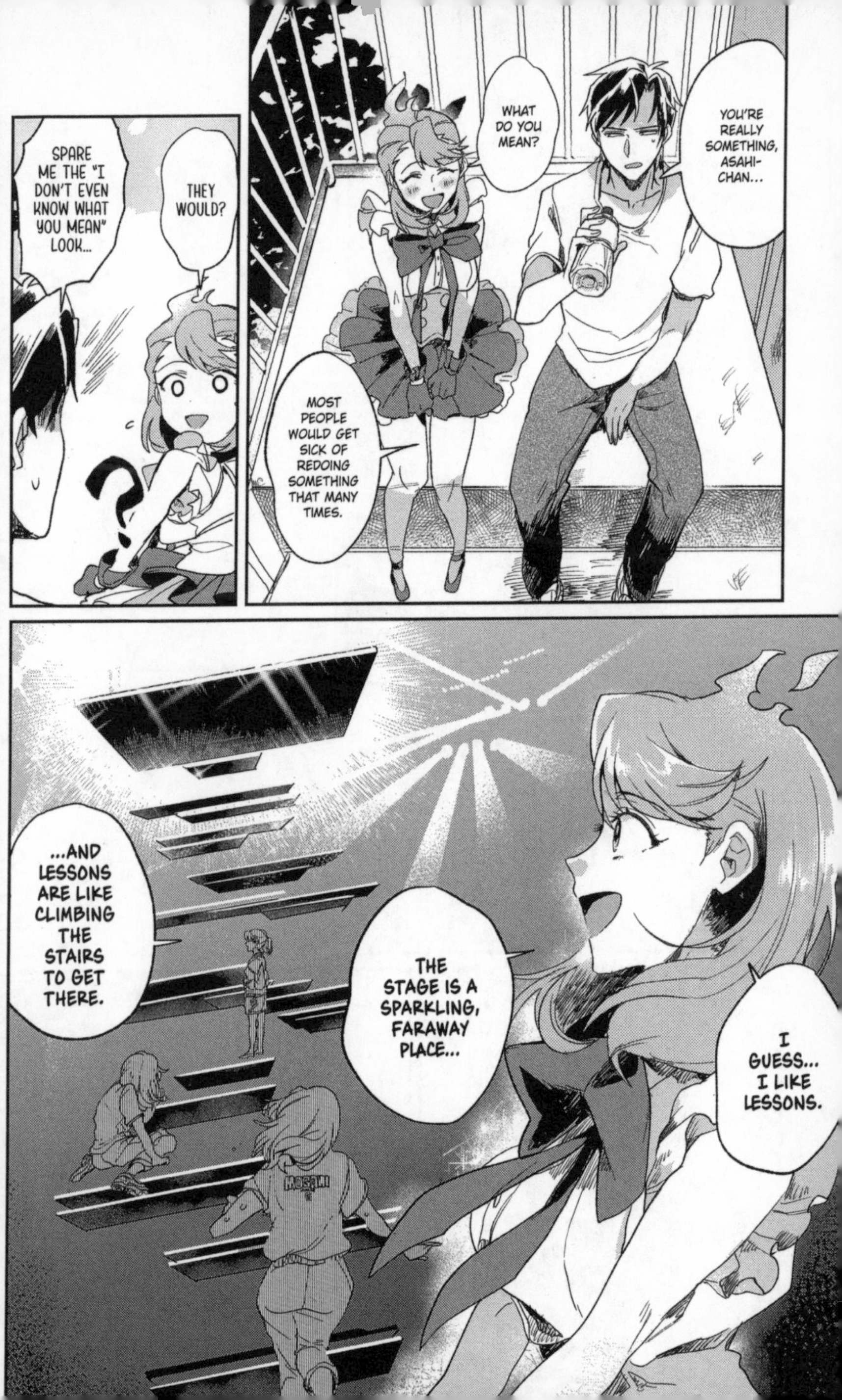
YOU'RE REALLY SOMETHING, ASAHI-CHAN...
WHAT DO YOU MEAN?
MOST PEOPLE WOULD GET SICK OF REDOING SOMETHING THAT MANY TIMES.
THEY WOULD?
SPARE ME THE "I DON'T EVEN KNOW WHAT YOU MEAN" LOOK...
I GUESS... I LIKE LESSONS.
THE STAGE IS A SPARKLING, FARAWAY PLACE...
...AND LESSONS ARE LIKE CLIMBING THE STAIRS TO GET THERE.

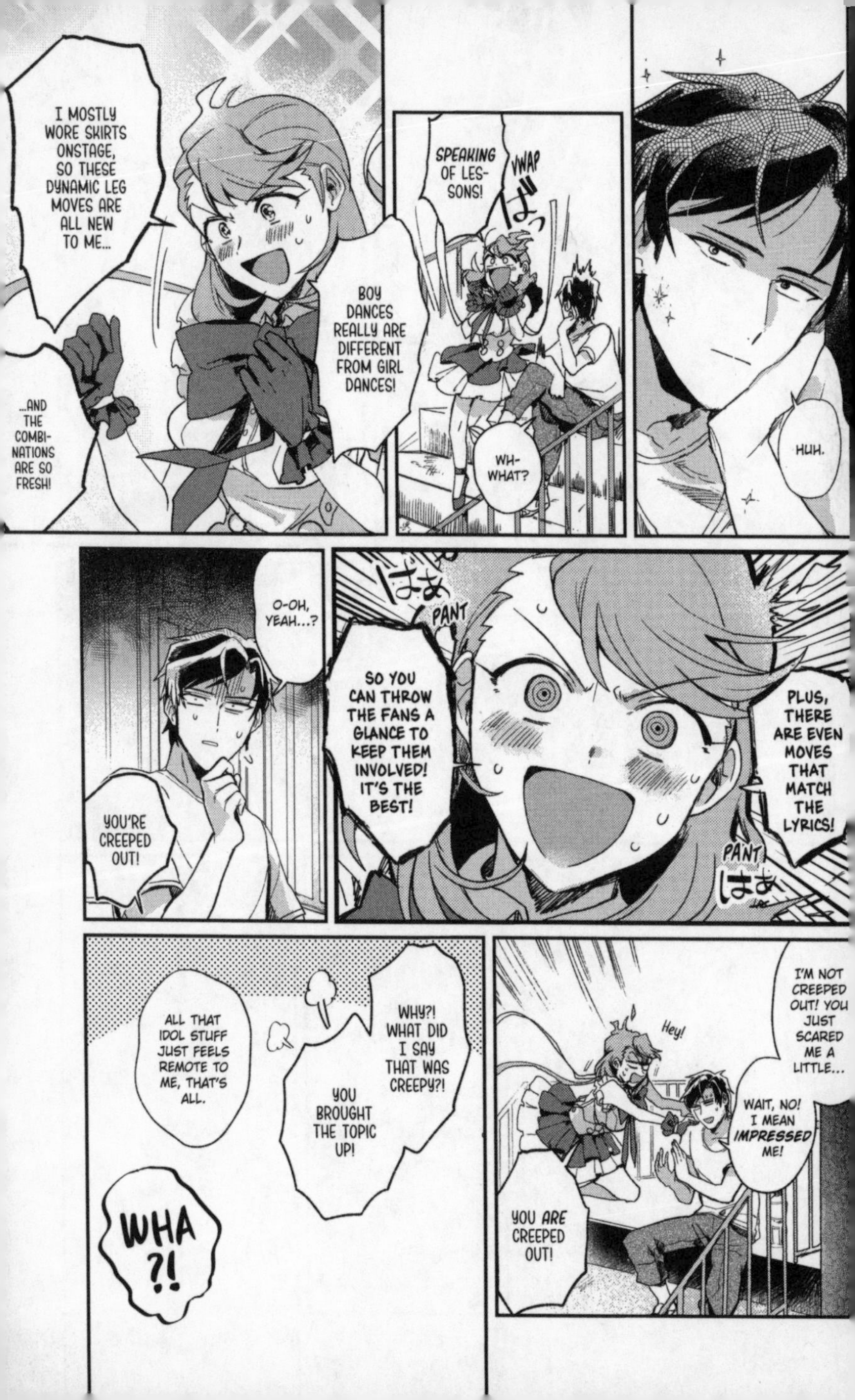
HUH.
SPEAKING OF LES-SONS!
VWAP
ばっ
BOY DANCES REALLY ARE DIFFERENT FROM GIRL DANCES!
WH-WHAT?
I MOSTLY WORE SKIRTS ONSTAGE, SO THESE DYNAMIC LEG MOVES ARE ALL NEW TO ME...
...AND THE COMBI-NATIONS ARE SO FRESH!
はあ
PANT
PLUS, THERE ARE EVEN MOVES THAT MATCH THE LYRICS!
SO YOU CAN THROW THE FANS A GLANCE TO KEEP THEM INVOLVED! IT'S THE BEST!
PANT
はあ
O-OH, YEAH...?
YOU'RE CREEPED OUT!
I'M NOT CREEPED OUT! YOU JUST SCARED ME A LITTLE...
WAIT, NO! I MEAN IMPRESSED ME!
Hey!
YOU ARE CREEPED OUT!
WHY?! WHAT DID I SAY THAT WAS CREEPY?!
ALL THAT IDOL STUFF JUST FEELS REMOTE TO ME, THAT'S ALL.
YOU BROUGHT THE TOPIC UP!
WHA ?!

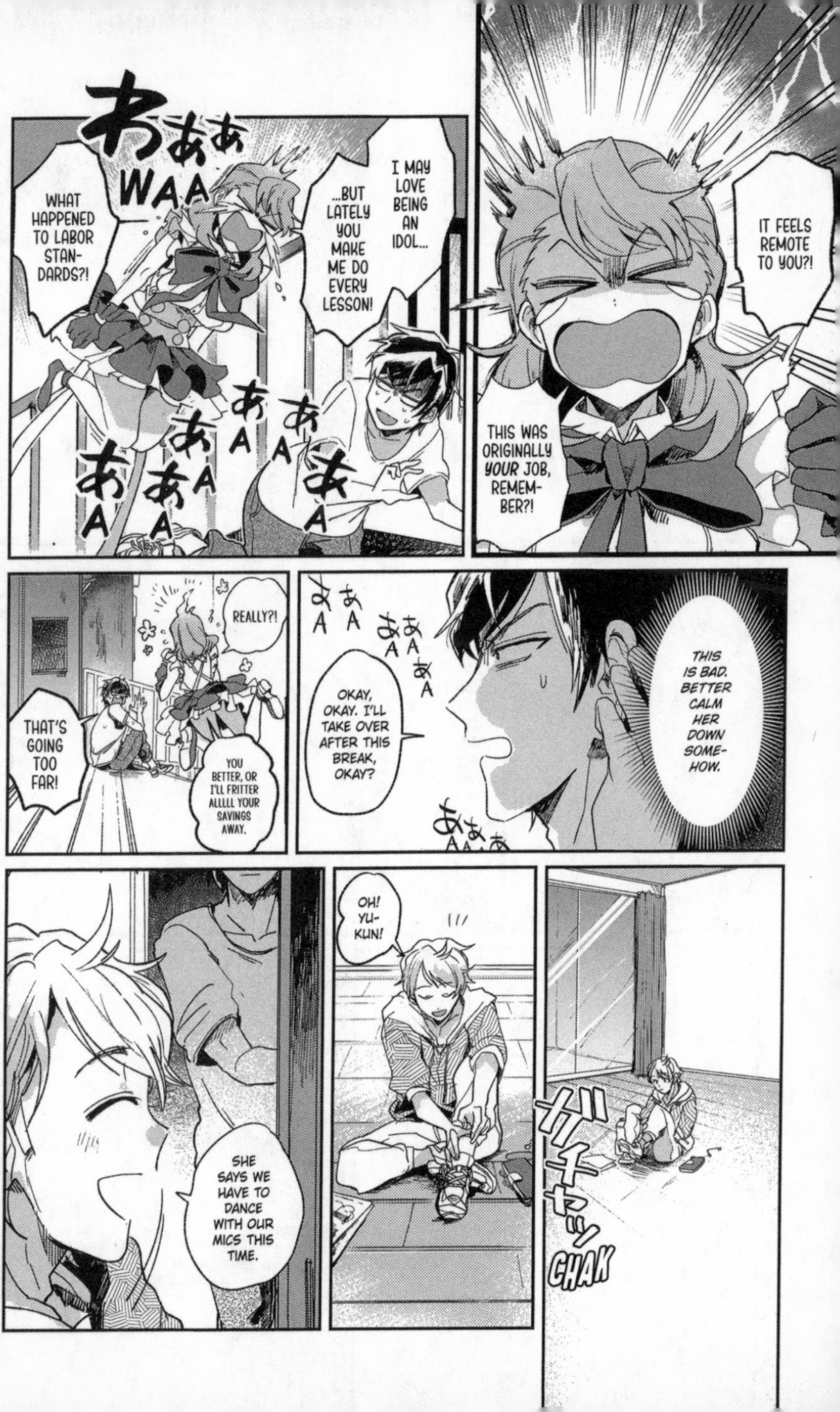
IT FEELS REMOTE TO YOU?!
THIS WAS ORIGINALLY YOUR JOB, REMEMBER?!
I MAY LOVE BEING AN IDOL...
...BUT LATELY YOU MAKE ME DO EVERY LESSON!
わあああ WAA
WHAT HAPPENED TO LABOR STANDARDS?!
あ A あ A あ A あ A あ A あ A
THIS IS BAD. BETTER CALM HER DOWN SOMEHOW.
ああ A A ああ A A あ A
OKAY, OKAY. I'LL TAKE OVER AFTER THIS BREAK, OKAY?
REALLY?!
YOU BETTER, OR I'LL FRITTER ALLLL YOUR SAVINGS AWAY.
THAT'S GOING TOO FAR!
ガチャッ CHAK
OH! YU-KUN!
SHE SAYS WE HAVE TO DANCE WITH OUR MICS THIS TIME.

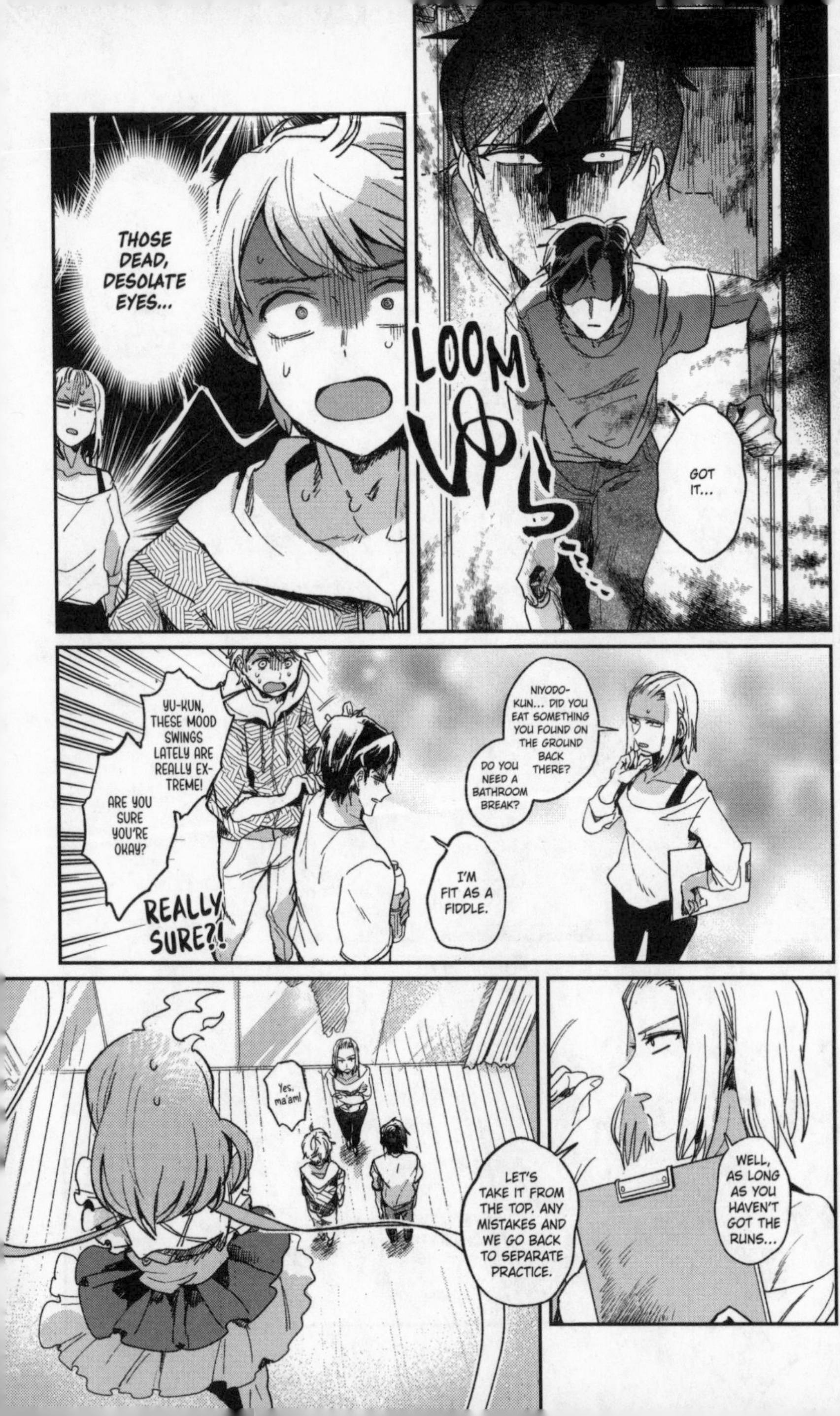
LOOM
GOT IT...
THOSE DEAD, DESOLATE EYES...
NIYODO-KUN... DID YOU EAT SOMETHING YOU FOUND ON THE GROUND BACK THERE?
DO YOU NEED A BATHROOM BREAK?
I'M FIT AS A FIDDLE.
YU-KUN, THESE MOOD SWINGS LATELY ARE REALLY EXTREME!
ARE YOU SURE YOU'RE OKAY?
REALLY SURE?!
WELL, AS LONG AS YOU HAVEN'T GOT THE RUNS...
LET'S TAKE IT FROM THE TOP. ANY MISTAKES AND WE GO BACK TO SEPARATE PRACTICE.
Yes, ma'am!

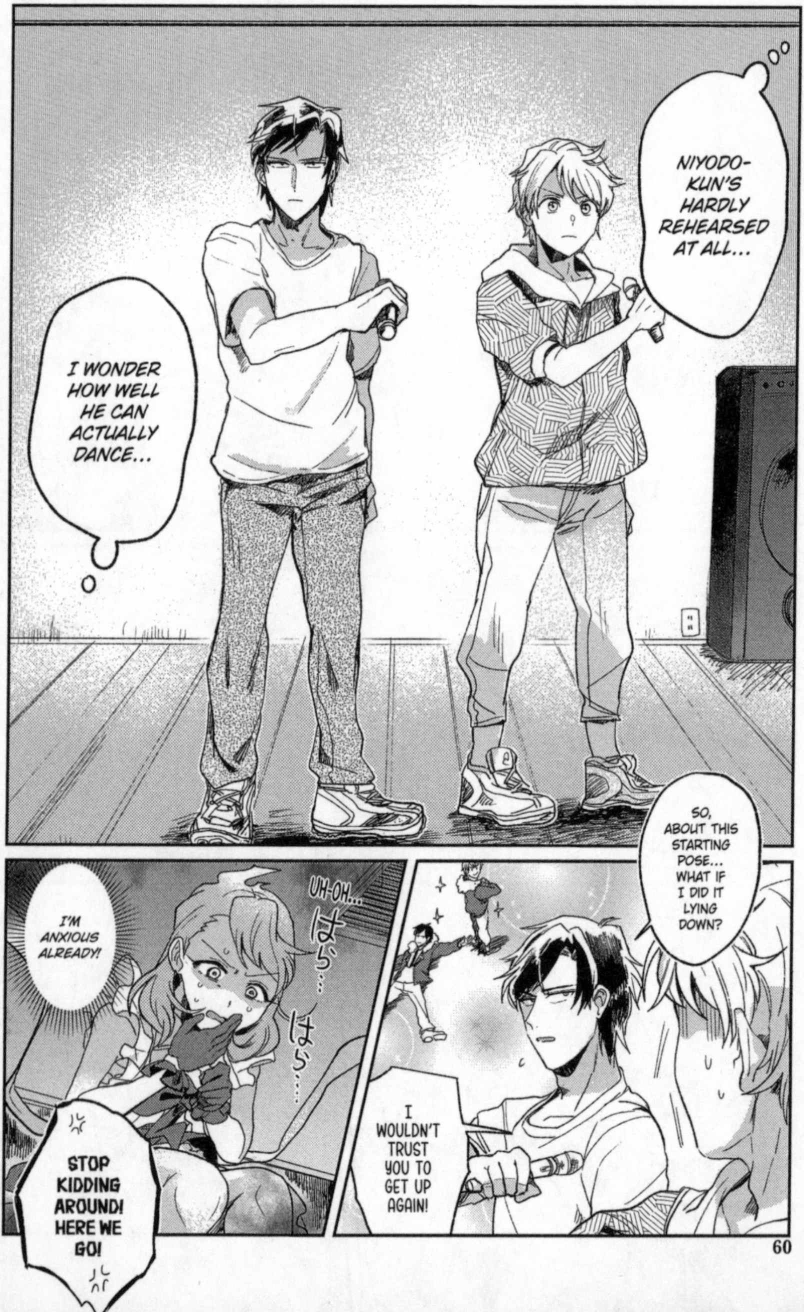

NIYODO-KUN'S HARDLY REHEARSED AT ALL...
I WONDER HOW WELL HE CAN ACTUALLY DANCE...
SO, ABOUT THIS STARTING POSE... WHAT IF I DID IT LYING DOWN?
I WOULDN'T TRUST YOU TO GET UP AGAIN!
UH-OH...
はら…
はら…
I'M ANXIOUS ALREADY!
STOP KIDDING AROUND! HERE WE GO!

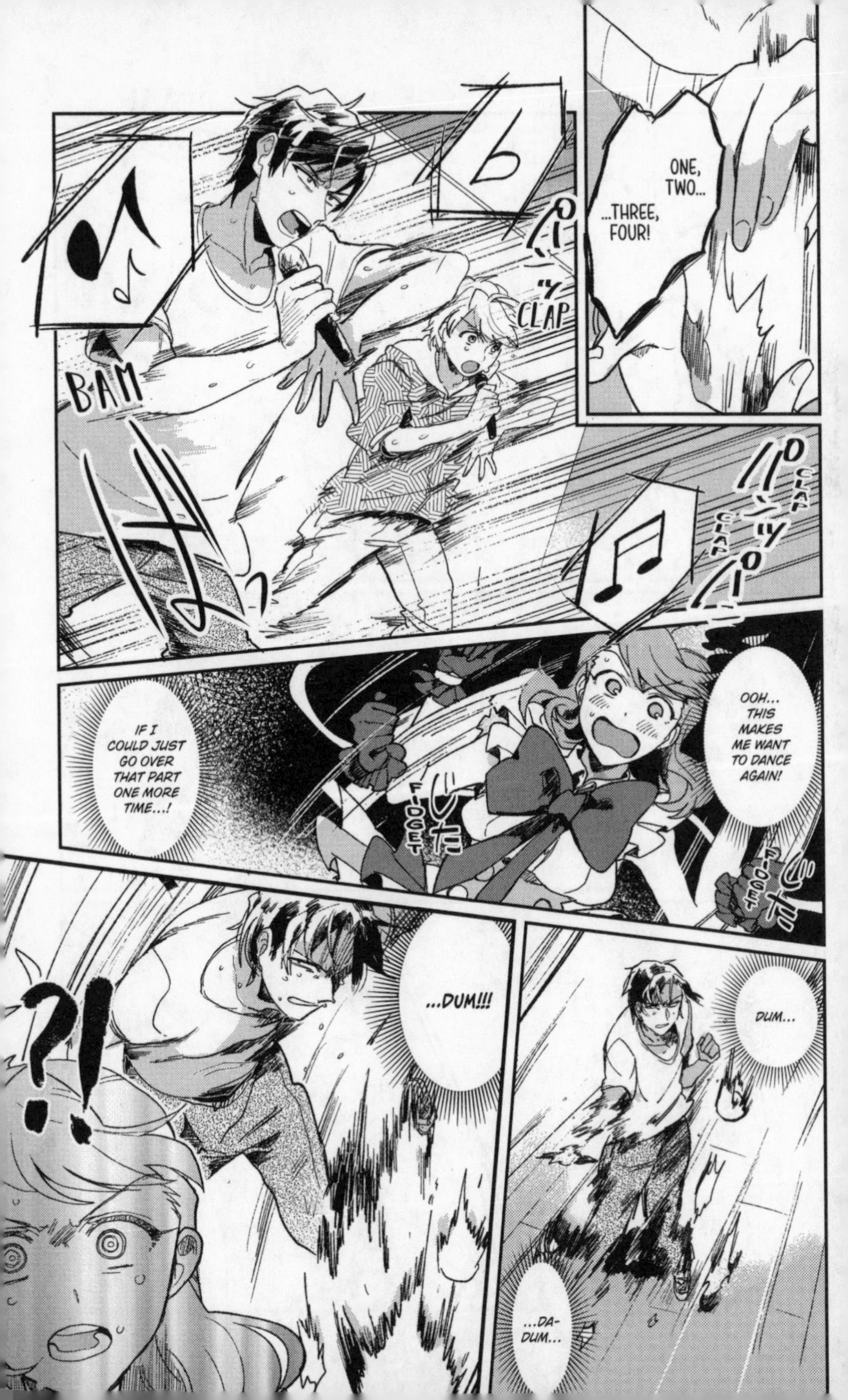
ONE, TWO...
...THREE, FOUR!
CLAP CLAP
CLAP
BAM
OOH... THIS MAKES ME WANT TO DANCE AGAIN!
FIDGET
IF I COULD JUST GO OVER THAT PART ONE MORE TIME...!
FIDGET
DUM...
...DA-DUM...
...DUM!!!
?!

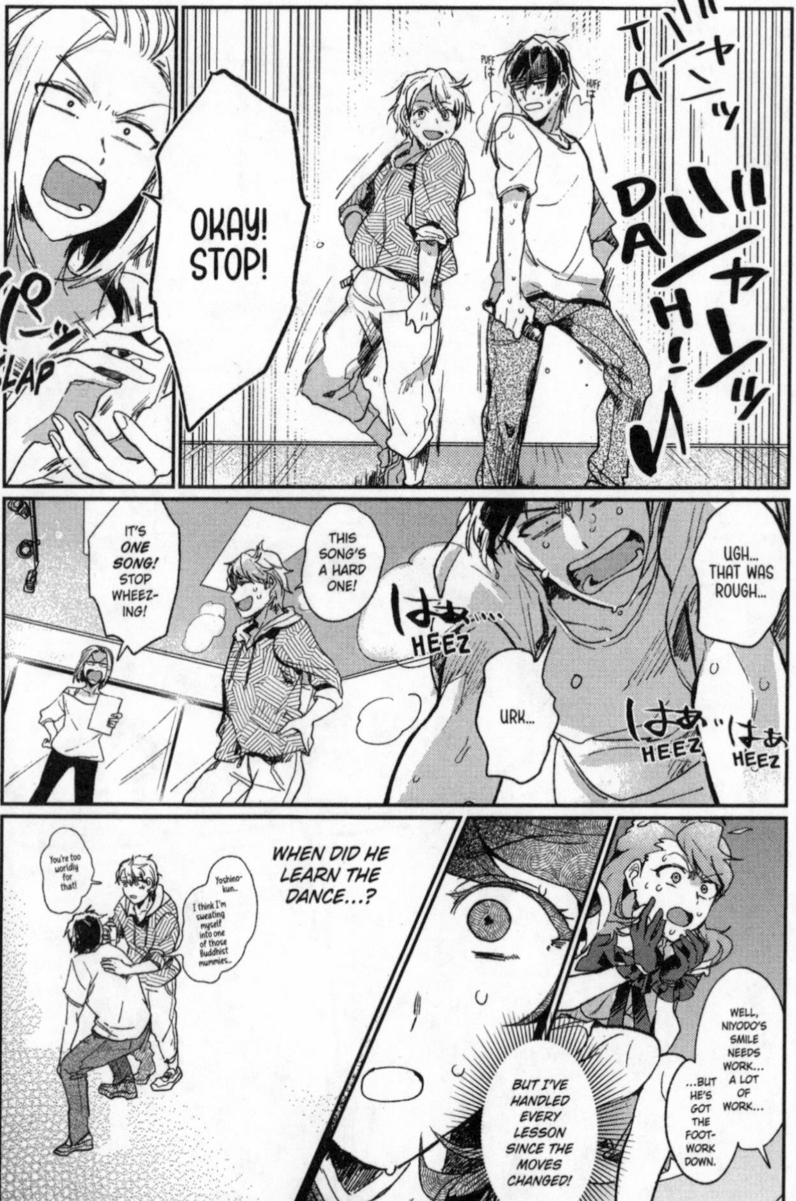
TAA
DAAH!!
PUFF
HUFF
OKAY! STOP!
CLAP
UGH... THAT WAS ROUGH...
HEEZ
URK...
HEEZ HEEZ
THIS SONG'S A HARD ONE!
IT'S ONE SONG! STOP WHEEZING!
WELL, NIYODO'S SMILE NEEDS WORK... A LOT OF WORK...
...BUT HE'S GOT THE FOOTWORK DOWN.
BUT I'VE HANDLED EVERY LESSON SINCE THE MOVES CHANGED!
WHEN DID HE LEARN THE DANCE...?
Yoshino-kun... I think I'm sweating myself into one of those Buddhist mummies...
You're too worldly for that!

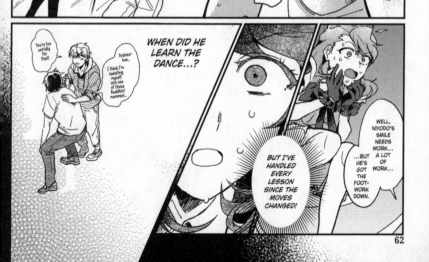

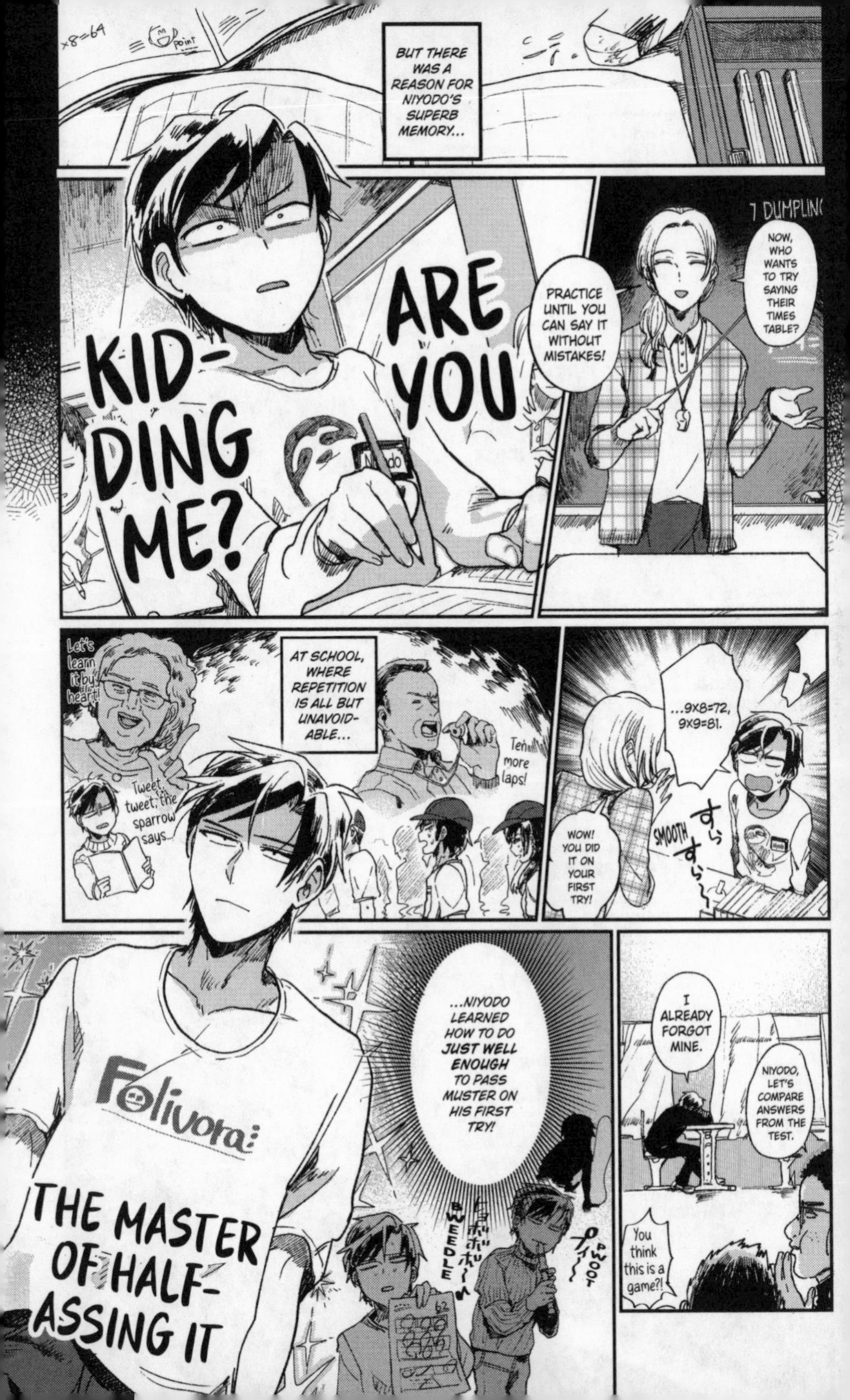
x8=64
BUT THERE WAS A REASON FOR NIYODO'S SUPERB MEMORY...
7 DUMPLING
NOW, WHO WANTS TO TRY SAYING THEIR TIMES TABLE?
PRACTICE UNTIL YOU CAN SAY IT WITHOUT MISTAKES!
ARE YOU KIDDING ME?
...9X8=72, 9X9=81.
WOW! YOU DID IT ON YOUR FIRST TRY!
SMOOTH
すら すら~
AT SCHOOL, WHERE REPETITION IS ALL BUT UNAVOIDABLE...
Ten more laps!
Let's learn it by heart!
Tweet, tweet, the sparrow says...
I ALREADY FORGOT MINE.
NIYODO, LET'S COMPARE ANSWERS FROM THE TEST.
You think this is a game?!
...NIYODO LEARNED HOW TO DO JUST WELL ENOUGH TO PASS MUSTER ON HIS FIRST TRY!
PWOOT
BWEEDLE
Folivora
THE MASTER OF HALF-ASSING IT

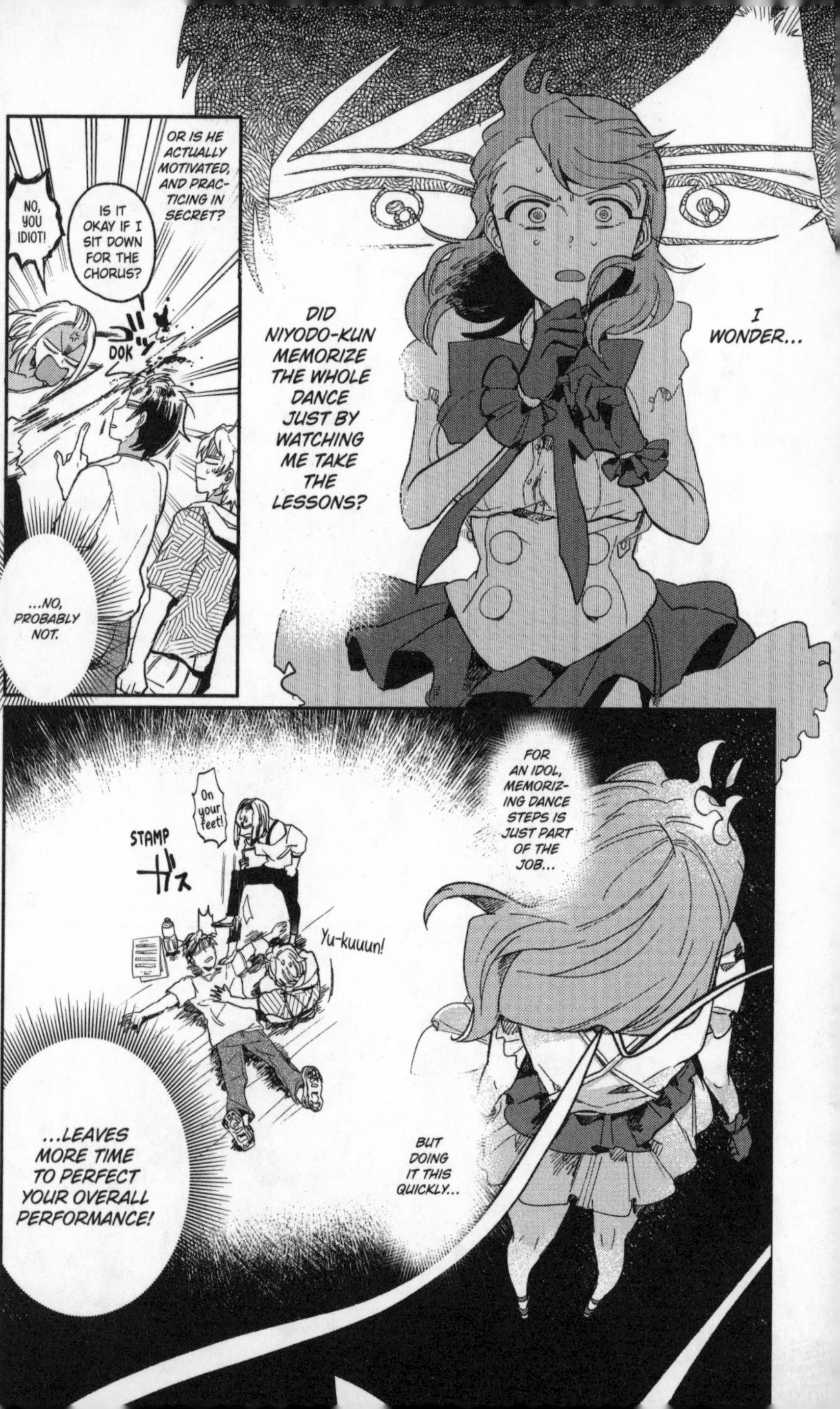
I WONDER...
DID NIYODO-KUN MEMORIZE THE WHOLE DANCE JUST BY WATCHING ME TAKE THE LESSONS?
OR IS HE ACTUALLY MOTIVATED, AND PRACTICING IN SECRET?
IS IT OKAY IF I SIT DOWN FOR THE CHORUS?
NO, YOU IDIOT!
DOK
...NO, PROBABLY NOT.
FOR AN IDOL, MEMORIZING DANCE STEPS IS JUST PART OF THE JOB...
BUT DOING IT THIS QUICKLY...
On your feet!
STAMP
Yu-kuuun!
...LEAVES MORE TIME TO PERFECT YOUR OVERALL PERFORMANCE!

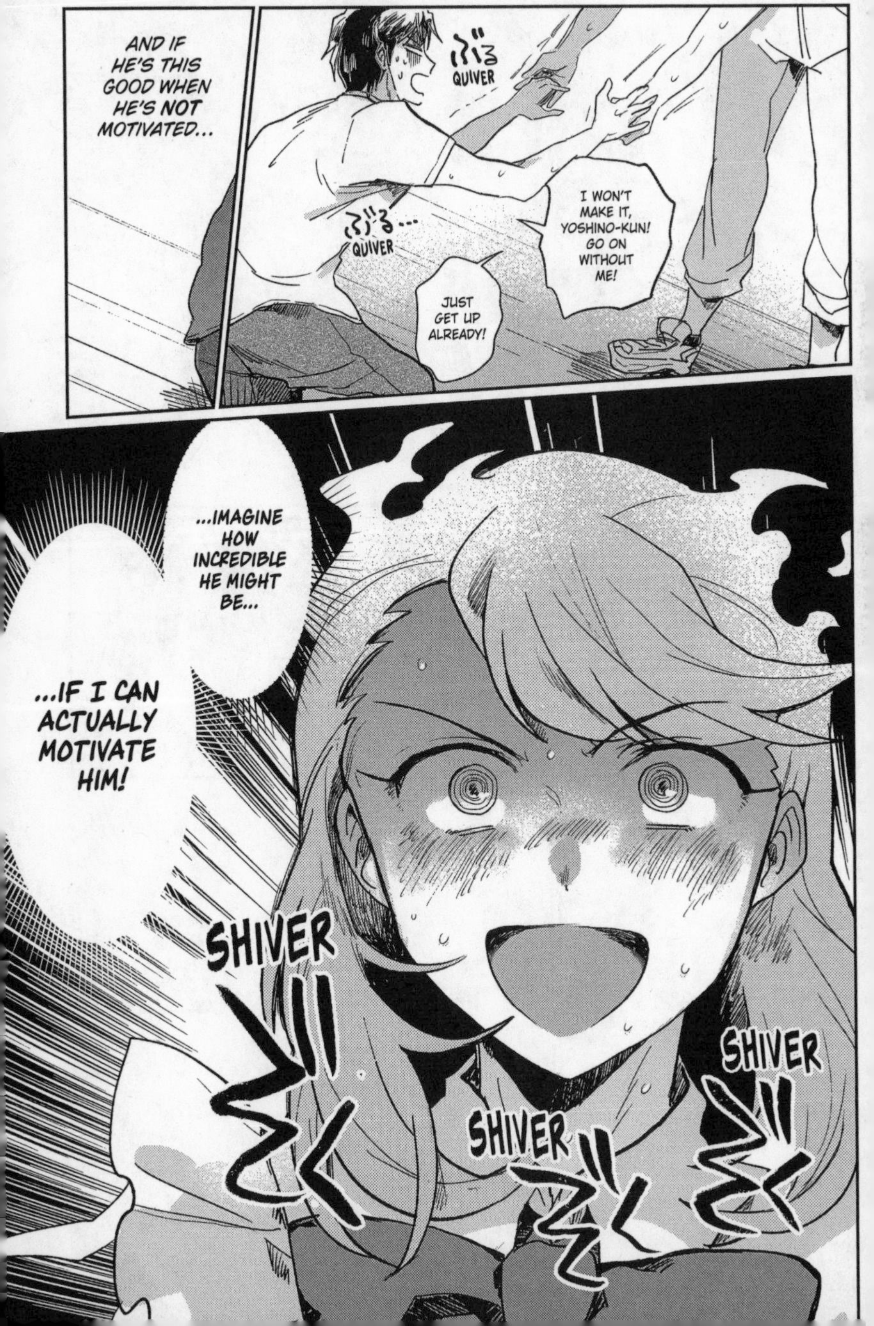
ぶる
QUIVER
I WON'T MAKE IT, YOSHINO-KUN! GO ON WITHOUT ME!
ぶる...
QUIVER
JUST GET UP ALREADY!
AND IF HE'S THIS GOOD WHEN HE'S NOT MOTIVATED...
...IMAGINE HOW INCREDIBLE HE MIGHT BE...
...IF I CAN ACTUALLY MOTIVATE HIM!
SHIVER
SHIVER
SHIVER

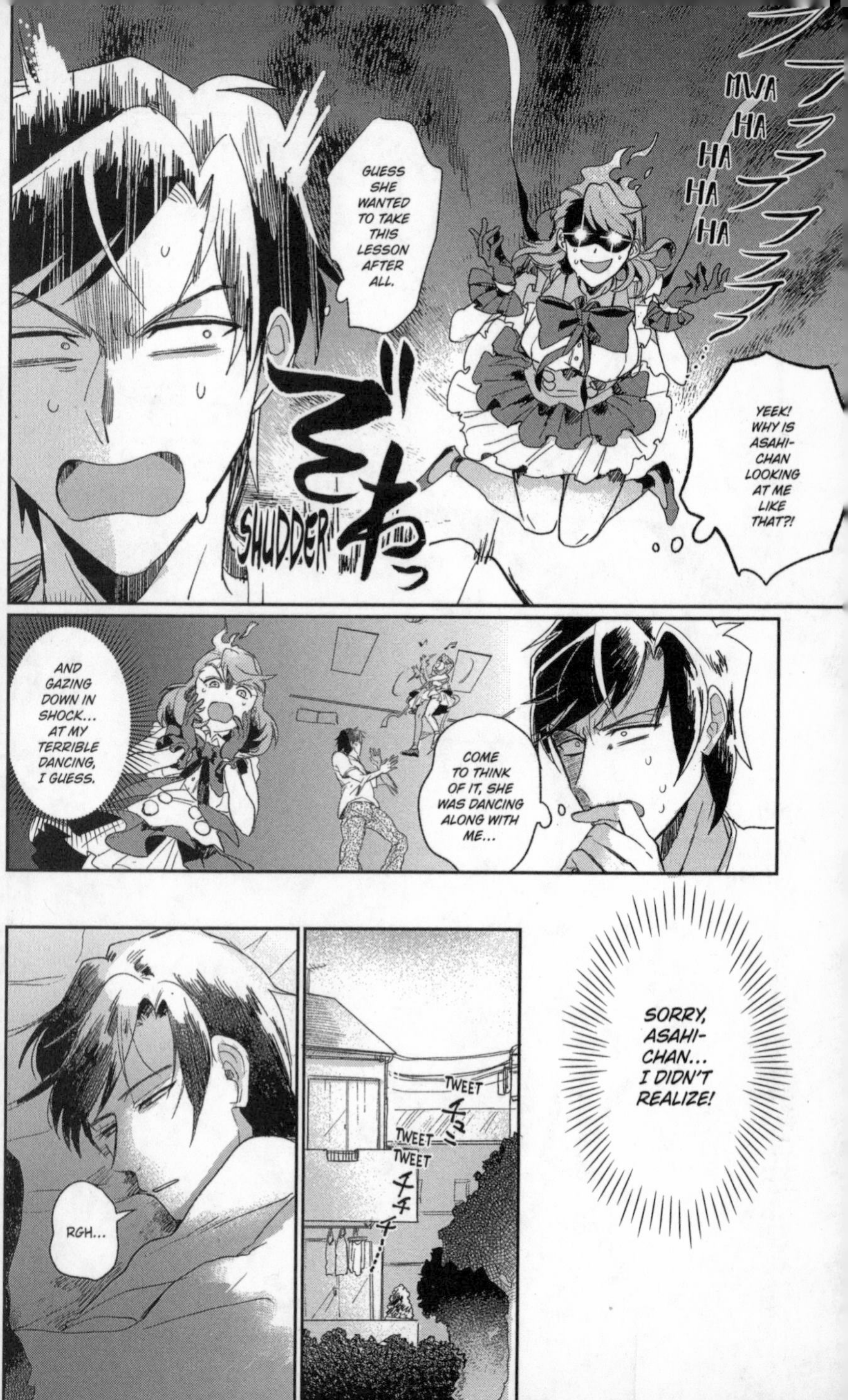
MWA HA HA HA HA
GUESS SHE WANTED TO TAKE THIS LESSON AFTER ALL.
SHUDDER
YEEK! WHY IS ASAHI-CHAN LOOKING AT ME LIKE THAT?!
COME TO THINK OF IT, SHE WAS DANCING ALONG WITH ME...
AND GAZING DOWN IN SHOCK... AT MY TERRIBLE DANCING, I GUESS.
SORRY, ASAHI-CHAN... I DIDN'T REALIZE!
TWEET
TWEET TWEET
RGH...

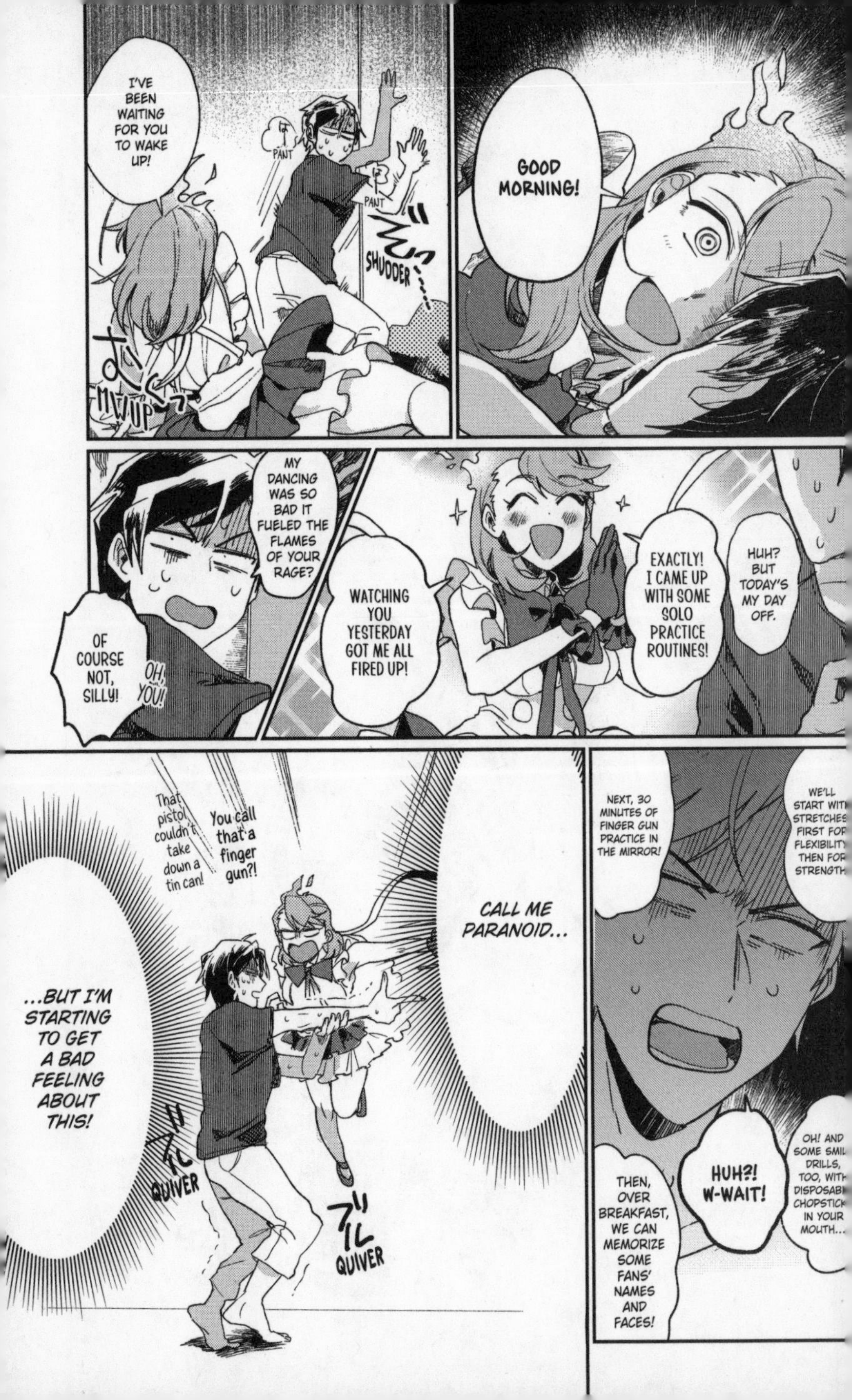
GOOD MORNING!
I'VE BEEN WAITING FOR YOU TO WAKE UP!
PANT
PANT
SHUDDER
FMWUP
HUH? BUT TODAY'S MY DAY OFF.
EXACTLY! I CAME UP WITH SOME SOLO PRACTICE ROUTINES!
WATCHING YOU YESTERDAY GOT ME ALL FIRED UP!
MY DANCING WAS SO BAD IT FUELED THE FLAMES OF YOUR RAGE?
OF COURSE NOT, SILLY!
OH, YOU!
WE'LL START WIT STRETCHES FIRST FO FLEXIBILIT THEN FO STRENGTH
NEXT, 30 MINUTES OF FINGER GUN PRACTICE IN THE MIRROR!
OH! AND SOME SMIL DRILLS, TOO, WITH DISPOSAB CHOPSTIC IN YOUR MOUTH...
HUH?! W-WAIT!
THEN, OVER BREAKFAST, WE CAN MEMORIZE SOME FANS' NAMES AND FACES!
CALL ME PARANOID...
...BUT I'M STARTING TO GET A BAD FEELING ABOUT THIS!
You call that a finger gun?!
That pistol couldn't take down a tin can!
QUIVER
QUIVER

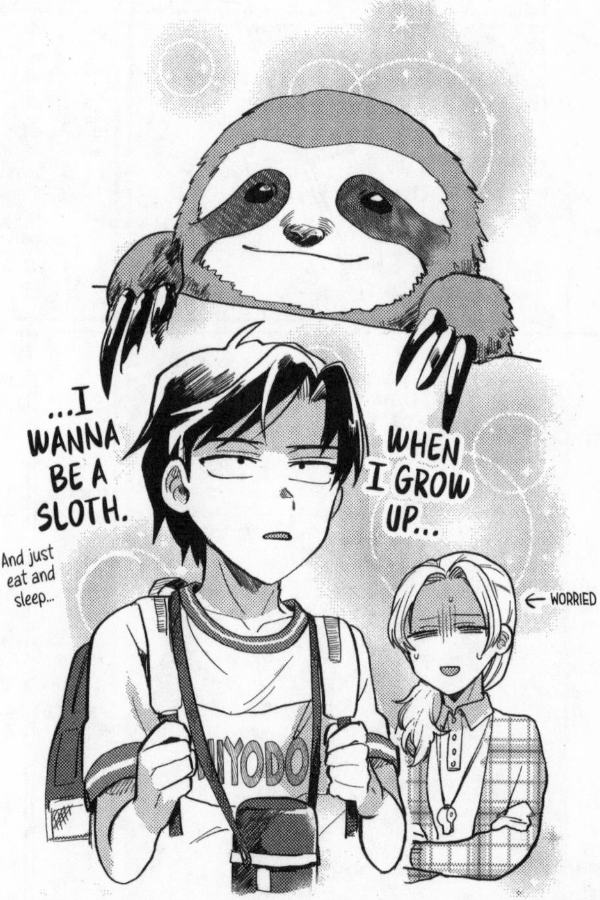
WHEN I GROW UP...
...I WANNA BE A SLOTH.
And just eat and sleep...
← WORRIED

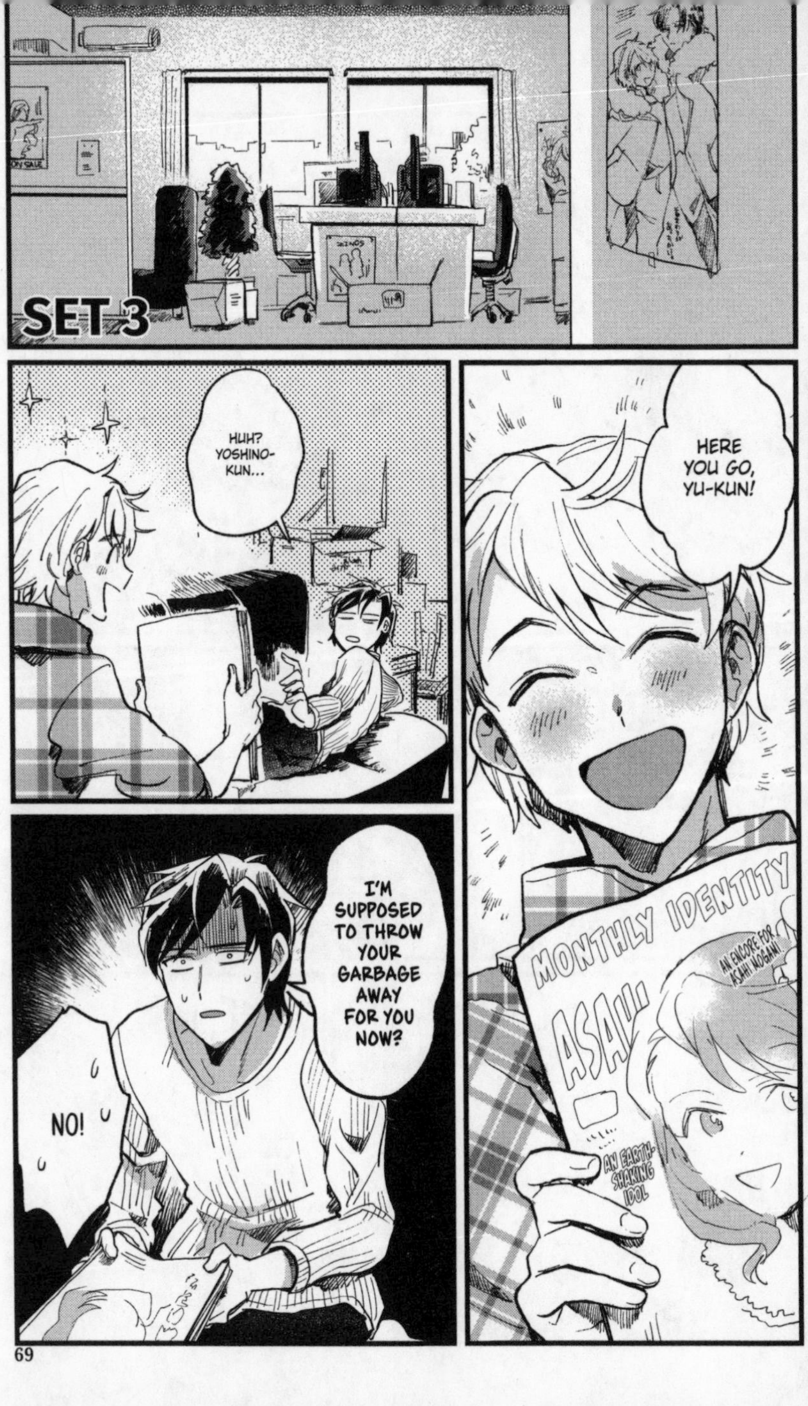
SET 3
HERE YOU GO, YU-KUN!
MONTHLY IDENTITY
AN ENCORE FOR ASAHI MOGAMI!
ASAHI
AN EARTH-SHAKING IDOL
HUH? YOSHINO-KUN...
I'M SUPPOSED TO THROW YOUR GARBAGE AWAY FOR YOU NOW?
NO!

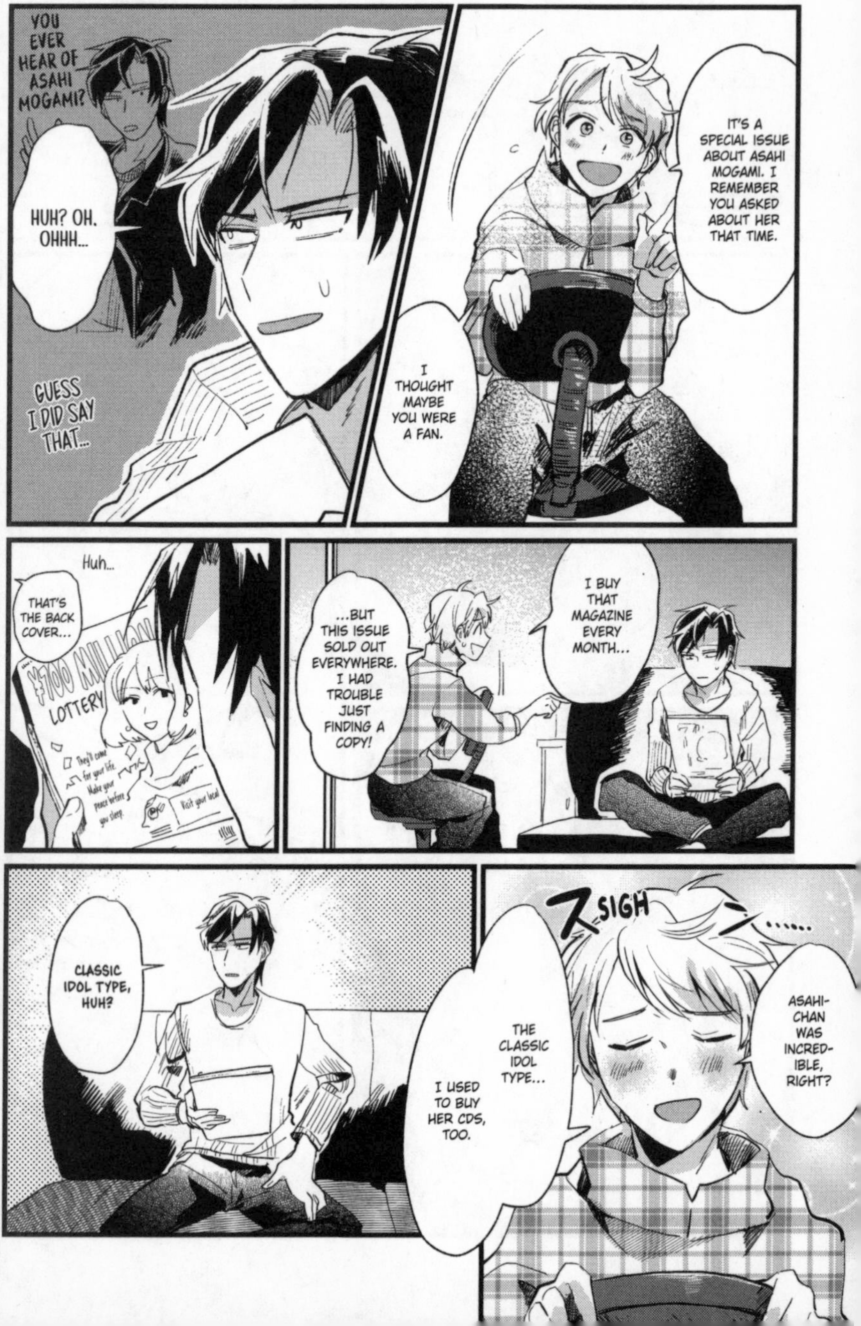
IT'S A SPECIAL ISSUE ABOUT ASAHI MOGAMI. I REMEMBER YOU ASKED ABOUT HER THAT TIME.
I THOUGHT MAYBE YOU WERE A FAN.
YOU EVER HEAR OF ASAHI MOGAMI?
HUH? OH. OHHH...
GUESS I DID SAY THAT...
I BUY THAT MAGAZINE EVERY MONTH...
...BUT THIS ISSUE SOLD OUT EVERYWHERE. I HAD TROUBLE JUST FINDING A COPY!
Huh...
THAT'S THE BACK COVER...
LOTTERY
They'll come for your life. Make your peace before you sleep.
Visit your local
SIGH
......
ASAHI-CHAN WAS INCREDIBLE, RIGHT?
THE CLASSIC IDOL TYPE...
I USED TO BUY HER CDS, TOO.
CLASSIC IDOL TYPE, HUH?

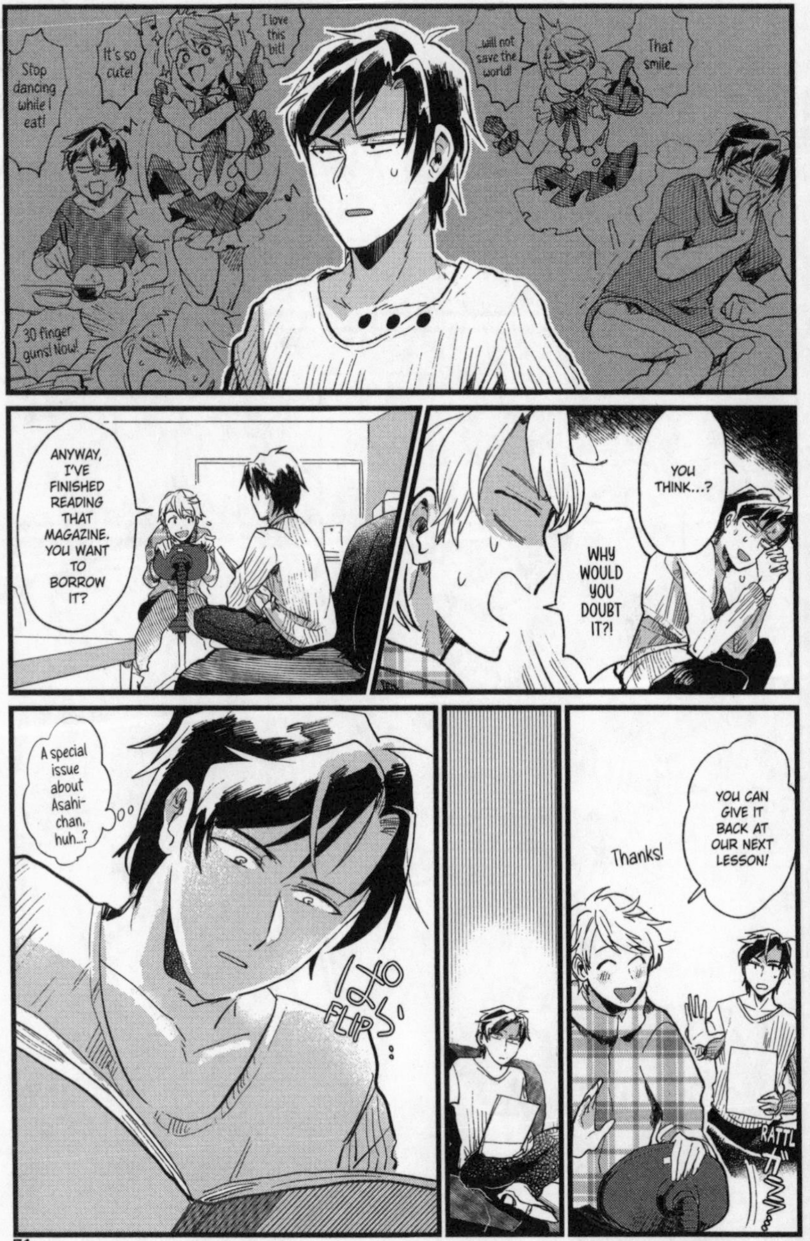
That smile...
...will not save the world!
I love this bit!
It's so cute!
Stop dancing while I eat!
30 finger guns! Now!
YOU THINK...?
WHY WOULD YOU DOUBT IT?!
ANYWAY, I'VE FINISHED READING THAT MAGAZINE. YOU WANT TO BORROW IT?
YOU CAN GIVE IT BACK AT OUR NEXT LESSON!
Thanks!
RATTL
A special issue about Asahi-chan, huh...?
FLIP

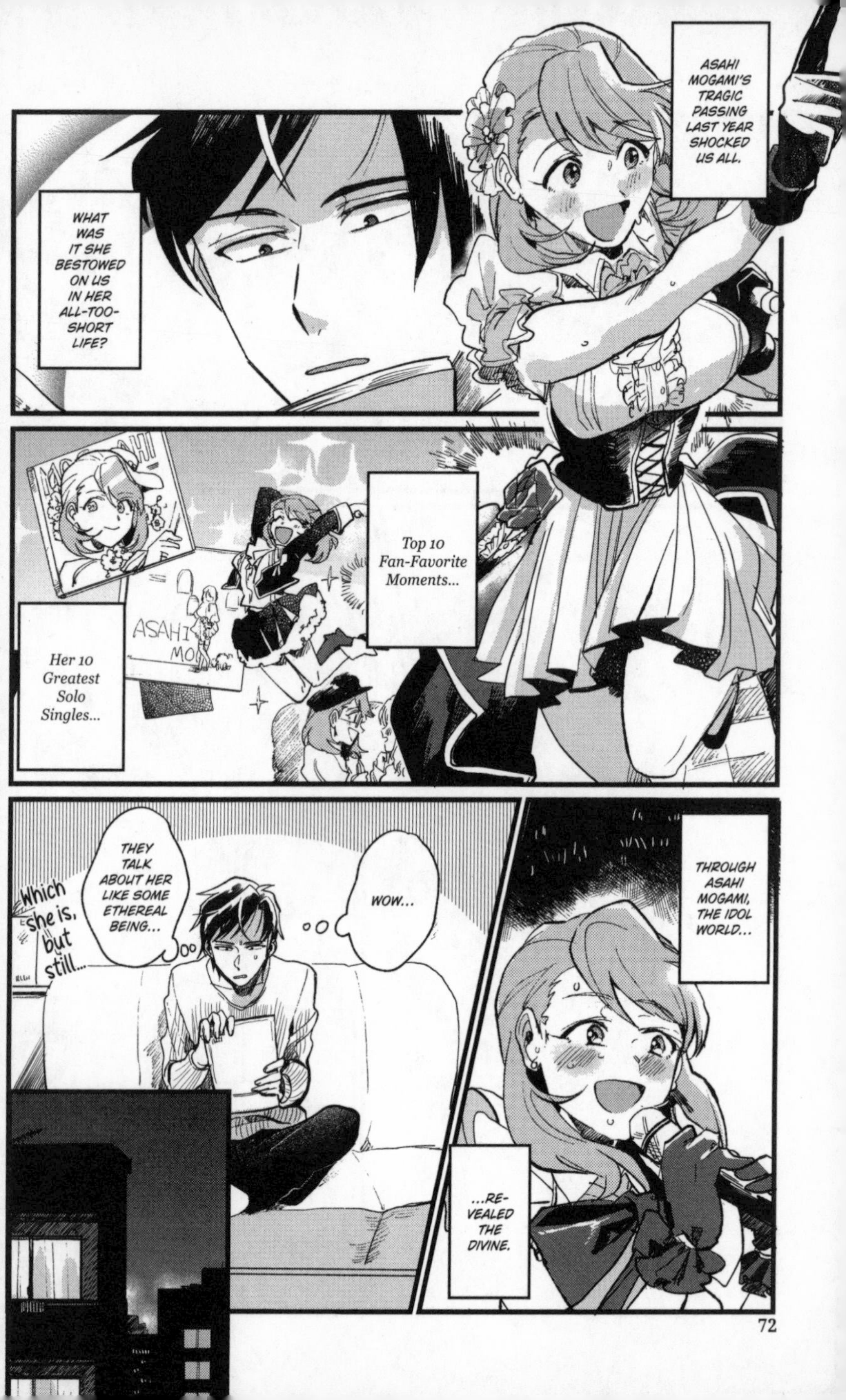
ASAHI MOGAMI'S TRAGIC PASSING LAST YEAR SHOCKED US ALL.
WHAT WAS IT SHE BESTOWED ON US IN HER ALL-TOO-SHORT LIFE?
Top 10 Fan-Favorite Moments...
ASAHI MO
Her 10 Greatest Solo Singles...
THROUGH ASAHI MOGAMI, THE IDOL WORLD...
...RE-VEALED THE DIVINE.
WOW...
THEY TALK ABOUT HER LIKE SOME ETHEREAL BEING...
Which she is, but still...

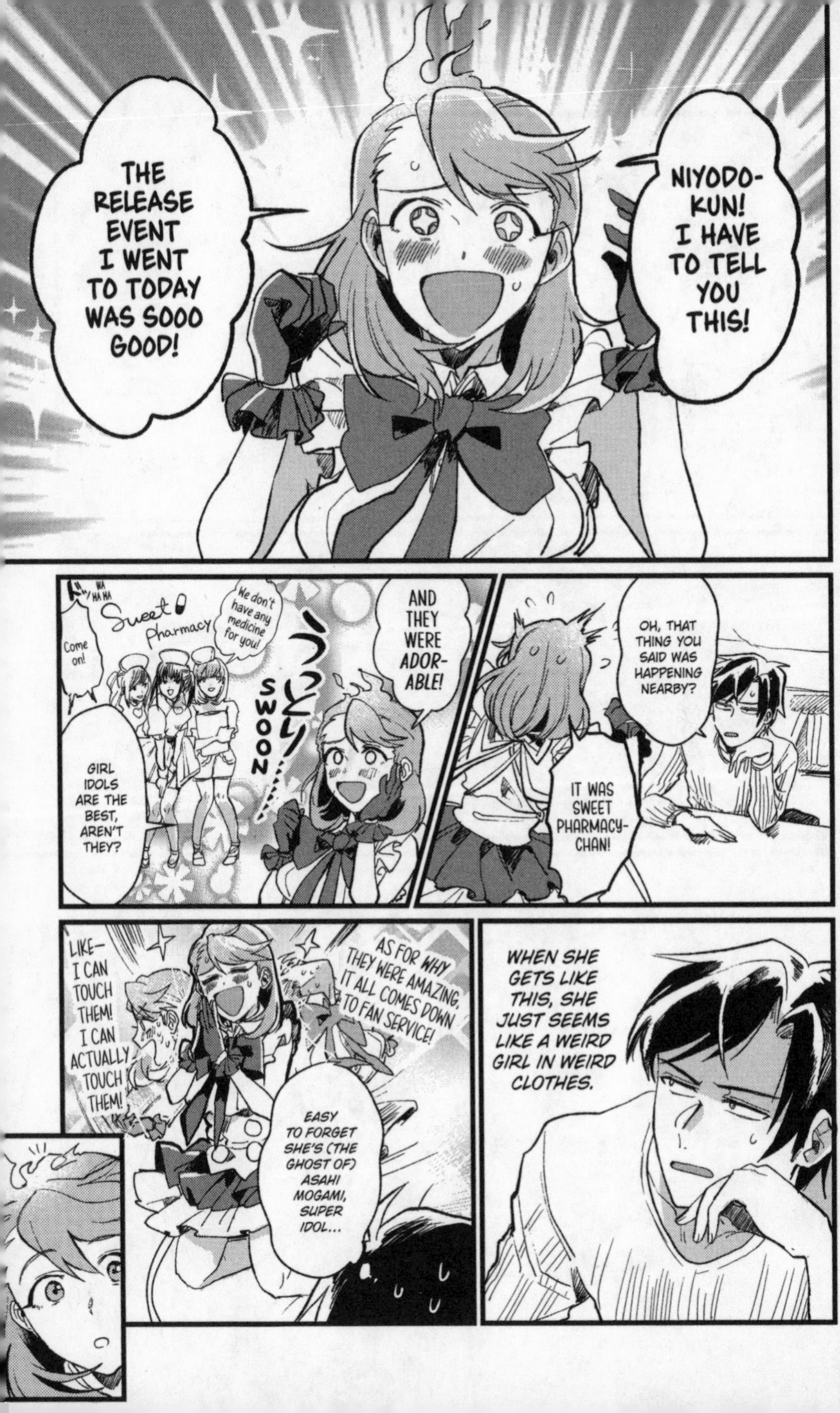
NIYODO-KUN! I HAVE TO TELL YOU THIS!
THE RELEASE EVENT I WENT TO TODAY WAS SOOO GOOD!
OH, THAT THING YOU SAID WAS HAPPENING NEARBY?
IT WAS SWEET PHARMACY-CHAN!
AND THEY WERE ADORABLE!
うっとり
SWOON
We don't have any medicine for you!
Sweet Pharmacy
WA HA HA
Come on!
GIRL IDOLS ARE THE BEST, AREN'T THEY?
WHEN SHE GETS LIKE THIS, SHE JUST SEEMS LIKE A WEIRD GIRL IN WEIRD CLOTHES.
AS FOR WHY THEY WERE AMAZING, IT ALL COMES DOWN TO FAN SERVICE!
LIKE— I CAN TOUCH THEM! I CAN ACTUALLY TOUCH THEM!
EASY TO FORGET SHE'S (THE GHOST OF) ASAHI MOGAMI, SUPER IDOL...

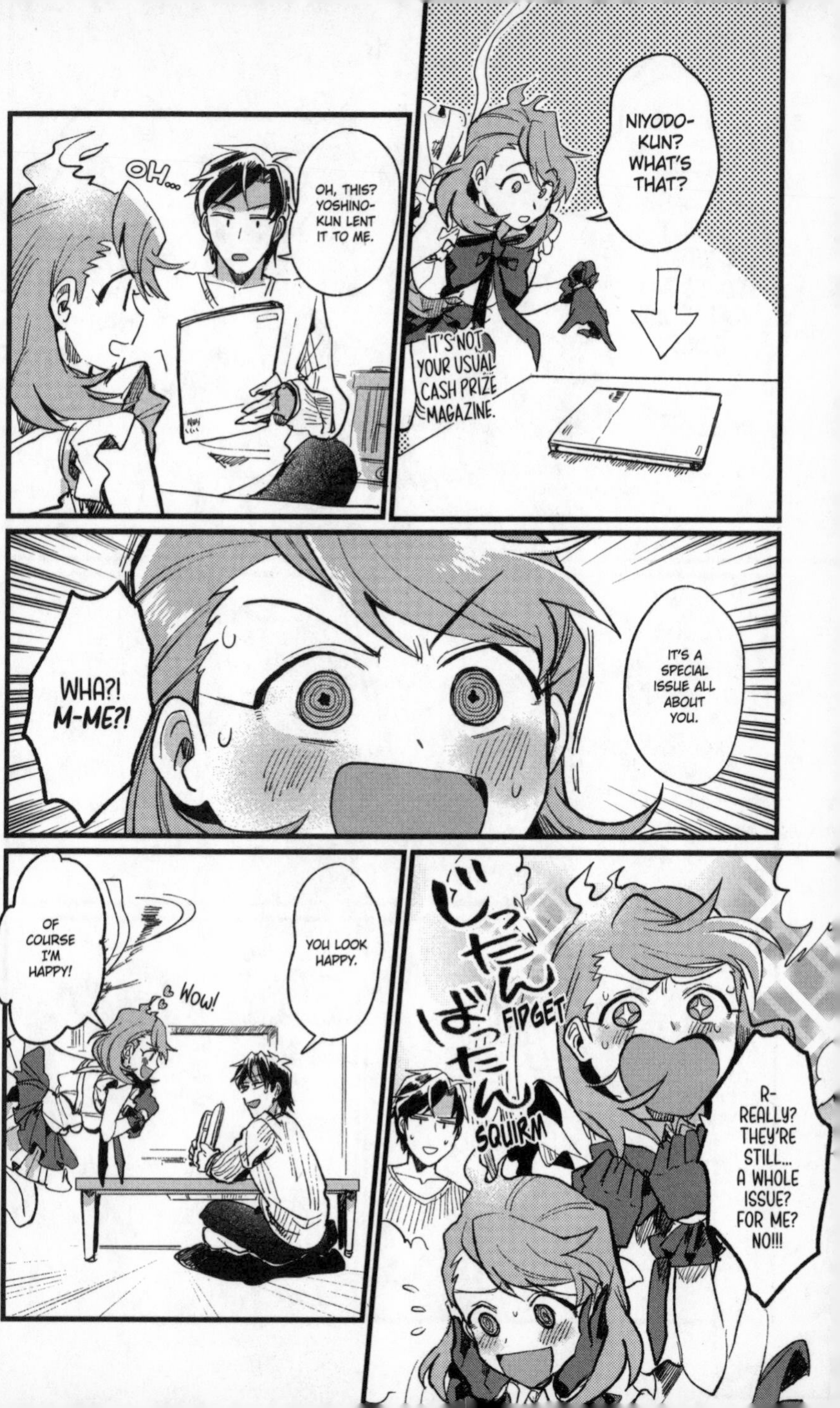
NIYODO-KUN? WHAT'S THAT?
IT'S NOT YOUR USUAL CASH PRIZE MAGAZINE.
OH, THIS? YOSHINO-KUN LENT IT TO ME.
OH...
IT'S A SPECIAL ISSUE ALL ABOUT YOU.
WHA?! M-ME?!
R-REALLY? THEY'RE STILL... A WHOLE ISSUE? FOR ME? NO!!!
じったん FIDGET
ばったん SQUIRM
YOU LOOK HAPPY.
OF COURSE I'M HAPPY!
WOW!

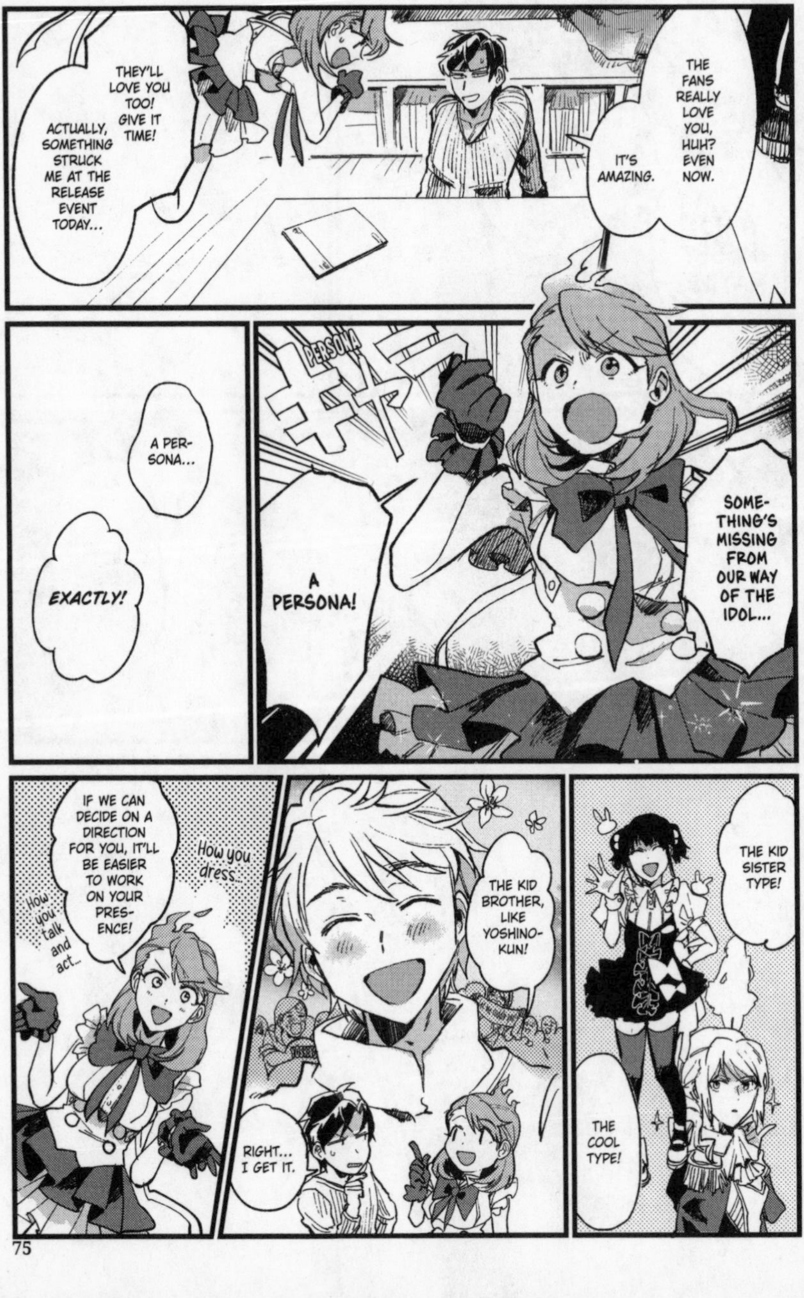
THE FANS REALLY LOVE YOU, HUH? EVEN NOW.
IT'S AMAZING.
THEY'LL LOVE YOU TOO! GIVE IT TIME!
ACTUALLY, SOMETHING STRUCK ME AT THE RELEASE EVENT TODAY...
SOMETHING'S MISSING FROM OUR WAY OF THE IDOL...
PERSONA
A PERSONA!
A PERSONA...
EXACTLY!
THE KID SISTER TYPE!
THE COOL TYPE!
THE KID BROTHER, LIKE YOSHINO-KUN!
RIGHT... I GET IT.
IF WE CAN DECIDE ON A DIRECTION FOR YOU, IT'LL BE EASIER TO WORK ON YOUR PRESENCE!
How you dress...
How you talk and act...

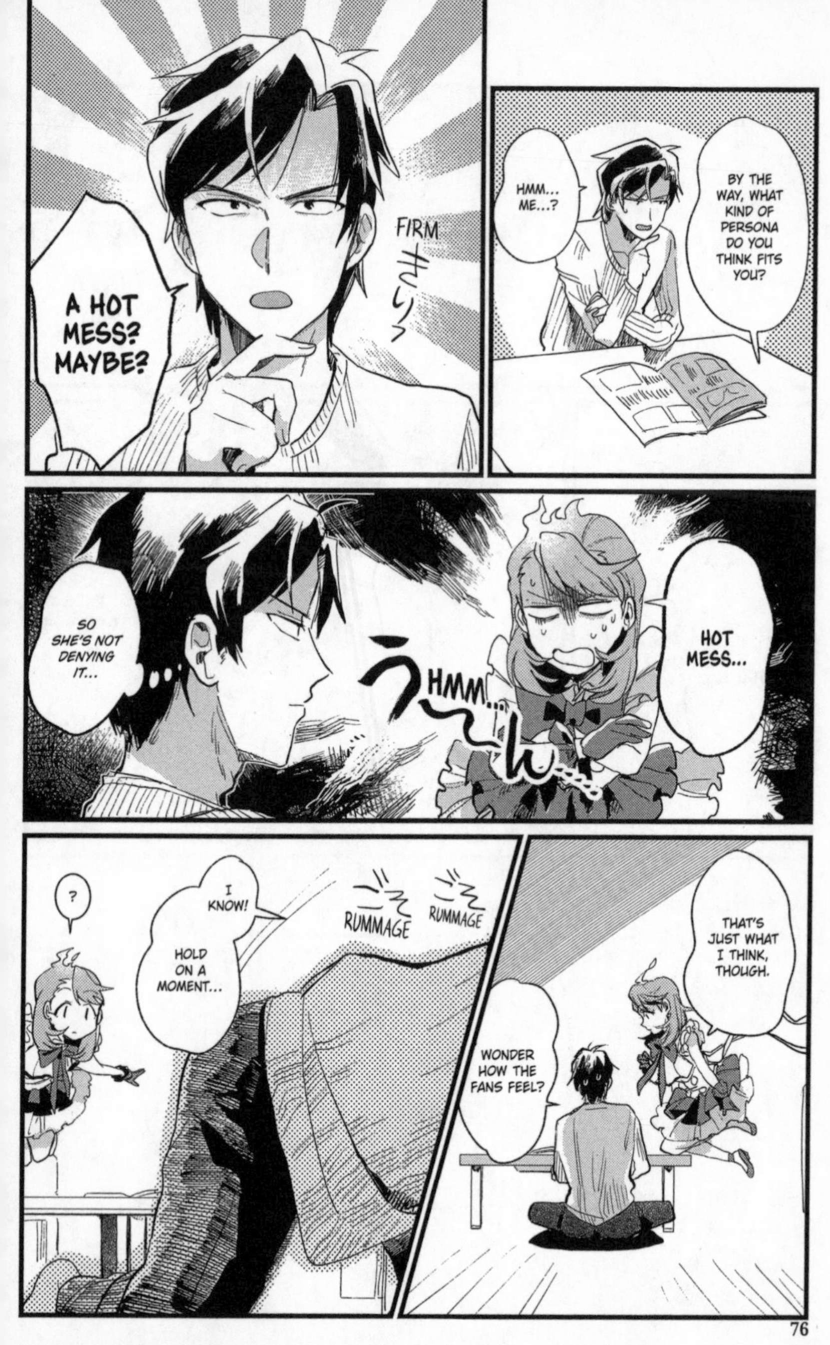
BY THE WAY, WHAT KIND OF PERSONA DO YOU THINK FITS YOU?
HMM... ME...?
FIRM
きりっ
A HOT MESS? MAYBE?
HOT MESS...
HMM...
SO SHE'S NOT DENYING IT...
THAT'S JUST WHAT I THINK, THOUGH.
WONDER HOW THE FANS FEEL?
ごそ
RUMMAGE
ごそ
RUMMAGE
I KNOW!
HOLD ON A MOMENT...
?

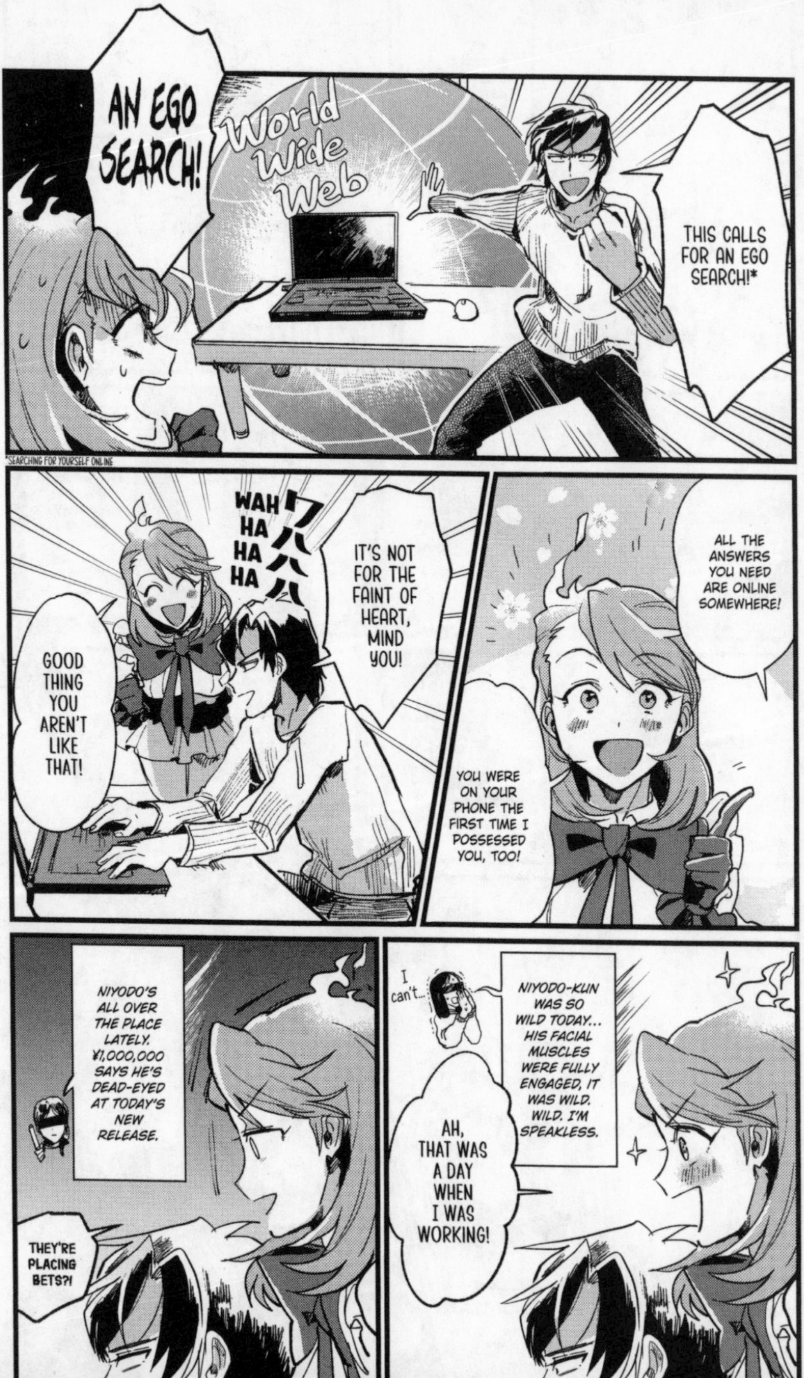
THIS CALLS FOR AN EGO SEARCH!*
World Wide Web
AN EGO SEARCH!
*SEARCHING FOR YOURSELF ONLINE
ALL THE ANSWERS YOU NEED ARE ONLINE SOMEWHERE!
YOU WERE ON YOUR PHONE THE FIRST TIME I POSSESSED YOU, TOO!
IT'S NOT FOR THE FAINT OF HEART, MIND YOU!
WAH HA HA HA
GOOD THING YOU AREN'T LIKE THAT!
NIYODO-KUN WAS SO WILD TODAY... HIS FACIAL MUSCLES WERE FULLY ENGAGED, IT WAS WILD. WILD. I'M SPEAKLESS.
I can't...
AH, THAT WAS A DAY WHEN I WAS WORKING!
NIYODO'S ALL OVER THE PLACE LATELY. ¥1,000,000 SAYS HE'S DEAD-EYED AT TODAY'S NEW RELEASE.
THEY'RE PLACING BETS?!

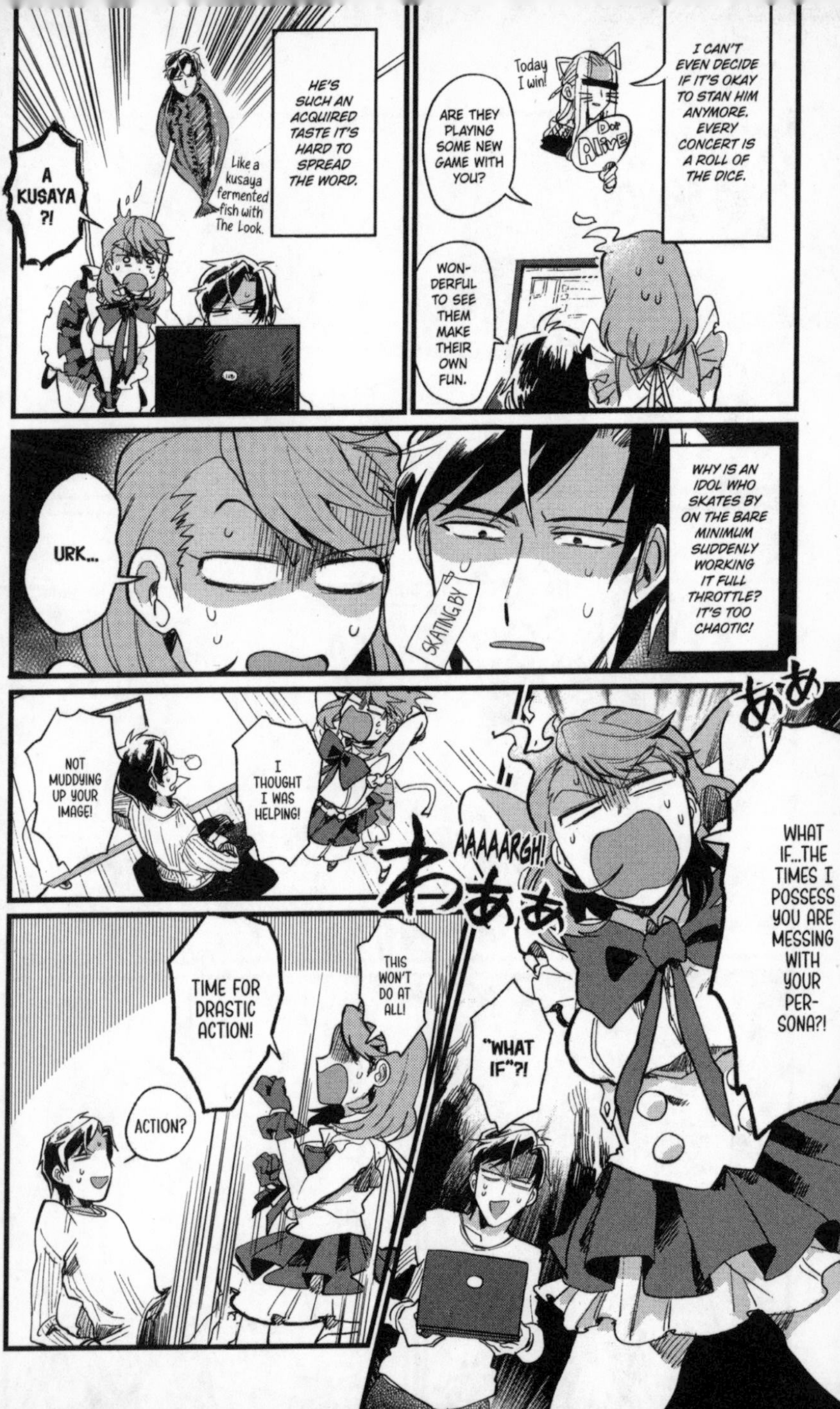
I CAN'T EVEN DECIDE IF IT'S OKAY TO STAN HIM ANYMORE. EVERY CONCERT IS A ROLL OF THE DICE.
Today I win!
DoP Alive
ARE THEY PLAYING SOME NEW GAME WITH YOU?
WONDERFUL TO SEE THEM MAKE THEIR OWN FUN.
HE'S SUCH AN ACQUIRED TASTE IT'S HARD TO SPREAD THE WORD.
Like a kusaya fermented fish with The Look.
A KUSAYA?!
WHY IS AN IDOL WHO SKATES BY ON THE BARE MINIMUM SUDDENLY WORKING IT FULL THROTTLE? IT'S TOO CHAOTIC!
SKATING BY
URK...
ああ
わあああ
AAAAARGH!
WHAT IF...THE TIMES I POSSESS YOU ARE MESSING WITH YOUR PERSONA?!
"WHAT IF"?!
I THOUGHT I WAS HELPING!
NOT MUDDYING UP YOUR IMAGE!
THIS WON'T DO AT ALL!
TIME FOR DRASTIC ACTION!
ACTION?

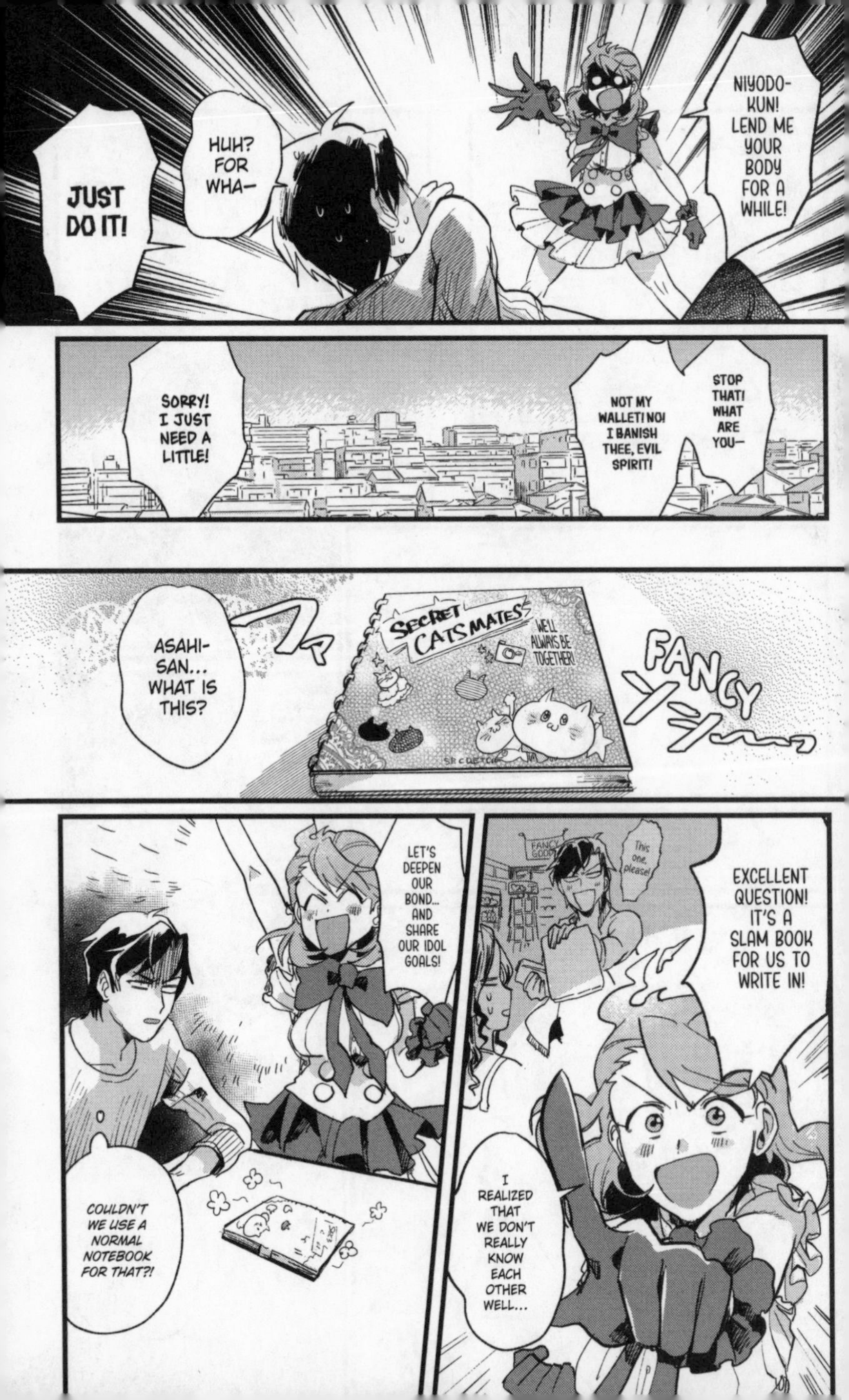
NIYODO-KUN! LEND ME YOUR BODY FOR A WHILE!
HUH? FOR WHA-
JUST DO IT!
STOP THAT! WHAT ARE YOU—
NOT MY WALLET! NO! I BANISH THEE, EVIL SPIRIT!
SORRY! I JUST NEED A LITTLE!
FANCY
SECRET CATSMATES
WE'LL ALWAYS BE TOGETHER!
ASAHI-SAN... WHAT IS THIS?
EXCELLENT QUESTION! IT'S A SLAM BOOK FOR US TO WRITE IN!
This one, please!
I REALIZED THAT WE DON'T REALLY KNOW EACH OTHER WELL...
LET'S DEEPEN OUR BOND... AND SHARE OUR IDOL GOALS!
COULDN'T WE USE A NORMAL NOTEBOOK FOR THAT?!

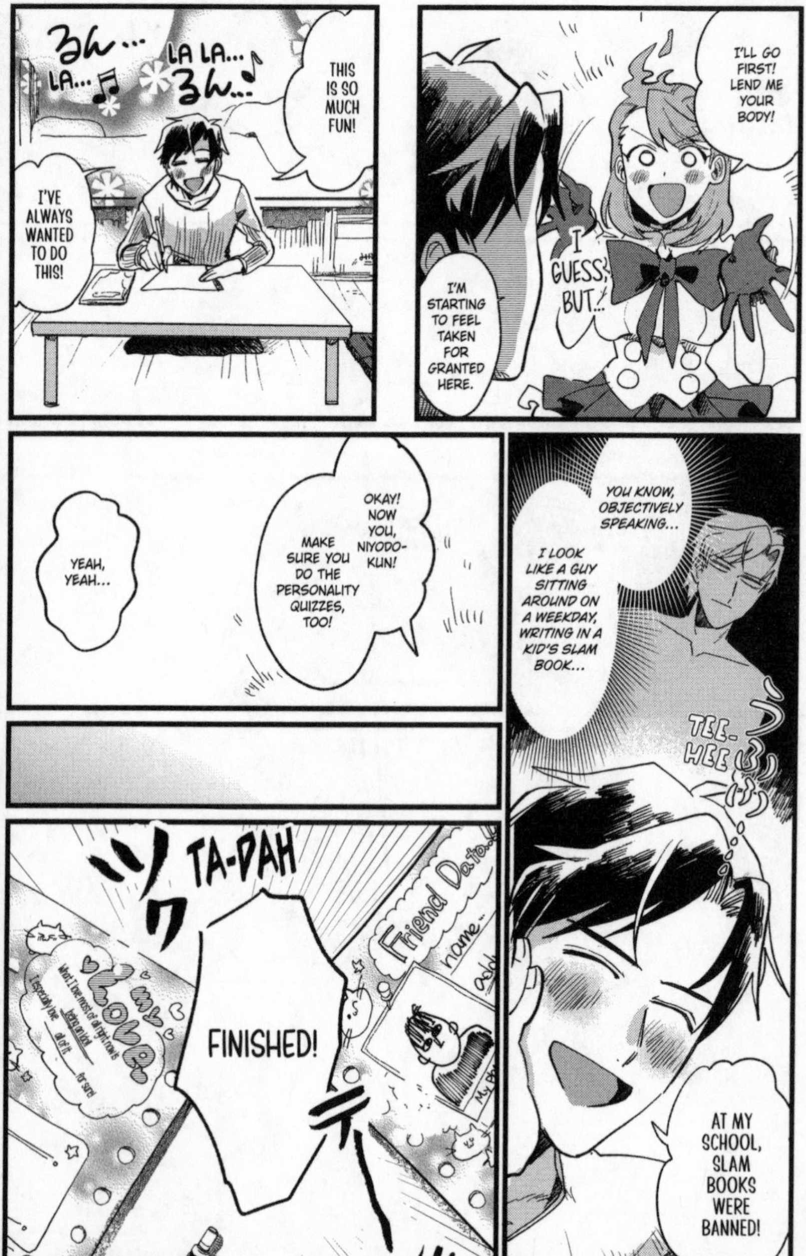
I'LL GO FIRST! LEND ME YOUR BODY!
I GUESS, BUT...
I'M STARTING TO FEEL TAKEN FOR GRANTED HERE.
るん… LA…♫
LA LA… るん…♪
THIS IS SO MUCH FUN!
I'VE ALWAYS WANTED TO DO THIS!
YOU KNOW, OBJECTIVELY SPEAKING…
I LOOK LIKE A GUY SITTING AROUND ON A WEEKDAY, WRITING IN A KID'S SLAM BOOK…
TEE-HEE うふふ
AT MY SCHOOL, SLAM BOOKS WERE BANNED!
OKAY! NOW YOU, NIYODO-KUN!
MAKE SURE YOU DO THE PERSONALITY QUIZZES, TOO!
YEAH, YEAH…
TA-DAH
FINISHED!
デーン!!
Friend Data
name…
my Love

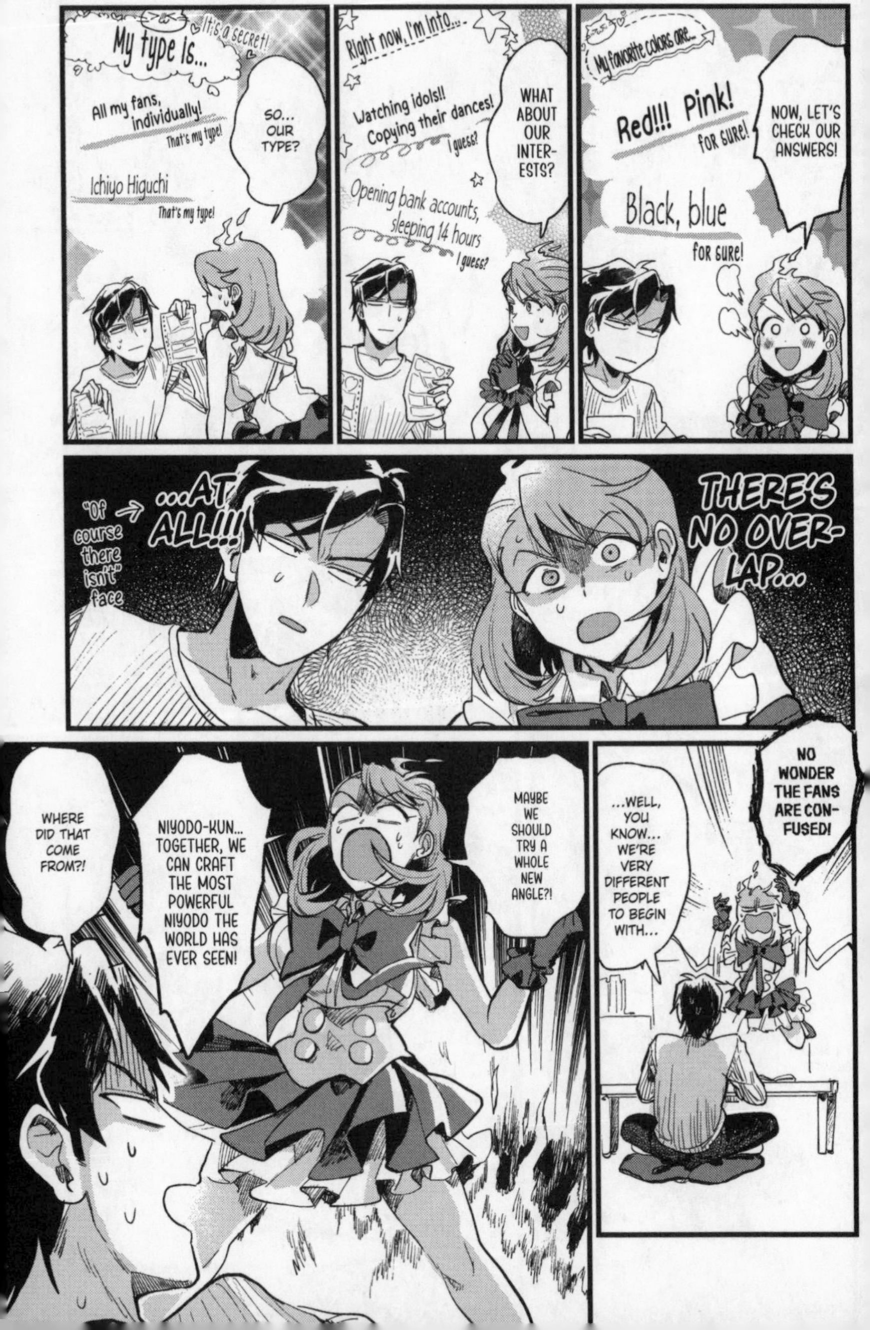
NOW, LET'S CHECK OUR ANSWERS!
My favorite colors are...
Red!!! Pink! for sure!
Black, blue for sure!
WHAT ABOUT OUR INTERESTS?
Right now, I'm into...
Watching idols!! Copying their dances! I guess?
Opening bank accounts, sleeping 14 hours I guess?
SO... OUR TYPE?
My type is... It's a secret!
All my fans, individually! That's my type!
Ichiyo Higuchi That's my type!
THERE'S NO OVER-LAP...
...AT ALL!!!
"Of course there isn't" face
NO WONDER THE FANS ARE CON-FUSED!
...WELL, YOU KNOW... WE'RE VERY DIFFERENT PEOPLE TO BEGIN WITH...
MAYBE WE SHOULD TRY A WHOLE NEW ANGLE?!
NIYODO-KUN... TOGETHER, WE CAN CRAFT THE MOST POWERFUL NIYODO THE WORLD HAS EVER SEEN!
WHERE DID THAT COME FROM?!

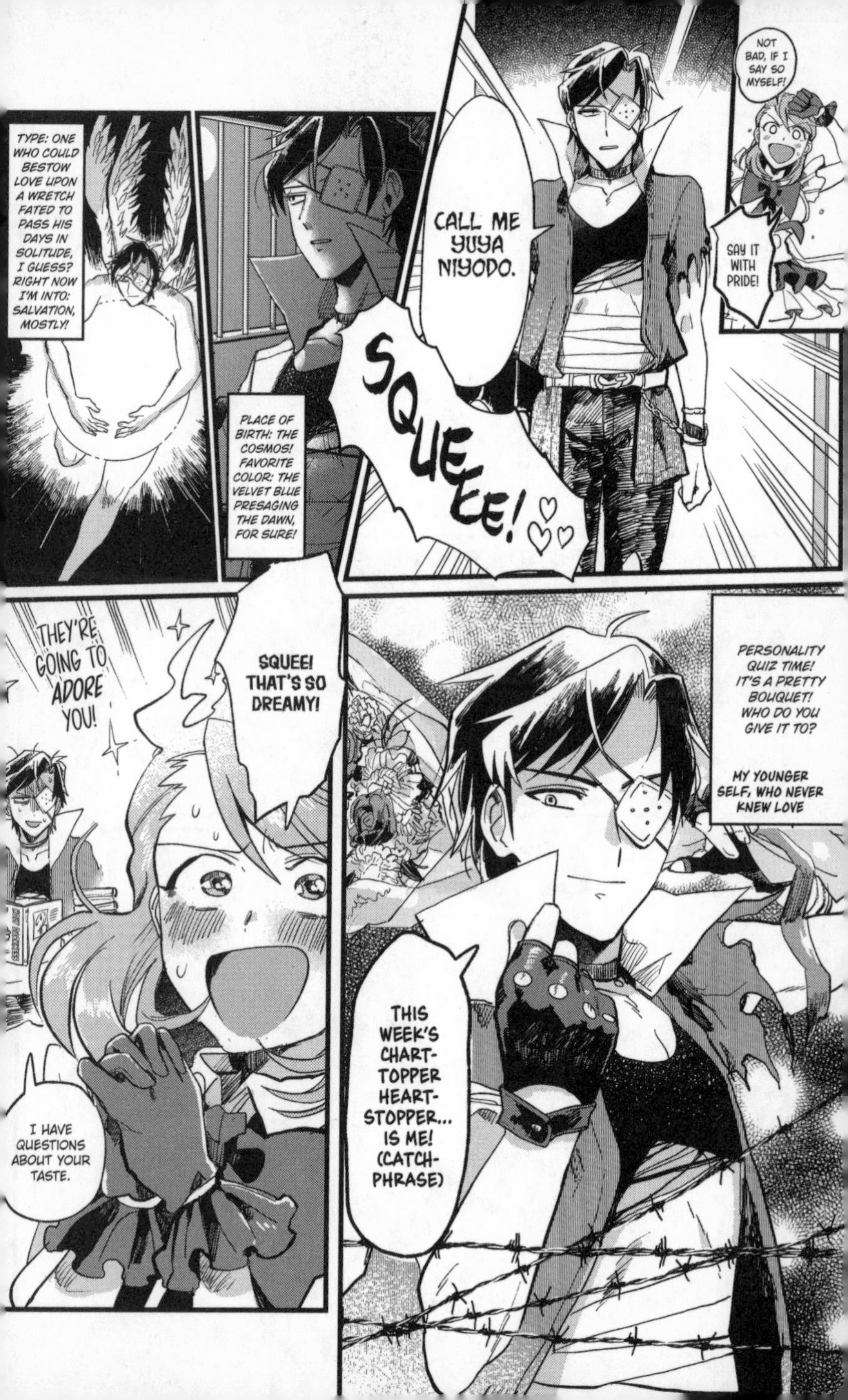
NOT BAD, IF I SAY SO MYSELF!
SAY IT WITH PRIDE!
CALL ME YUYA NIYODO.
SQUEEEE!
PLACE OF BIRTH: THE COSMOS! FAVORITE COLOR: THE VELVET BLUE PRESAGING THE DAWN, FOR SURE!
TYPE: ONE WHO COULD BESTOW LOVE UPON A WRETCH FATED TO PASS HIS DAYS IN SOLITUDE, I GUESS? RIGHT NOW I'M INTO: SALVATION, MOSTLY!
PERSONALITY QUIZ TIME! IT'S A PRETTY BOUQUET! WHO DO YOU GIVE IT TO?
MY YOUNGER SELF, WHO NEVER KNEW LOVE
THIS WEEK'S CHART-TOPPER HEART-STOPPER... IS ME! (CATCH-PHRASE)
SQUEE! THAT'S SO DREAMY!
THEY'RE GOING TO ADORE YOU!
I HAVE QUESTIONS ABOUT YOUR TASTE.

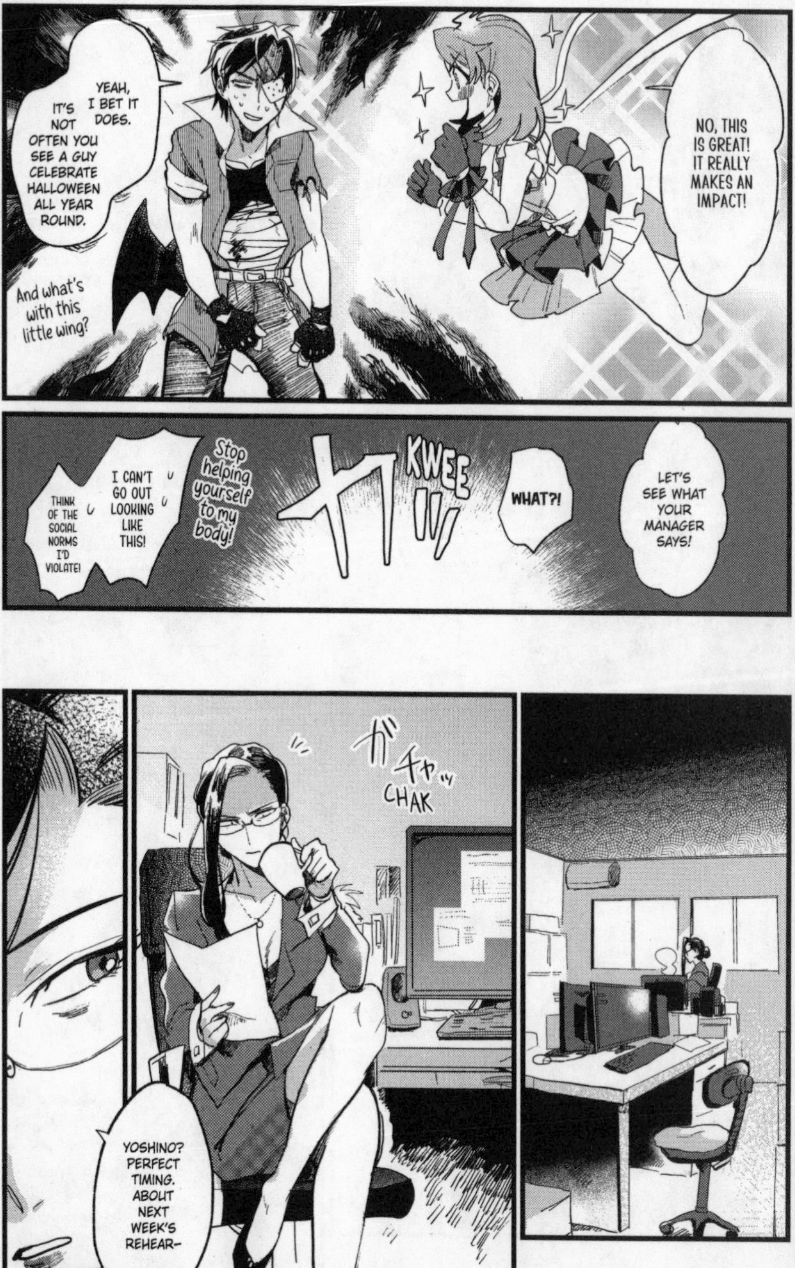
NO, THIS IS GREAT! IT REALLY MAKES AN IMPACT!
YEAH, I BET IT DOES.
IT'S NOT OFTEN YOU SEE A GUY CELEBRATE HALLOWEEN ALL YEAR ROUND.
And what's with this little wing?
LET'S SEE WHAT YOUR MANAGER SAYS!
WHAT?!
KWEE
Stop helping yourself to my body!
I CAN'T GO OUT LOOKING LIKE THIS!
THINK OF THE SOCIAL NORMS I'D VIOLATE!
ガチャッ
CHAK
YOSHINO? PERFECT TIMING. ABOUT NEXT WEEK'S REHEAR-

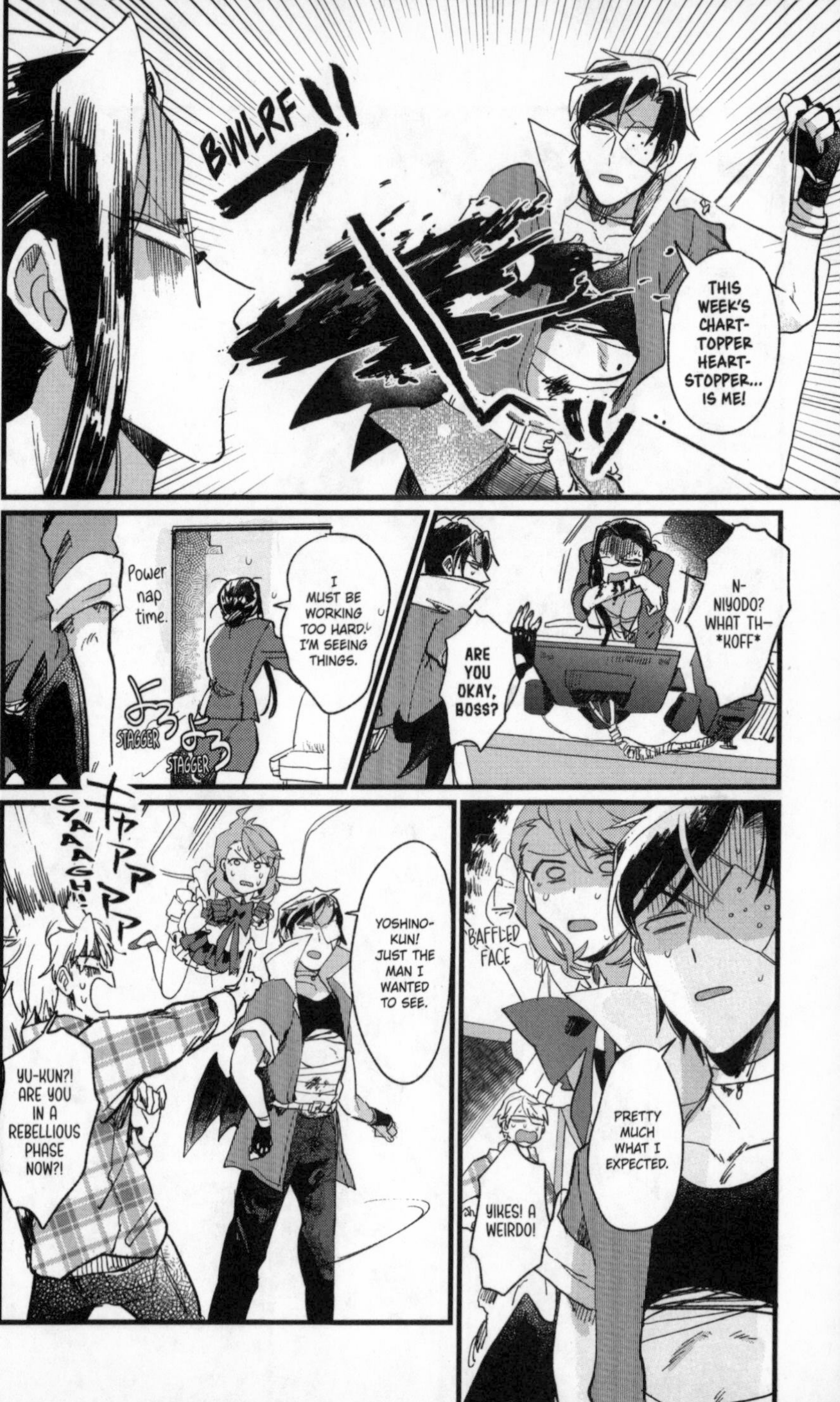
THIS WEEK'S CHART-TOPPER HEART-STOPPER... IS ME!
BWLRF
N-NIYODO? WHAT TH— *KOFF*
ARE YOU OKAY, BOSS?
I MUST BE WORKING TOO HARD. I'M SEEING THINGS.
Power nap time.
よろよろ
STAGGER STAGGER
BAFFLED FACE
PRETTY MUCH WHAT I EXPECTED.
YIKES! A WEIRDO!
キャアア
GYAAAGH!!
YOSHINO-KUN! JUST THE MAN I WANTED TO SEE.
YU-KUN?! ARE YOU IN A REBELLIOUS PHASE NOW?!

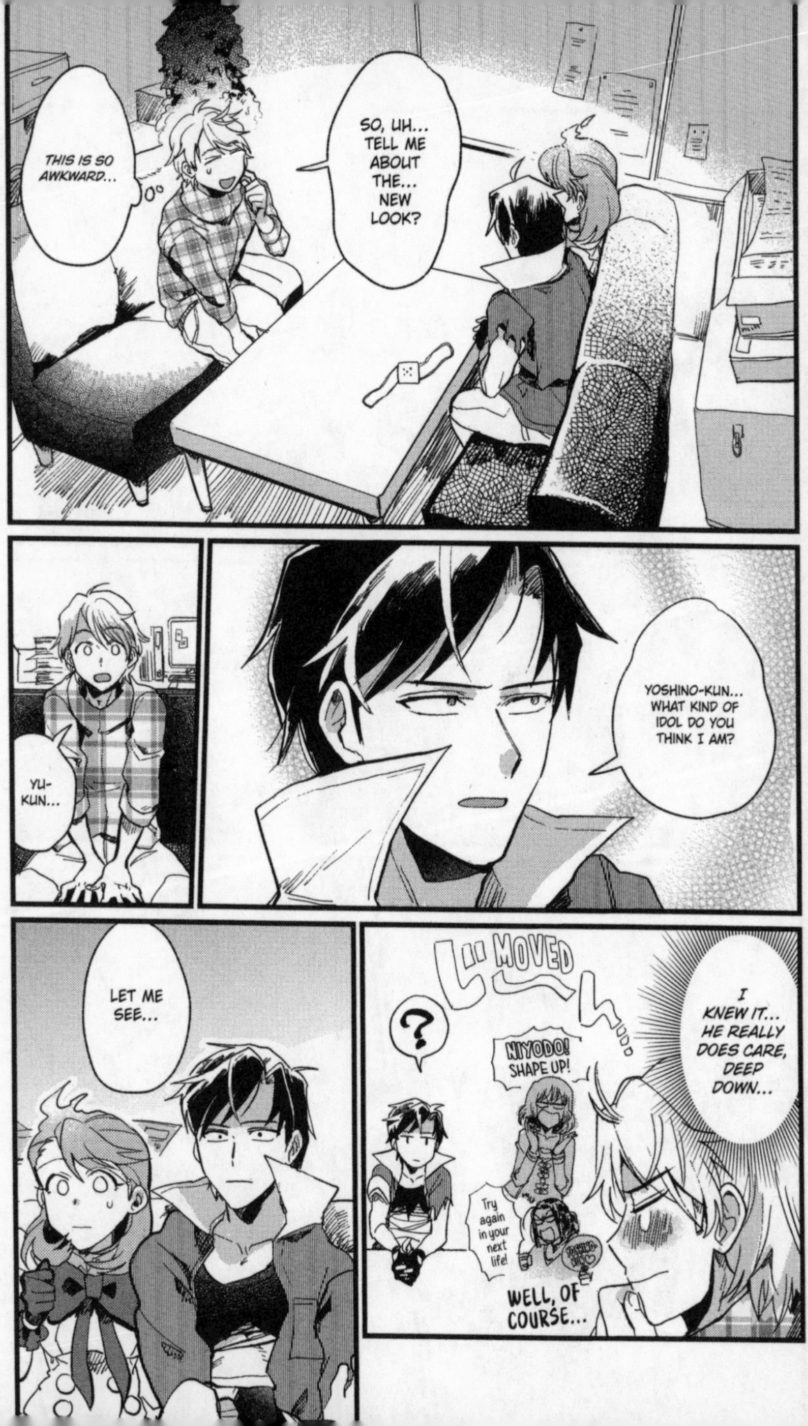
SO, UH... TELL ME ABOUT THE... NEW LOOK?
THIS IS SO AWKWARD...
YOSHINO-KUN... WHAT KIND OF IDOL DO YOU THINK I AM?
YU-KUN...
I KNEW IT... HE REALLY DOES CARE, DEEP DOWN...
MOVED
?
NIYODO! SHAPE UP!
Try again in your next life!
WELL, OF COURSE...
LET ME SEE...

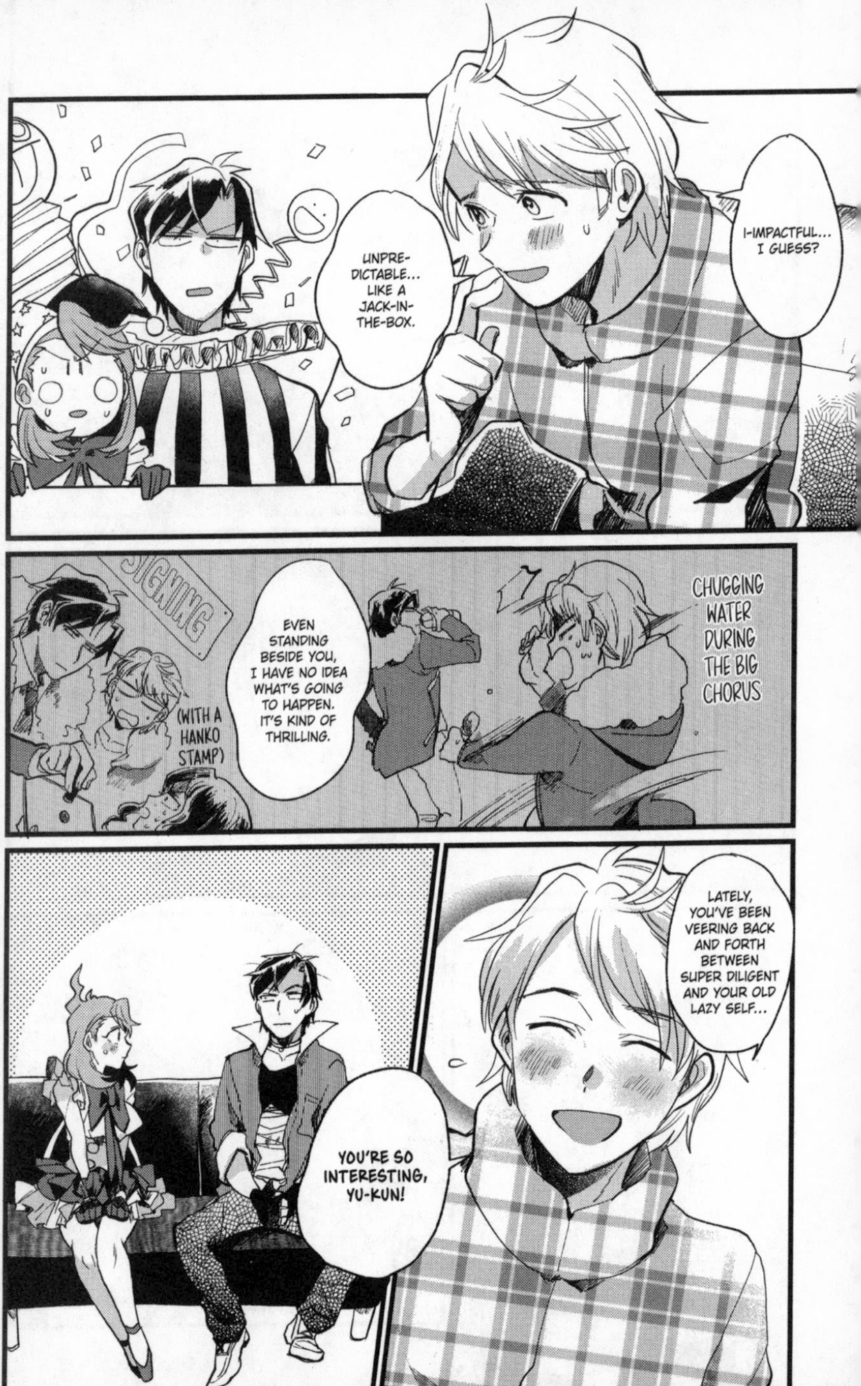
I-IMPACTFUL… I GUESS?
UNPRE-DICTABLE… LIKE A JACK-IN-THE-BOX.
CHUGGING WATER DURING THE BIG CHORUS
EVEN STANDING BESIDE YOU, I HAVE NO IDEA WHAT'S GOING TO HAPPEN. IT'S KIND OF THRILLING.
(WITH A HANKO STAMP)
SIGNING
LATELY, YOU'VE BEEN VEERING BACK AND FORTH BETWEEN SUPER DILIGENT AND YOUR OLD LAZY SELF…
YOU'RE SO INTERESTING, YU-KUN!

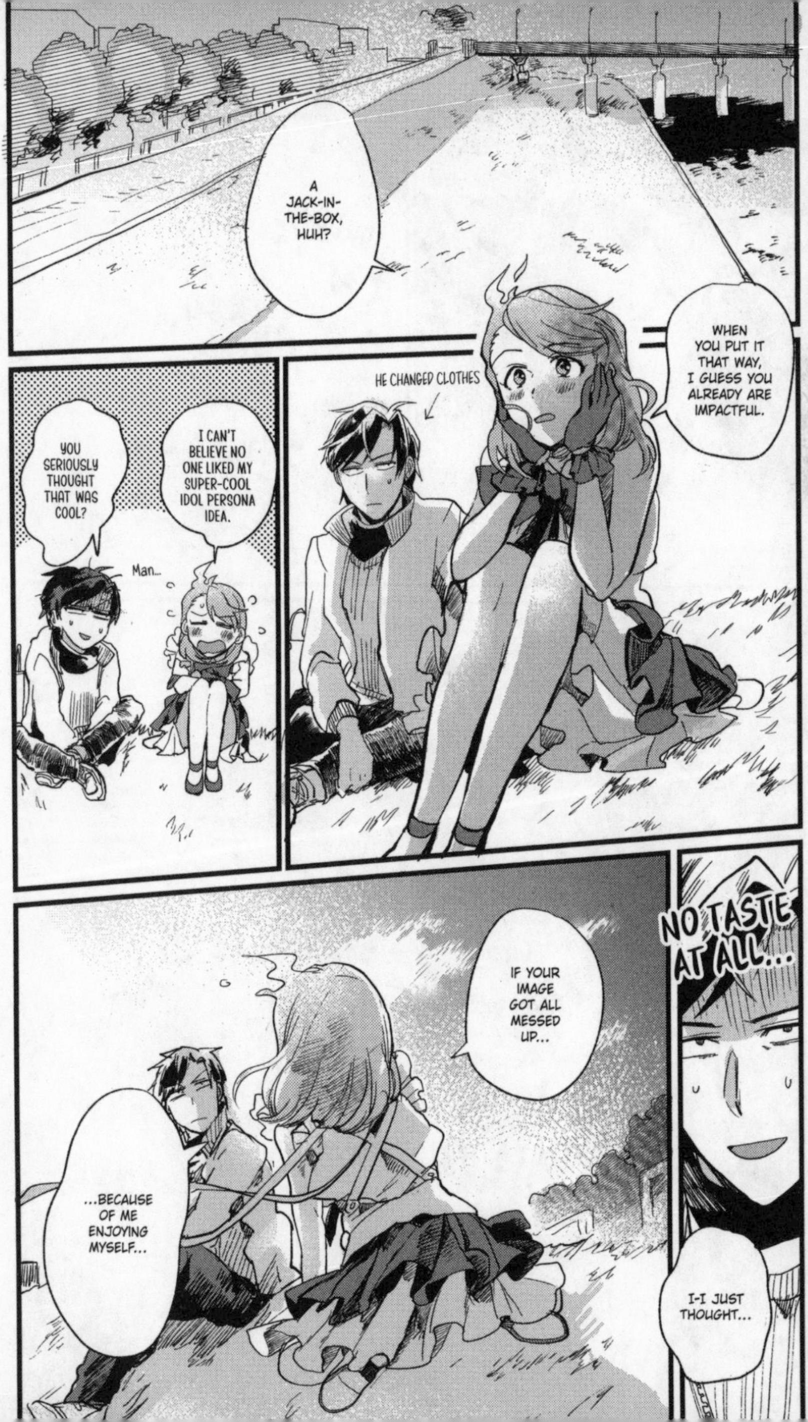
A JACK-IN-THE-BOX, HUH?
WHEN YOU PUT IT THAT WAY, I GUESS YOU ALREADY ARE IMPACTFUL.
HE CHANGED CLOTHES
I CAN'T BELIEVE NO ONE LIKED MY SUPER-COOL IDOL PERSONA IDEA.
YOU SERIOUSLY THOUGHT THAT WAS COOL?
Man...
NO TASTE AT ALL...
I-I JUST THOUGHT...
IF YOUR IMAGE GOT ALL MESSED UP...
...BECAUSE OF ME ENJOYING MYSELF...

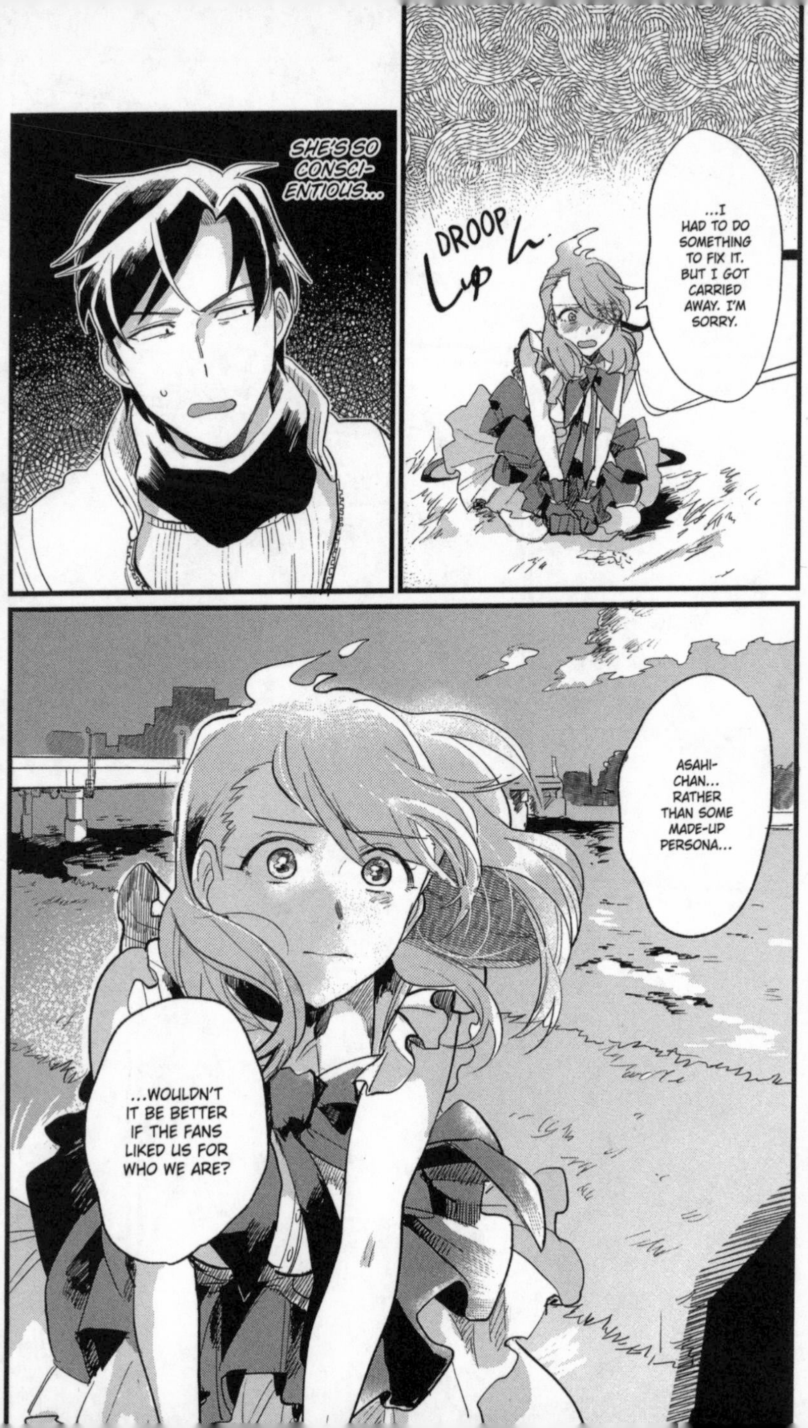
DROOP
...I HAD TO DO SOMETHING TO FIX IT. BUT I GOT CARRIED AWAY. I'M SORRY.
SHE'S SO CONSCI-ENTIOUS...
ASAHI-CHAN... RATHER THAN SOME MADE-UP PERSONA...
...WOULDN'T IT BE BETTER IF THE FANS LIKED US FOR WHO WE ARE?

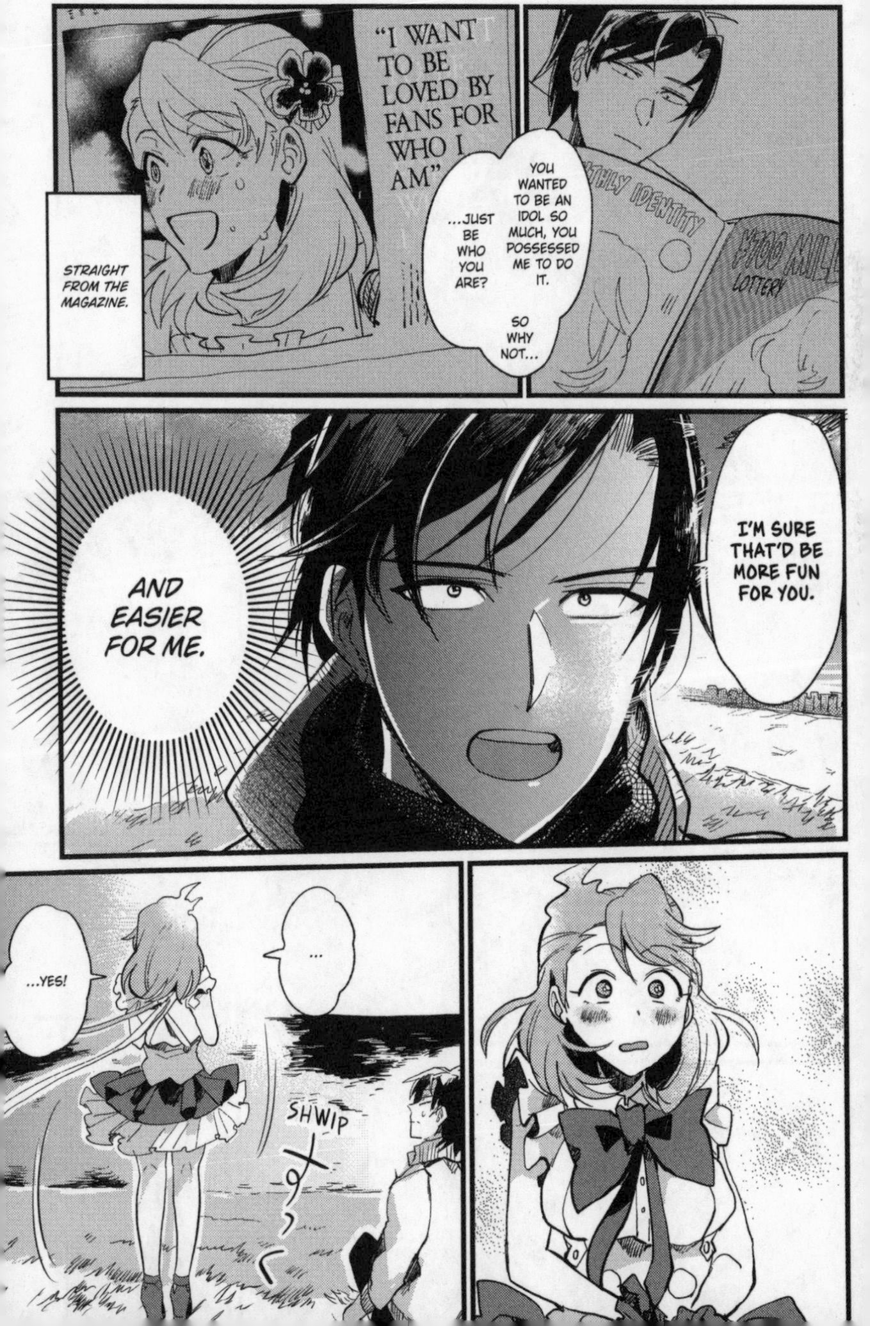
YOU WANTED TO BE AN IDOL SO MUCH, YOU POSSESSED ME TO DO IT.
SO WHY NOT...
...JUST BE WHO YOU ARE?
LOTTERY
"I WANT TO BE LOVED BY FANS FOR WHO I AM"
STRAIGHT FROM THE MAGAZINE.
I'M SURE THAT'D BE MORE FUN FOR YOU.
AND EASIER FOR ME.
...
...YES!
SHWIP

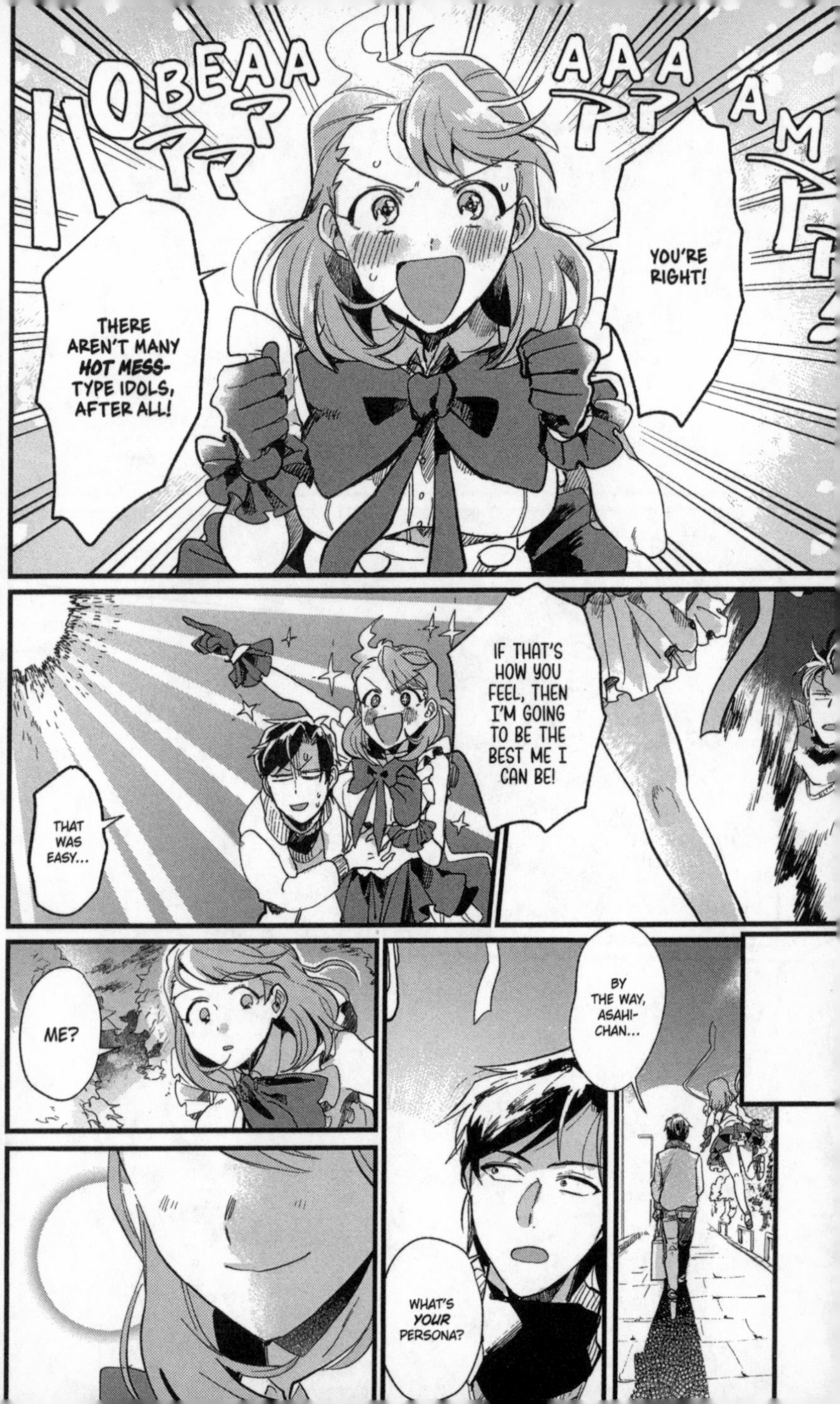
OBEAAA
AAA
AM
YOU'RE RIGHT!
THERE AREN'T MANY HOT MESS-TYPE IDOLS, AFTER ALL!
IF THAT'S HOW YOU FEEL, THEN I'M GOING TO BE THE BEST ME I CAN BE!
THAT WAS EASY...
BY THE WAY, ASAHI-CHAN...
WHAT'S YOUR PERSONA?
ME?

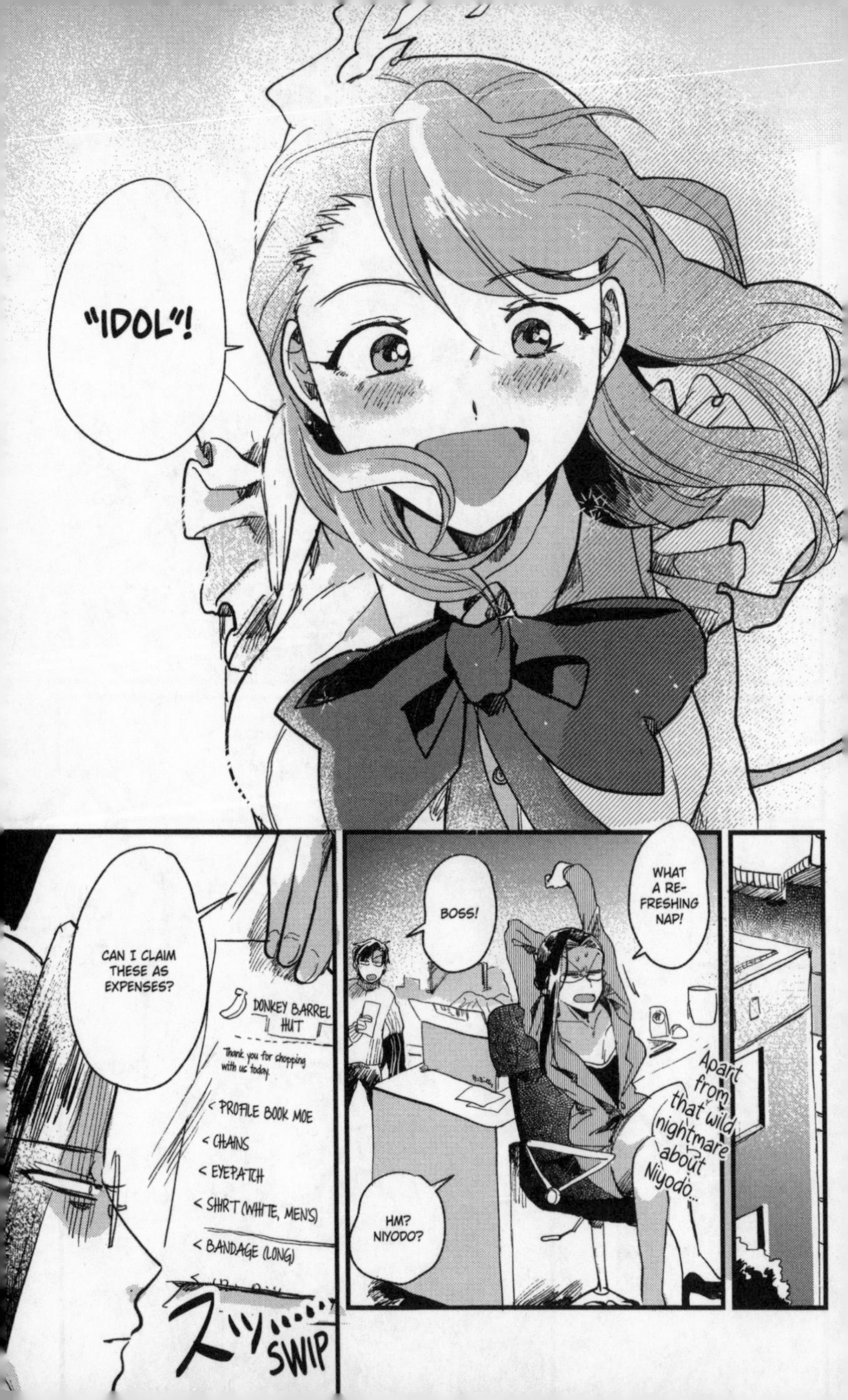
"IDOL"!
WHAT A RE-FRESHING NAP!
BOSS!
Apart from that wild nightmare about Niyodo...
HM? NIYODO?
CAN I CLAIM THESE AS EXPENSES?
DONKEY BARREL HUT
Thank you for shopping with us today.
< PROFILE BOOK MOE
< CHAINS
< EYEPATCH
< SHIRT (WHITE, MEN'S)
< BANDAGE (LONG)
スッ…
SWIP

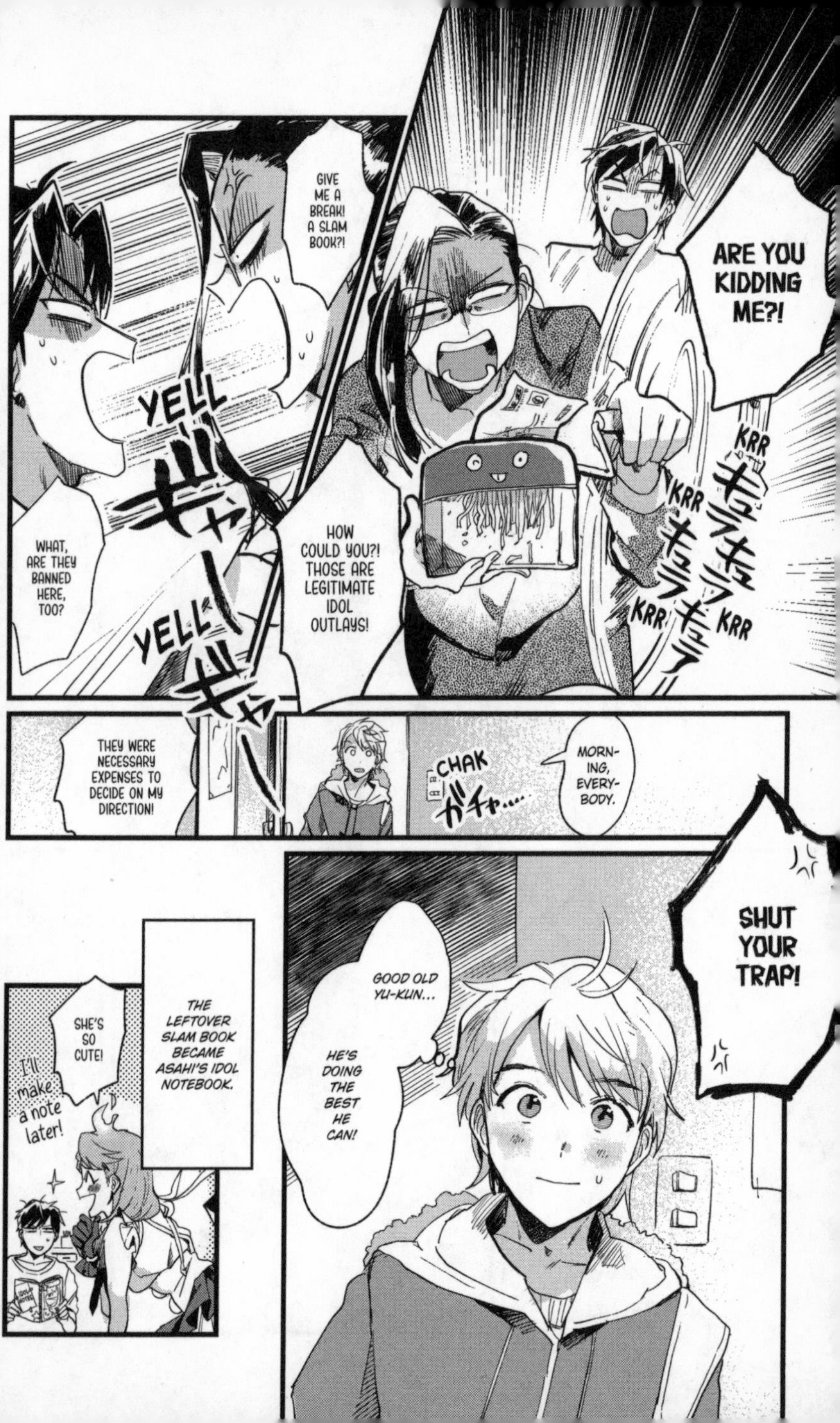
ARE YOU KIDDING ME?!
KRR KRR KRR KRR
HOW COULD YOU?! THOSE ARE LEGITIMATE IDOL OUTLAYS!
GIVE ME A BREAK! A SLAM BOOK?!
YELL
WHAT, ARE THEY BANNED HERE, TOO?
YELL
MORNING, EVERYBODY.
CHAK
THEY WERE NECESSARY EXPENSES TO DECIDE ON MY DIRECTION!
SHUT YOUR TRAP!
GOOD OLD YU-KUN...
HE'S DOING THE BEST HE CAN!
THE LEFTOVER SLAM BOOK BECAME ASAHI'S IDOL NOTEBOOK.
SHE'S SO CUTE!
I'll make a note later!

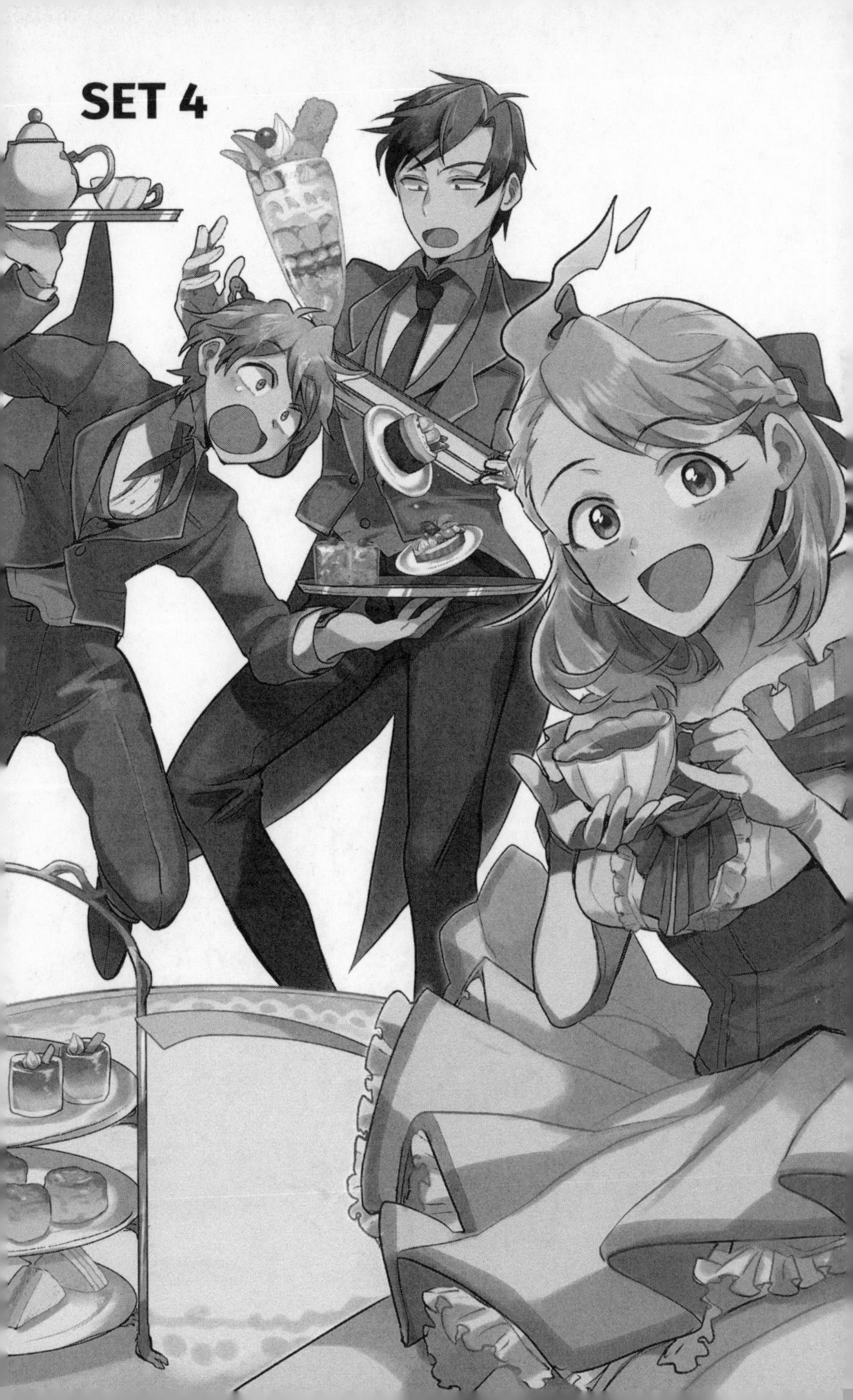
SET 4

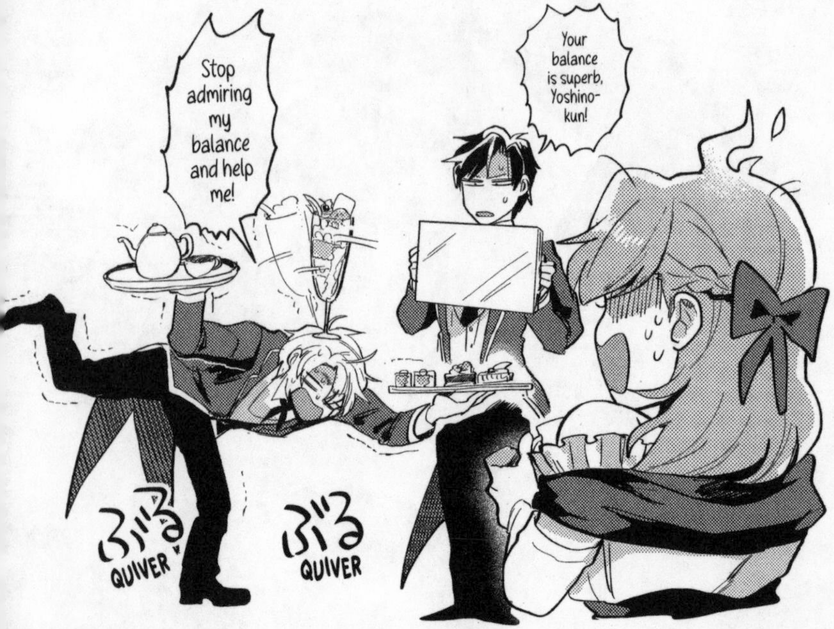
Your balance is superb, Yoshino-kun!
Stop admiring my balance and help me!
ぶる
QUIVER
ぶる
QUIVER

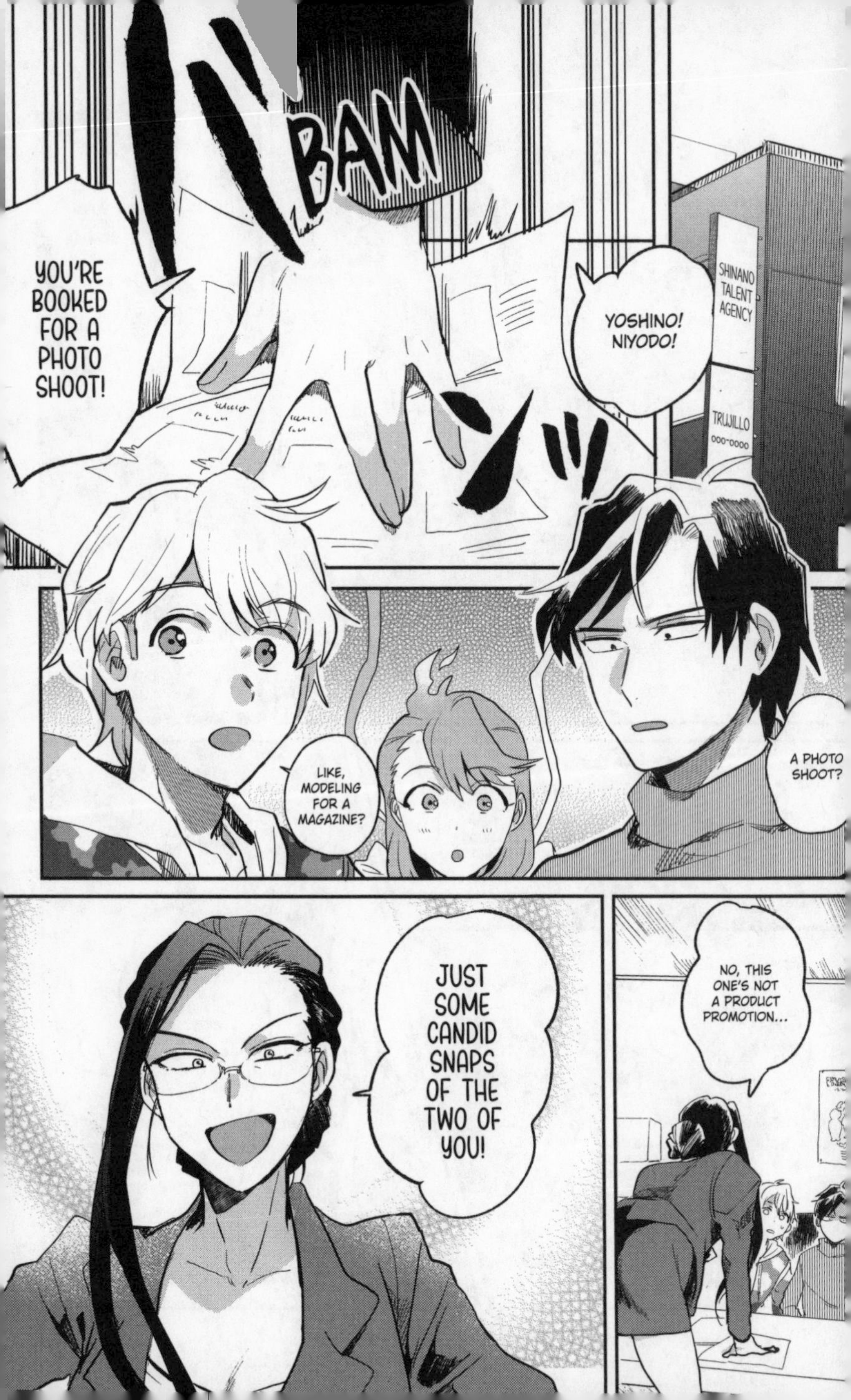
BAM
SHINANO TALENT AGENCY
TRUJILLO 000-0000
YOSHINO! NIYODO!
YOU'RE BOOKED FOR A PHOTO SHOOT!
A PHOTO SHOOT?
LIKE, MODELING FOR A MAGAZINE?
NO, THIS ONE'S NOT A PRODUCT PROMOTION...
JUST SOME CANDID SNAPS OF THE TWO OF YOU!

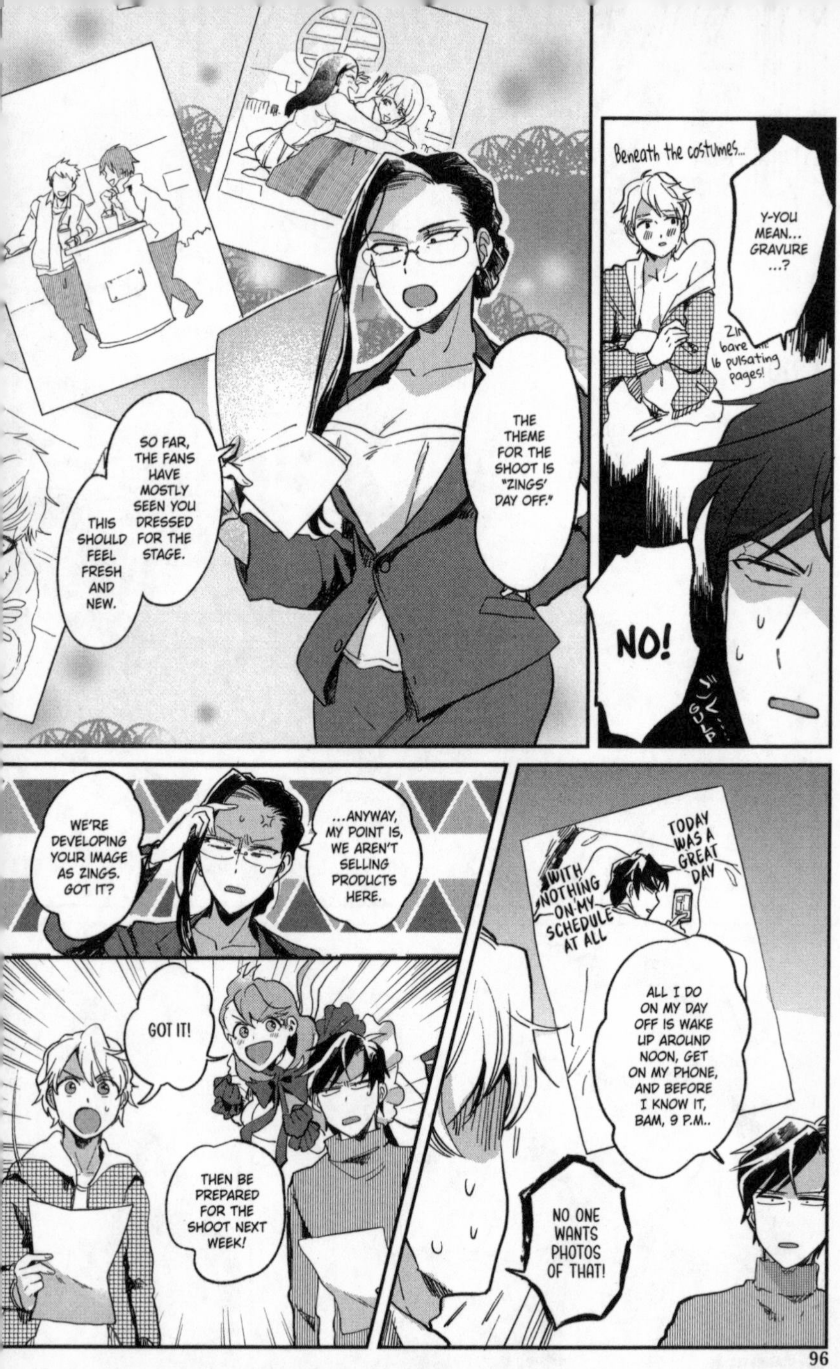
Beneath the costumes...
Y-YOU MEAN... GRAVURE ...?
16 pulsating pages!
NO!
GULP
THE THEME FOR THE SHOOT IS "ZINGS' DAY OFF."
SO FAR, THE FANS HAVE MOSTLY SEEN YOU DRESSED FOR THE STAGE.
THIS SHOULD FEEL FRESH AND NEW.
TODAY WAS A GREAT DAY
WITH NOTHING ON MY SCHEDULE AT ALL
ALL I DO ON MY DAY OFF IS WAKE UP AROUND NOON, GET ON MY PHONE, AND BEFORE I KNOW IT, BAM, 9 P.M..
NO ONE WANTS PHOTOS OF THAT!
...ANYWAY, MY POINT IS, WE AREN'T SELLING PRODUCTS HERE.
WE'RE DEVELOPING YOUR IMAGE AS ZINGS. GOT IT?
GOT IT!
THEN BE PREPARED FOR THE SHOOT NEXT WEEK!

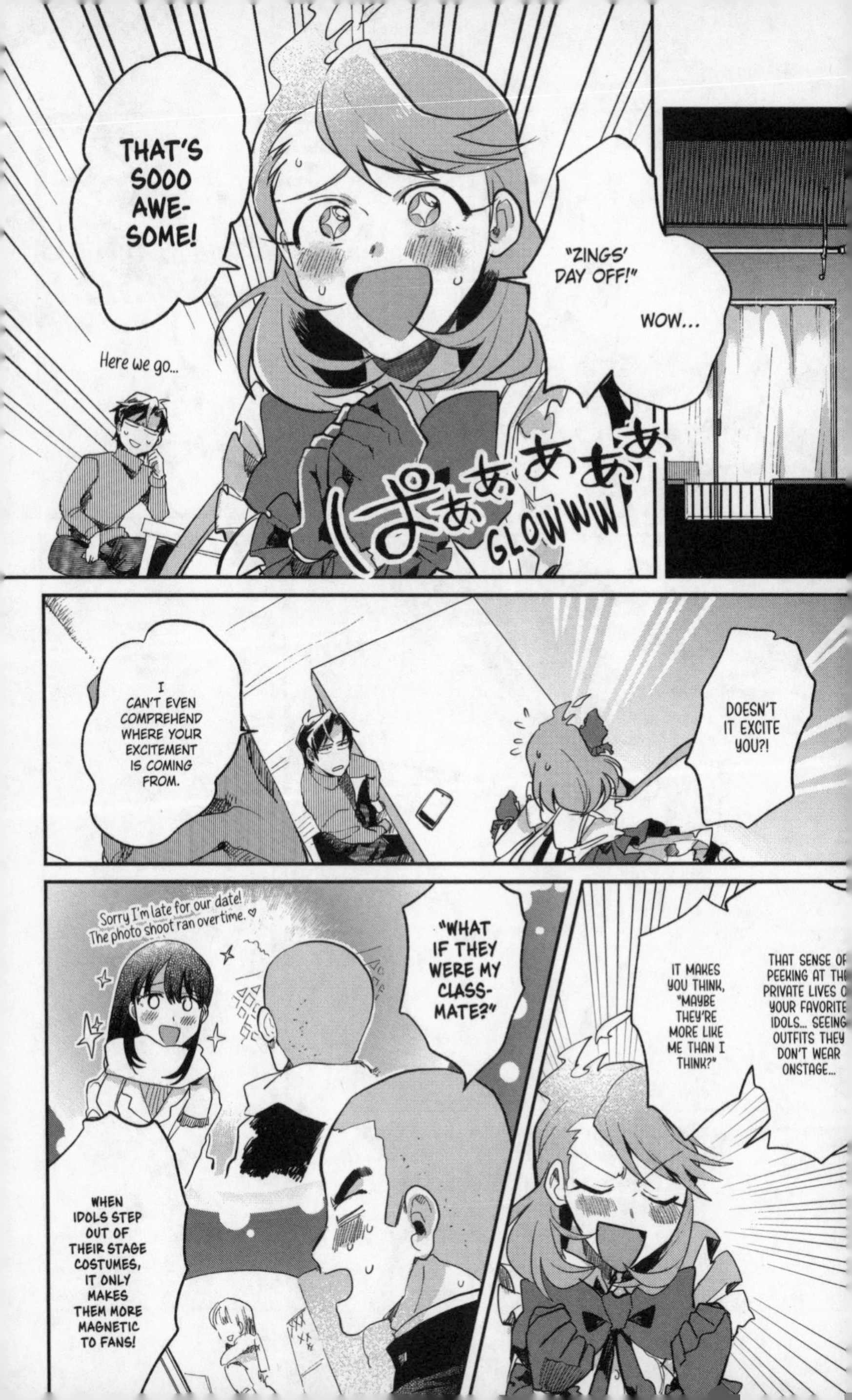
"ZINGS' DAY OFF!" WOW...
THAT'S SOOO AWESOME!
ぱぁあああああ
GLOWWW
Here we go...
DOESN'T IT EXCITE YOU?!
I CAN'T EVEN COMPREHEND WHERE YOUR EXCITEMENT IS COMING FROM.
THAT SENSE OF PEEKING AT THE PRIVATE LIVES O YOUR FAVORITE IDOLS... SEEING OUTFITS THEY DON'T WEAR ONSTAGE...
IT MAKES YOU THINK, "MAYBE THEY'RE MORE LIKE ME THAN I THINK?"
"WHAT IF THEY WERE MY CLASSMATE?"
Sorry I'm late for our date! The photo shoot ran overtime. ♡
WHEN IDOLS STEP OUT OF THEIR STAGE COSTUMES, IT ONLY MAKES THEM MORE MAGNETIC TO FANS!

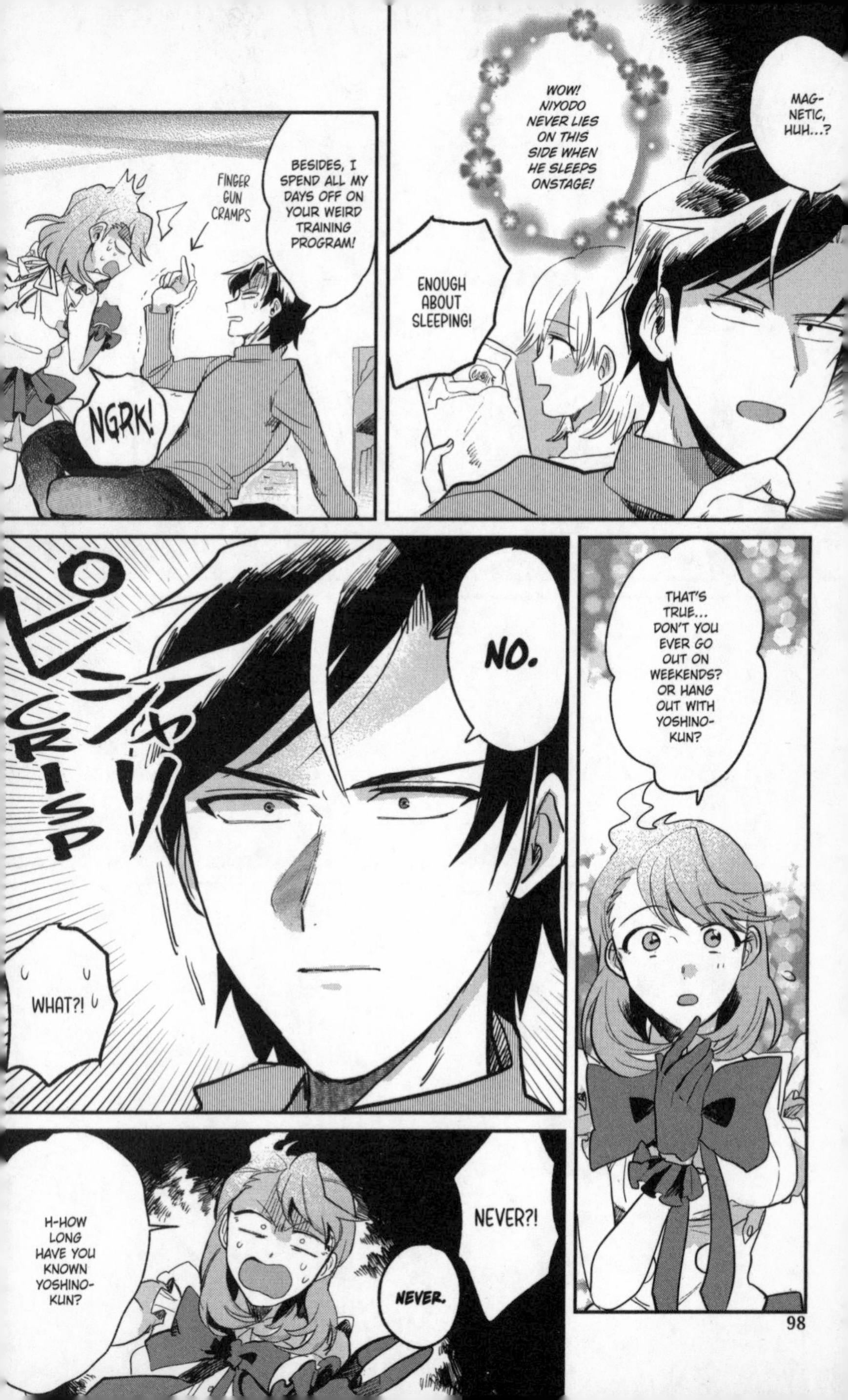
MAG-
NETIC,
HUH...?
WOW! NIYODO NEVER LIES ON THIS SIDE WHEN HE SLEEPS ONSTAGE!
ENOUGH ABOUT SLEEPING!
BESIDES, I SPEND ALL MY DAYS OFF ON YOUR WEIRD TRAINING PROGRAM!
FINGER GUN CRAMPS
NGRK!
THAT'S TRUE... DON'T YOU EVER GO OUT ON WEEKENDS? OR HANG OUT WITH YOSHINO-KUN?
NO.
CRISP
WHAT?!
NEVER?!
NEVER.
H-HOW LONG HAVE YOU KNOWN YOSHINO-KUN?

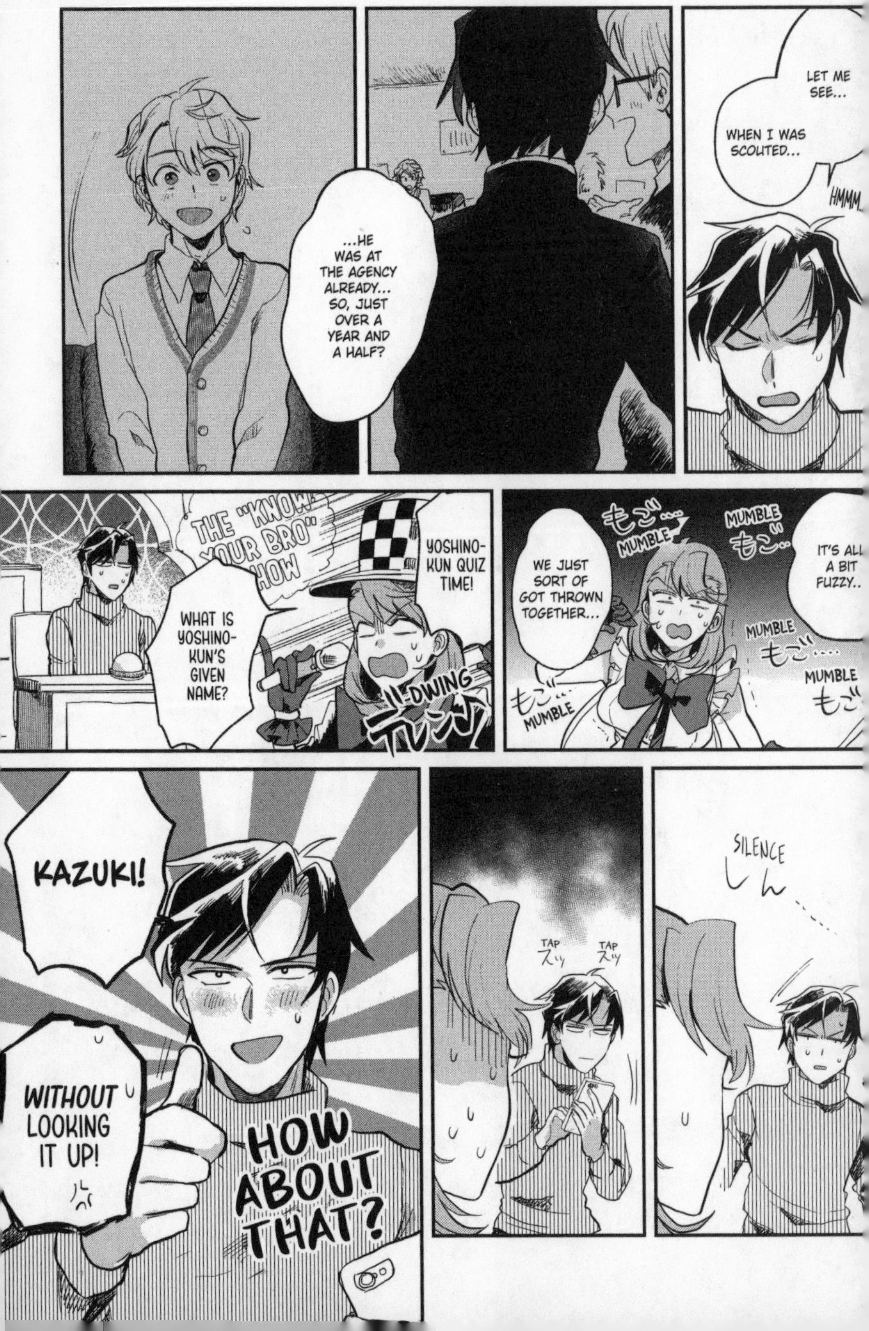
LET ME SEE...
WHEN I WAS SCOUTED...
HMMM..
...HE WAS AT THE AGENCY ALREADY... SO, JUST OVER A YEAR AND A HALF?
IT'S ALL A BIT FUZZY..
MUMBLE もご...
MUMBLE もご....
MUMBLE もご...
WE JUST SORT OF GOT THROWN TOGETHER...
もご... MUMBLE
もご... MUMBLE
YOSHINO-KUN QUIZ TIME!
THE "KNOW YOUR BRO" HOW
WHAT IS YOSHINO-KUN'S GIVEN NAME?
DWING テレーン
SILENCE しん
TAP ズッ
TAP ズッ
KAZUKI!
WITHOUT LOOKING IT UP!
HOW ABOUT THAT?

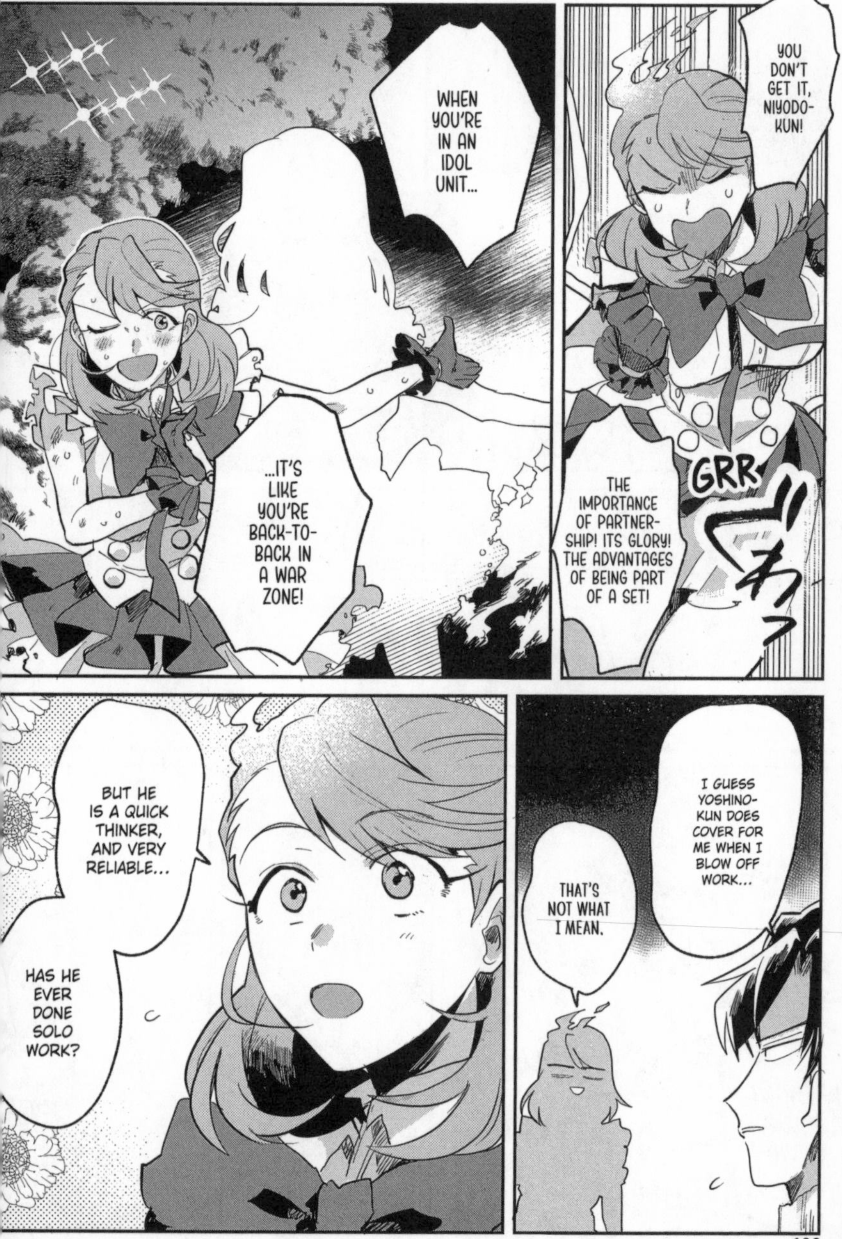
YOU DON'T GET IT, NIYODO-KUN!
THE IMPORTANCE OF PARTNERSHIP! ITS GLORY! THE ADVANTAGES OF BEING PART OF A SET!
GRR
WHEN YOU'RE IN AN IDOL UNIT...
...IT'S LIKE YOU'RE BACK-TO-BACK IN A WAR ZONE!
I GUESS YOSHINO-KUN DOES COVER FOR ME WHEN I BLOW OFF WORK...
THAT'S NOT WHAT I MEAN.
BUT HE IS A QUICK THINKER, AND VERY RELIABLE...
HAS HE EVER DONE SOLO WORK?

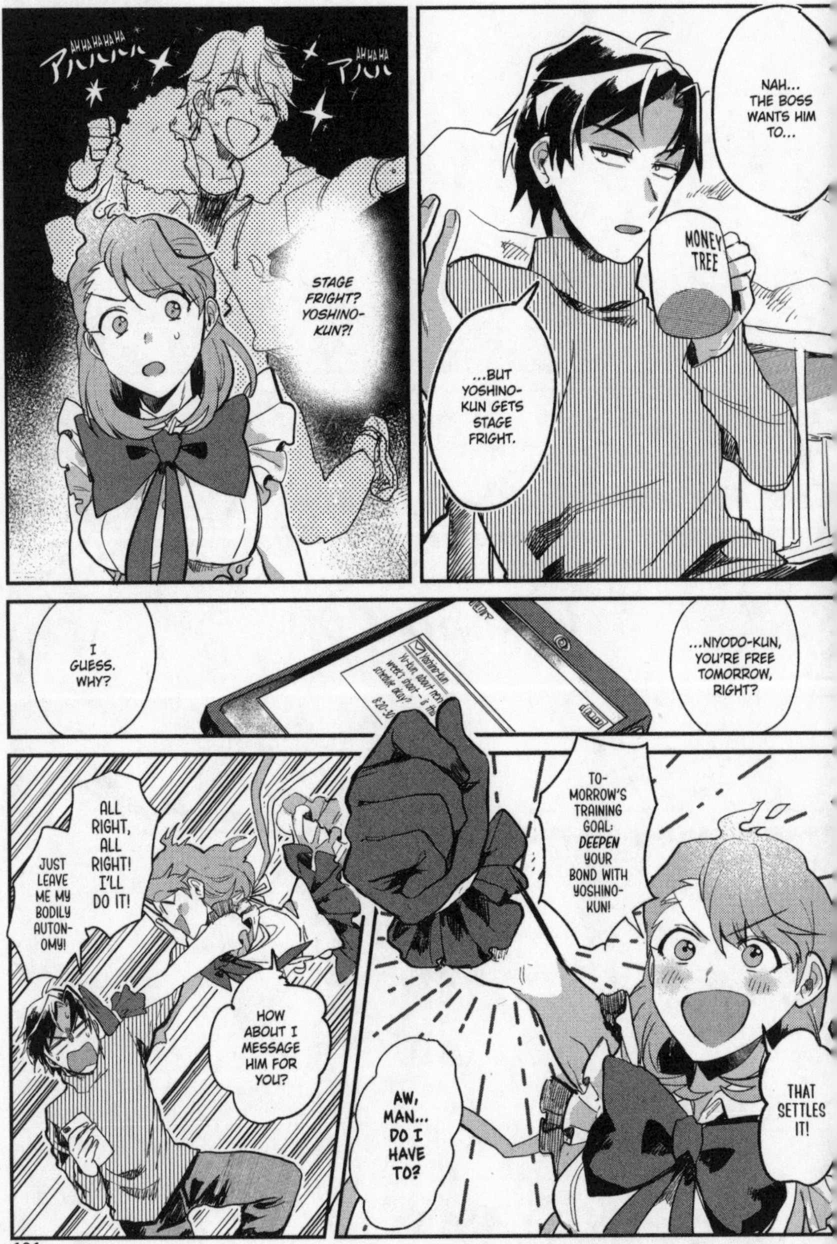
NAH... THE BOSS WANTS HIM TO...
MONEY TREE
...BUT YOSHINO-KUN GETS STAGE FRIGHT.
AH HA HA HA HA
AH HA HA
STAGE FRIGHT? YOSHINO-KUN?!
...NIYODO-KUN, YOU'RE FREE TOMORROW, RIGHT?
I GUESS. WHY?
THAT SETTLES IT!
TO-MORROW'S TRAINING GOAL: DEEPEN YOUR BOND WITH YOSHINO-KUN!
AW, MAN... DO I HAVE TO?
HOW ABOUT I MESSAGE HIM FOR YOU?
ALL RIGHT, ALL RIGHT! I'LL DO IT!
JUST LEAVE ME MY BODILY AUTON-OMY!

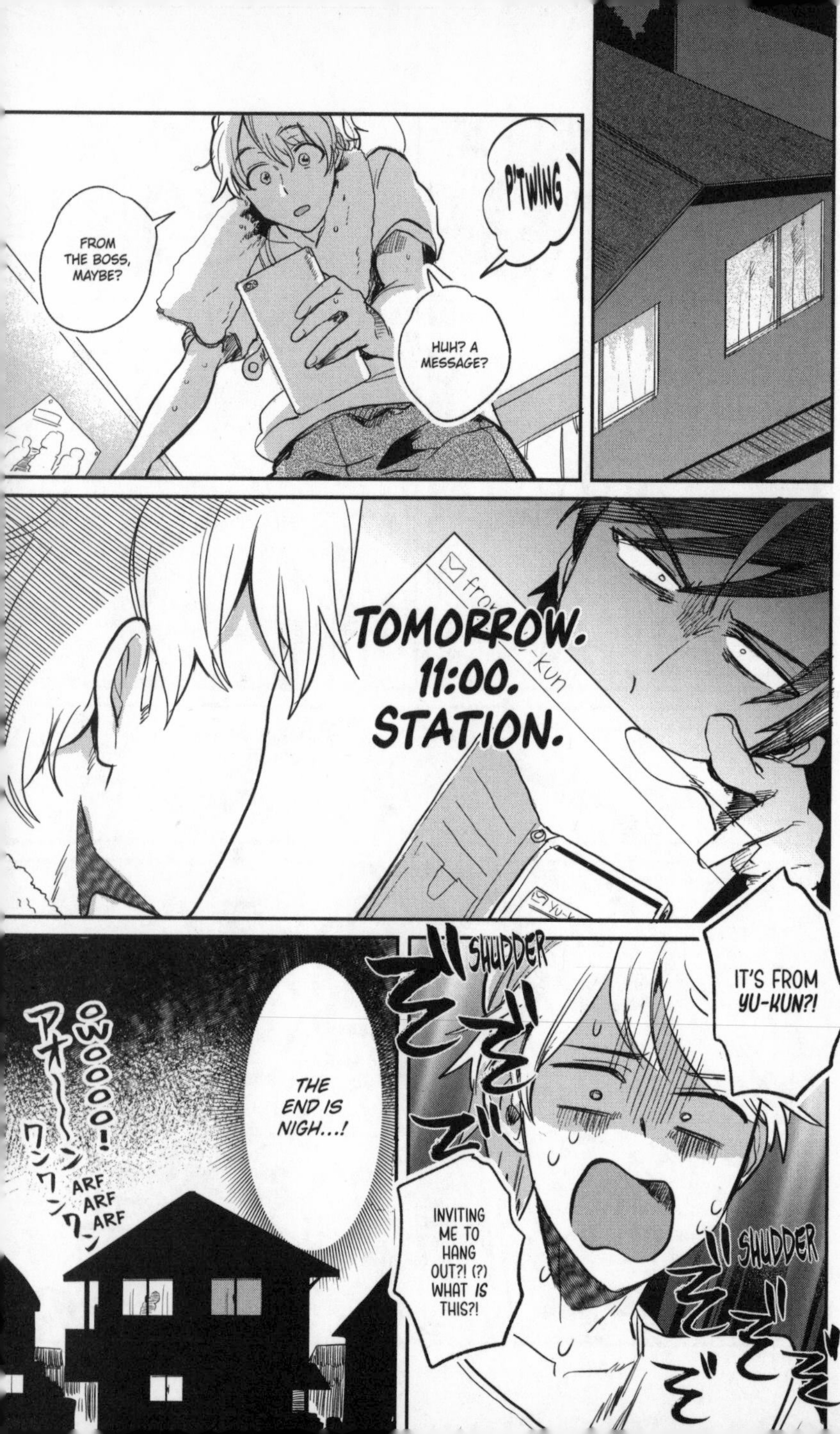
P'TWING
HUH? A MESSAGE?
FROM THE BOSS, MAYBE?
TOMORROW. 11:00. STATION.
SHUDDER
ぞぞぞ
IT'S FROM YU-KUN?!
INVITING ME TO HANG OUT?! (?) WHAT IS THIS?!
SHUDDER
ぞぞぞ
THE END IS NIGH...!
AWOOOOO!
アオーン
ARF ARF ARF
ワンワンワン

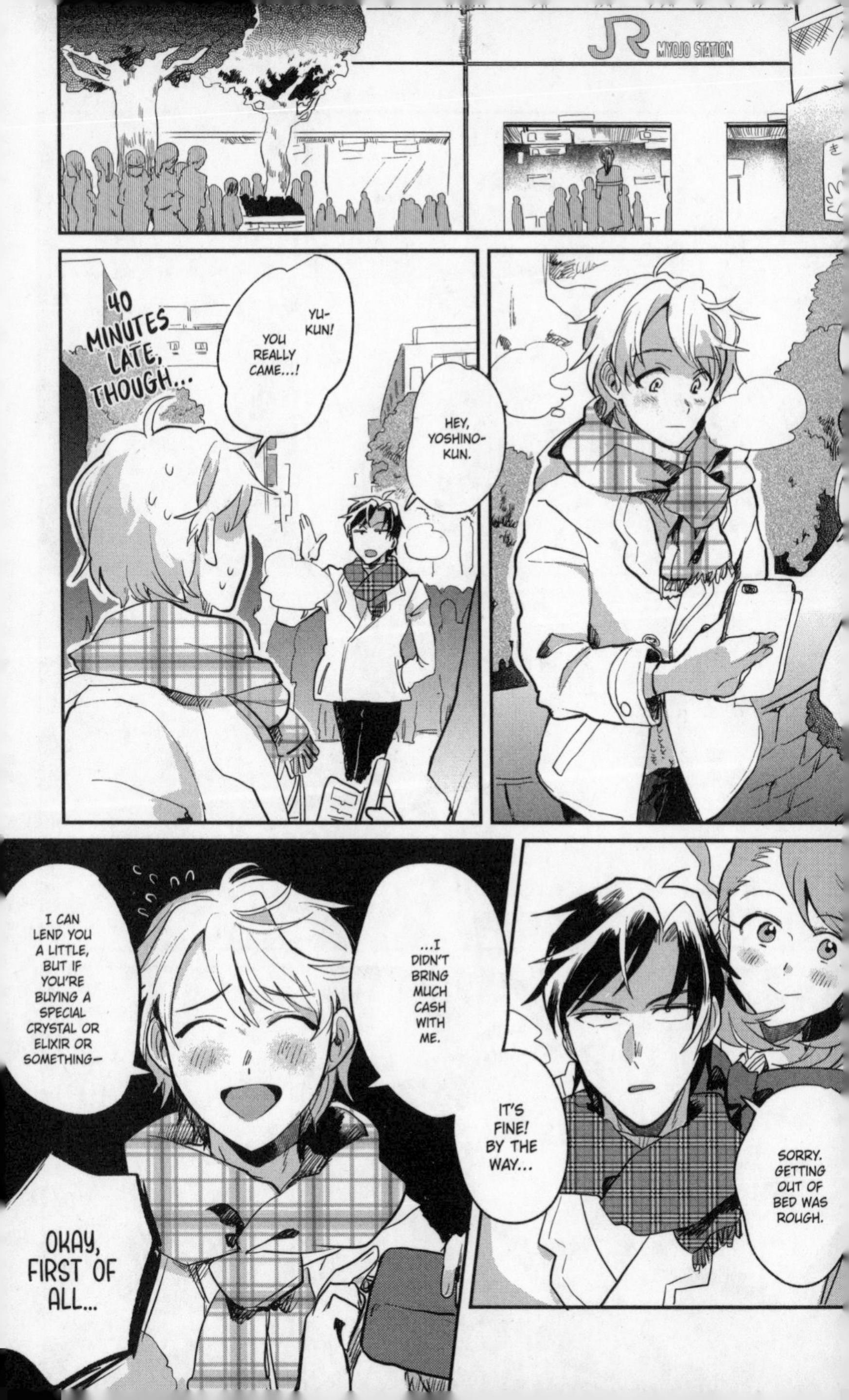

MYOJO STATION
YU-KUN! YOU REALLY CAME...!
HEY, YOSHINO-KUN.
40 MINUTES LATE, THOUGH...
SORRY. GETTING OUT OF BED WAS ROUGH.
IT'S FINE! BY THE WAY...
...I DIDN'T BRING MUCH CASH WITH ME.
I CAN LEND YOU A LITTLE, BUT IF YOU'RE BUYING A SPECIAL CRYSTAL OR ELIXIR OR SOMETHING—
OKAY, FIRST OF ALL...

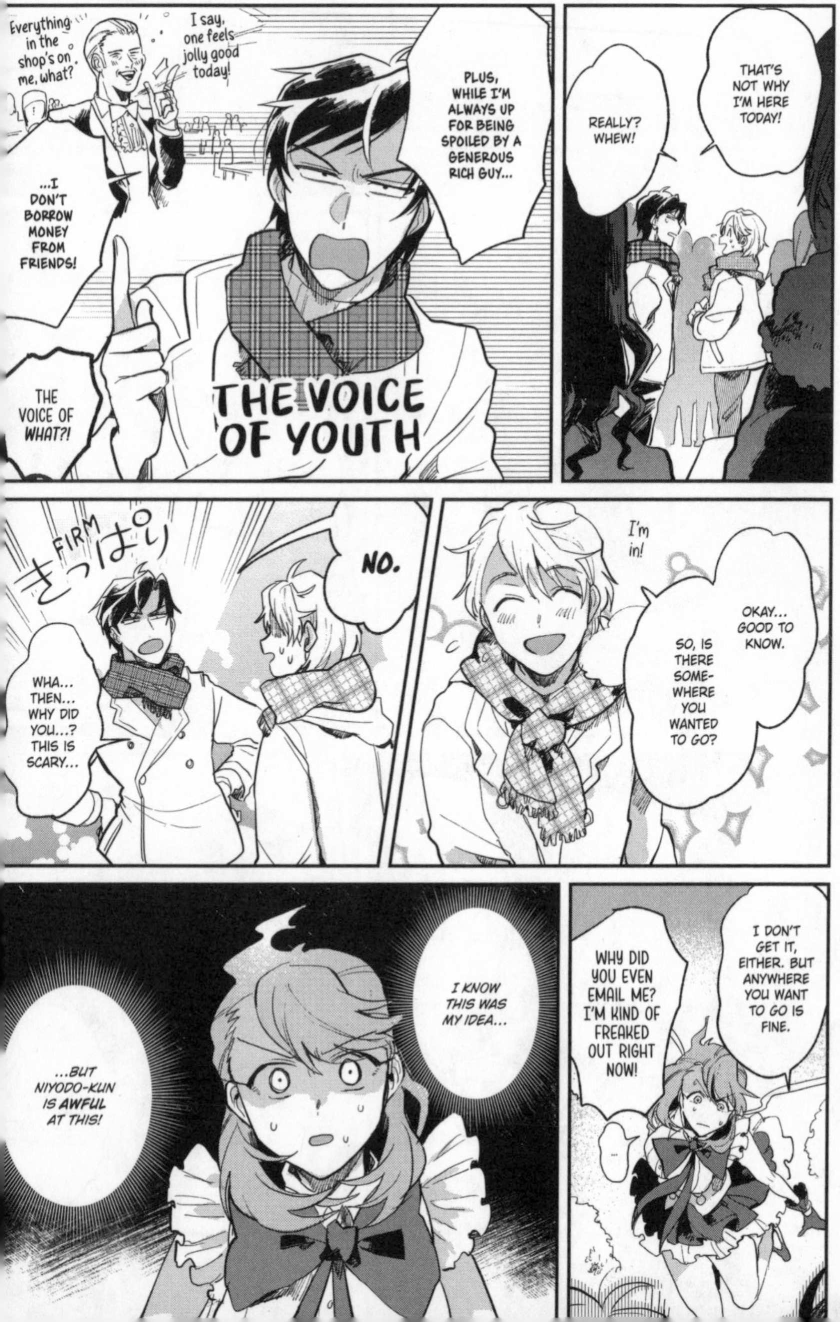
THAT'S NOT WHY I'M HERE TODAY!
REALLY? WHEW!
PLUS, WHILE I'M ALWAYS UP FOR BEING SPOILED BY A GENEROUS RICH GUY...
I say, one feels jolly good today!
Everything in the shop's on me, what?
...I DON'T BORROW MONEY FROM FRIENDS!
THE VOICE OF YOUTH
THE VOICE OF WHAT?!
I'm in!
OKAY... GOOD TO KNOW.
SO, IS THERE SOMEWHERE YOU WANTED TO GO?
NO.
FIRM
きっぱり
WHA... THEN... WHY DID YOU...? THIS IS SCARY...
I DON'T GET IT, EITHER. BUT ANYWHERE YOU WANT TO GO IS FINE.
WHY DID YOU EVEN EMAIL ME? I'M KIND OF FREAKED OUT RIGHT NOW!
...
I KNOW THIS WAS MY IDEA...
...BUT NIYODO-KUN IS AWFUL AT THIS!

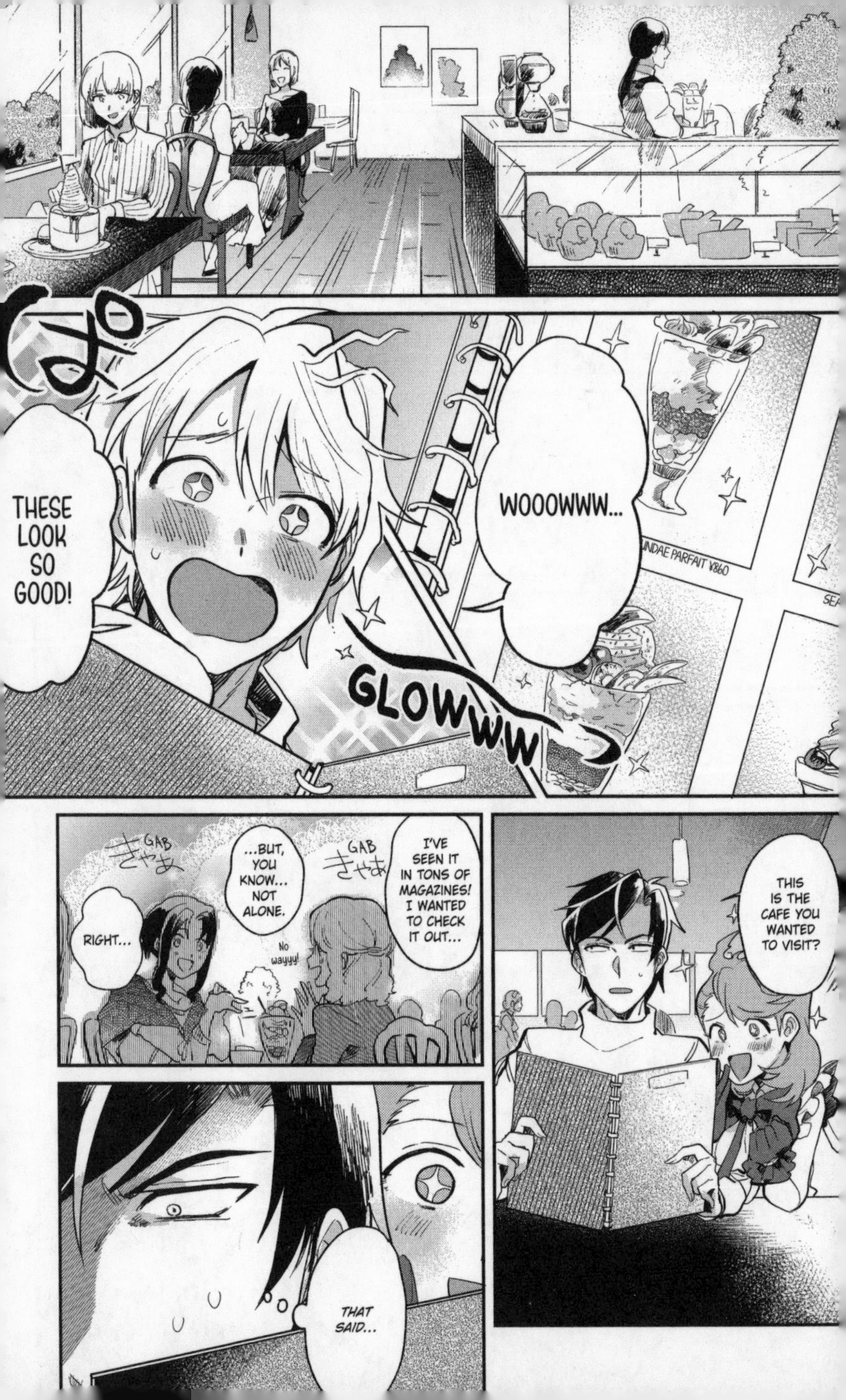
ぱっ
WOOOWWW...
THESE LOOK SO GOOD!
NDAE PARFAIT ¥860
GLOWWWW
THIS IS THE CAFE YOU WANTED TO VISIT?
I'VE SEEN IT IN TONS OF MAGAZINES! I WANTED TO CHECK IT OUT...
GAB きゃあ
...BUT, YOU KNOW... NOT ALONE.
No wayyy!
GAB きゃあ
RIGHT...
THAT SAID...

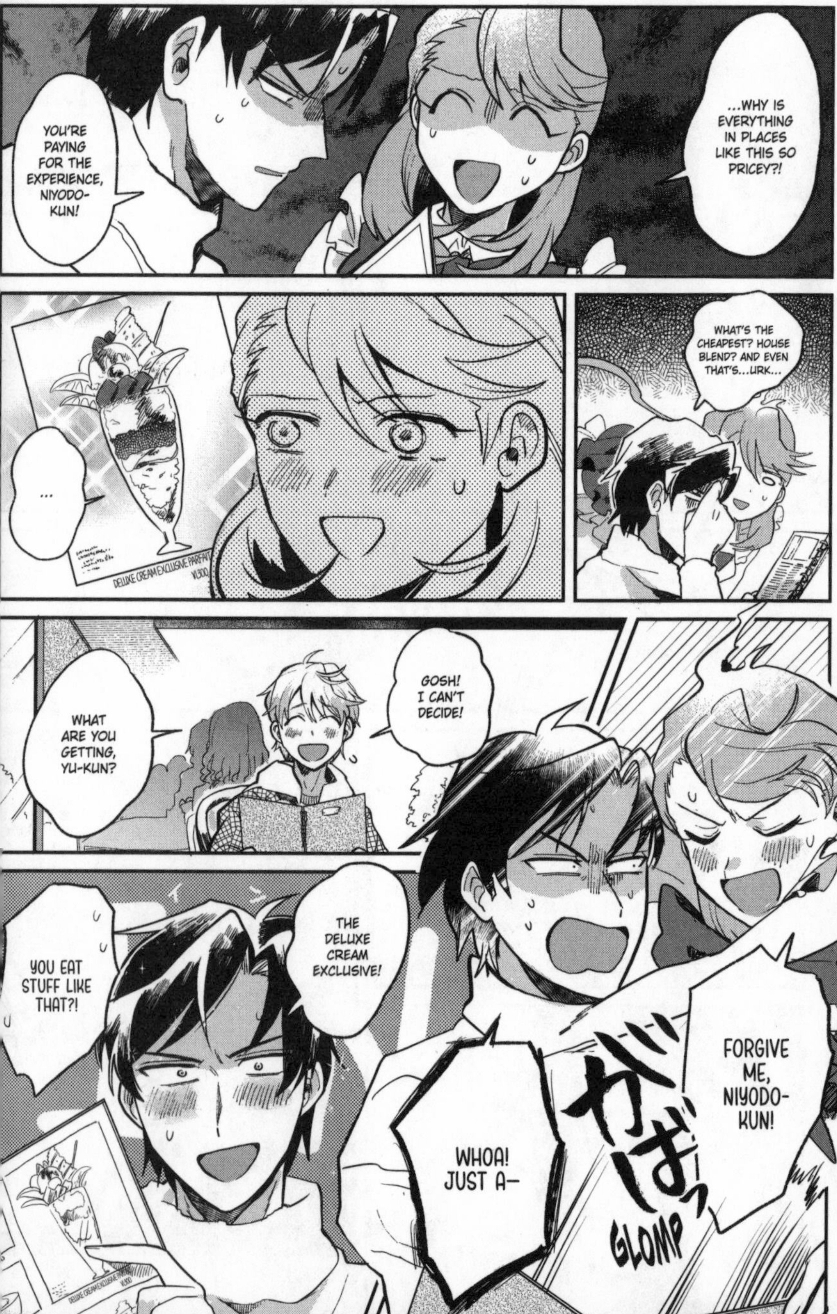
...WHY IS EVERYTHING IN PLACES LIKE THIS SO PRICEY?!
YOU'RE PAYING FOR THE EXPERIENCE, NIYODO-KUN!
WHAT'S THE CHEAPEST? HOUSE BLEND? AND EVEN THAT'S...URK...
DELUXE CREAM EXCLUSIVE PARFAIT ¥1,300
...
FORGIVE ME, NIYODO-KUN!
がばっ GLOMP
WHOA! JUST A—
GOSH! I CAN'T DECIDE!
WHAT ARE YOU GETTING, YU-KUN?
THE DELUXE CREAM EXCLUSIVE!
YOU EAT STUFF LIKE THAT?!
DELUXE CREAM EXCLUSIVE PARFAIT ¥1,300

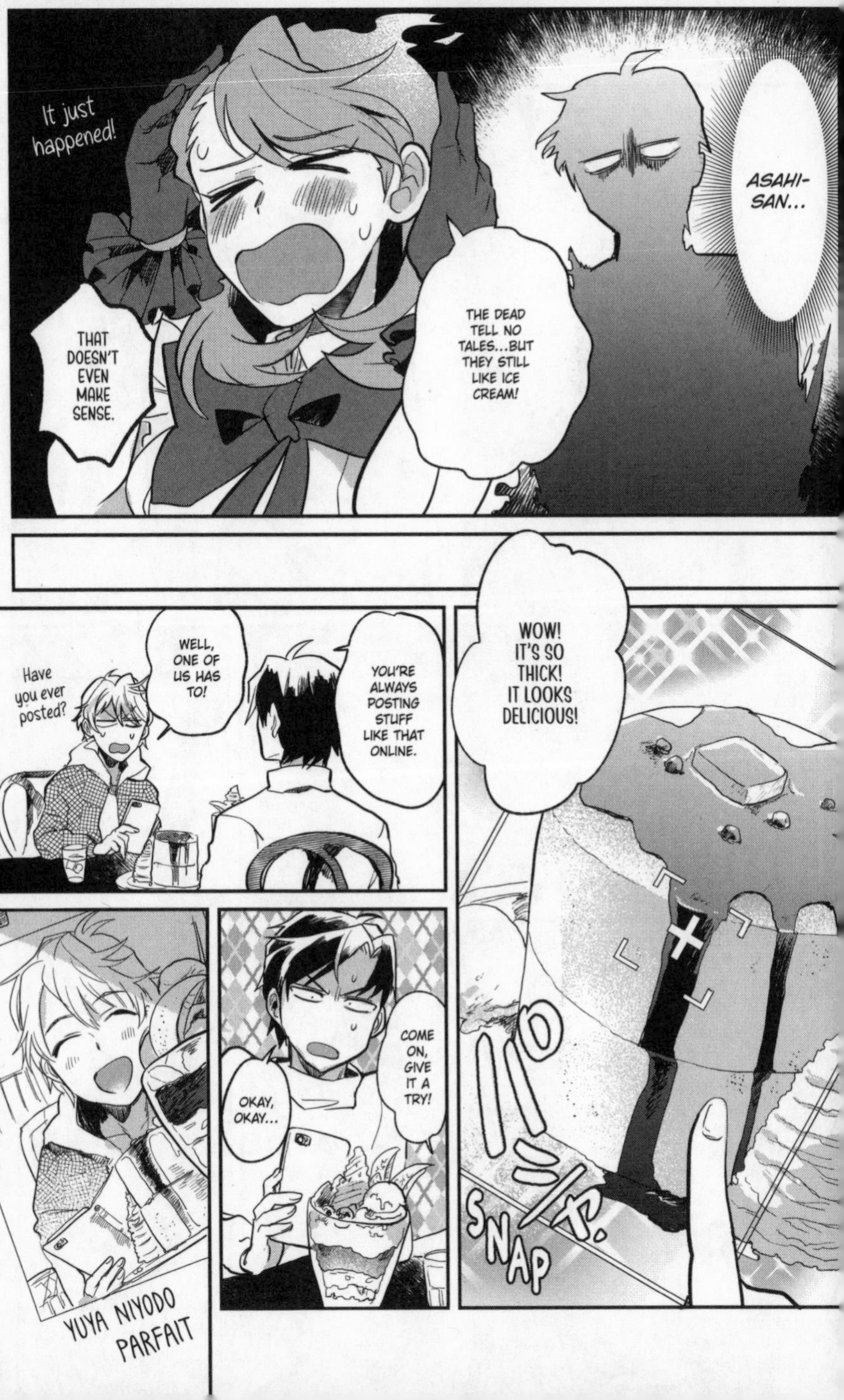
ASAHI-SAN...
THE DEAD TELL NO TALES...BUT THEY STILL LIKE ICE CREAM!
It just happened!
THAT DOESN'T EVEN MAKE SENSE.
WOW! IT'S SO THICK! IT LOOKS DELICIOUS!
SNAP
YOU'RE ALWAYS POSTING STUFF LIKE THAT ONLINE.
WELL, ONE OF US HAS TO!
Have you ever posted?
COME ON, GIVE IT A TRY!
OKAY, OKAY...
YUYA NIYODO PARFAIT

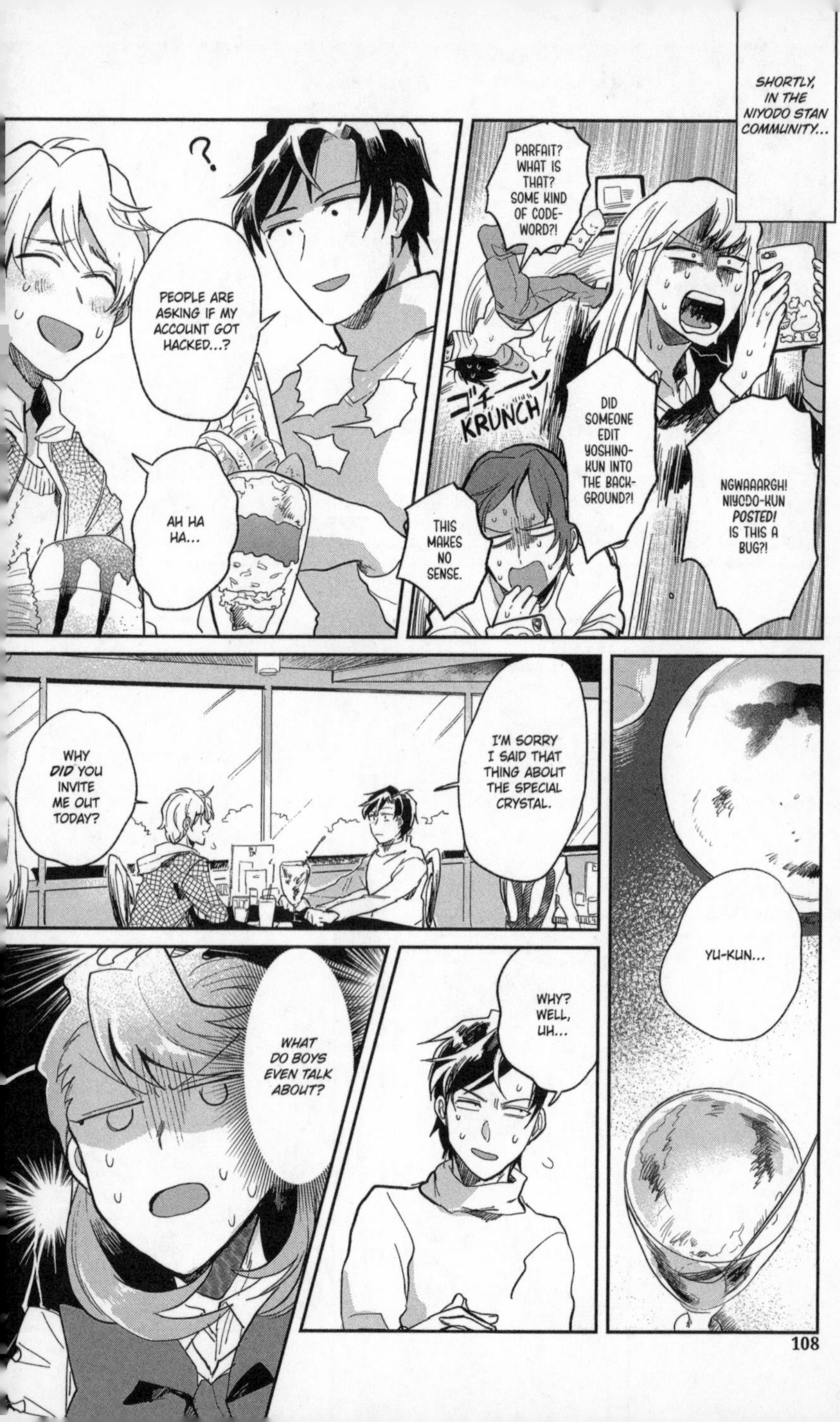
SHORTLY, IN THE NIYODO STAN COMMUNITY...
NGWAAARGH! NIYODO-KUN *POSTED!* IS THIS A BUG?!
PARFAIT? WHAT IS THAT? SOME KIND OF CODE-WORD?!
KRUNCH
DID SOMEONE EDIT YOSHINO-KUN INTO THE BACK-GROUND?!
THIS MAKES NO SENSE.
PEOPLE ARE ASKING IF MY ACCOUNT GOT HACKED...?
AH HA HA...
YU-KUN...
I'M SORRY I SAID THAT THING ABOUT THE SPECIAL CRYSTAL.
WHY *DID* YOU INVITE ME OUT TODAY?
WHY? WELL, UH...
WHAT DO BOYS EVEN TALK ABOUT?

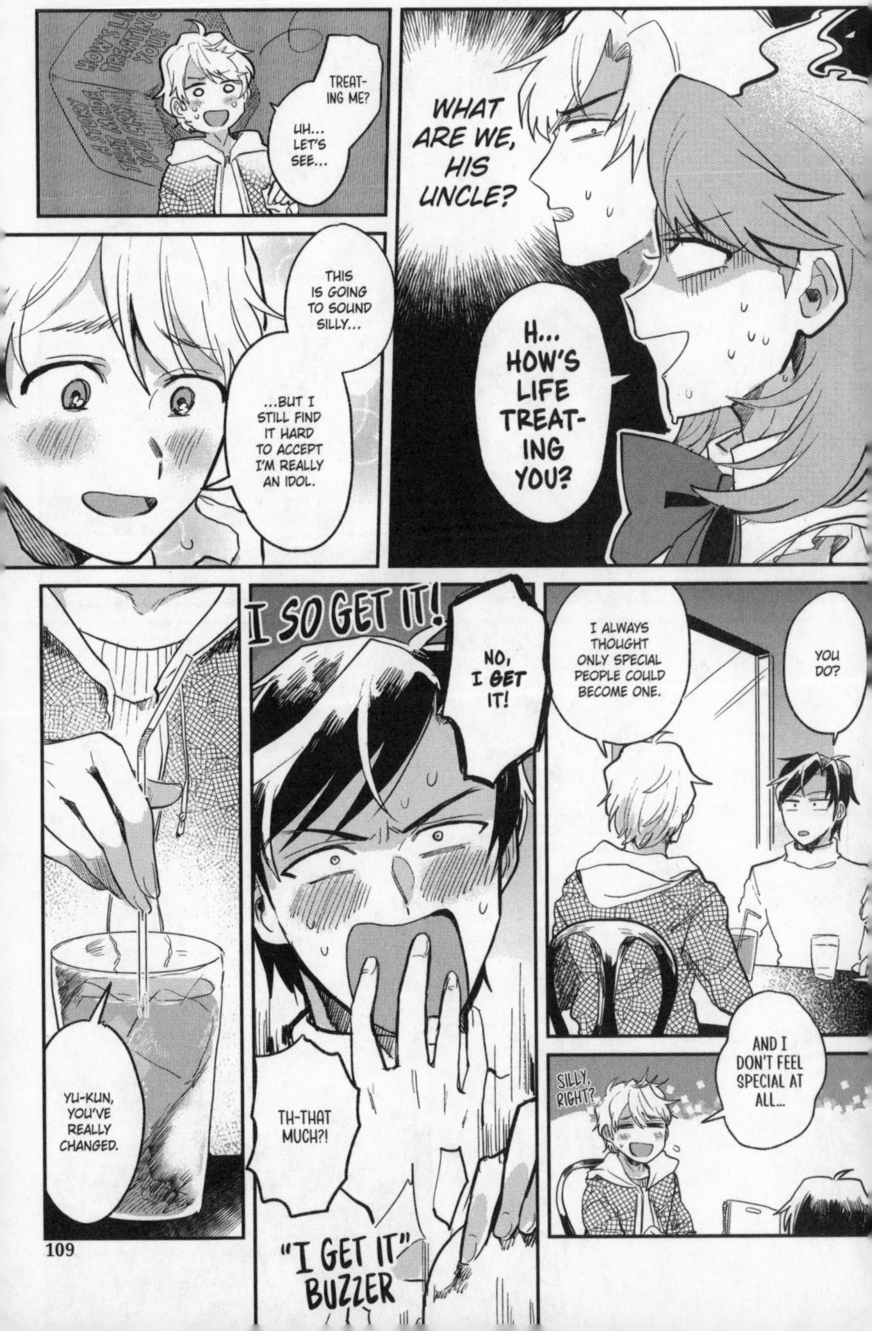

WHAT ARE WE, HIS UNCLE?
H... HOW'S LIFE TREAT-ING YOU?
TREAT-ING ME?
UH... LET'S SEE...
THIS IS GOING TO SOUND SILLY...
...BUT I STILL FIND IT HARD TO ACCEPT I'M REALLY AN IDOL.
YOU DO?
I ALWAYS THOUGHT ONLY SPECIAL PEOPLE COULD BECOME ONE.
AND I DON'T FEEL SPECIAL AT ALL...
SILLY, RIGHT?
NO, I GET IT!
I SO GET IT!
TH-THAT MUCH?!
"I GET IT" BUZZER
YU-KUN, YOU'VE REALLY CHANGED.

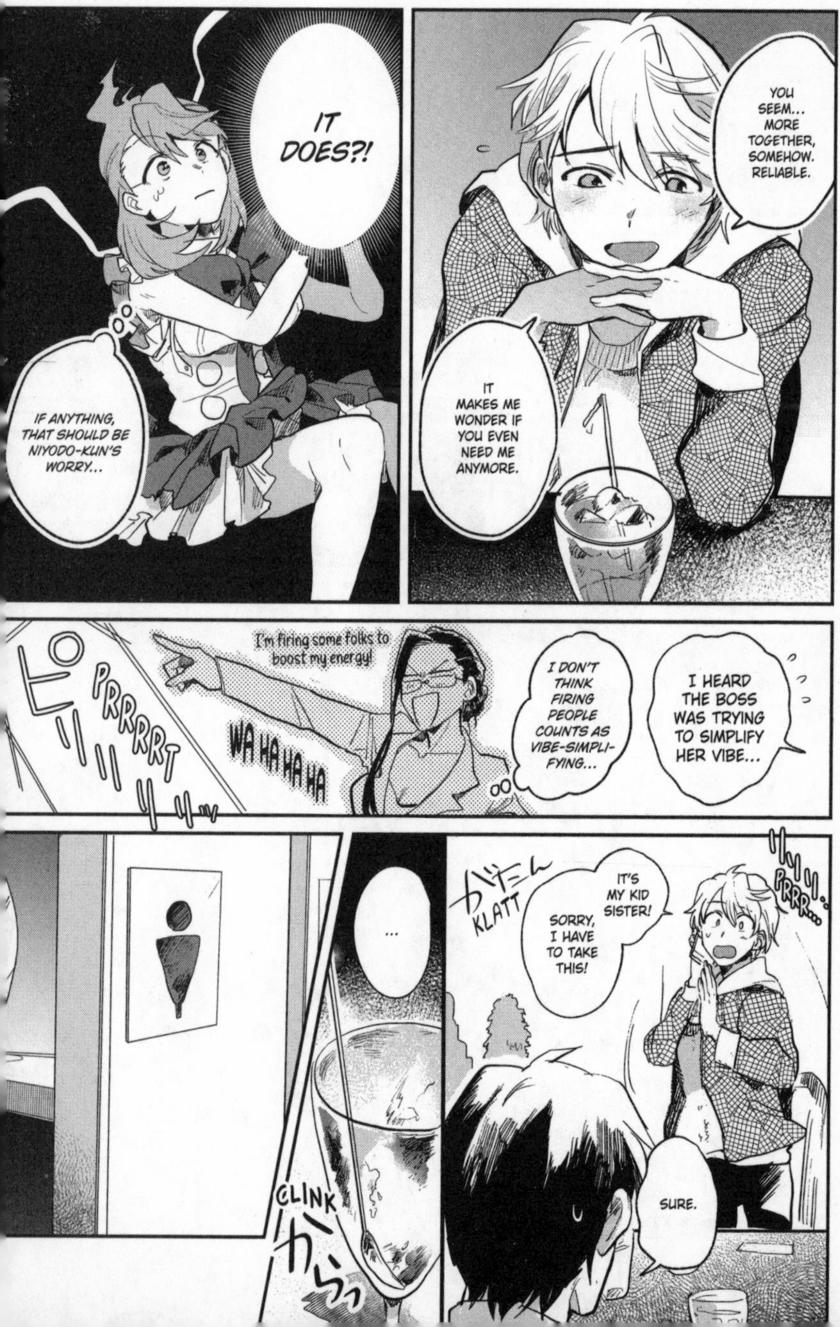

YOU SEEM... MORE TOGETHER, SOMEHOW. RELIABLE.
IT MAKES ME WONDER IF YOU EVEN NEED ME ANYMORE.
IT DOES?!
IF ANYTHING, THAT SHOULD BE NIYODO-KUN'S WORRY...
I HEARD THE BOSS WAS TRYING TO SIMPLIFY HER VIBE...
I DON'T THINK FIRING PEOPLE COUNTS AS VIBE-SIMPLI-FYING...
I'm firing some folks to boost my energy!
WA HA HA HA
PRRRRRT
PRRRR...
KLATT
IT'S MY KID SISTER!
SORRY, I HAVE TO TAKE THIS!
SURE.
...
CLINK

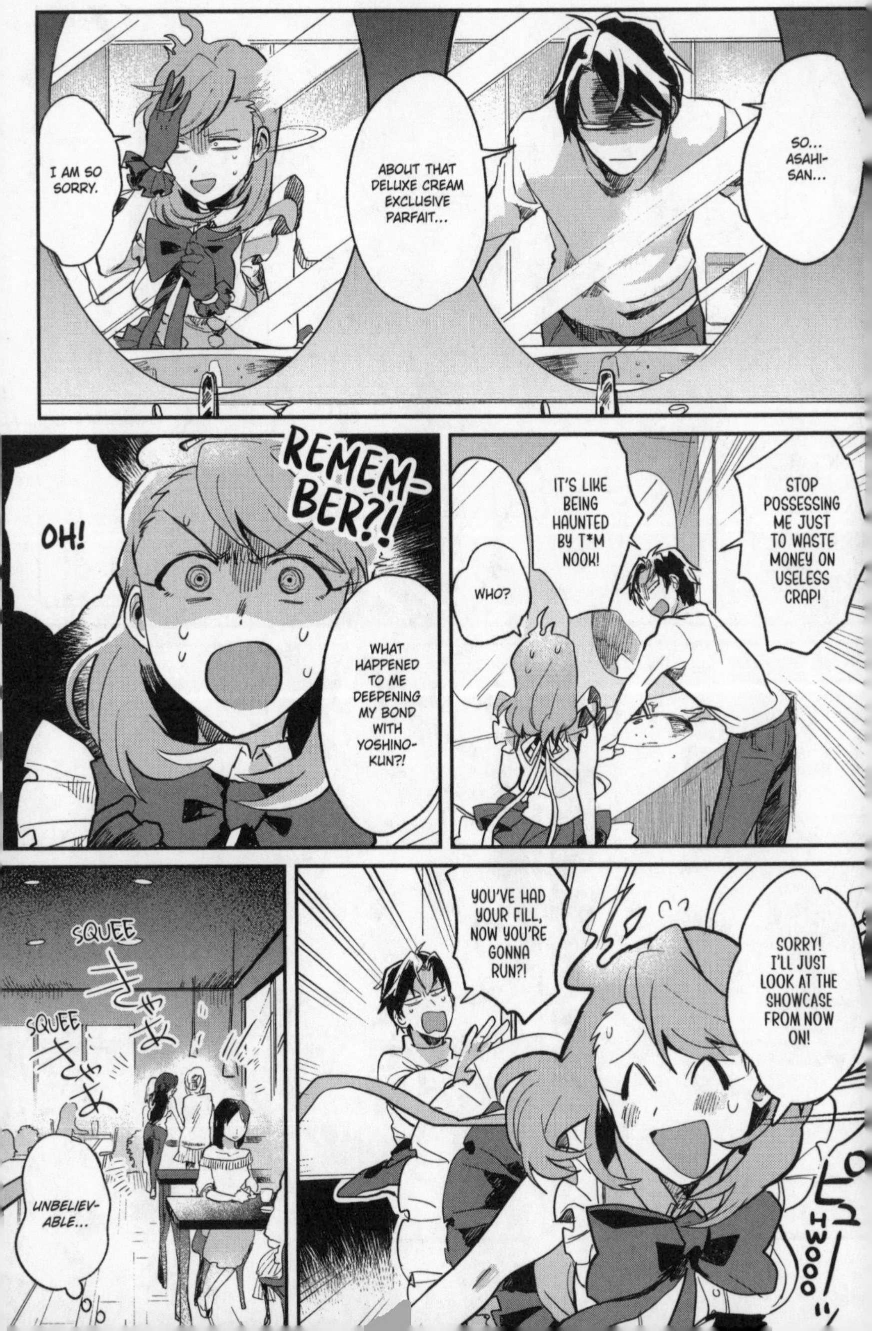
SO... ASAHI-SAN...
ABOUT THAT DELUXE CREAM EXCLUSIVE PARFAIT...
I AM SO SORRY.
STOP POSSESSING ME JUST TO WASTE MONEY ON USELESS CRAP!
IT'S LIKE BEING HAUNTED BY T*M NOOK!
WHO?
REMEM-BER?!
WHAT HAPPENED TO ME DEEPENING MY BOND WITH YOSHINO-KUN?!
OH!
SORRY! I'LL JUST LOOK AT THE SHOWCASE FROM NOW ON!
YOU'VE HAD YOUR FILL, NOW YOU'RE GONNA RUN?!
WHOOOO!!
SQUEE
きゃあ
SQUEE
きゃあ
UNBELIEV-ABLE...

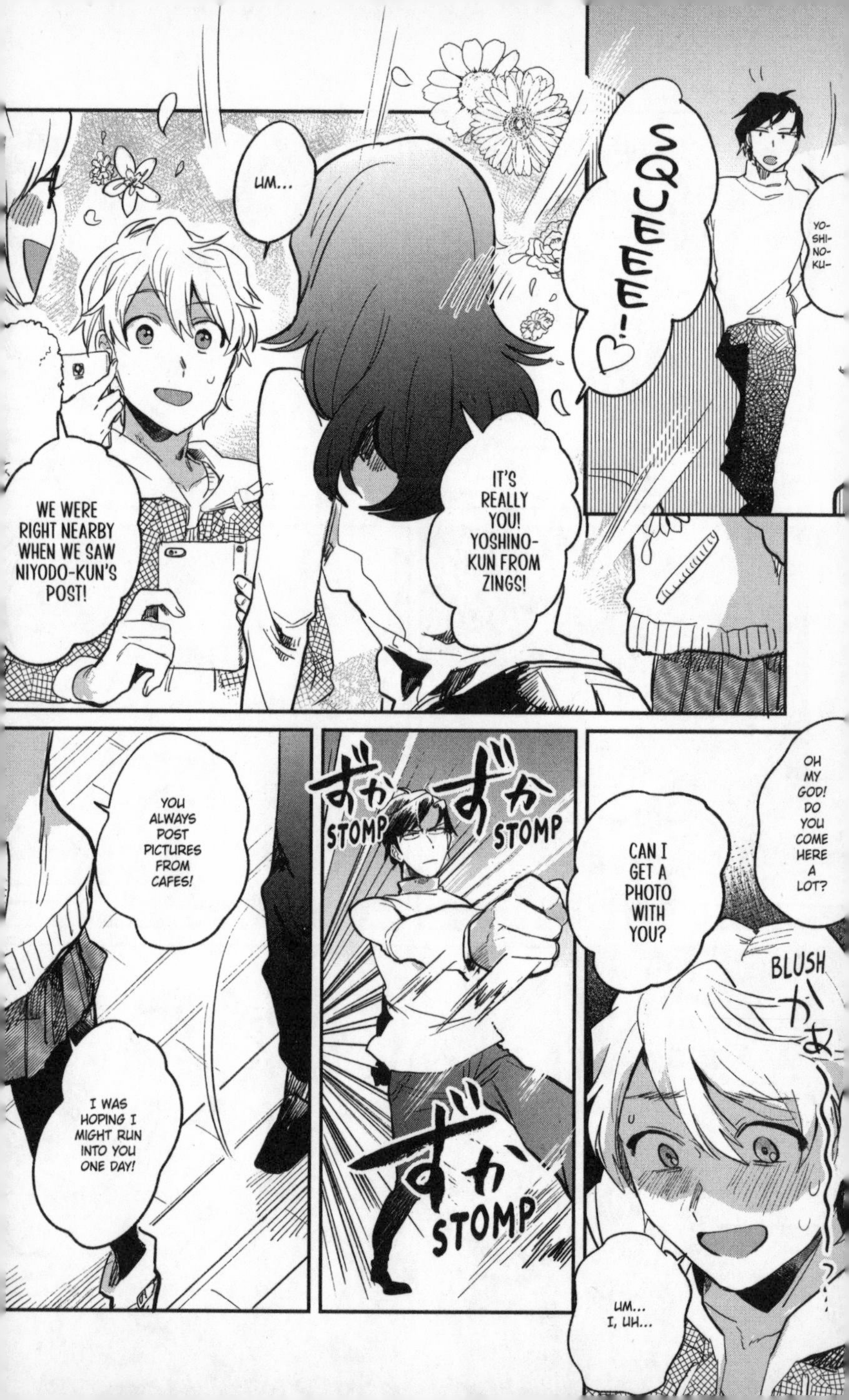
YO-SHI-NO-KU-
SQUEEE!♡
IT'S REALLY YOU! YOSHINO-KUN FROM ZINGS!
UM...
WE WERE RIGHT NEARBY WHEN WE SAW NIYODO-KUN'S POST!
OH MY GOD! DO YOU COME HERE A LOT?
CAN I GET A PHOTO WITH YOU?
BLUSH
UM... I, UH...
ずか STOMP
ずか STOMP
ずか STOMP
YOU ALWAYS POST PICTURES FROM CAFES!
I WAS HOPING I MIGHT RUN INTO YOU ONE DAY!

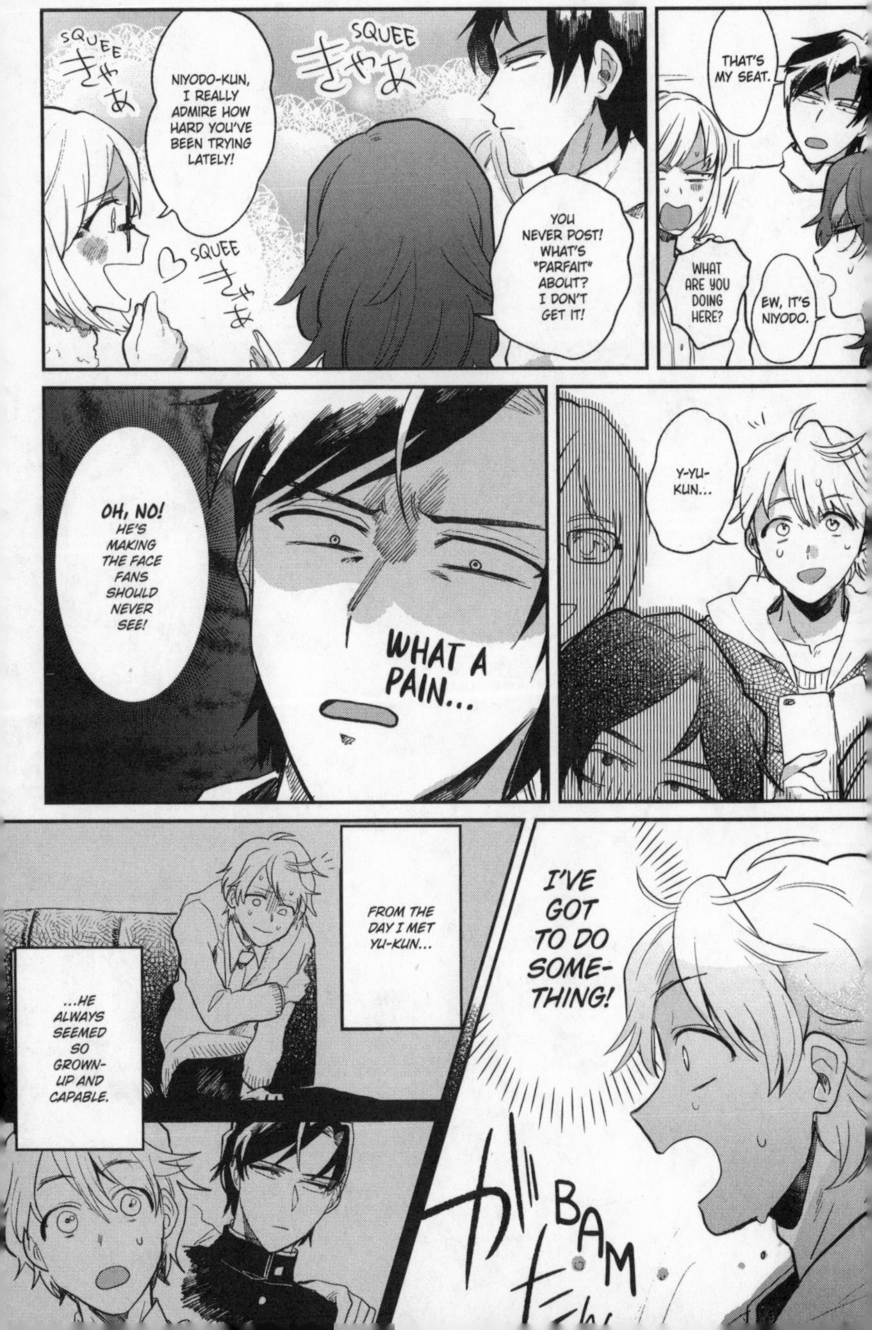
THAT'S MY SEAT.
EW, IT'S NIYODO.
WHAT ARE YOU DOING HERE?
SQUEE きゃあ
NIYODO-KUN, I REALLY ADMIRE HOW HARD YOU'VE BEEN TRYING LATELY!
SQUEE きゃあ
YOU NEVER POST! WHAT'S "PARFAIT" ABOUT? I DON'T GET IT!
SQUEE きゃぁ
Y-YU-KUN...
OH, NO! HE'S MAKING THE FACE FANS SHOULD NEVER SEE!
WHAT A PAIN...
I'VE GOT TO DO SOME-THING!
BAM
FROM THE DAY I MET YU-KUN...
...HE ALWAYS SEEMED SO GROWN-UP AND CAPABLE.

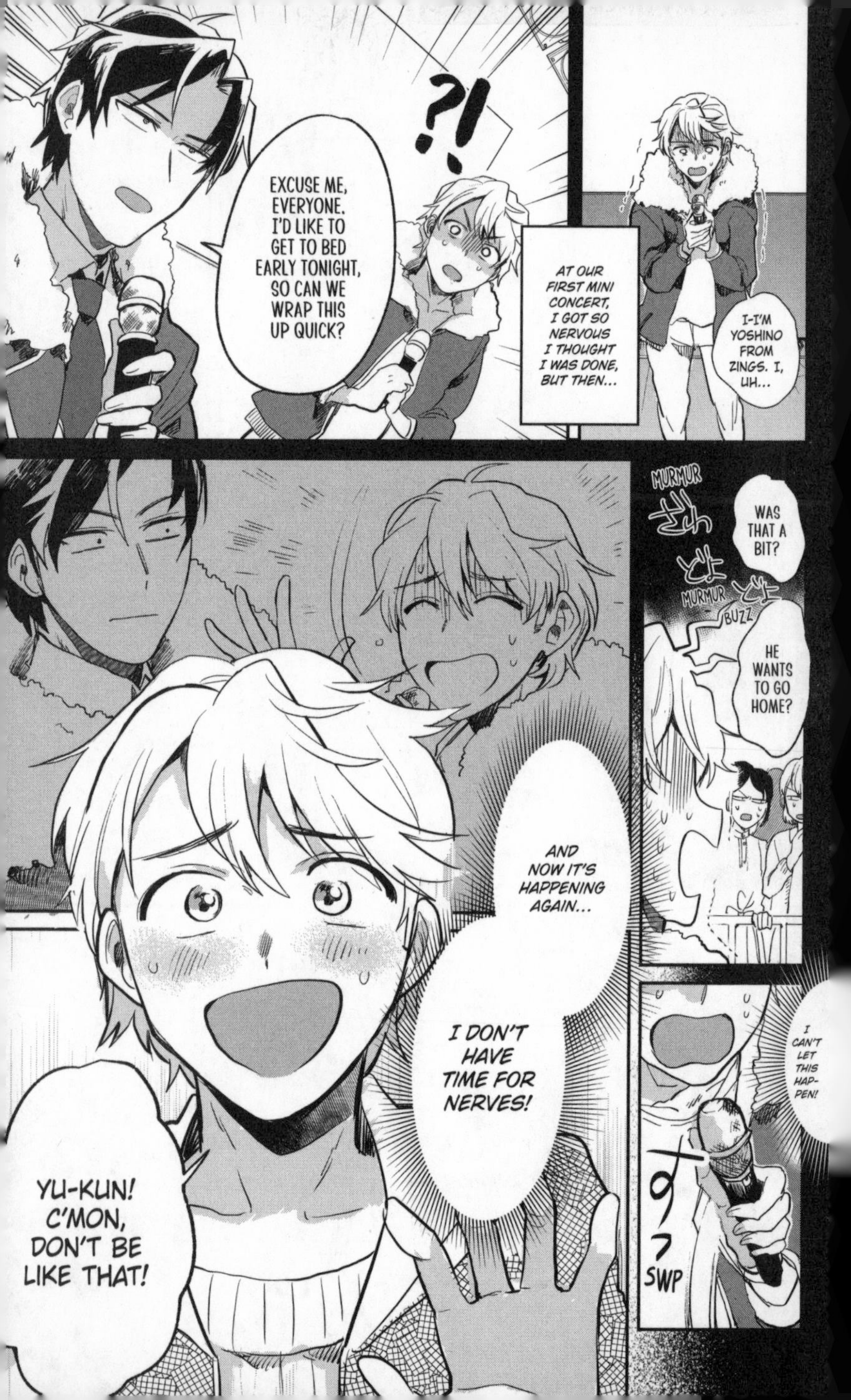
AT OUR FIRST MINI CONCERT, I GOT SO NERVOUS I THOUGHT I WAS DONE, BUT THEN...
I-I'M YOSHINO FROM ZINGS. I, UH...
?!
EXCUSE ME, EVERYONE. I'D LIKE TO GET TO BED EARLY TONIGHT, SO CAN WE WRAP THIS UP QUICK?
MURMUR
WAS THAT A BIT?
MURMUR
BUZZ
HE WANTS TO GO HOME?
I CAN'T LET THIS HAP-PEN!
SWP
AND NOW IT'S HAPPENING AGAIN...
I DON'T HAVE TIME FOR NERVES!
YU-KUN! C'MON, DON'T BE LIKE THAT!

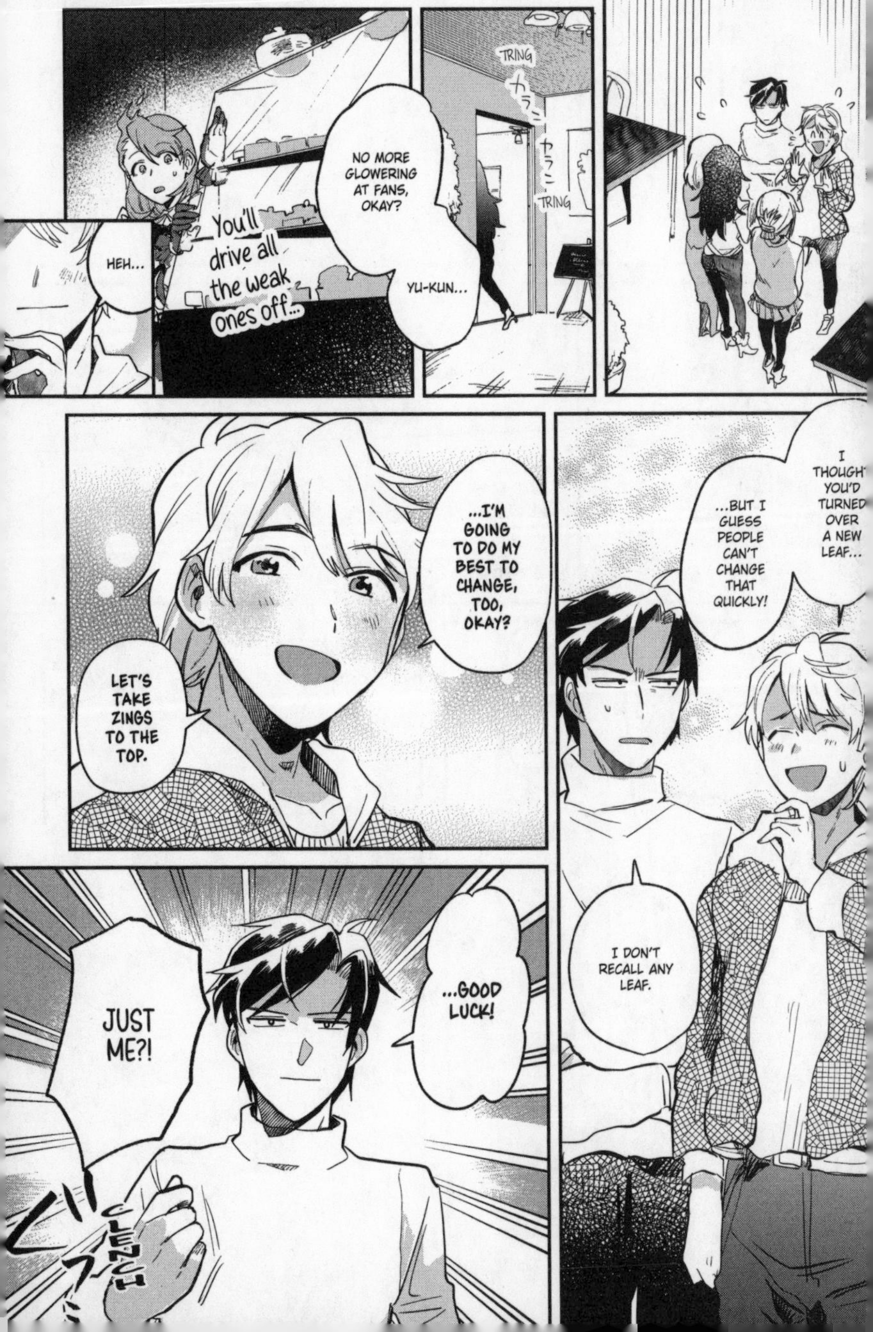
TRING
カラン
カラン
TRING
NO MORE GLOWERING AT FANS, OKAY?
YU-KUN...
You'll drive all the weak ones off...
HEH...
I THOUGHT YOU'D TURNED OVER A NEW LEAF...
...BUT I GUESS PEOPLE CAN'T CHANGE THAT QUICKLY!
I DON'T RECALL ANY LEAF.
...I'M GOING TO DO MY BEST TO CHANGE, TOO, OKAY?
LET'S TAKE ZINGS TO THE TOP.
...GOOD LUCK!
JUST ME?!
CLENCH

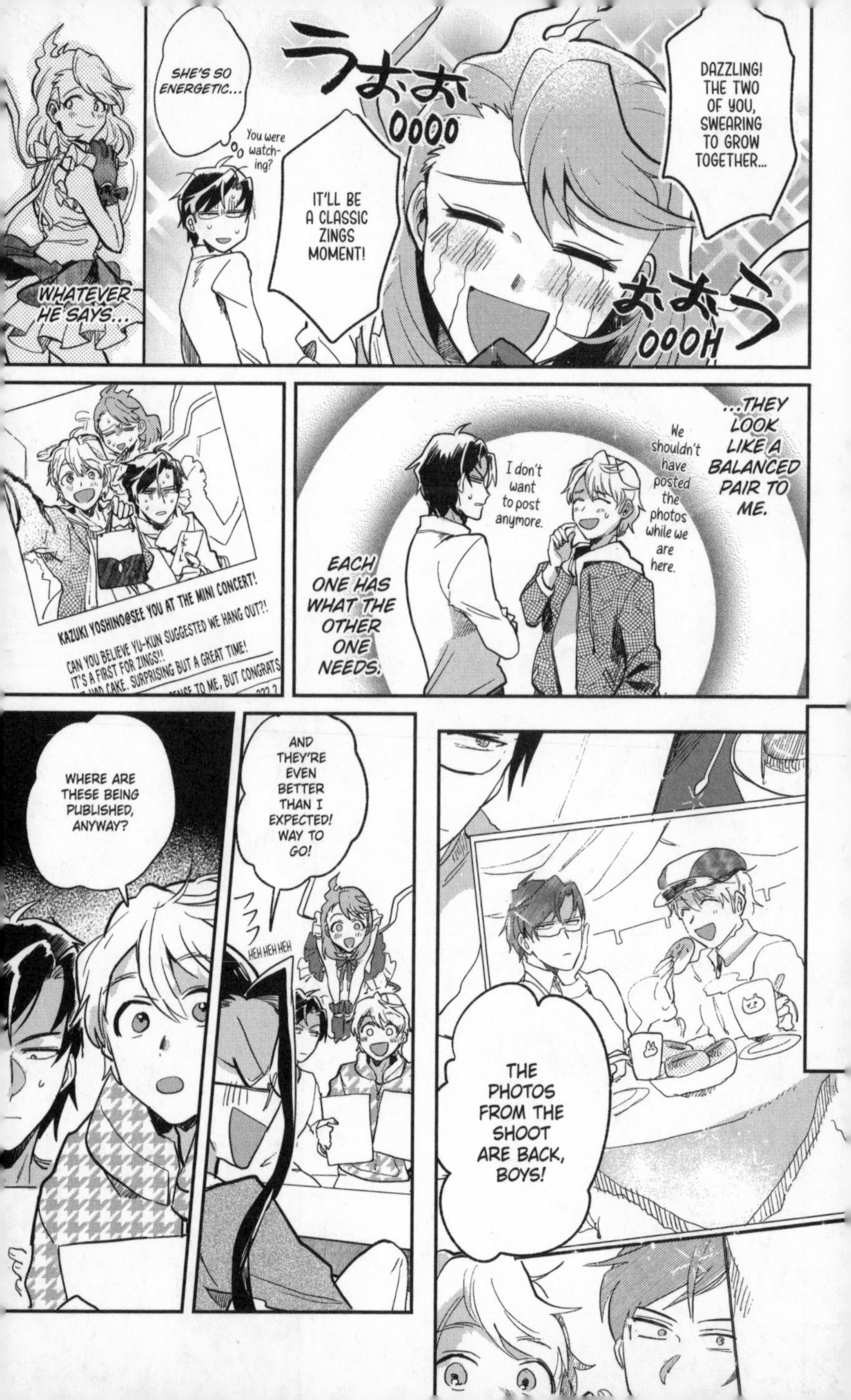
DAZZLING! THE TWO OF YOU, SWEARING TO GROW TOGETHER...
うおおお OOOO
おおう OOOH
SHE'S SO ENERGETIC...
IT'LL BE A CLASSIC ZINGS MOMENT!
You were watching?
WHATEVER HE SAYS...
...THEY LOOK LIKE A BALANCED PAIR TO ME.
We shouldn't have posted the photos while we are here.
I don't want to post anymore.
EACH ONE HAS WHAT THE OTHER ONE NEEDS.
KAZUKI YOSHINO@SEE YOU AT THE MINI CONCERT!
CAN YOU BELIEVE YU-KUN SUGGESTED WE HANG OUT?!
IT'S A FIRST FOR ZINGS!!
SURPRISING BUT A GREAT TIME!
THE PHOTOS FROM THE SHOOT ARE BACK, BOYS!
AND THEY'RE EVEN BETTER THAN I EXPECTED! WAY TO GO!
HEH HEH HEH
WHERE ARE THESE BEING PUBLISHED, ANYWAY?

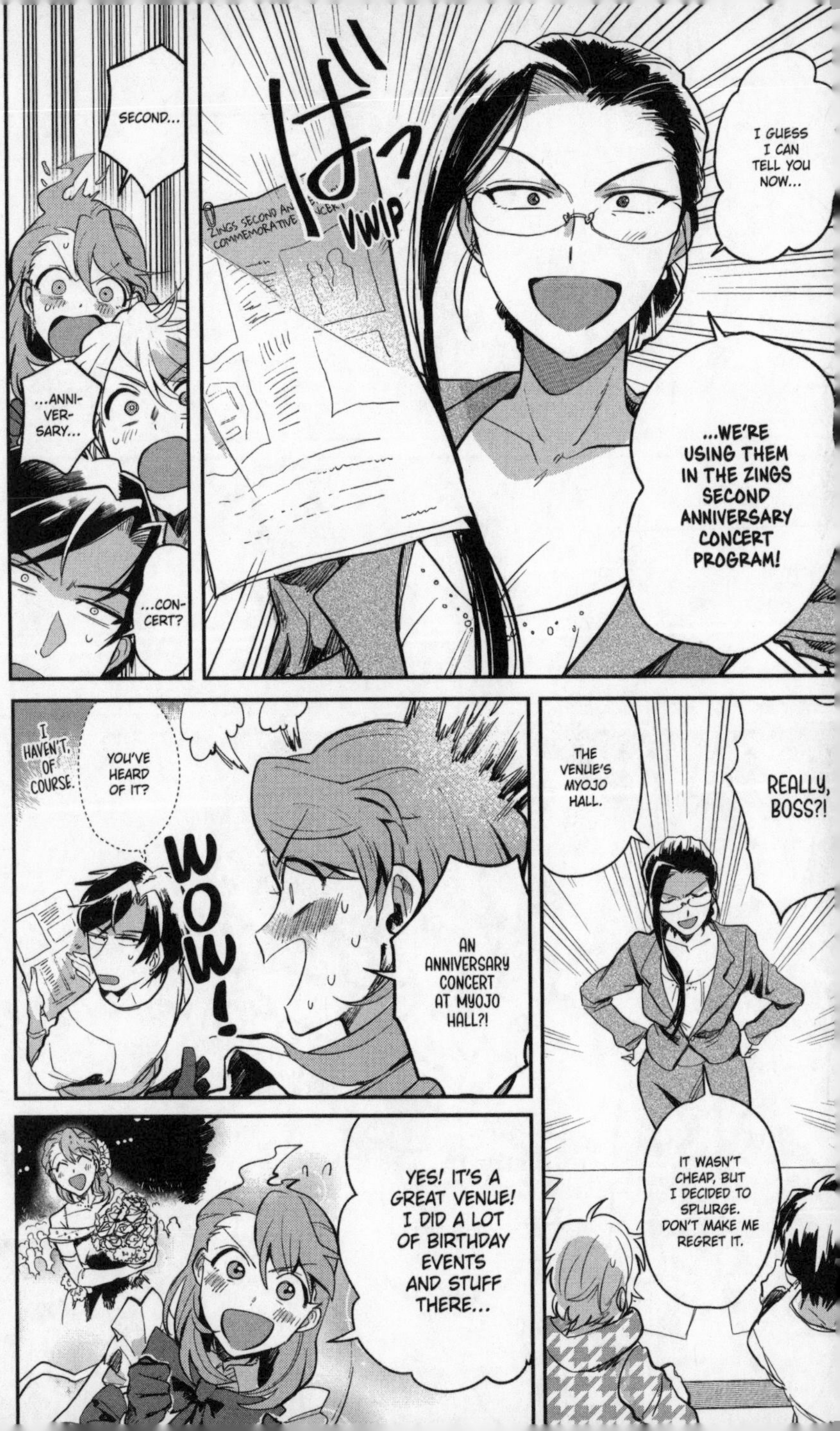
I GUESS I CAN TELL YOU NOW...
ばっ
VWIP
...WE'RE USING THEM IN THE ZINGS SECOND ANNIVERSARY CONCERT PROGRAM!
SECOND...
...ANNI-VER-SARY...
...CON-CERT?
REALLY, BOSS?!
THE VENUE'S MYOJO HALL.
IT WASN'T CHEAP, BUT I DECIDED TO SPLURGE. DON'T MAKE ME REGRET IT.
AN ANNIVERSARY CONCERT AT MYOJO HALL?!
WOW!
YOU'VE HEARD OF IT?
I HAVEN'T, OF COURSE.
YES! IT'S A GREAT VENUE! I DID A LOT OF BIRTHDAY EVENTS AND STUFF THERE...

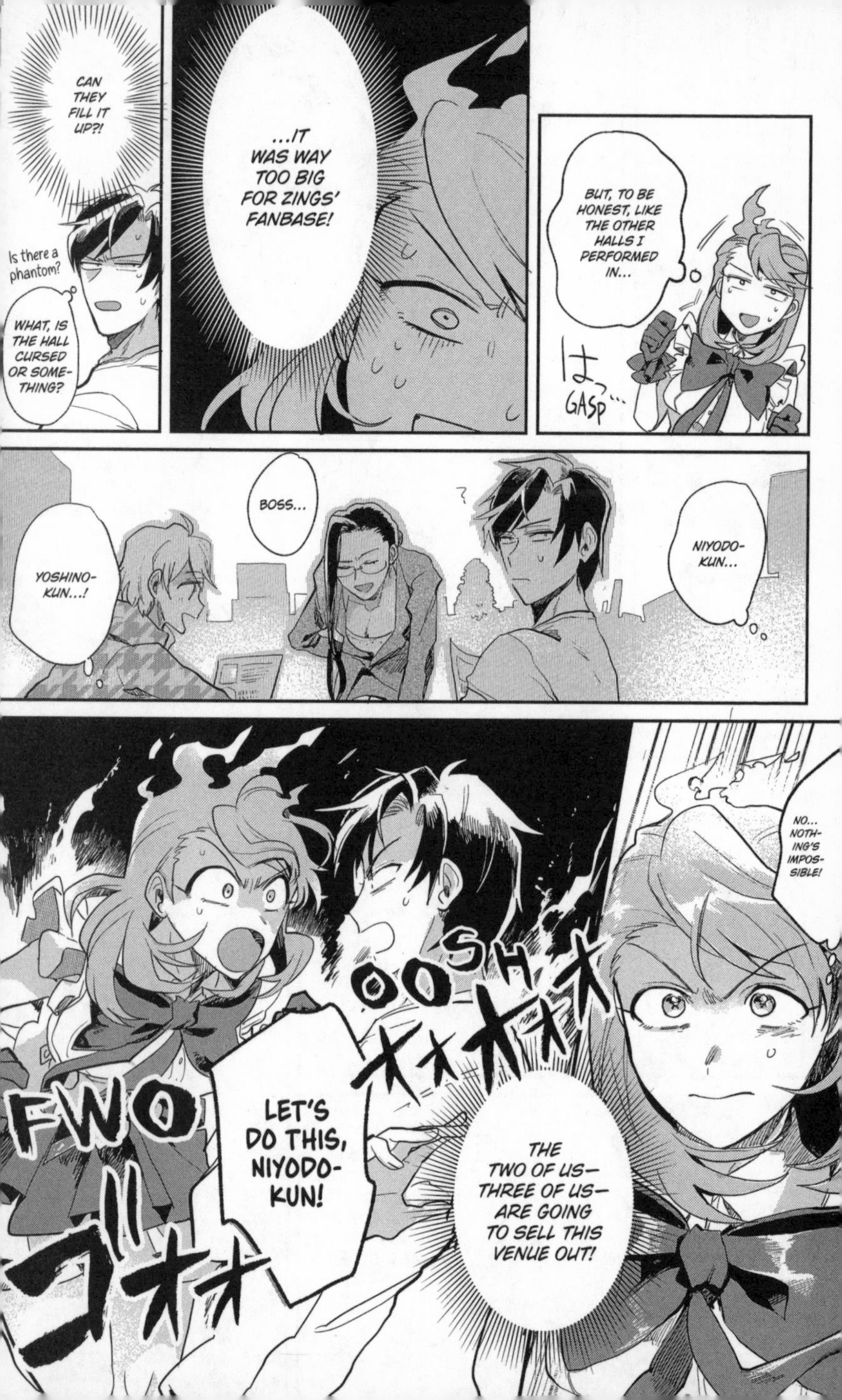
BUT, TO BE HONEST, LIKE THE OTHER HALLS I PERFORMED IN...
はっ GASP...
...IT WAS WAY TOO BIG FOR ZINGS' FANBASE!
CAN THEY FILL IT UP?!
Is there a phantom?
WHAT, IS THE HALL CURSED OR SOMETHING?
NIYODO-KUN...
BOSS...
YOSHINO-KUN...!
NO... NOTHING'S IMPOSSIBLE!
THE TWO OF US— THREE OF US— ARE GOING TO SELL THIS VENUE OUT!
OOSH オオオオオ
LET'S DO THIS, NIYODO-KUN!
FWO ゴオオ

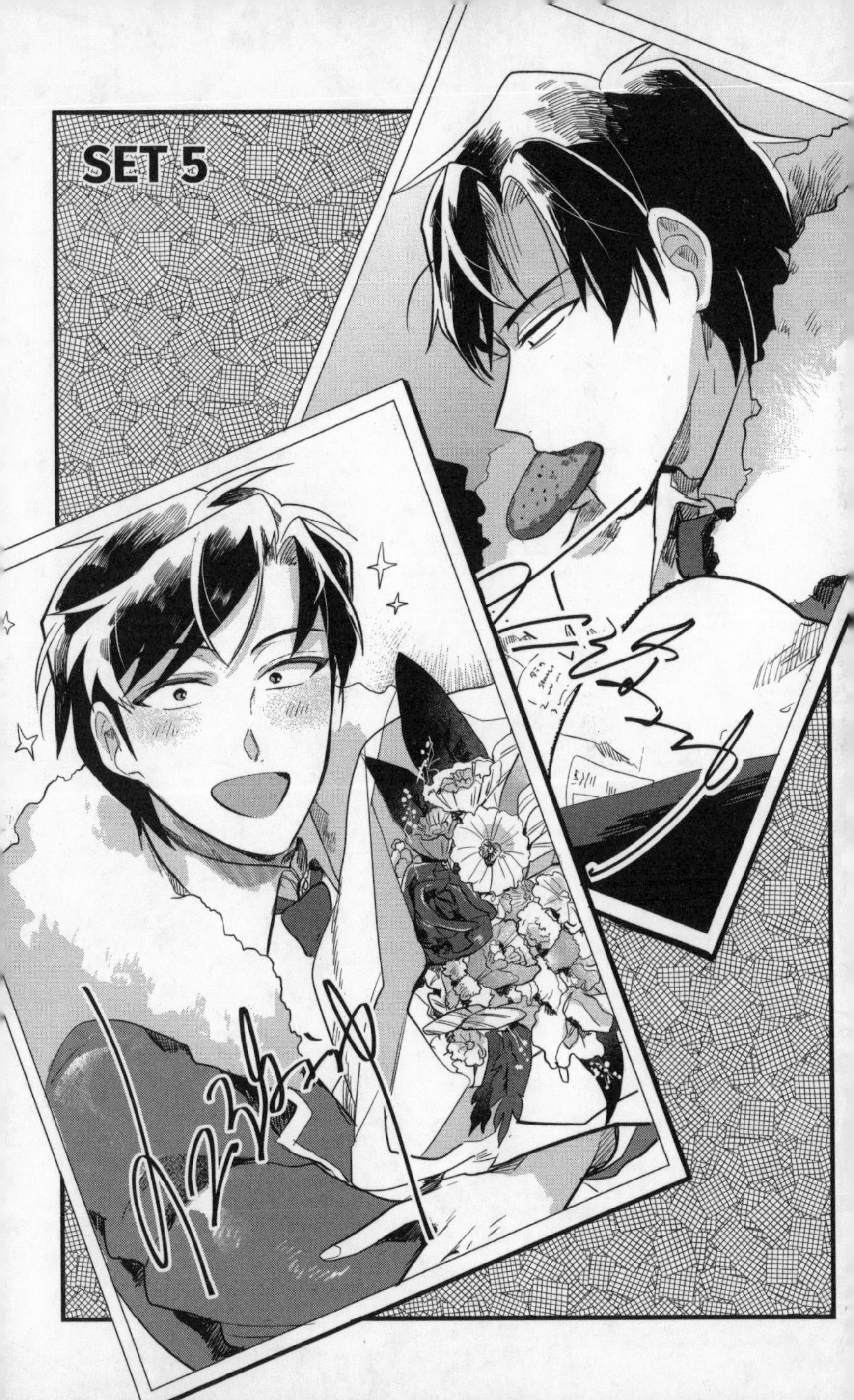
SET 5

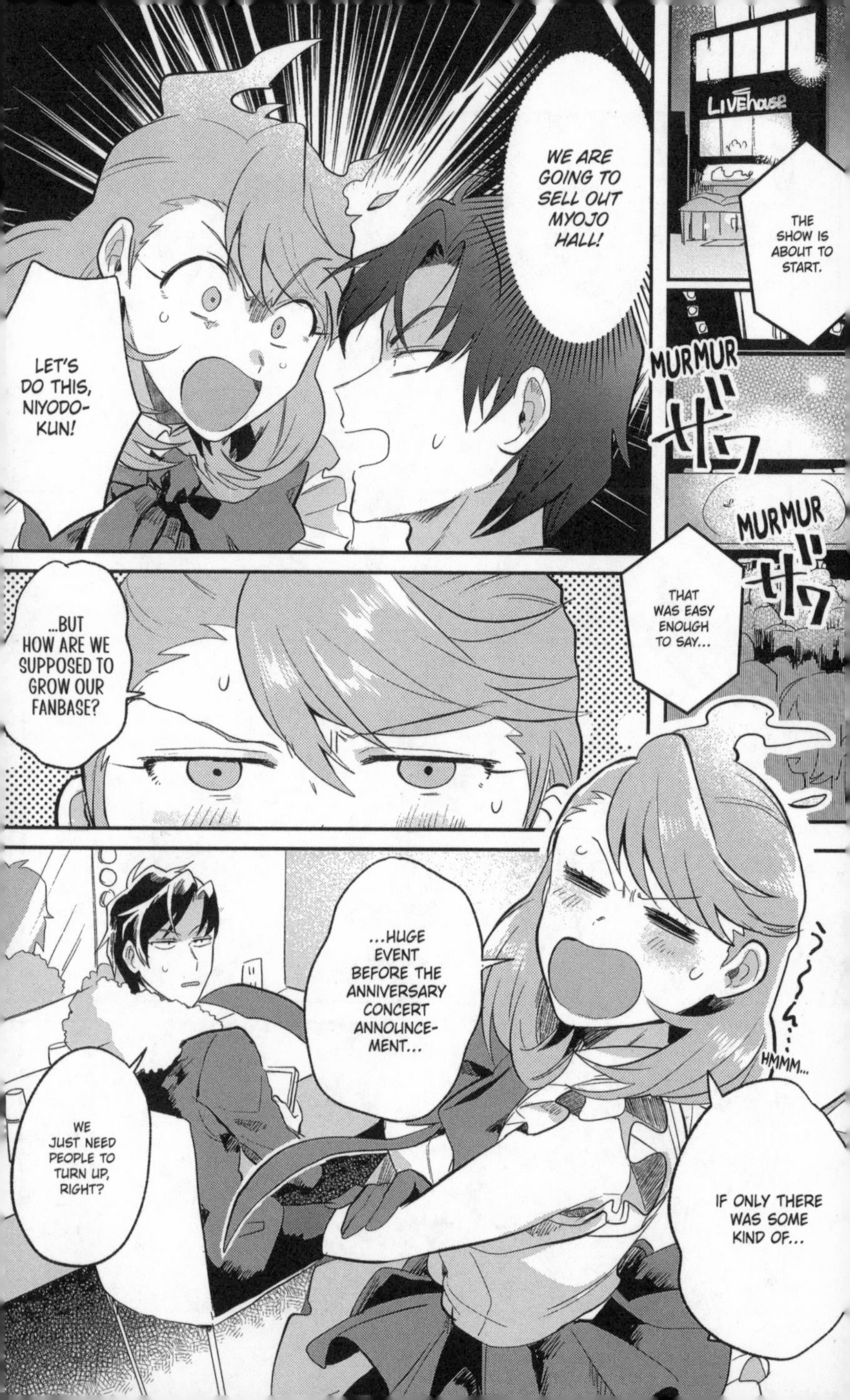
LIVEhouse
THE SHOW IS ABOUT TO START.
MURMUR
ザワ
WE ARE GOING TO SELL OUT MYOJO HALL!
LET'S DO THIS, NIYODO-KUN!
MURMUR
ザワ
THAT WAS EASY ENOUGH TO SAY...
...BUT HOW ARE WE SUPPOSED TO GROW OUR FANBASE?
HMMM...
IF ONLY THERE WAS SOME KIND OF...
...HUGE EVENT BEFORE THE ANNIVERSARY CONCERT ANNOUNCEMENT...
WE JUST NEED PEOPLE TO TURN UP, RIGHT?

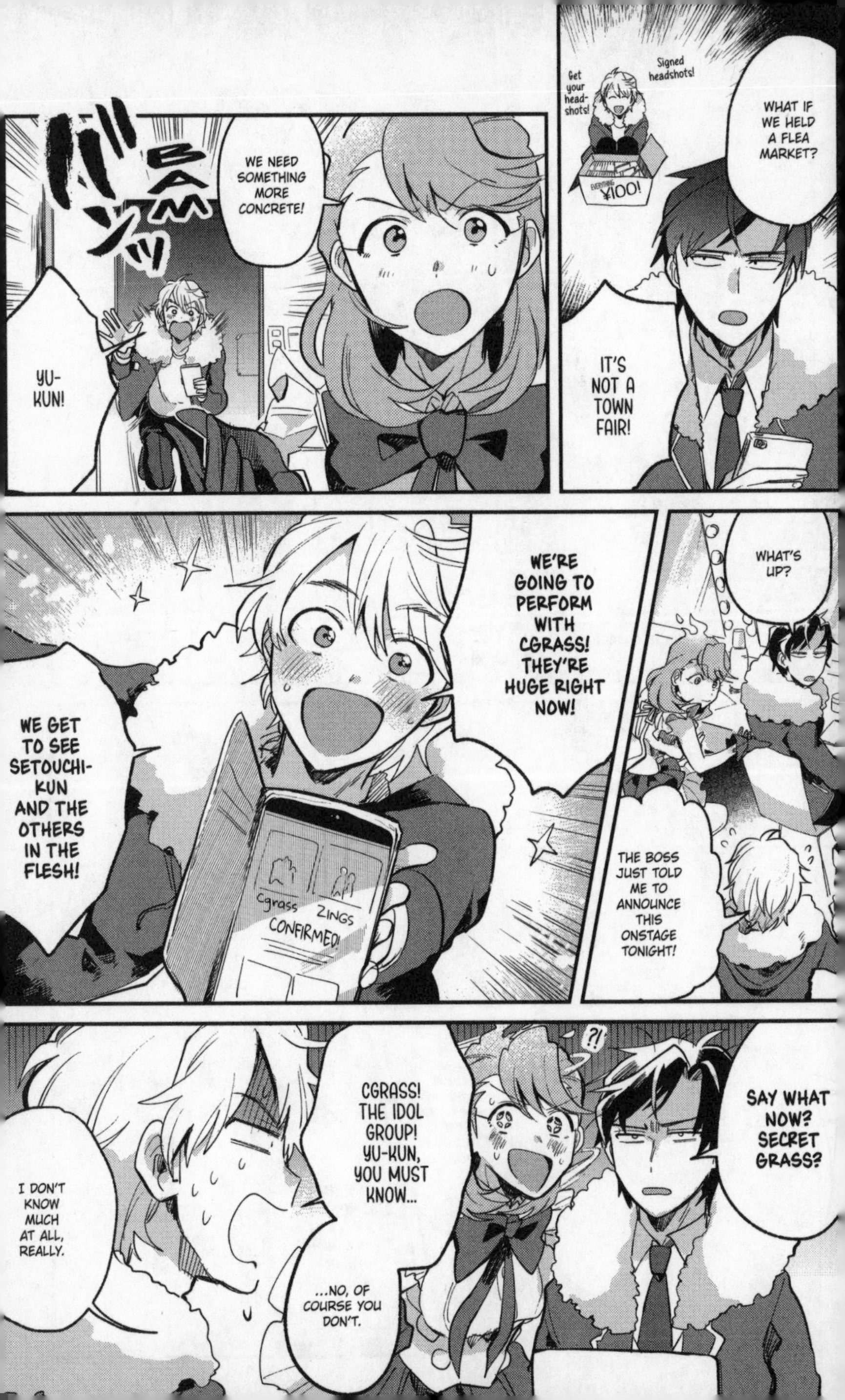

Signed headshots!
Get your head-shots!
EVERYTHING ¥100!
WHAT IF WE HELD A FLEA MARKET?
IT'S NOT A TOWN FAIR!
WE NEED SOMETHING MORE CONCRETE!
バンッ
BAM
YU-KUN!
WHAT'S UP?
THE BOSS JUST TOLD ME TO ANNOUNCE THIS ONSTAGE TONIGHT!
WE'RE GOING TO PERFORM WITH CGRASS! THEY'RE HUGE RIGHT NOW!
Cgrass
ZINGS
CONFIRMED!
WE GET TO SEE SETOUCHI-KUN AND THE OTHERS IN THE FLESH!
SAY WHAT NOW? SECRET GRASS?
?!
CGRASS! THE IDOL GROUP! YU-KUN, YOU MUST KNOW...
...NO, OF COURSE YOU DON'T.
I DON'T KNOW MUCH AT ALL, REALLY.

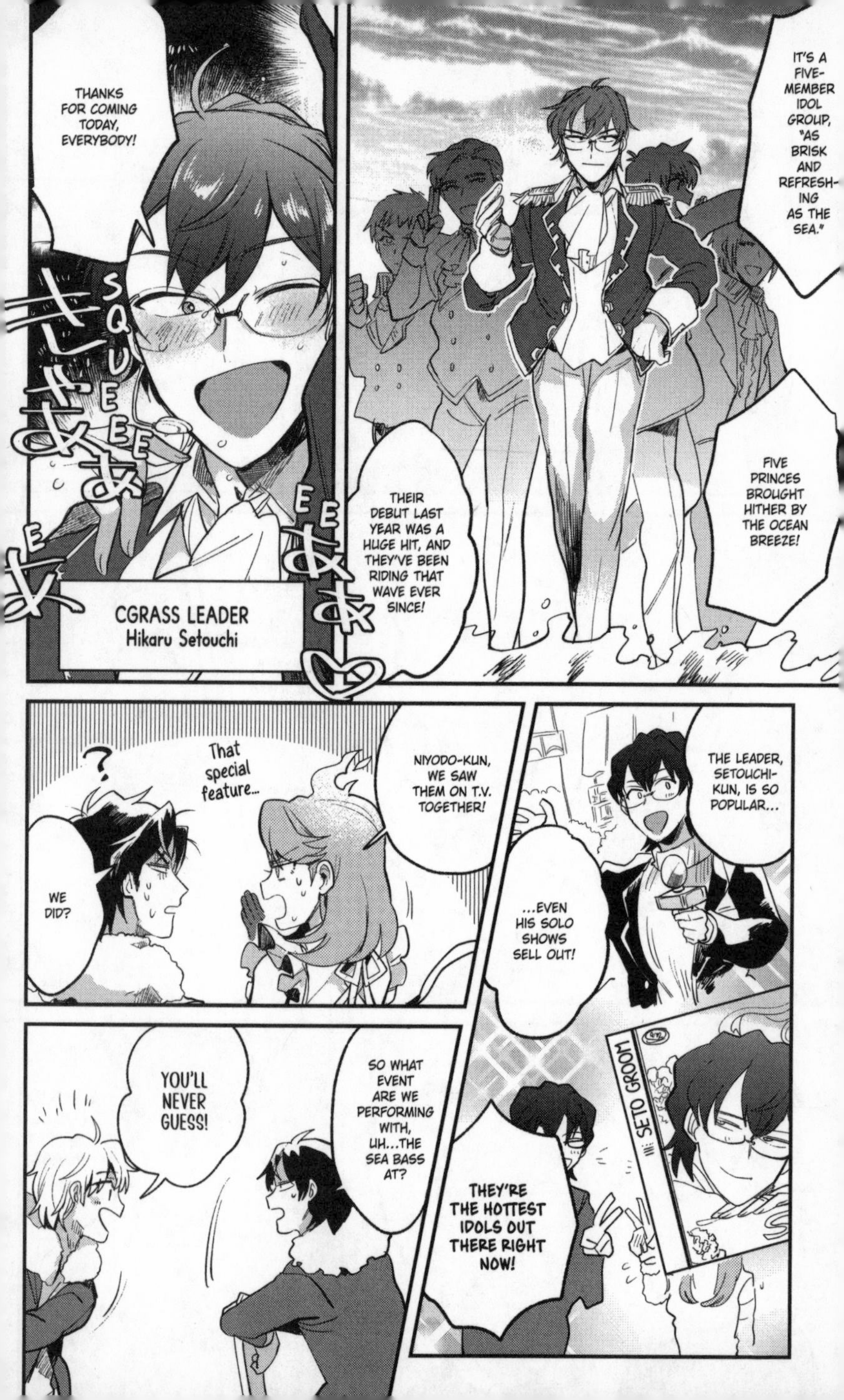
IT'S A FIVE-MEMBER IDOL GROUP, "AS BRISK AND REFRESHING AS THE SEA."
FIVE PRINCES BROUGHT HITHER BY THE OCEAN BREEZE!
THEIR DEBUT LAST YEAR WAS A HUGE HIT, AND THEY'VE BEEN RIDING THAT WAVE EVER SINCE!
EE
ああ♡
THANKS FOR COMING TODAY, EVERYBODY!
SQUEEEE
きゃあああ
E
CGRASS LEADER
Hikaru Setouchi
THE LEADER, SETOUCHI-KUN, IS SO POPULAR...
...EVEN HIS SOLO SHOWS SELL OUT!
NIYODO-KUN, WE SAW THEM ON T.V. TOGETHER!
That special feature...
?
WE DID?
SETO GROOM
THEY'RE THE HOTTEST IDOLS OUT THERE RIGHT NOW!
SO WHAT EVENT ARE WE PERFORMING WITH, UH...THE SEA BASS AT?
YOU'LL NEVER GUESS!

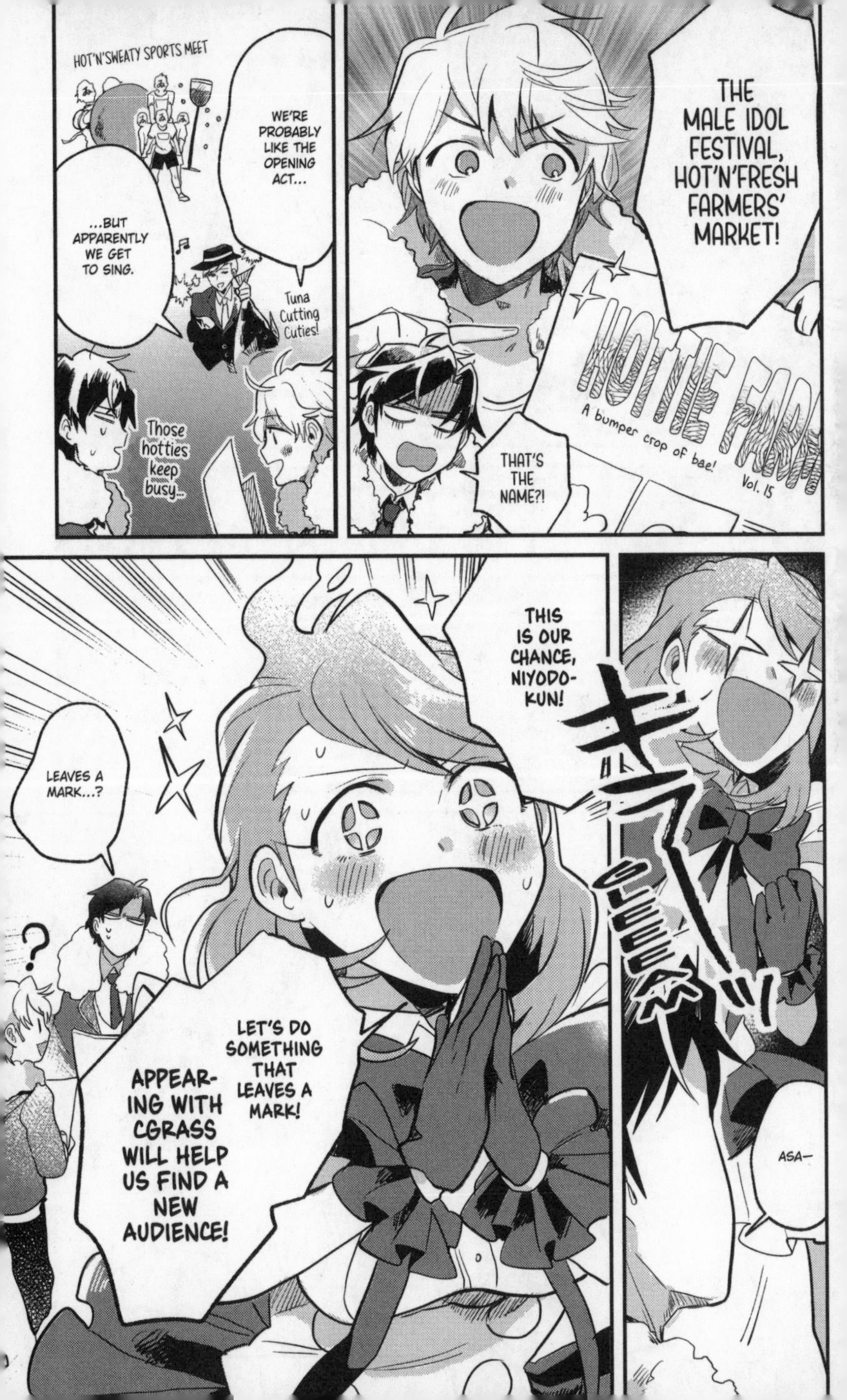
THE MALE IDOL FESTIVAL, HOT'N'FRESH FARMERS' MARKET!
A bumper crop of bae!
Vol. 15
THAT'S THE NAME?!
WE'RE PROBABLY LIKE THE OPENING ACT...
HOT'N'SWEATY SPORTS MEET
Tuna Cutting Cuties!
...BUT APPARENTLY WE GET TO SING.
Those hotties keep busy...
THIS IS OUR CHANCE, NIYODO-KUN!
GLEEE!!
ASA—
LET'S DO SOMETHING THAT LEAVES A MARK!
APPEARING WITH CGRASS WILL HELP US FIND A NEW AUDIENCE!
LEAVES A MARK...?
?

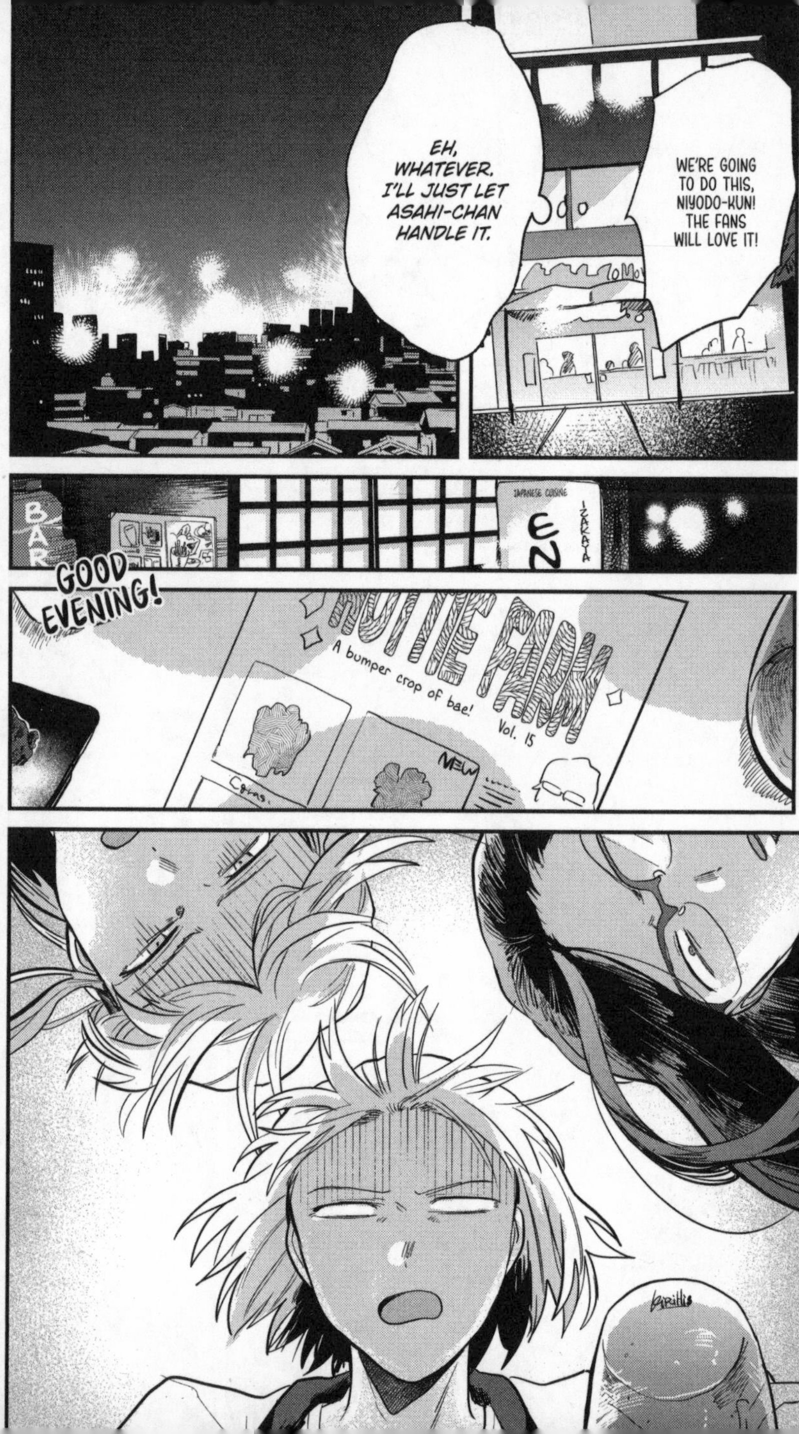
WE'RE GOING TO DO THIS, NIYODO-KUN! THE FANS WILL LOVE IT!
EH, WHATEVER. I'LL JUST LET ASAHI-CHAN HANDLE IT.
JAPANESE CUISINE
EN
IZAKAYA
BAR
GOOD EVENING!
HOTTIE FARM
A bumper crop of bae!
Vol. 15
NEW

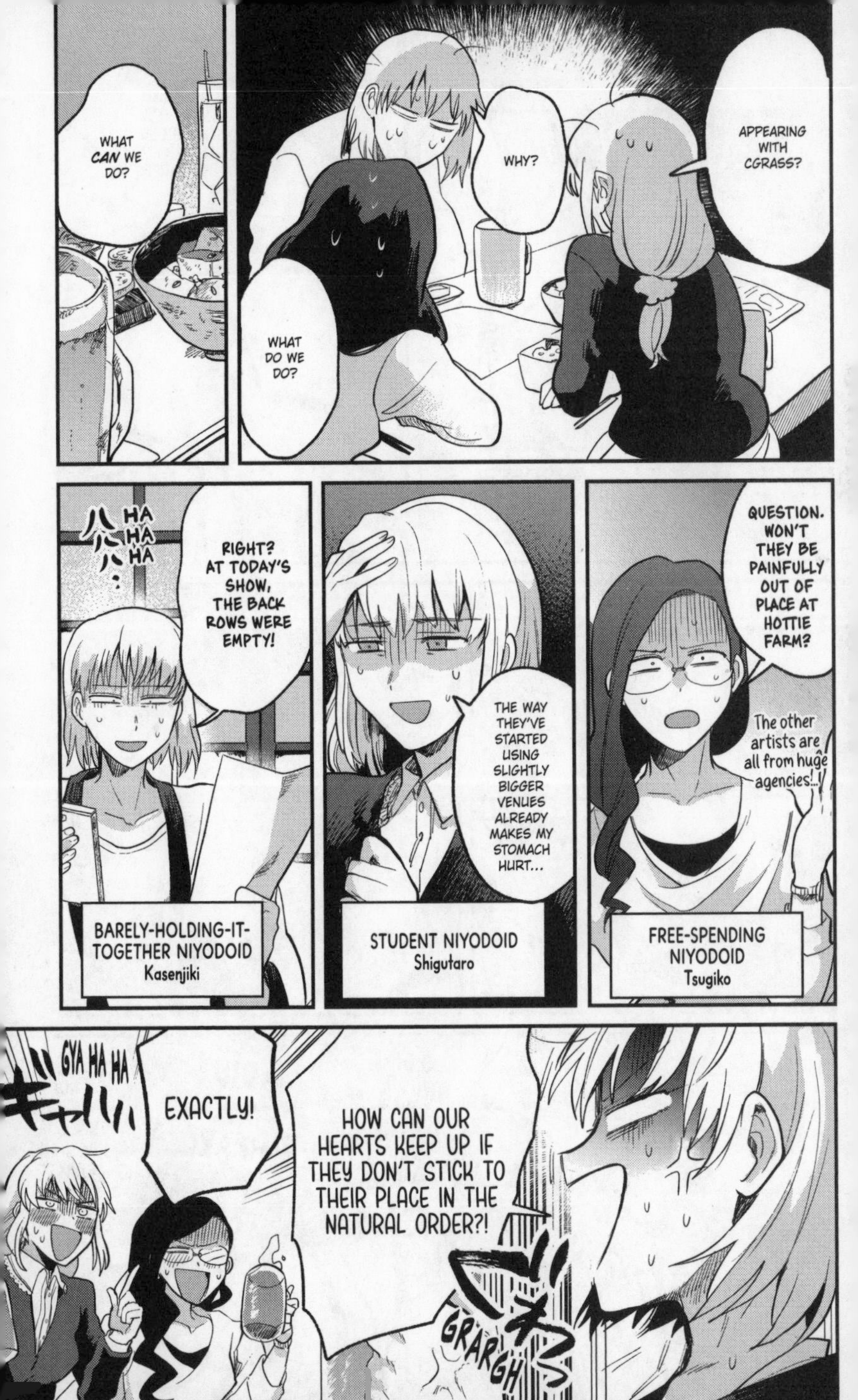
APPEARING WITH CGRASS?
WHY?
WHAT DO WE DO?
WHAT CAN WE DO?
QUESTION. WON'T THEY BE PAINFULLY OUT OF PLACE AT HOTTIE FARM?
The other artists are all from huge agencies!..!
FREE-SPENDING NIYODOID
Tsugiko
THE WAY THEY'VE STARTED USING SLIGHTLY BIGGER VENUES ALREADY MAKES MY STOMACH HURT...
STUDENT NIYODOID
Shigutaro
RIGHT? AT TODAY'S SHOW, THE BACK ROWS WERE EMPTY!
HA HA HA
BARELY-HOLDING-IT-TOGETHER NIYODOID
Kasenjiki
GRARGH
HOW CAN OUR HEARTS KEEP UP IF THEY DON'T STICK TO THEIR PLACE IN THE NATURAL ORDER?!
EXACTLY!
GYA HA HA

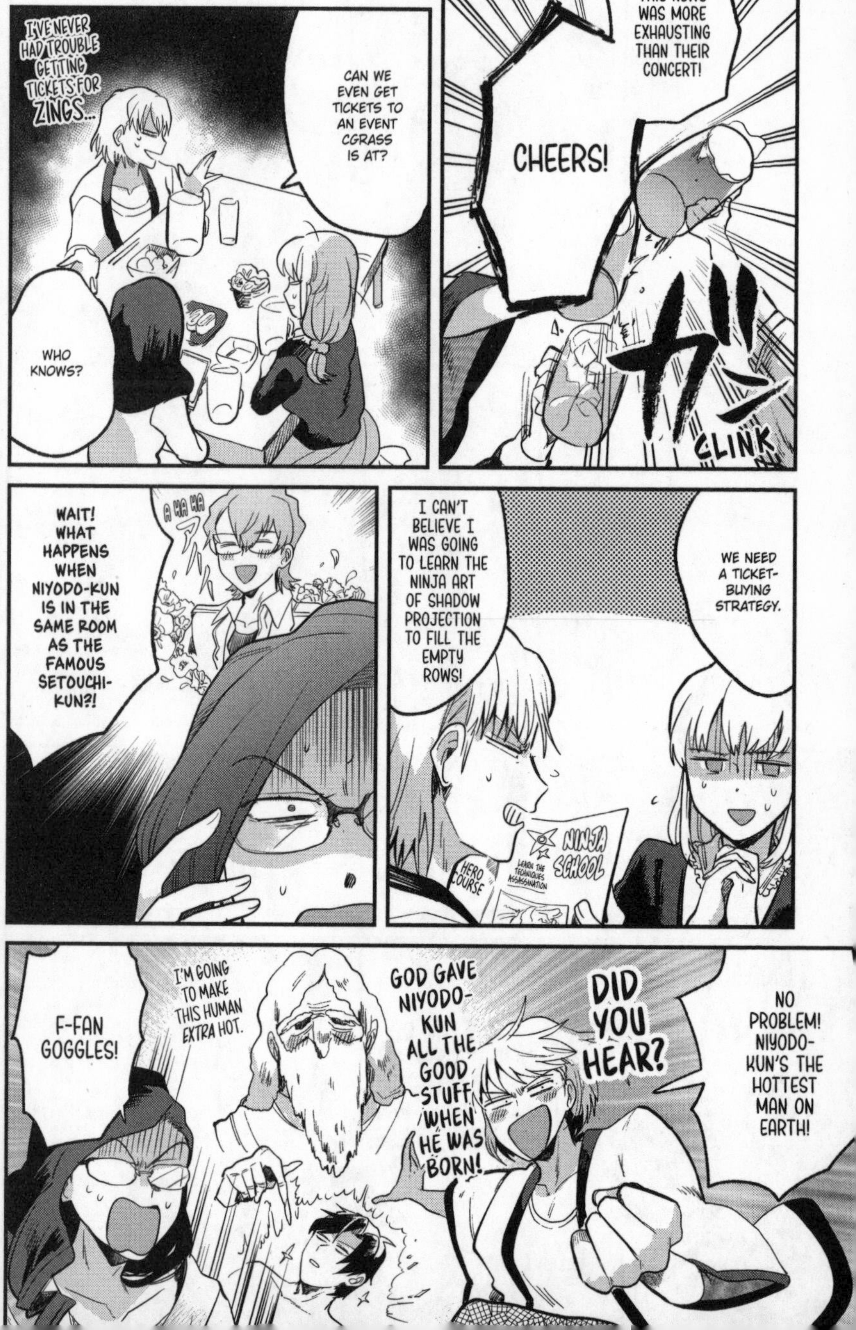
THIS NEWS WAS MORE EXHAUSTING THAN THEIR CONCERT!
CHEERS!
CLINK
CAN WE EVEN GET TICKETS TO AN EVENT CGRASS IS AT?
I'VE NEVER HAD TROUBLE GETTING TICKETS FOR ZINGS...
WHO KNOWS?
WE NEED A TICKET-BUYING STRATEGY.
I CAN'T BELIEVE I WAS GOING TO LEARN THE NINJA ART OF SHADOW PROJECTION TO FILL THE EMPTY ROWS!
NINJA SCHOOL
LEARN THE TECHNIQUES ASSASSINATION
HERO COURSE
A HA HA
WAIT! WHAT HAPPENS WHEN NIYODO-KUN IS IN THE SAME ROOM AS THE FAMOUS SETOUCHI-KUN?!
NO PROBLEM! NIYODO-KUN'S THE HOTTEST MAN ON EARTH!
DID YOU HEAR?
GOD GAVE NIYODO-KUN ALL THE GOOD STUFF WHEN HE WAS BORN!
I'M GOING TO MAKE THIS HUMAN EXTRA HOT.
F-FAN GOGGLES!

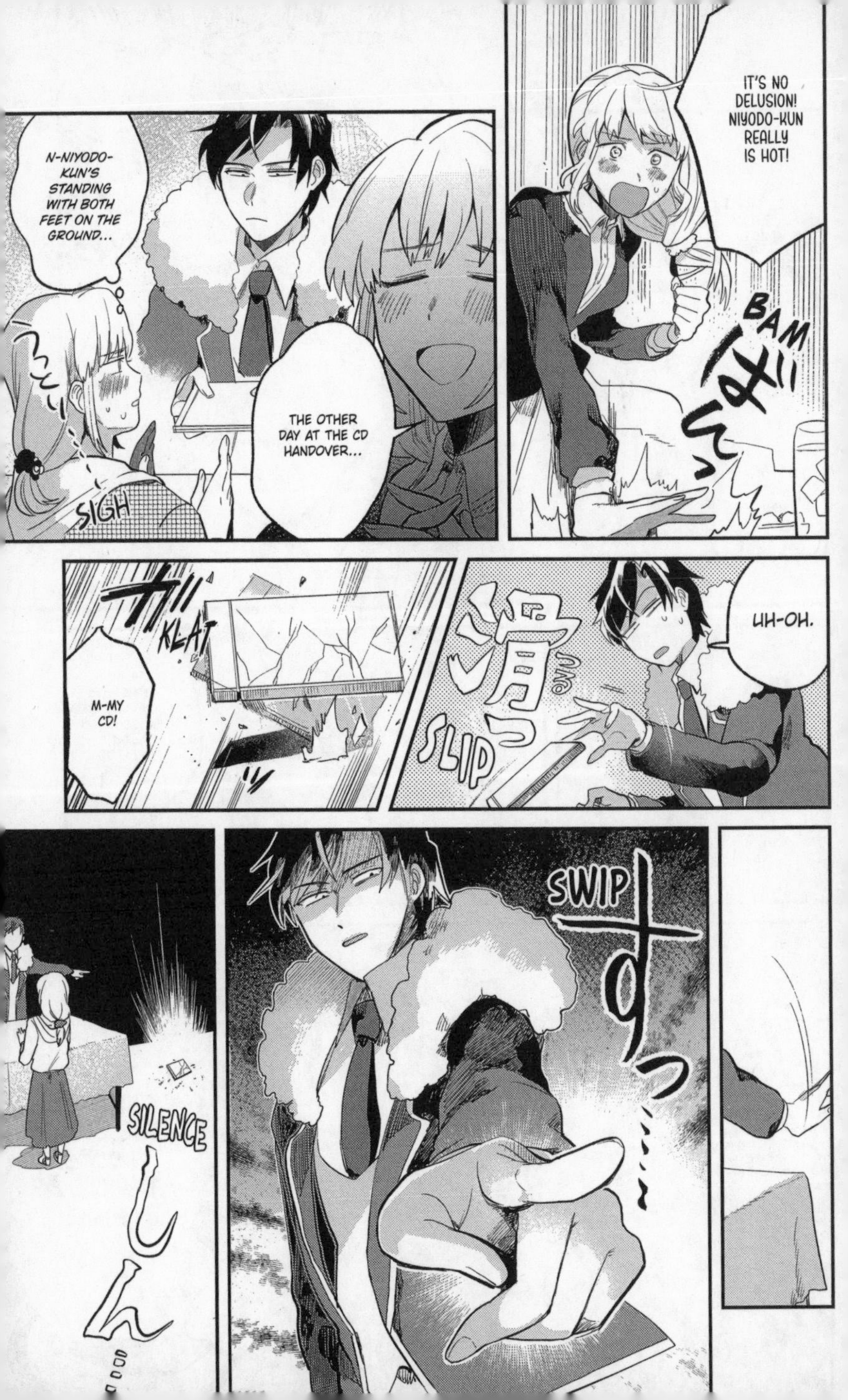
IT'S NO DELUSION! NIYODO-KUN REALLY IS HOT!
BAM
ばんっ
N-NIYODO-KUN'S STANDING WITH BOTH FEET ON THE GROUND...
THE OTHER DAY AT THE CD HANDOVER...
SIGH
UH-OH.
滑っ
つるっ
SLIP
M-MY CD!
KLAT
SWIP
すっ
SILENCE
しん

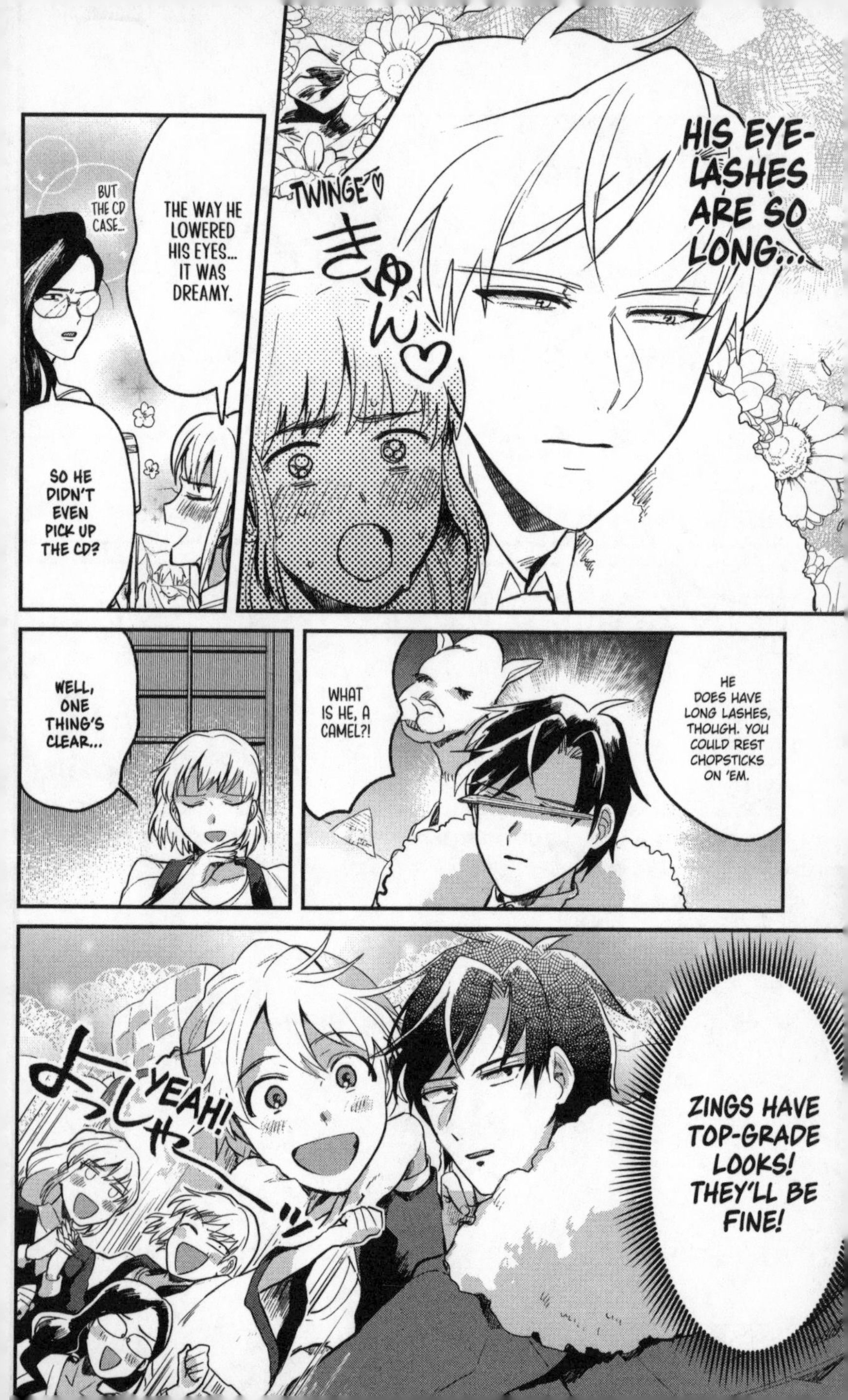
HIS EYE-LASHES ARE SO LONG...
TWINGE♡
きゅん♡
THE WAY HE LOWERED HIS EYES... IT WAS DREAMY.
BUT THE CD CASE...
SO HE DIDN'T EVEN PICK UP THE CD?
HE DOES HAVE LONG LASHES, THOUGH. YOU COULD REST CHOPSTICKS ON 'EM.
WHAT IS HE, A CAMEL?!
WELL, ONE THING'S CLEAR...
ZINGS HAVE TOP-GRADE LOOKS! THEY'LL BE FINE!
YEAH!
よっしゃーッ

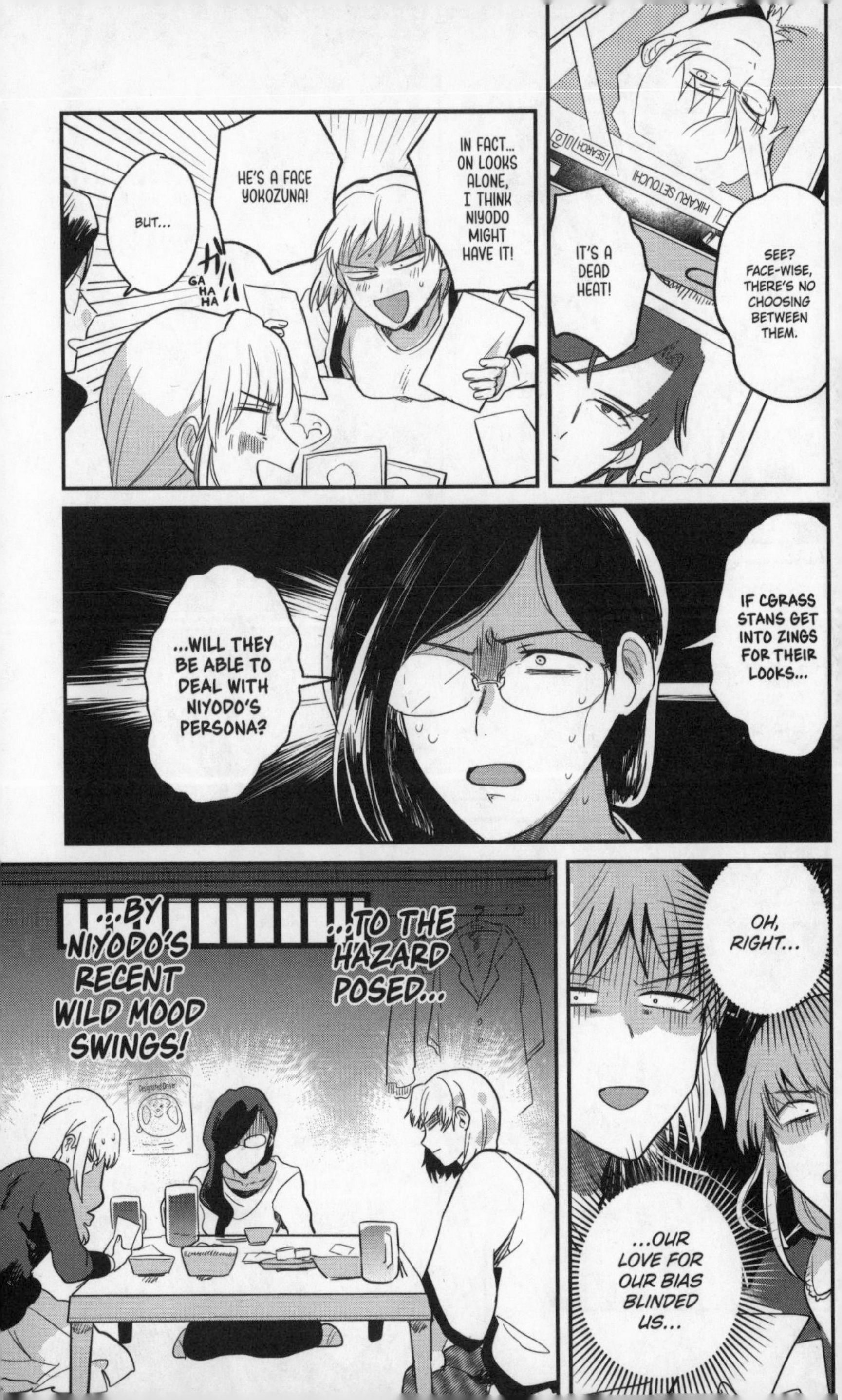
HIKARU SETOUCHI
SEARCH
SEE? FACE-WISE, THERE'S NO CHOOSING BETWEEN THEM.
IT'S A DEAD HEAT!
IN FACT... ON LOOKS ALONE, I THINK NIYODO MIGHT HAVE IT!
HE'S A FACE YOKOZUNA!
GA HA HA
BUT...
IF CGRASS STANS GET INTO ZINGS FOR THEIR LOOKS...
...WILL THEY BE ABLE TO DEAL WITH NIYODO'S PERSONA?
OH, RIGHT...
...OUR LOVE FOR OUR BIAS BLINDED US...
...TO THE HAZARD POSED...
...BY NIYODO'S RECENT WILD MOOD SWINGS!

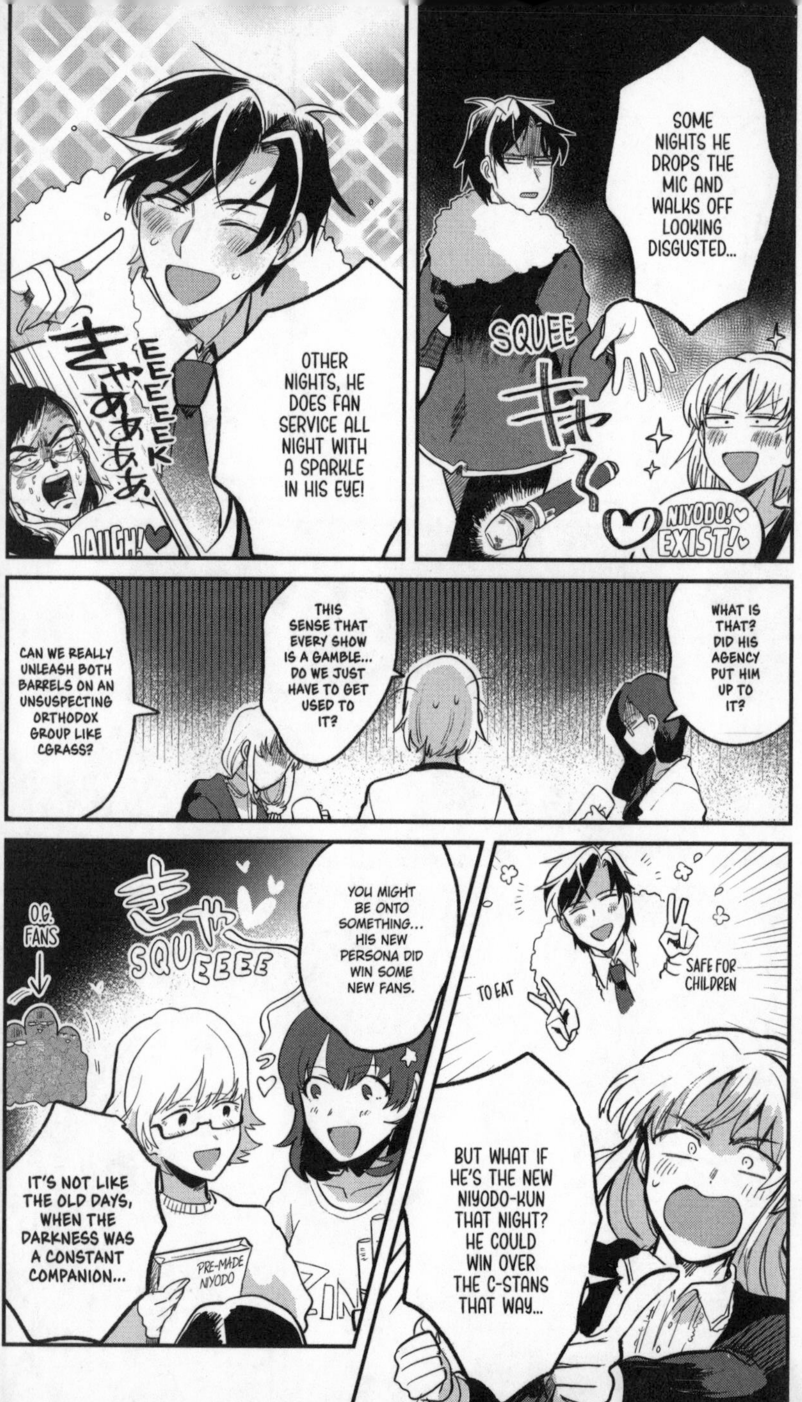
SOME NIGHTS HE DROPS THE MIC AND WALKS OFF LOOKING DISGUSTED...
SQUEE
キャ~
NIYODO!♥ EXIST!♥
OTHER NIGHTS, HE DOES FAN SERVICE ALL NIGHT WITH A SPARKLE IN HIS EYE!
きゃあああ
EEEEEK
LAUGH!♥
WHAT IS THAT? DID HIS AGENCY PUT HIM UP TO IT?
THIS SENSE THAT EVERY SHOW IS A GAMBLE... DO WE JUST HAVE TO GET USED TO IT?
CAN WE REALLY UNLEASH BOTH BARRELS ON AN UNSUSPECTING ORTHODOX GROUP LIKE CGRASS?
SAFE FOR CHILDREN
TO EAT
BUT WHAT IF HE'S THE NEW NIYODO-KUN THAT NIGHT? HE COULD WIN OVER THE C-STANS THAT WAY...
YOU MIGHT BE ONTO SOMETHING... HIS NEW PERSONA DID WIN SOME NEW FANS.
きゃ
SQUEEEE
O.G. FANS
IT'S NOT LIKE THE OLD DAYS, WHEN THE DARKNESS WAS A CONSTANT COMPANION...
PRE-MADE NIYODO

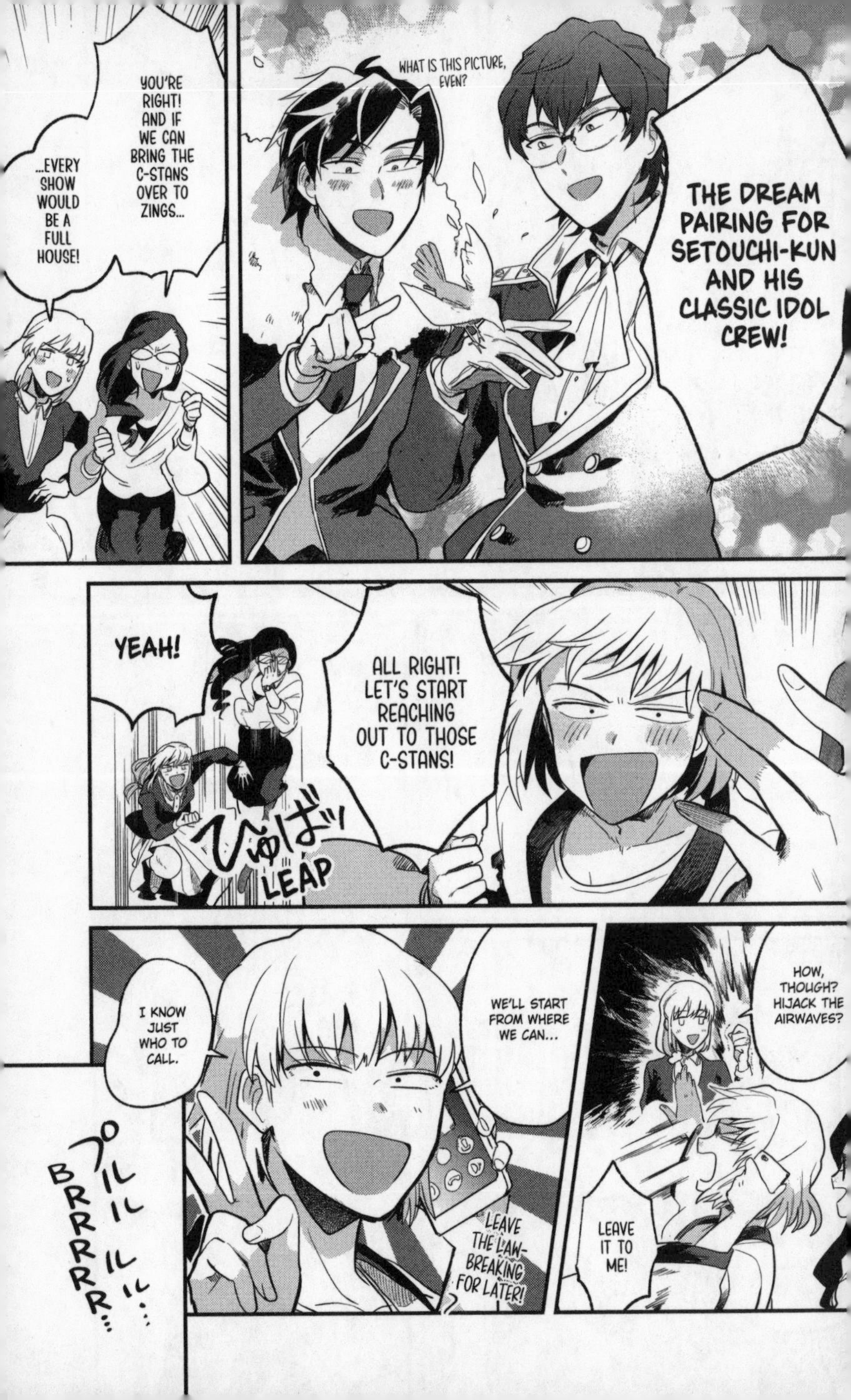
THE DREAM PAIRING FOR SETOUCHI-KUN AND HIS CLASSIC IDOL CREW!
WHAT IS THIS PICTURE, EVEN?
YOU'RE RIGHT! AND IF WE CAN BRING THE C-STANS OVER TO ZINGS...
...EVERY SHOW WOULD BE A FULL HOUSE!
ALL RIGHT! LET'S START REACHING OUT TO THOSE C-STANS!
YEAH!
ひゅばっ
LEAP
HOW, THOUGH? HIJACK THE AIRWAVES?
LEAVE IT TO ME!
WE'LL START FROM WHERE WE CAN...
I KNOW JUST WHO TO CALL.
LEAVE THE LAW-BREAKING FOR LATER!
プルルルル…
BRRRRR...

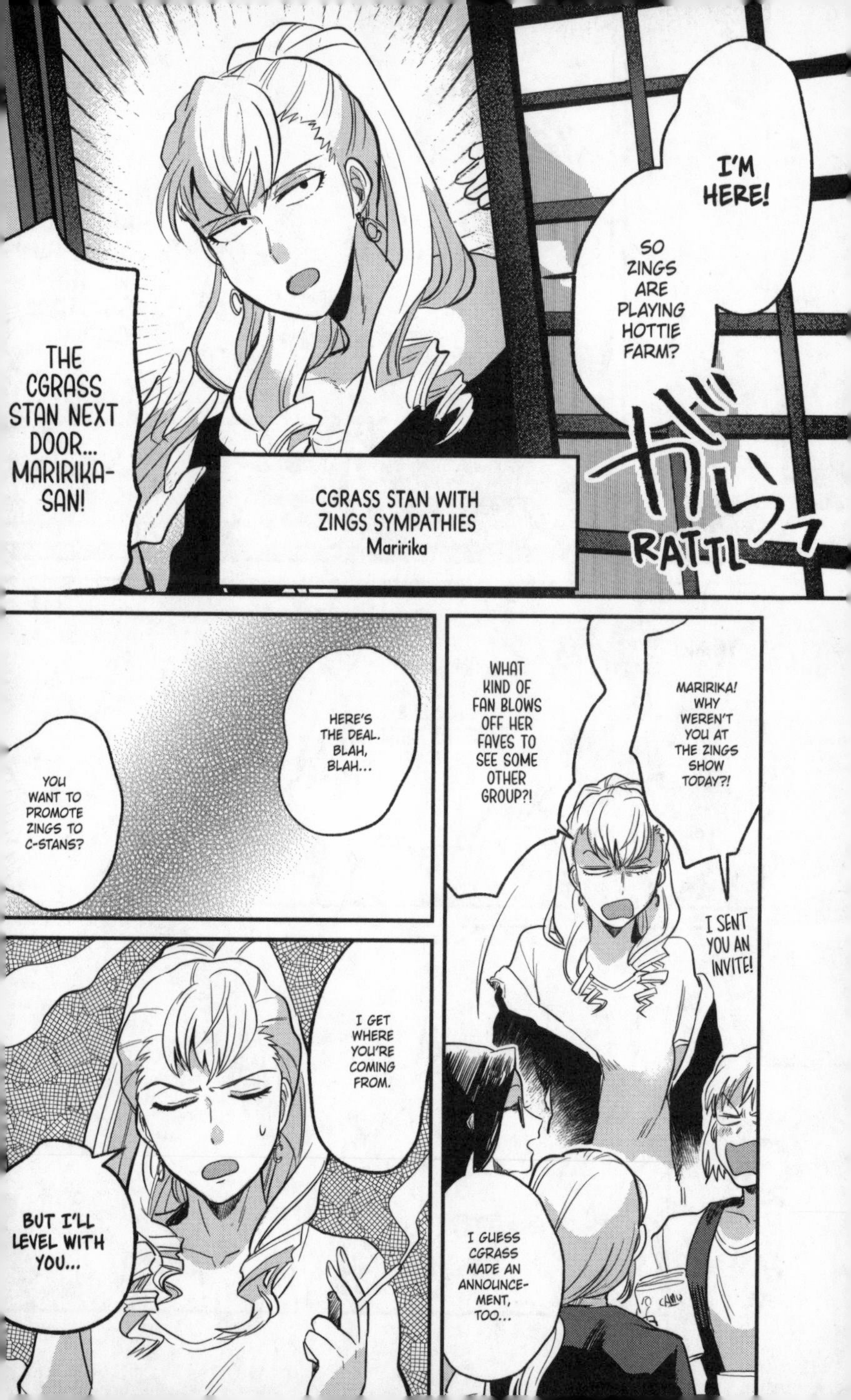
I'M HERE!
SO ZINGS ARE PLAYING HOTTIE FARM?
がらっ
RAT-TL
CGRASS STAN WITH ZINGS SYMPATHIES
Maririka
THE CGRASS STAN NEXT DOOR... MARIRIKA-SAN!
MARIRIKA! WHY WEREN'T YOU AT THE ZINGS SHOW TODAY?!
WHAT KIND OF FAN BLOWS OFF HER FAVES TO SEE SOME OTHER GROUP?!
I SENT YOU AN INVITE!
I GUESS CGRASS MADE AN ANNOUNCE-MENT, TOO...
HERE'S THE DEAL. BLAH, BLAH...
YOU WANT TO PROMOTE ZINGS TO C-STANS?
I GET WHERE YOU'RE COMING FROM.
BUT I'LL LEVEL WITH YOU...

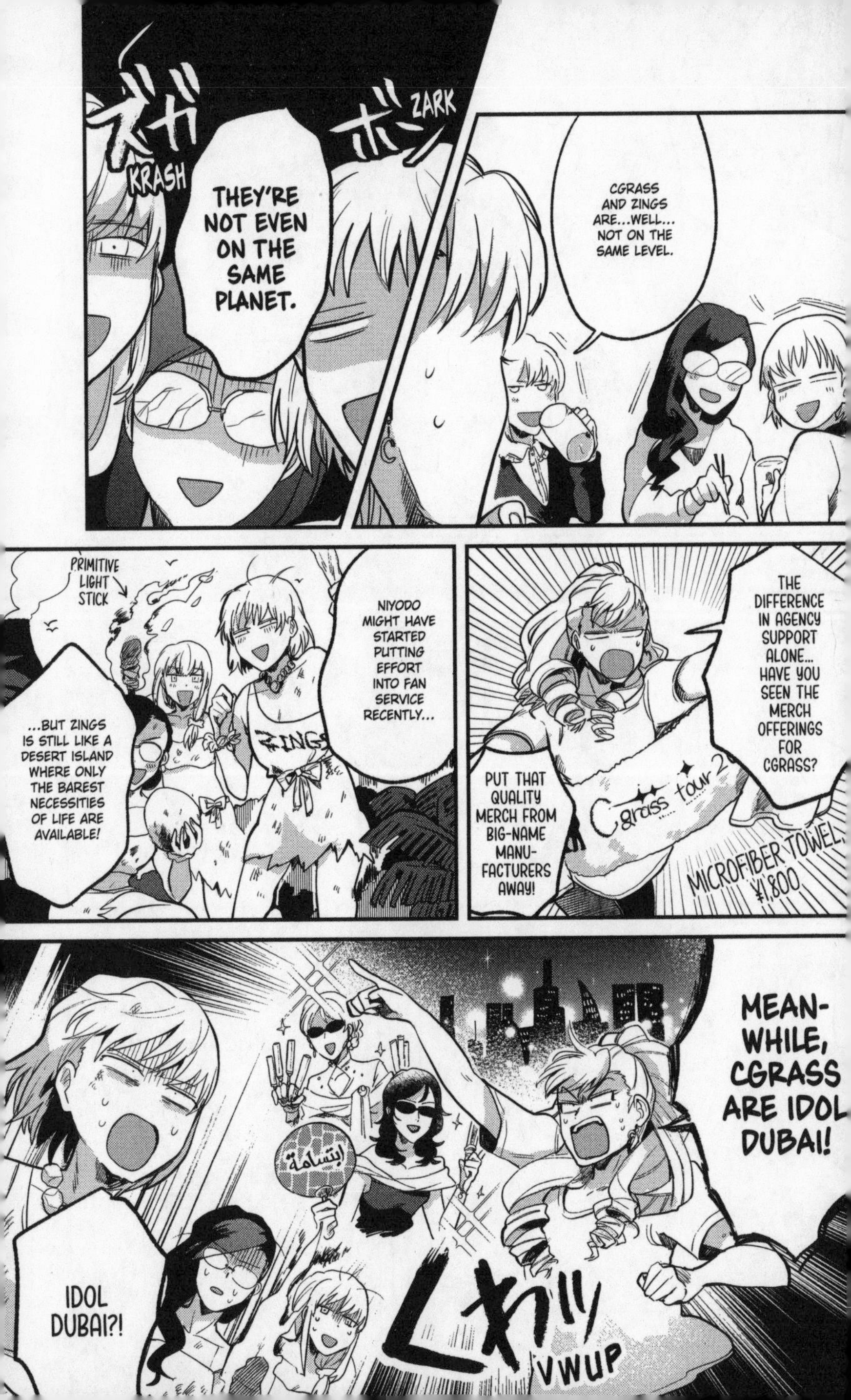

CGRASS AND ZINGS ARE...WELL... NOT ON THE SAME LEVEL.
ZARK
KRASH
THEY'RE NOT EVEN ON THE SAME PLANET.
THE DIFFERENCE IN AGENCY SUPPORT ALONE... HAVE YOU SEEN THE MERCH OFFERINGS FOR CGRASS?
PUT THAT QUALITY MERCH FROM BIG-NAME MANU-FACTURERS AWAY!
Cgrass tour 2
MICROFIBER TOWEL, ¥1,800
NIYODO MIGHT HAVE STARTED PUTTING EFFORT INTO FAN SERVICE RECENTLY...
PRIMITIVE LIGHT STICK
ZINGS
...BUT ZINGS IS STILL LIKE A DESERT ISLAND WHERE ONLY THE BAREST NECESSITIES OF LIFE ARE AVAILABLE!
MEAN-WHILE, CGRASS ARE IDOL DUBAI!
ابتسامة
IDOL DUBAI?!
VWUP

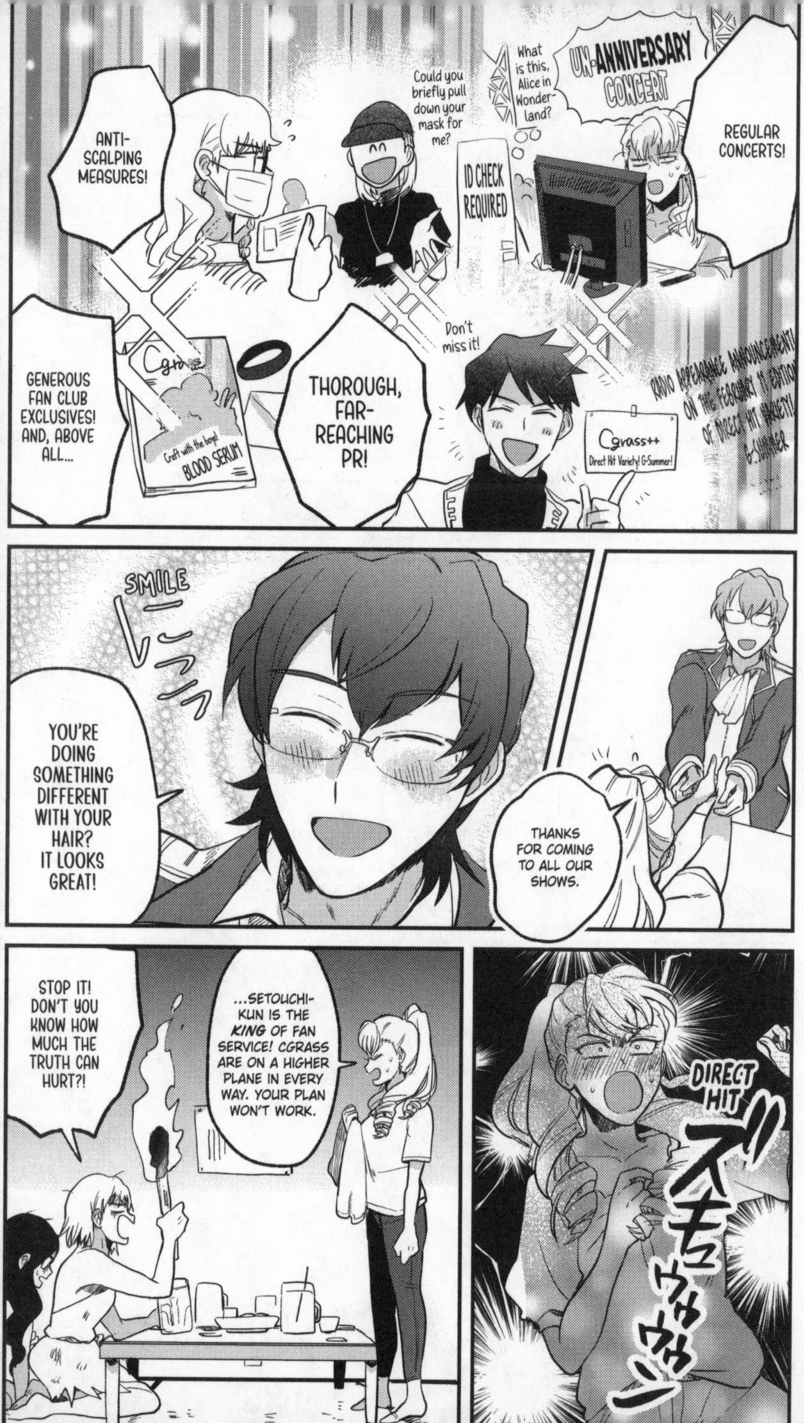
REGULAR CONCERTS!
UN-ANNIVERSARY CONCERT
What is this, Alice in Wonderland?
ID CHECK REQUIRED
Could you briefly pull down your mask for me?
ANTI-SCALPING MEASURES!
RADIO APPEARANCE ANNOUNCEMENT! ON THE FEBRUARY 11 EDITION OF DIRECT HIT VARIETY! G-SUMMER
Cgrass++
Direct Hit Variety! G-Summer!
Don't miss it!
THOROUGH, FAR-REACHING PR!
Cgrass
Craft with the boys!
BLOOD SERUM
GENEROUS FAN CLUB EXCLUSIVES! AND, ABOVE ALL...
THANKS FOR COMING TO ALL OUR SHOWS.
SMILE
YOU'RE DOING SOMETHING DIFFERENT WITH YOUR HAIR? IT LOOKS GREAT!
DIRECT HIT
...SETOUCHI-KUN IS THE *KING* OF FAN SERVICE! CGRASS ARE ON A HIGHER PLANE IN EVERY WAY. YOUR PLAN WON'T WORK.
STOP IT! DON'T YOU KNOW HOW MUCH THE TRUTH CAN HURT?!

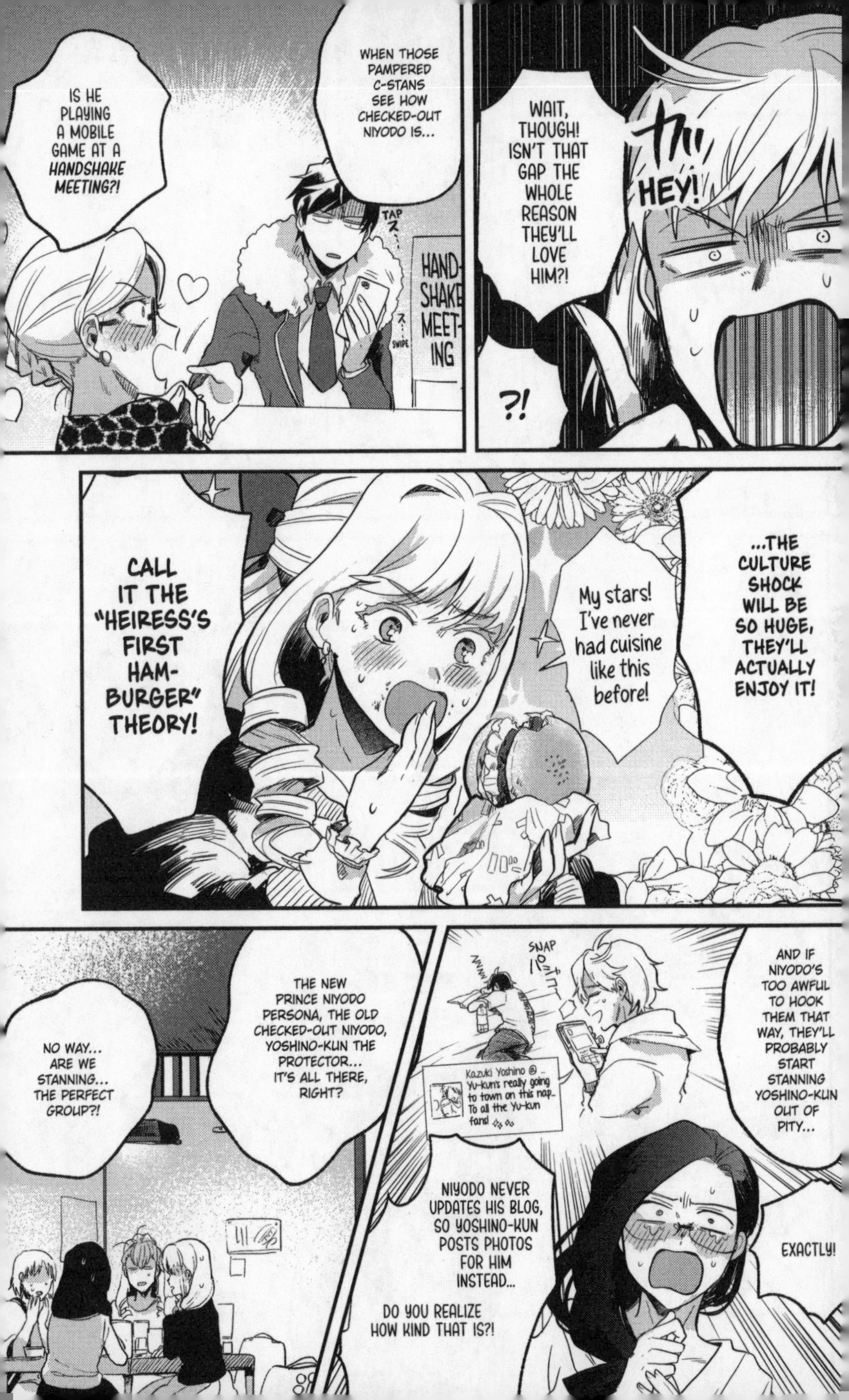
HEY!
WAIT, THOUGH! ISN'T THAT GAP THE WHOLE REASON THEY'LL LOVE HIM?!
?!
WHEN THOSE PAMPERED C-STANS SEE HOW CHECKED-OUT NIYODO IS...
IS HE PLAYING A MOBILE GAME AT A HANDSHAKE MEETING?!
TAP
SWIPE
HAND-SHAKE MEET-ING
...THE CULTURE SHOCK WILL BE SO HUGE, THEY'LL ACTUALLY ENJOY IT!
My stars! I've never had cuisine like this before!
CALL IT THE "HEIRESS'S FIRST HAMBURGER" THEORY!
AND IF NIYODO'S TOO AWFUL TO HOOK THEM THAT WAY, THEY'LL PROBABLY START STANNING YOSHINO-KUN OUT OF PITY...
SNAP
Kazuki Yoshino @... Yu-kun's really going to town on this nap... To all the Yu-kun fans!
EXACTLY!
NIYODO NEVER UPDATES HIS BLOG, SO YOSHINO-KUN POSTS PHOTOS FOR HIM INSTEAD...
DO YOU REALIZE HOW KIND THAT IS?!
THE NEW PRINCE NIYODO PERSONA, THE OLD CHECKED-OUT NIYODO, YOSHINO-KUN THE PROTECTOR... IT'S ALL THERE, RIGHT?
NO WAY... ARE WE STANNING... THE PERFECT GROUP?!

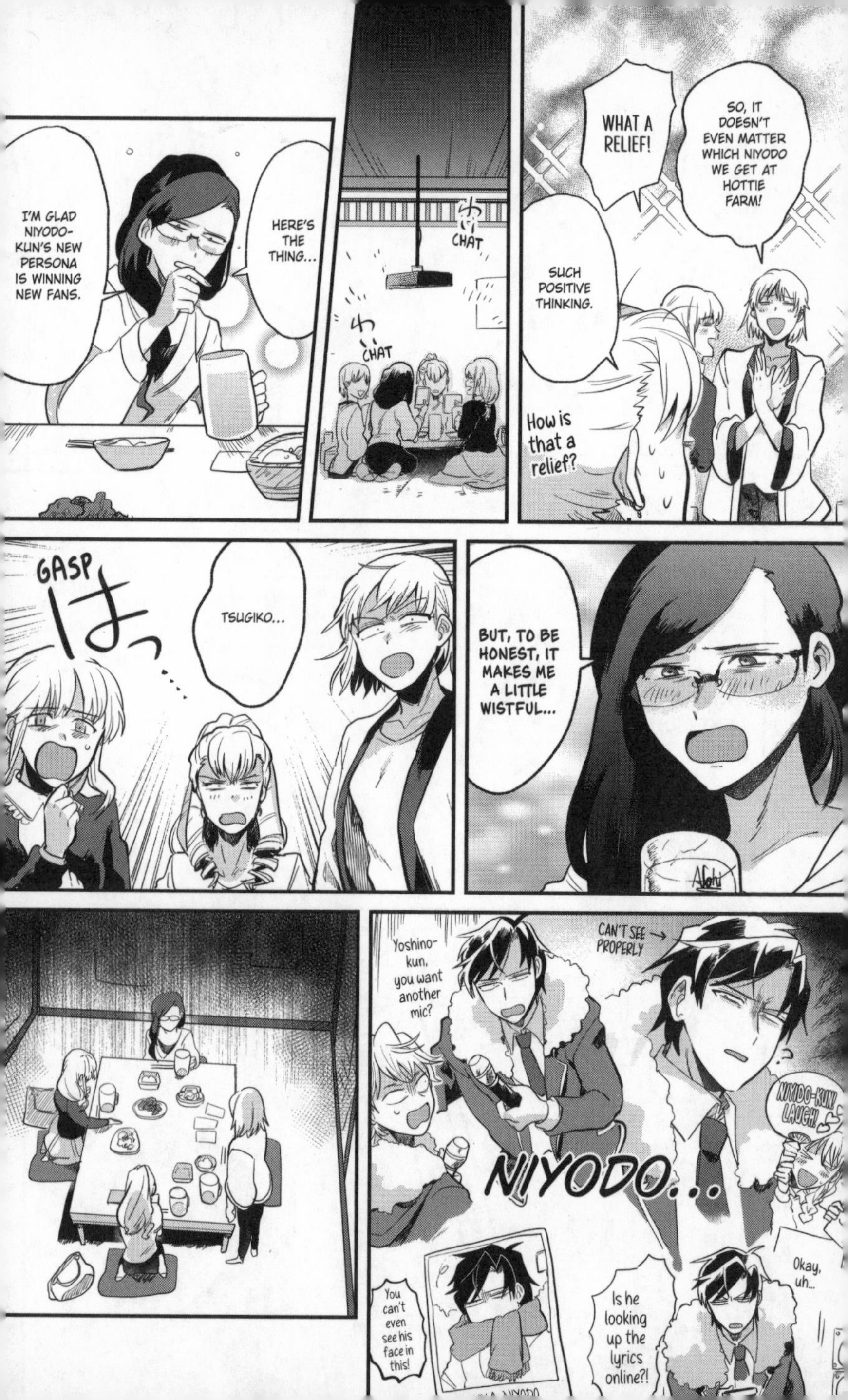
SO, IT DOESN'T EVEN MATTER WHICH NIYODO WE GET AT HOTTIE FARM!
WHAT A RELIEF!
SUCH POSITIVE THINKING.
How is that a relief?
わ
CHAT
わ
CHAT
HERE'S THE THING...
I'M GLAD NIYODO-KUN'S NEW PERSONA IS WINNING NEW FANS.
BUT, TO BE HONEST, IT MAKES ME A LITTLE WISTFUL...
TSUGIKO...
GASP
はっ
CAN'T SEE PROPERLY
Yoshino-kun, you want another mic?
NIYODO-KUN! LAUGH!
NIYODO...
Okay, uh...
Is he looking up the lyrics online?!
You can't even see his face in this!

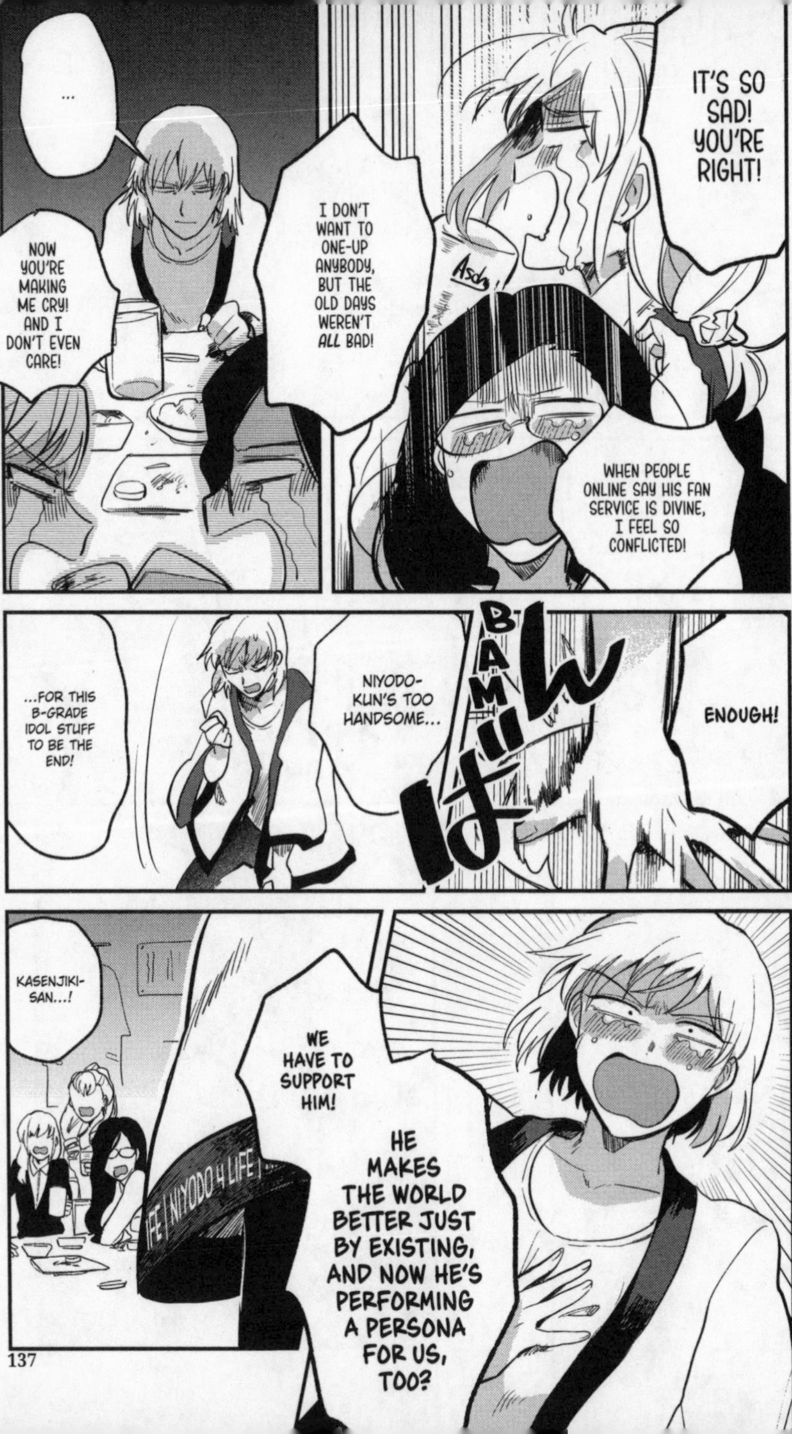
IT'S SO SAD! YOU'RE RIGHT!
WHEN PEOPLE ONLINE SAY HIS FAN SERVICE IS DIVINE, I FEEL SO CONFLICTED!
I DON'T WANT TO ONE-UP ANYBODY, BUT THE OLD DAYS WEREN'T ALL BAD!
...
NOW YOU'RE MAKING ME CRY! AND I DON'T EVEN CARE!
ENOUGH!
BAMM!!
NIYODO-KUN'S TOO HANDSOME...
...FOR THIS B-GRADE IDOL STUFF TO BE THE END!
HE MAKES THE WORLD BETTER JUST BY EXISTING, AND NOW HE'S PERFORMING A PERSONA FOR US, TOO?
WE HAVE TO SUPPORT HIM!
KASENJIKI-SAN...!

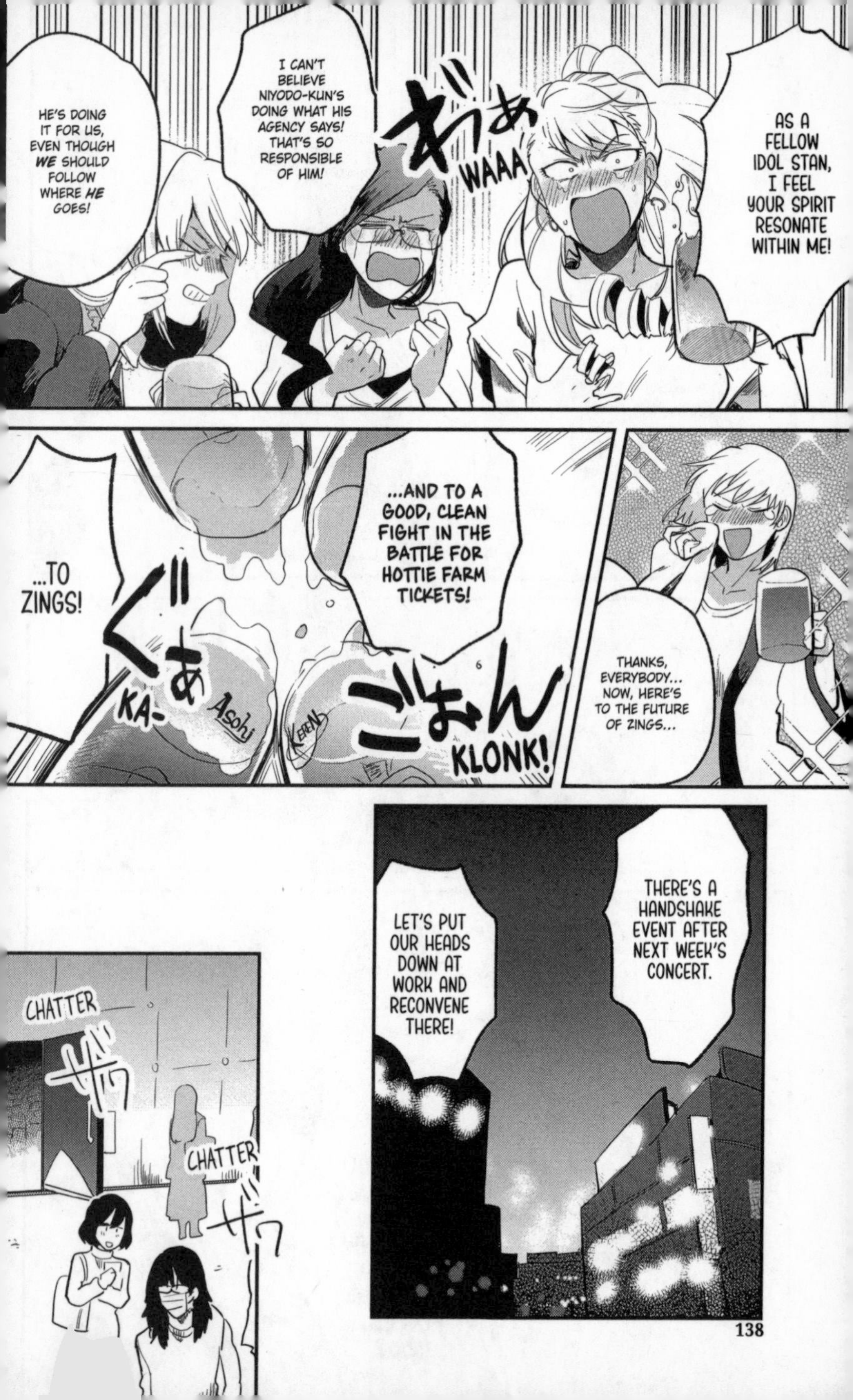
AS A FELLOW IDOL STAN, I FEEL YOUR SPIRIT RESONATE WITHIN ME!
WAAA
I CAN'T BELIEVE NIYODO-KUN'S DOING WHAT HIS AGENCY SAYS! THAT'S SO RESPONSIBLE OF HIM!
HE'S DOING IT FOR US, EVEN THOUGH WE SHOULD FOLLOW WHERE HE GOES!
THANKS, EVERYBODY... NOW, HERE'S TO THE FUTURE OF ZINGS...
...AND TO A GOOD, CLEAN FIGHT IN THE BATTLE FOR HOTTIE FARM TICKETS!
KLONK!
...TO ZINGS!
KA-
THERE'S A HANDSHAKE EVENT AFTER NEXT WEEK'S CONCERT.
LET'S PUT OUR HEADS DOWN AT WORK AND RECONVENE THERE!
CHATTER
CHATTER

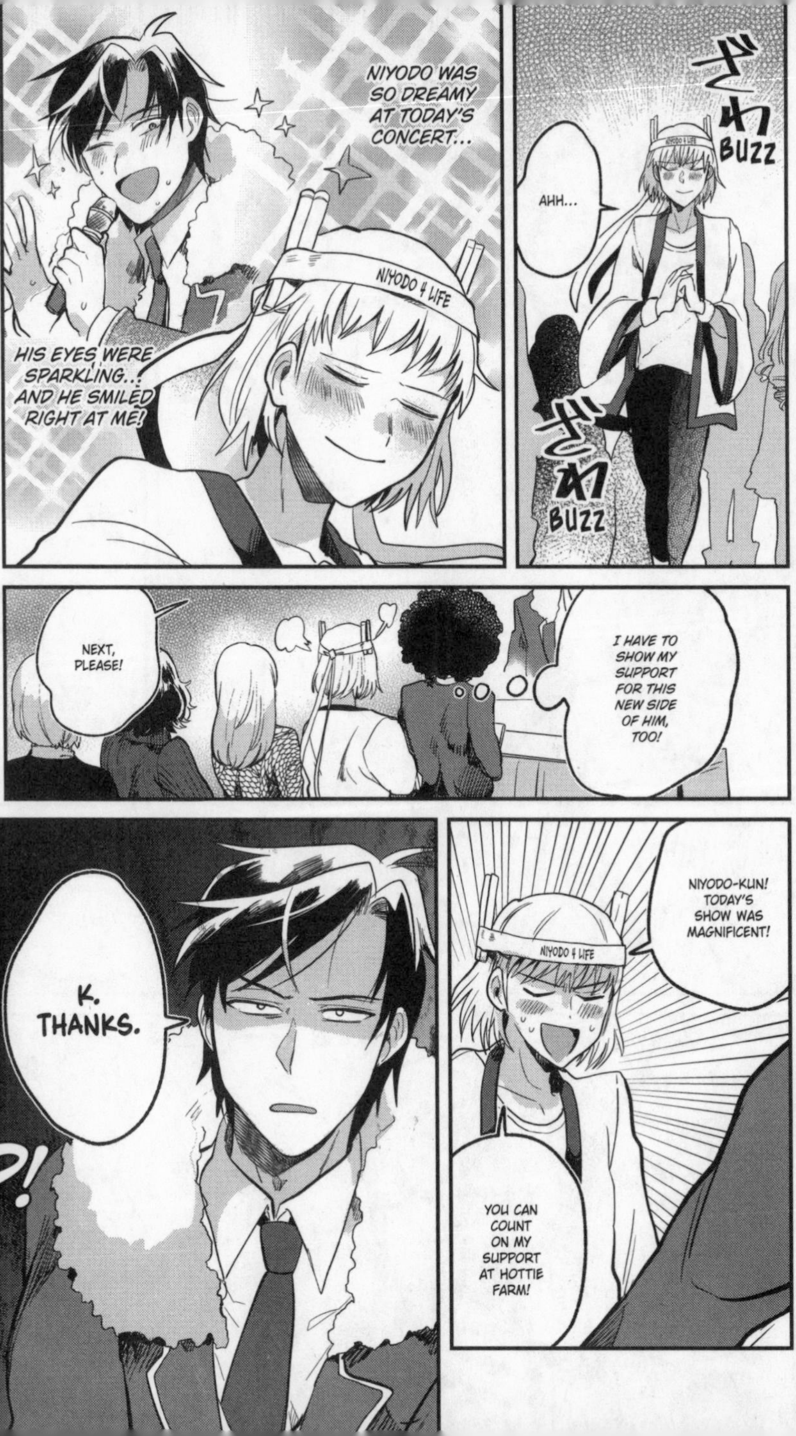
BUZZ
AHH...
BUZZ
NIYODO WAS SO DREAMY AT TODAY'S CONCERT...
NIYODO 4 LIFE
HIS EYES WERE SPARKLING... AND HE SMILED RIGHT AT ME!
I HAVE TO SHOW MY SUPPORT FOR THIS NEW SIDE OF HIM, TOO!
NEXT, PLEASE!
NIYODO-KUN! TODAY'S SHOW WAS MAGNIFICENT!
NIYODO 4 LIFE
YOU CAN COUNT ON MY SUPPORT AT HOTTIE FARM!
K. THANKS.
?!

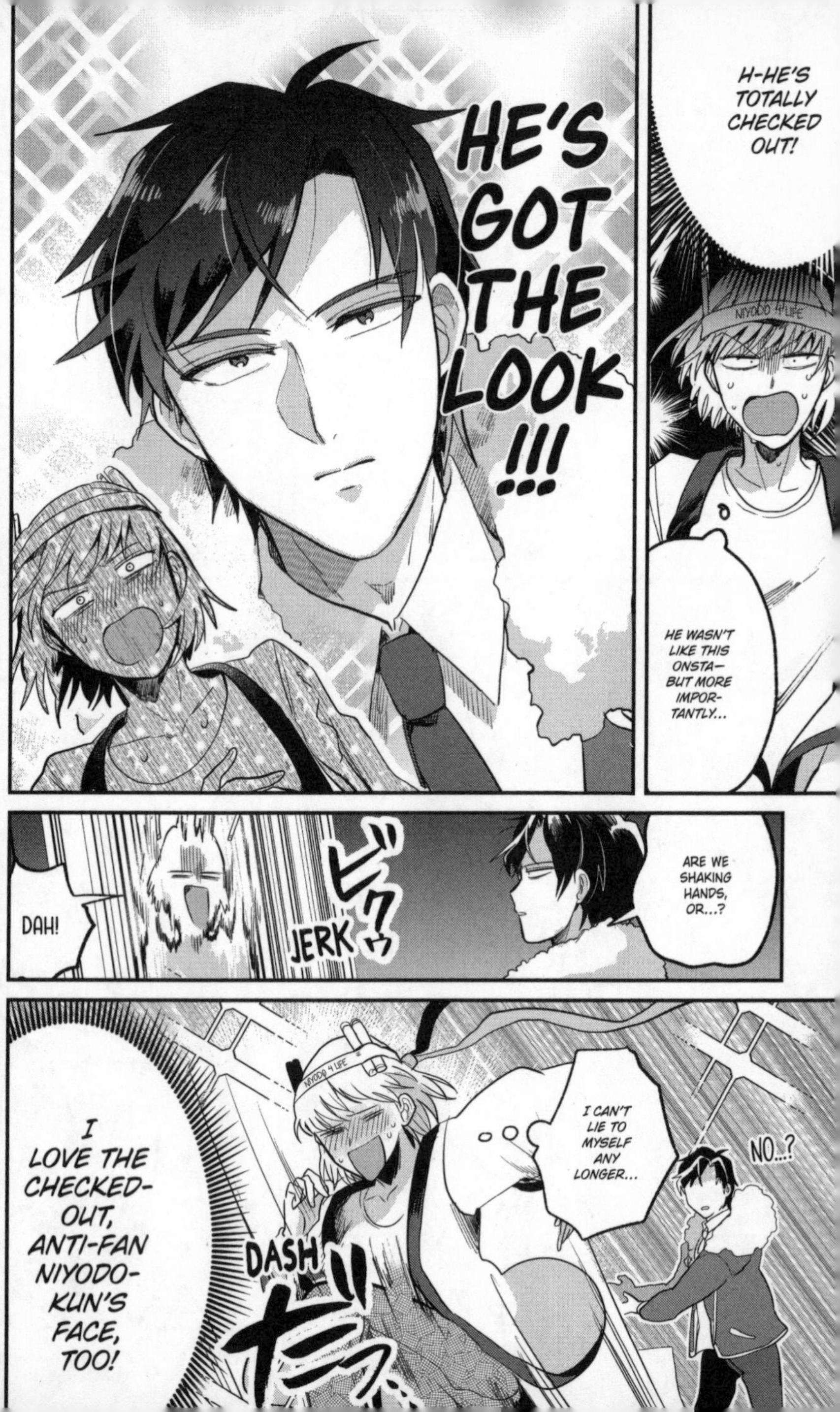
H-HE'S TOTALLY CHECKED OUT!
NIYODO 4 LIFE
HE WASN'T LIKE THIS ONSTA— BUT MORE IMPORTANTLY...
HE'S GOT THE LOOK!!!
ARE WE SHAKING HANDS, OR...?
JERK
DAH!
NO...?
I CAN'T LIE TO MYSELF ANY LONGER...
NIYODO 4 LIFE
DASH
I LOVE THE CHECKED-OUT, ANTI-FAN NIYODO-KUN'S FACE, TOO!

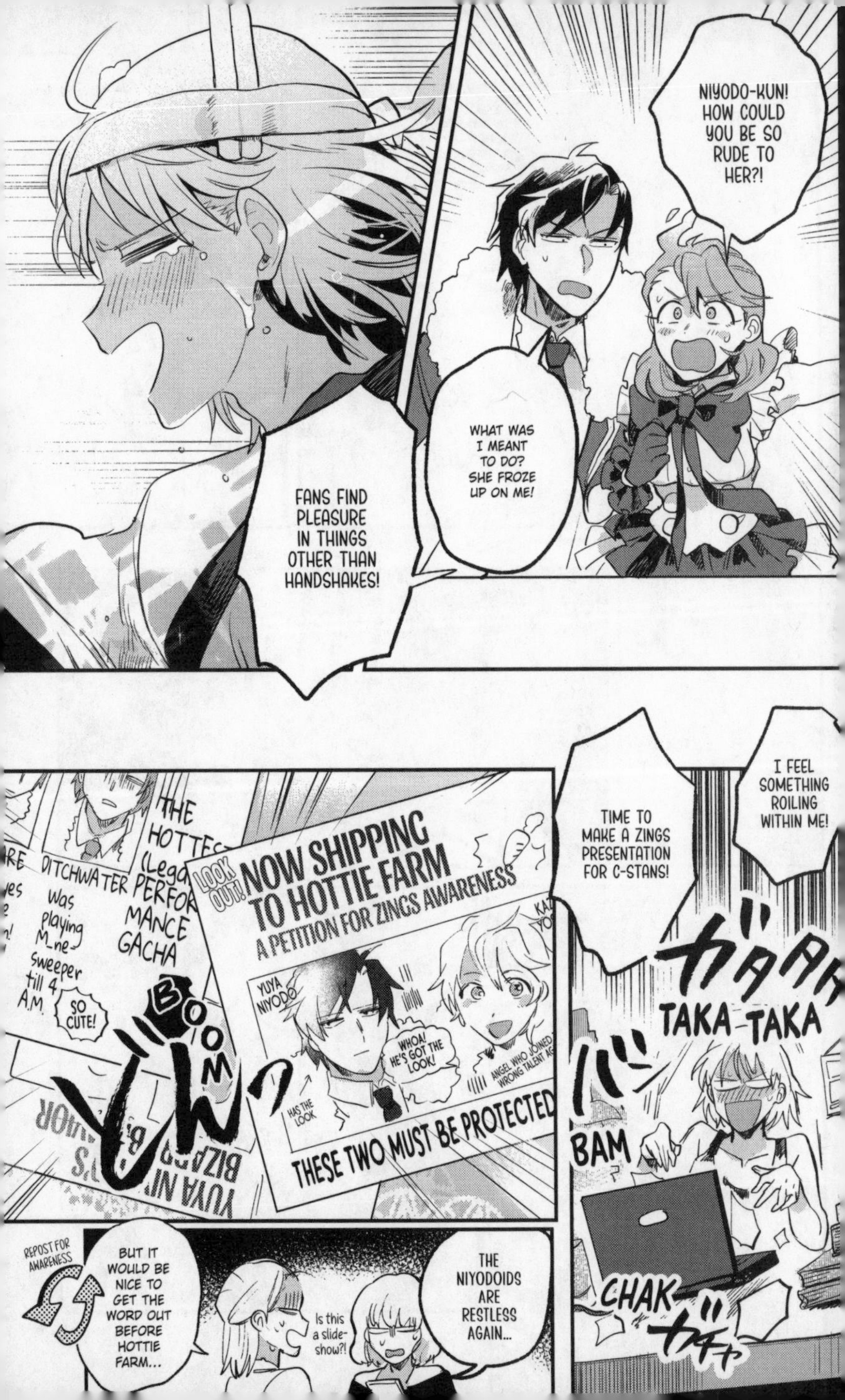
NIYODO-KUN! HOW COULD YOU BE SO RUDE TO HER?!
WHAT WAS I MEANT TO DO? SHE FROZE UP ON ME!
FANS FIND PLEASURE IN THINGS OTHER THAN HANDSHAKES!
I FEEL SOMETHING ROILING WITHIN ME!
TIME TO MAKE A ZINGS PRESENTATION FOR C-STANS!
TAKA-TAKA
BAM
CHAK
LOOK OUT!
NOW SHIPPING TO HOTTIE FARM
A PETITION FOR ZINGS AWARENESS
YUYA NIYODO
WHOA! HE'S GOT THE LOOK!
HAS THE LOOK
THESE TWO MUST BE PROTECTED
THE HOTTEST (Legal) PERFORMANCE GACHA
DITCHWATER
Was playing M_ne-sweeper till 4 A.M.
SO CUTE!
BOOM
THE NIYODOIDS ARE RESTLESS AGAIN...
Is this a slide-show?!
BUT IT WOULD BE NICE TO GET THE WORD OUT BEFORE HOTTIE FARM...
REPOST FOR AWARENESS

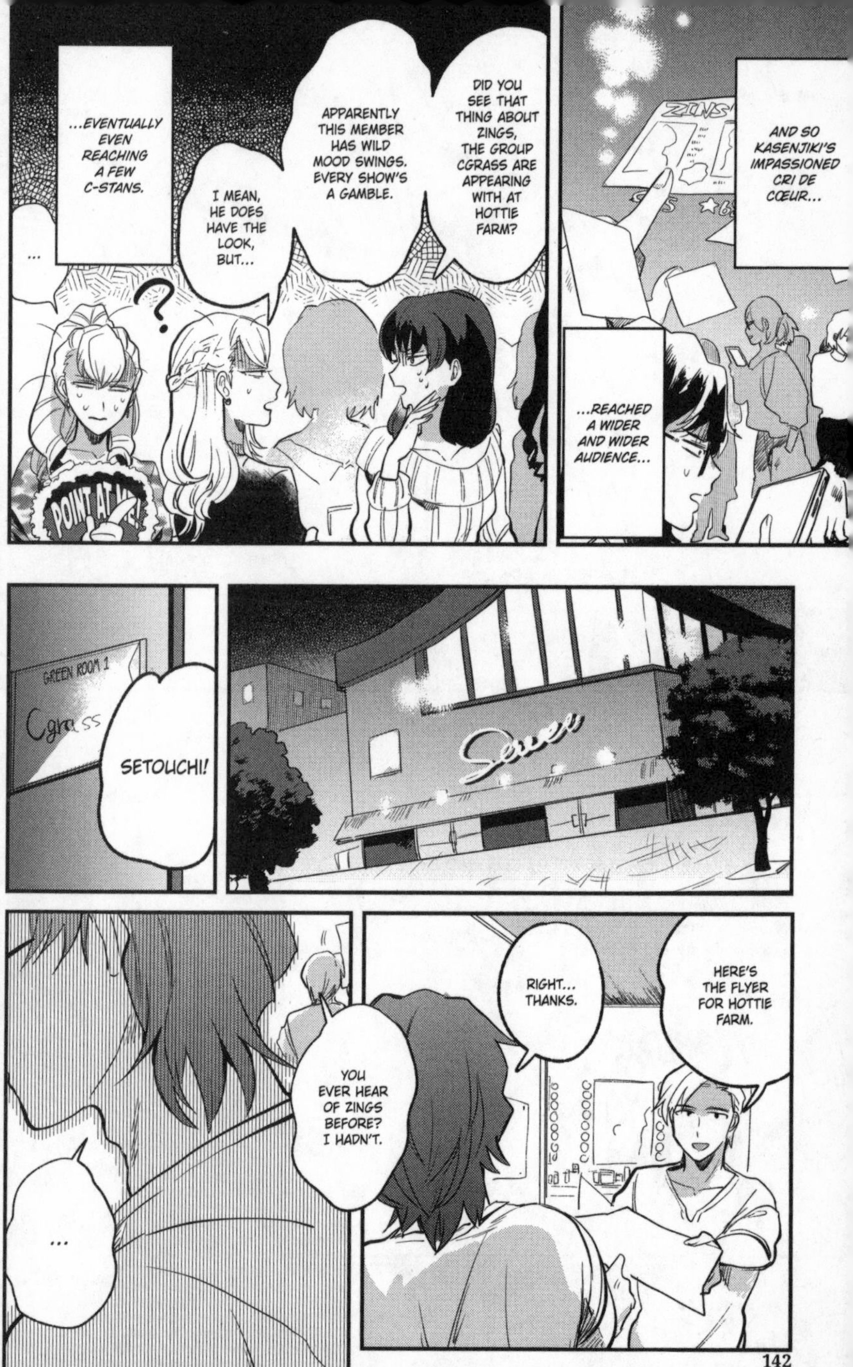
AND SO KASENJIKI'S IMPASSIONED CRI DE CŒUR...
...REACHED A WIDER AND WIDER AUDIENCE...
...EVENTUALLY EVEN REACHING A FEW C-STANS.
DID YOU SEE THAT THING ABOUT ZINGS, THE GROUP CGRASS ARE APPEARING WITH AT HOTTIE FARM?
APPARENTLY THIS MEMBER HAS WILD MOOD SWINGS. EVERY SHOW'S A GAMBLE.
I MEAN, HE DOES HAVE THE LOOK, BUT...
...
POINT AT ME!
GREEN ROOM 1
Cgrass
SETOUCHI!
HERE'S THE FLYER FOR HOTTIE FARM.
RIGHT... THANKS.
YOU EVER HEAR OF ZINGS BEFORE? I HADN'T.
...

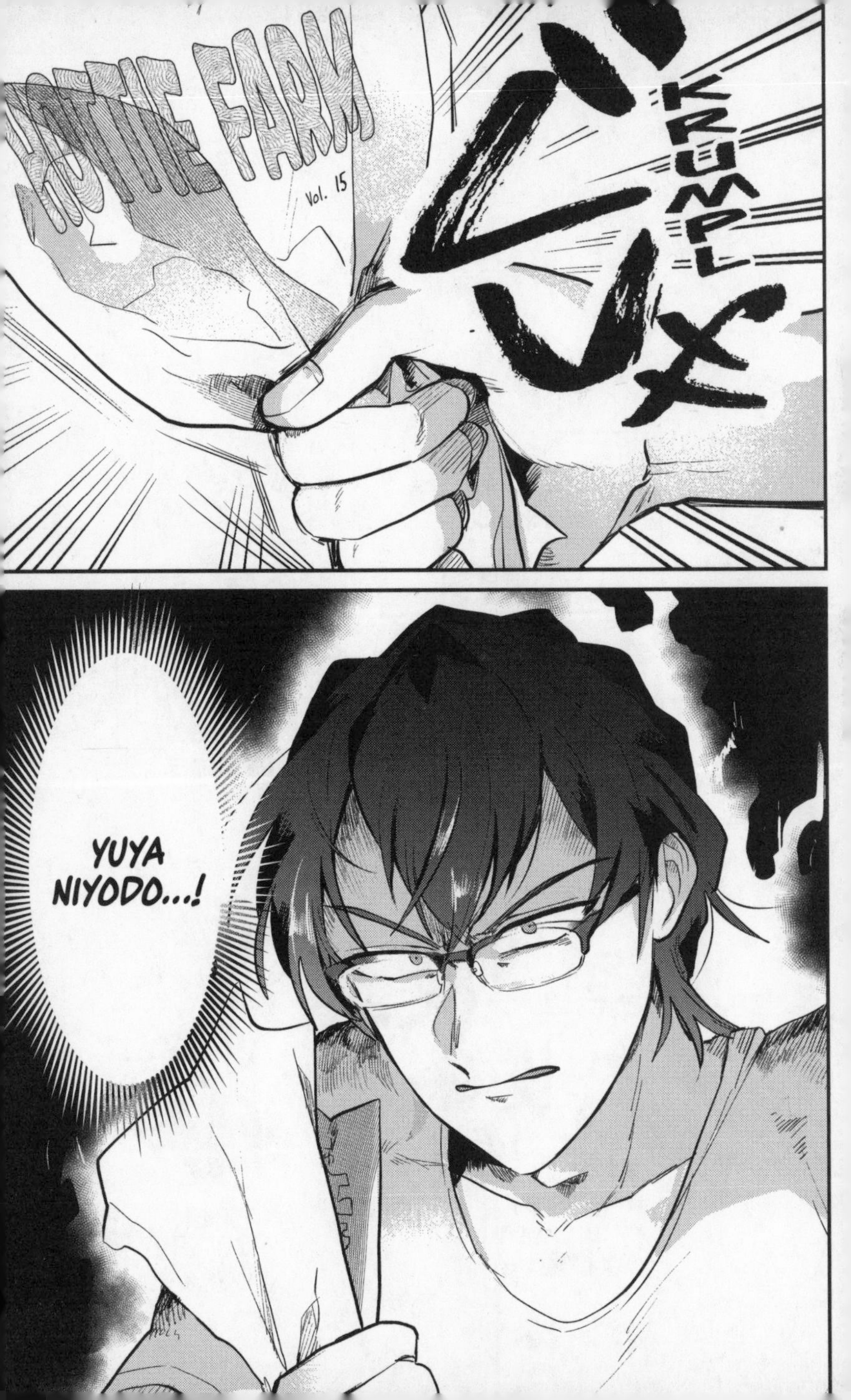
HOTTIE FARM
Vol. 15
KRUMPL
YUYA NIYODO...!

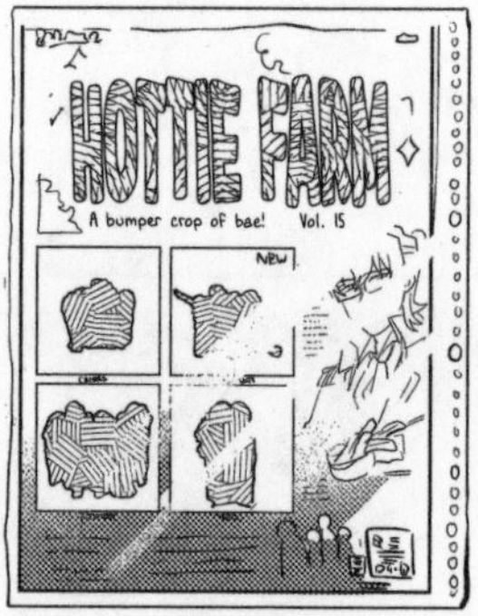
HOTTIE FARM
A bumper crop of bae!
Vol. 15
NEW
FOR THE ARCHIVES

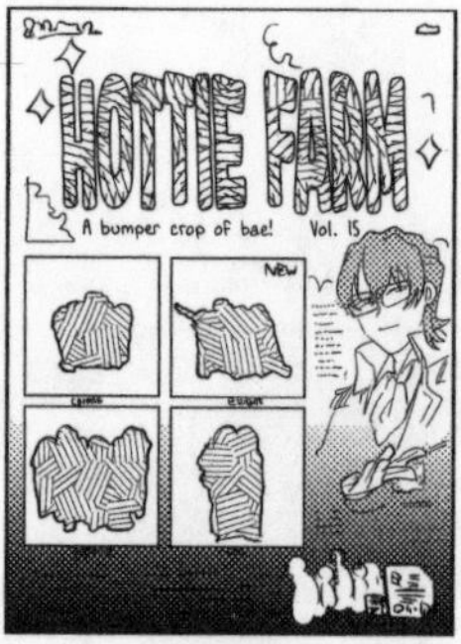
HOTTIE FARM
A bumper crop of bae!
Vol. 15
NEW
FOR READING

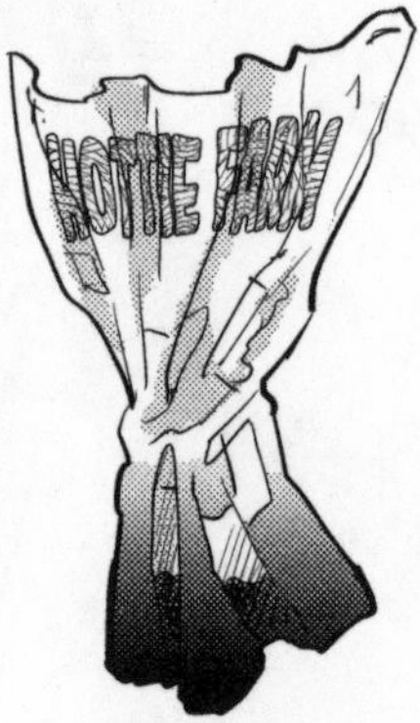
HOTTIE FARM
FORMERLY
SETOUCHI'S FLYER
(NOW GARBAGE)

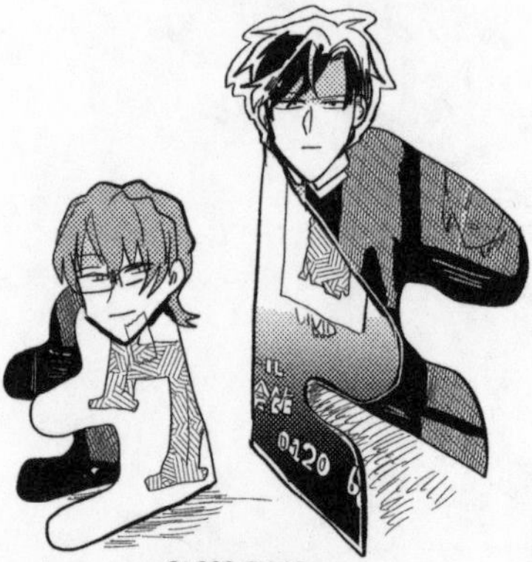
PAPER SUMO
WRESTLERS MADE FROM
LEFTOVER FLYER

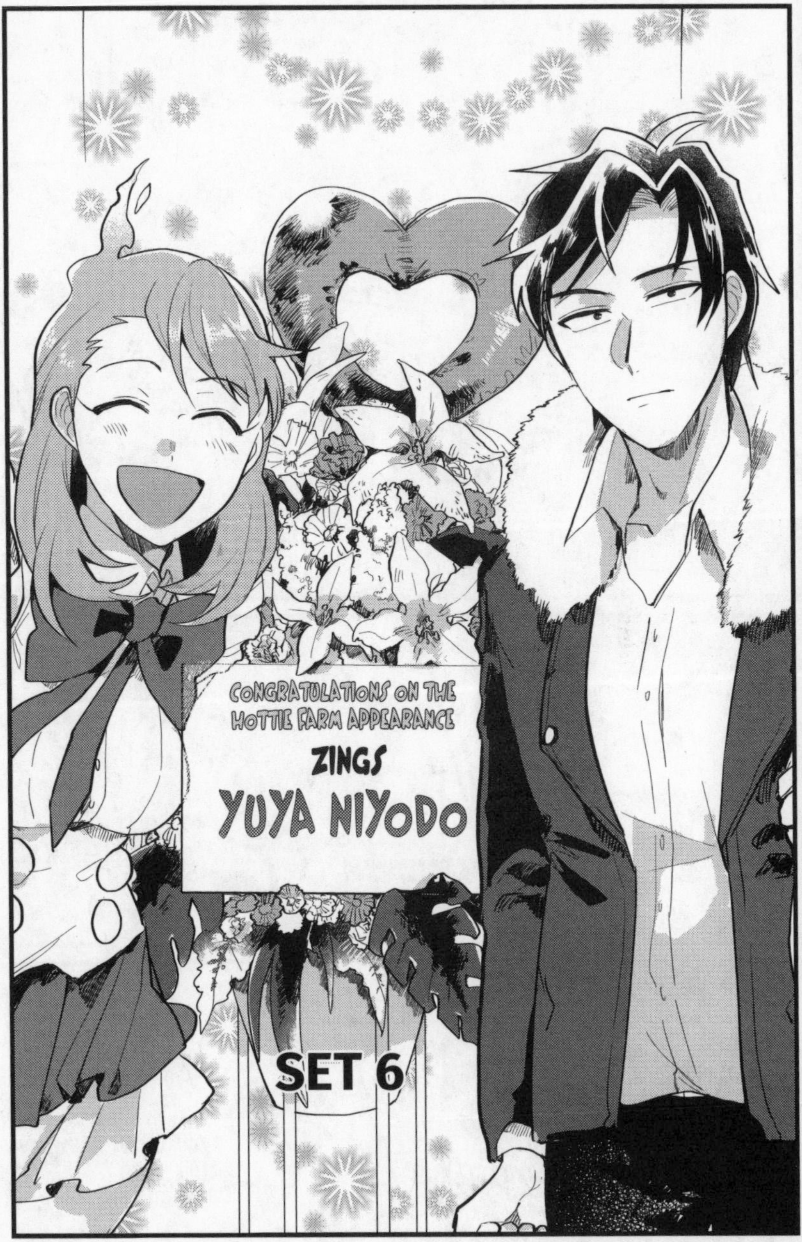
CONGRATULATIONS ON THE
HOTTIE FARM APPEARANCE
ZINGS
YUYA NIYODO
SET 6

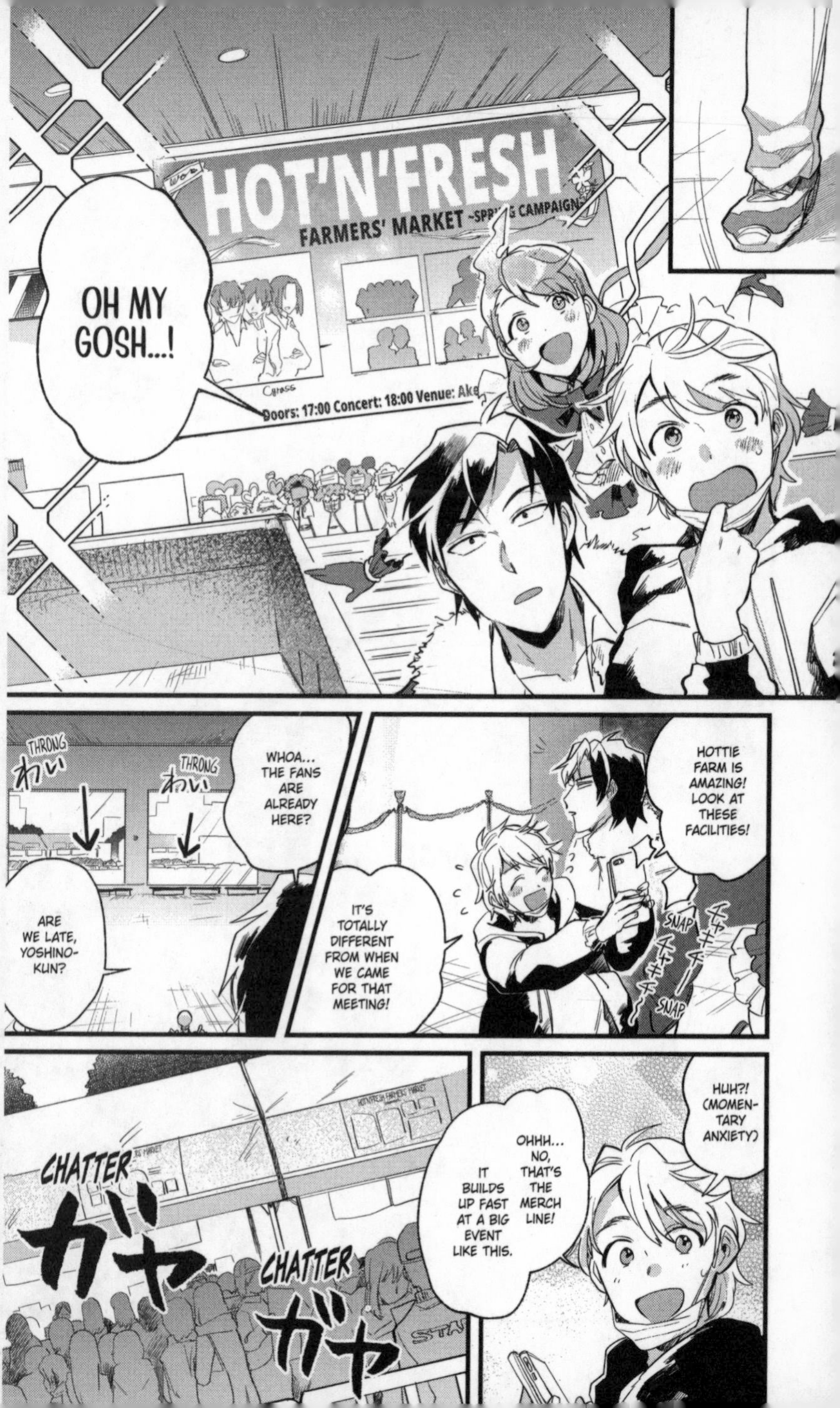
HOT'N'FRESH
FARMERS' MARKET
Doors: 17:00 Concert: 18:00 Venue: Ake
OH MY GOSH...!
HOTTIE FARM IS AMAZING! LOOK AT THESE FACILITIES!
IT'S TOTALLY DIFFERENT FROM WHEN WE CAME FOR THAT MEETING!
SNAP チャキ SNAP チャキ
WHOA... THE FANS ARE ALREADY HERE?
THRONG わい
THRONG わい
ARE WE LATE, YOSHINO-KUN?
HUH?! (MOMENTARY ANXIETY)
OHHH... NO, THAT'S THE MERCH LINE!
IT BUILDS UP FAST AT A BIG EVENT LIKE THIS.
CHATTER ガヤ
CHATTER ガヤ

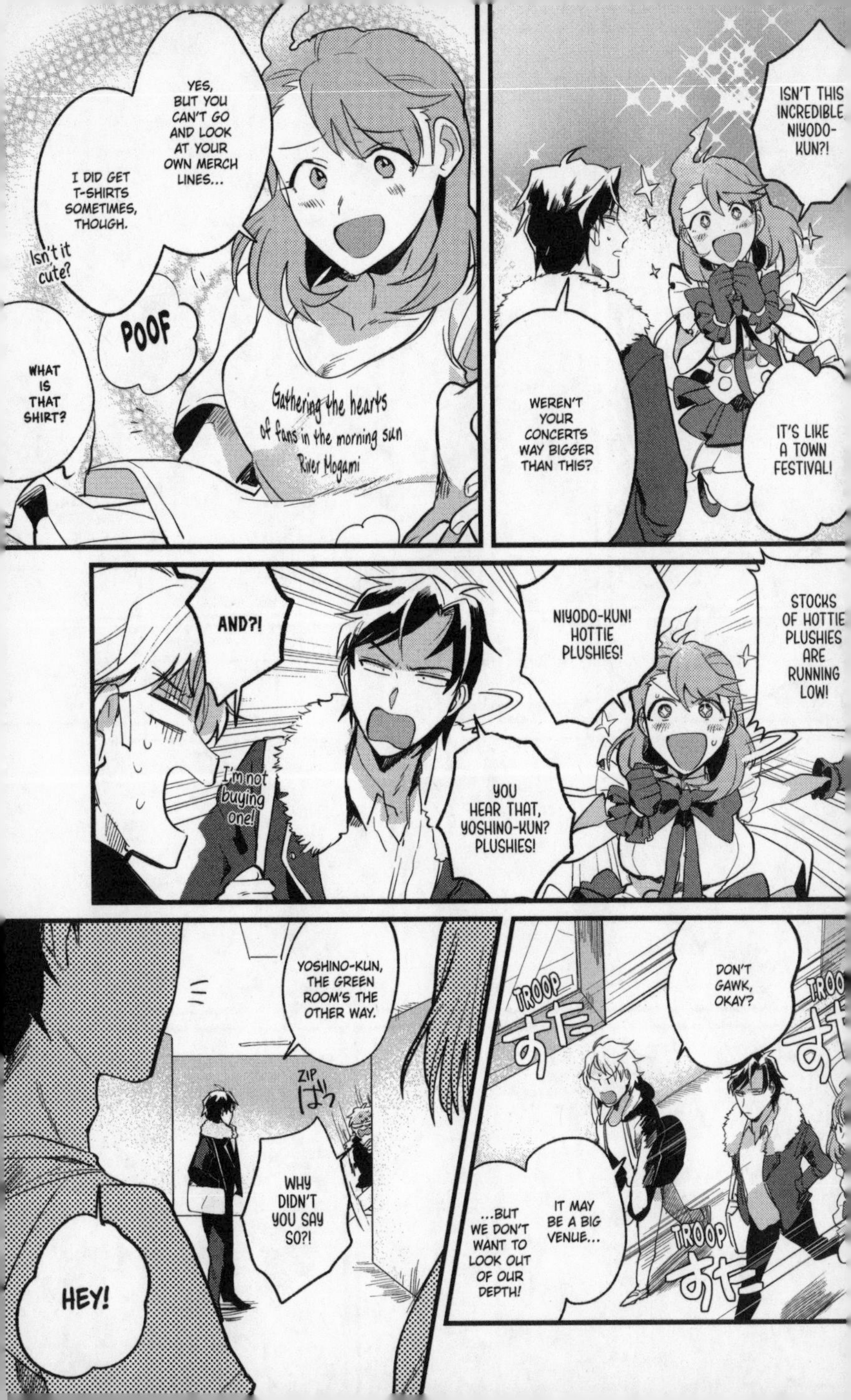
ISN'T THIS INCREDIBLE NIYODO-KUN?!
IT'S LIKE A TOWN FESTIVAL!
WEREN'T YOUR CONCERTS WAY BIGGER THAN THIS?
YES, BUT YOU CAN'T GO AND LOOK AT YOUR OWN MERCH LINES...
I DID GET T-SHIRTS SOMETIMES, THOUGH.
Isn't it cute?
POOF
Gathering the hearts of fans in the morning sun River Mogami
WHAT IS THAT SHIRT?
STOCKS OF HOTTIE PLUSHIES ARE RUNNING LOW!
NIYODO-KUN! HOTTIE PLUSHIES!
YOU HEAR THAT, YOSHINO-KUN? PLUSHIES!
AND?!
I'm not buying one!
DON'T GAWK, OKAY?
TROOP
IT MAY BE A BIG VENUE...
...BUT WE DON'T WANT TO LOOK OUT OF OUR DEPTH!
TROOP
YOSHINO-KUN, THE GREEN ROOM'S THE OTHER WAY.
ZIP
ばっ
WHY DIDN'T YOU SAY SO?!
HEY!

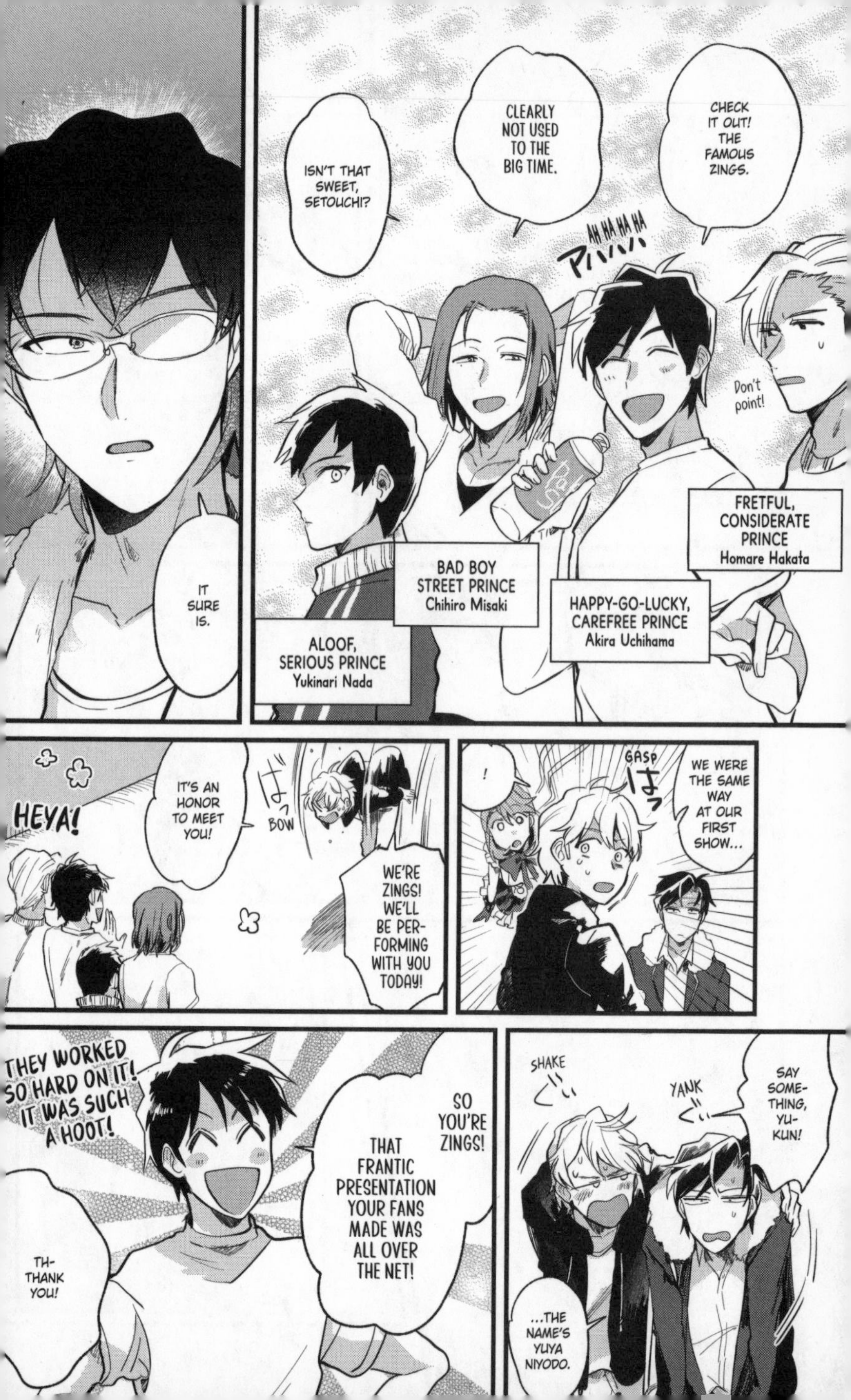
CHECK IT OUT! THE FAMOUS ZINGS.
CLEARLY NOT USED TO THE BIG TIME.
ISN'T THAT SWEET, SETOUCHI!?
AH HA HA HA
アハハ
Don't point!
FRETFUL, CONSIDERATE PRINCE Homare Hakata
BAD BOY STREET PRINCE Chihiro Misaki
HAPPY-GO-LUCKY, CAREFREE PRINCE Akira Uchihama
ALOOF, SERIOUS PRINCE Yukinari Nada
IT SURE IS.
WE WERE THE SAME WAY AT OUR FIRST SHOW...
GASP
はっ
!
IT'S AN HONOR TO MEET YOU!
ばっ
BOW
HEYA!
WE'RE ZINGS! WE'LL BE PERFORMING WITH YOU TODAY!
SAY SOMETHING, YU-KUN!
YANK
ぐい
SHAKE
ぐい
...THE NAME'S YUYA NIYODO.
SO YOU'RE ZINGS!
THAT FRANTIC PRESENTATION YOUR FANS MADE WAS ALL OVER THE NET!
THEY WORKED SO HARD ON IT! IT WAS SUCH A HOOT!
TH-THANK YOU!

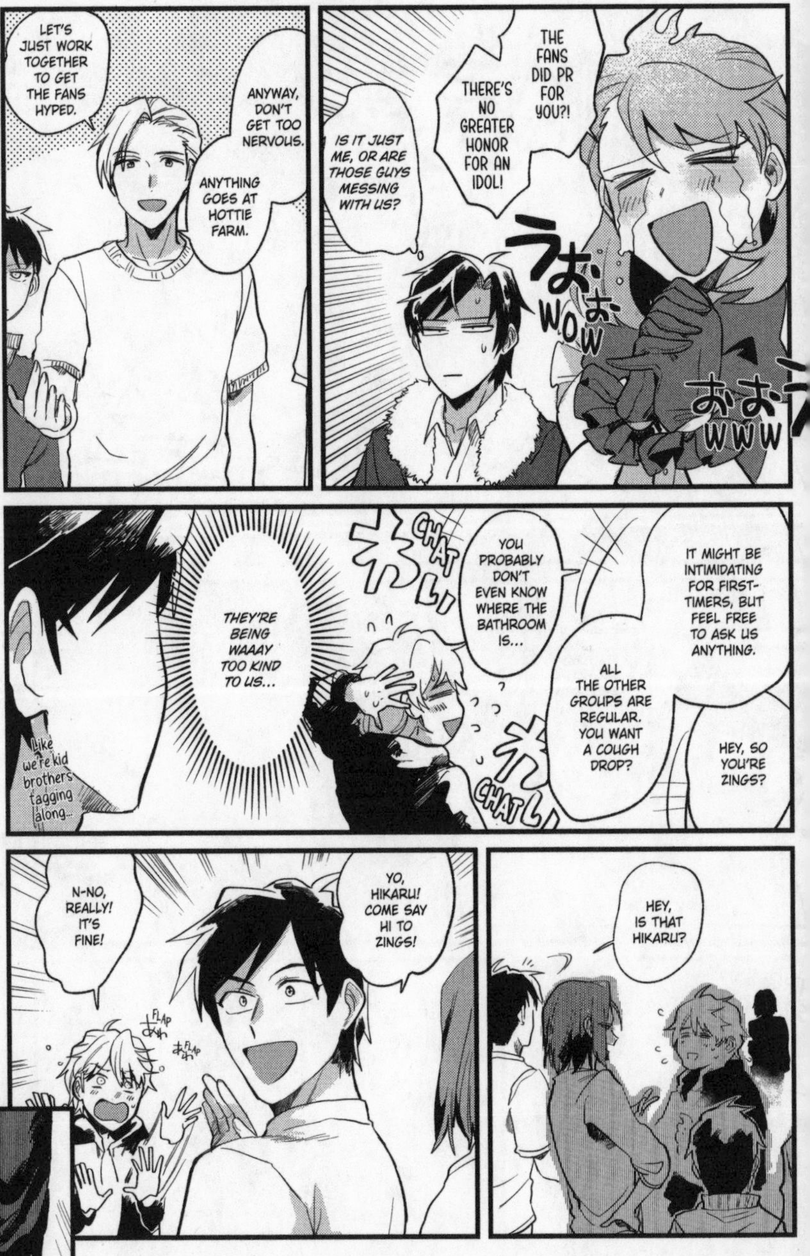
THE FANS DID PR FOR YOU?!
THERE'S NO GREATER HONOR FOR AN IDOL!
IS IT JUST ME, OR ARE THOSE GUYS MESSING WITH US?
うぉぉ WOW
おおう WWW
ANYWAY, DON'T GET TOO NERVOUS.
ANYTHING GOES AT HOTTIE FARM.
LET'S JUST WORK TOGETHER TO GET THE FANS HYPED.
IT MIGHT BE INTIMIDATING FOR FIRST-TIMERS, BUT FEEL FREE TO ASK US ANYTHING.
HEY, SO YOU'RE ZINGS?
YOU PROBABLY DON'T EVEN KNOW WHERE THE BATHROOM IS...
ALL THE OTHER GROUPS ARE REGULAR. YOU WANT A COUGH DROP?
わい CHAT
わい CHAT
THEY'RE BEING WAAAY TOO KIND TO US...
Like we're kid brothers tagging along...
HEY, IS THAT HIKARU?
YO, HIKARU! COME SAY HI TO ZINGS!
N-NO, REALLY! IT'S FINE!
あわ FLAP
あわ FLAP

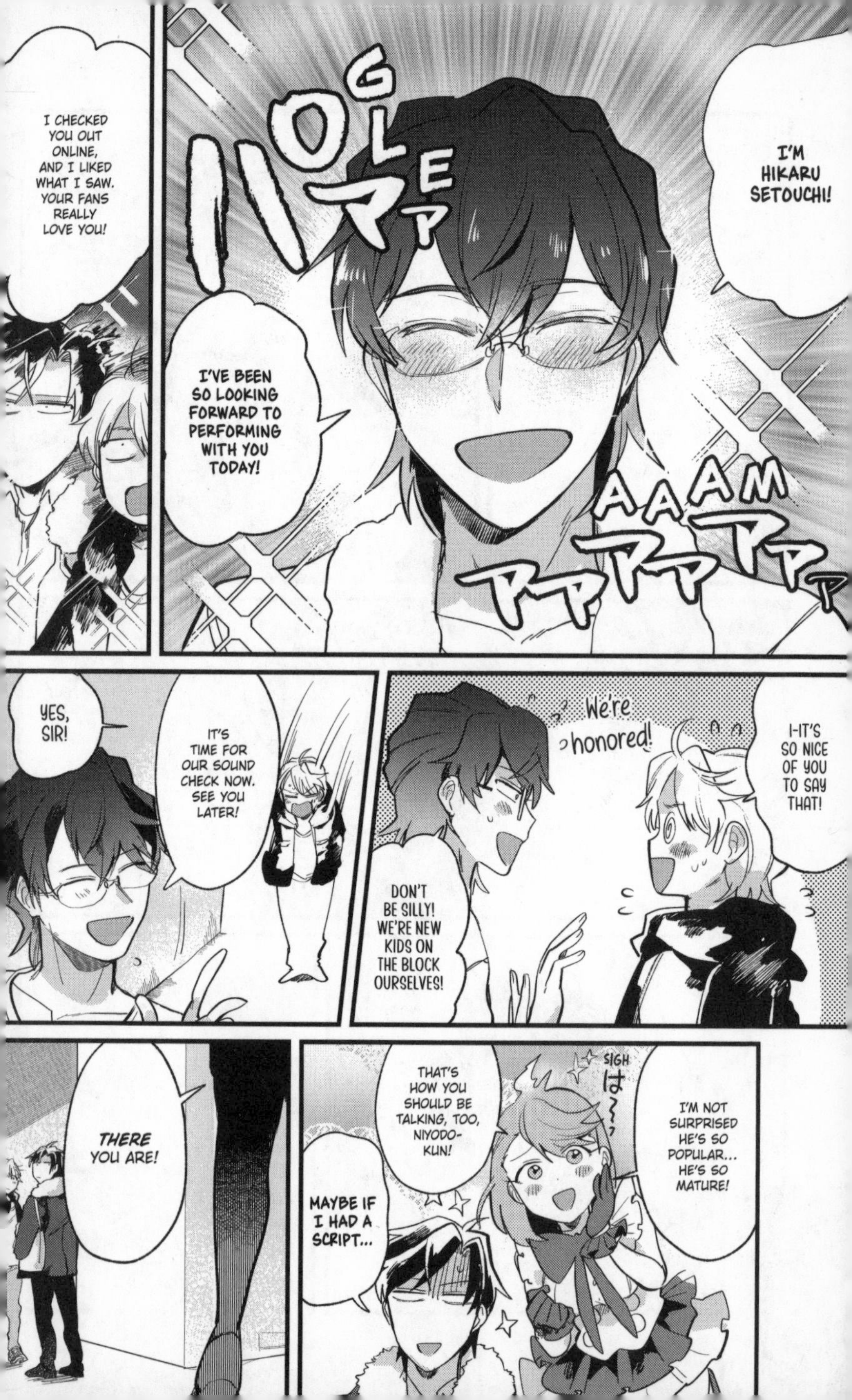
I'M HIKARU SETOUCHI!
I'VE BEEN SO LOOKING FORWARD TO PERFORMING WITH YOU TODAY!
I CHECKED YOU OUT ONLINE, AND I LIKED WHAT I SAW. YOUR FANS REALLY LOVE YOU!
I-IT'S SO NICE OF YOU TO SAY THAT!
We're honored!
DON'T BE SILLY! WE'RE NEW KIDS ON THE BLOCK OURSELVES!
IT'S TIME FOR OUR SOUND CHECK NOW. SEE YOU LATER!
YES, SIR!
I'M NOT SURPRISED HE'S SO POPULAR... HE'S SO MATURE!
SIGH
THAT'S HOW YOU SHOULD BE TALKING, TOO, NIYODO-KUN!
MAYBE IF I HAD A SCRIPT...
THERE YOU ARE!

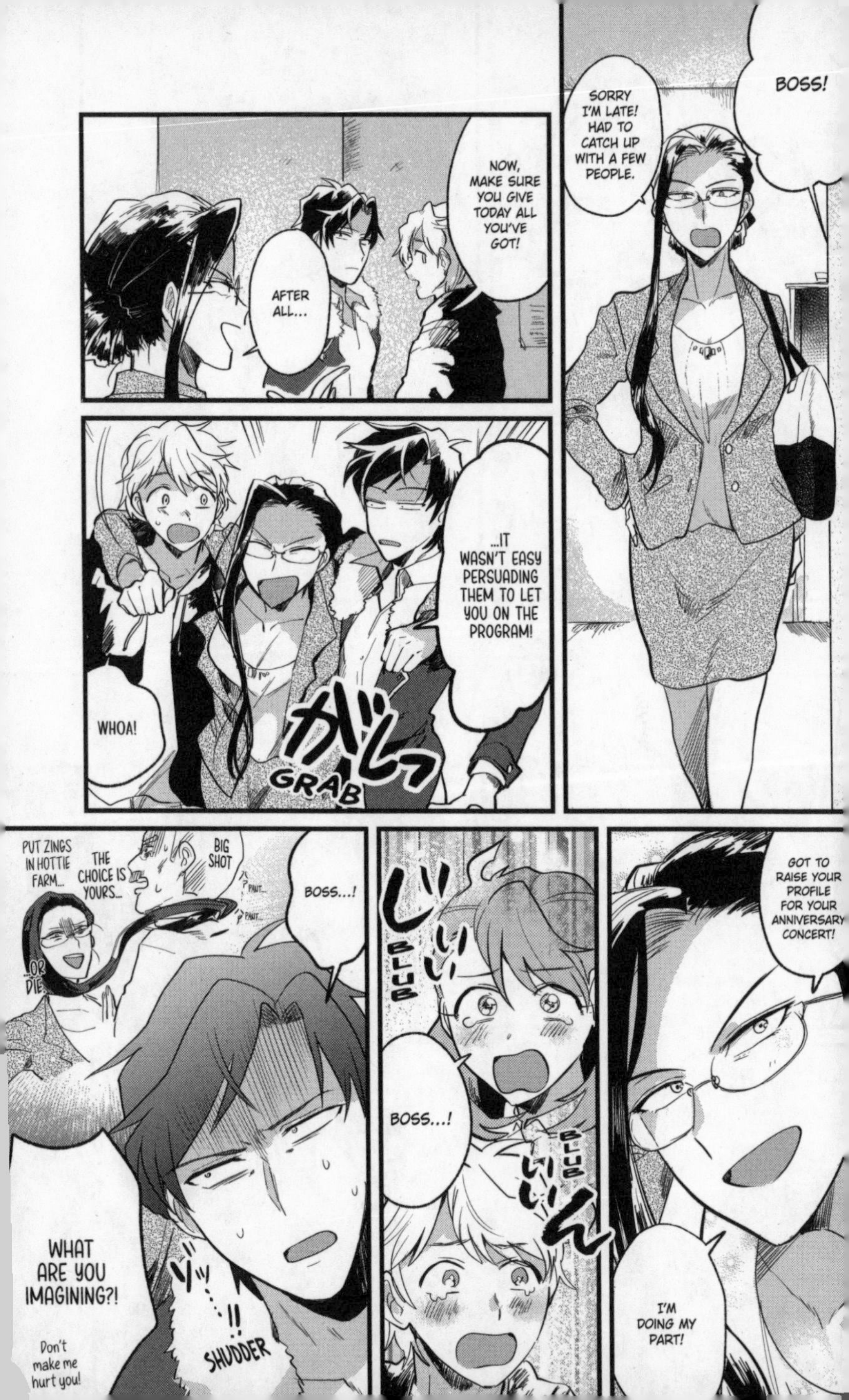
BOSS!
SORRY I'M LATE! HAD TO CATCH UP WITH A FEW PEOPLE.
NOW, MAKE SURE YOU GIVE TODAY ALL YOU'VE GOT!
AFTER ALL...
...IT WASN'T EASY PERSUADING THEM TO LET YOU ON THE PROGRAM!
がしっ
GRAB
WHOA!
GOT TO RAISE YOUR PROFILE FOR YOUR ANNIVERSARY CONCERT!
I'M DOING MY PART!
BLUB
BOSS...!
BLUB
BOSS...!
BIG SHOT
THE CHOICE IS YOURS...
PUT ZINGS IN HOTTIE FARM...
...OR DIE
PANT...
PANT...
WHAT ARE YOU IMAGINING?!
...!!
SHUDDER
Don't make me hurt you!

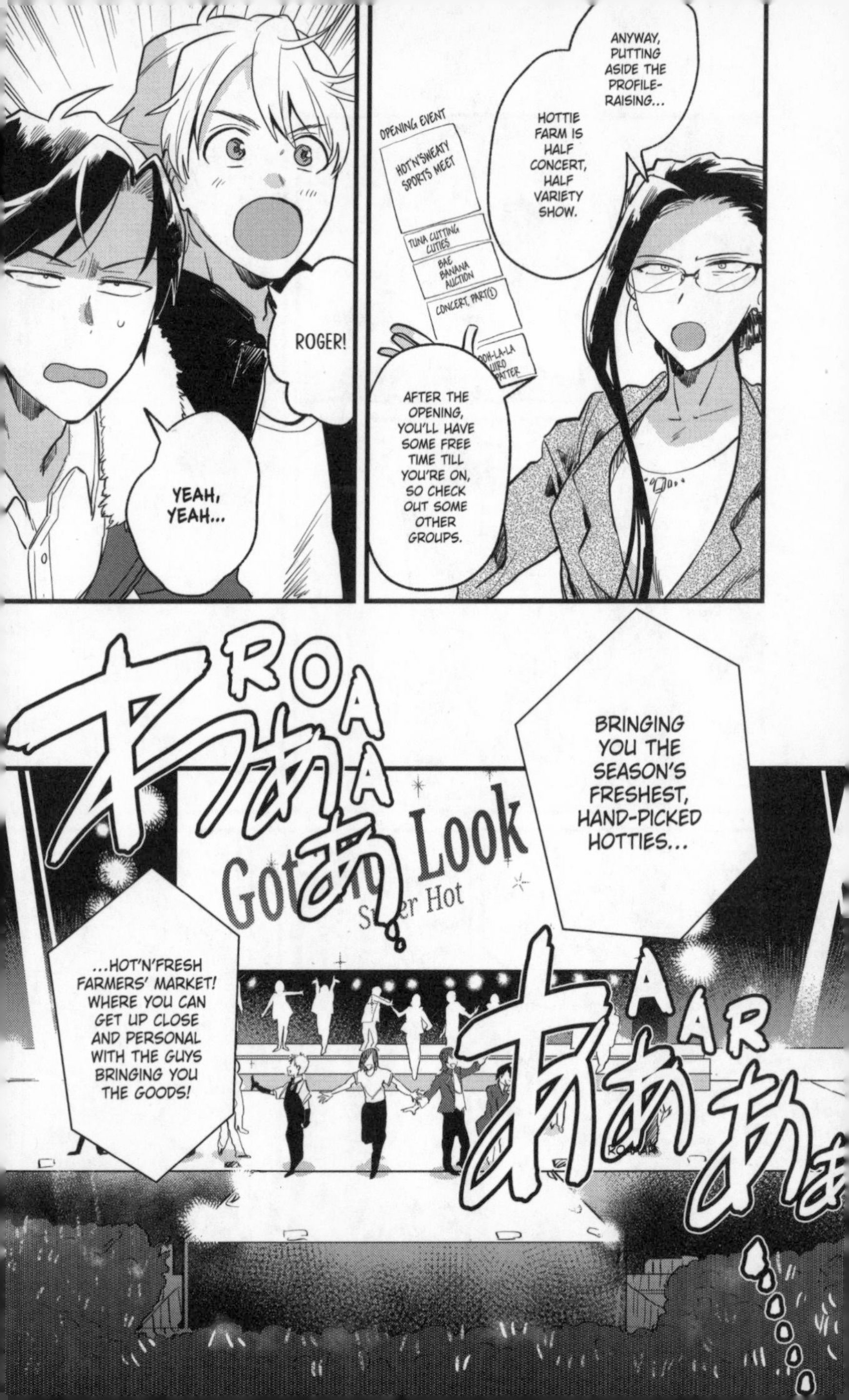
ANYWAY, PUTTING ASIDE THE PROFILE-RAISING...
HOTTIE FARM IS HALF CONCERT, HALF VARIETY SHOW.
OPENING EVENT
HOT'N'SWEATY SPORTS MEET
TUNA CUTTING CUTIES
BAE BANANA AUCTION
CONCERT, PART①
AFTER THE OPENING, YOU'LL HAVE SOME FREE TIME TILL YOU'RE ON, SO CHECK OUT SOME OTHER GROUPS.
ROGER!
YEAH, YEAH...
BRINGING YOU THE SEASON'S FRESHEST, HAND-PICKED HOTTIES...
ROAA
Look
...HOT'N'FRESH FARMERS' MARKET! WHERE YOU CAN GET UP CLOSE AND PERSONAL WITH THE GUYS BRINGING YOU THE GOODS!
AAR

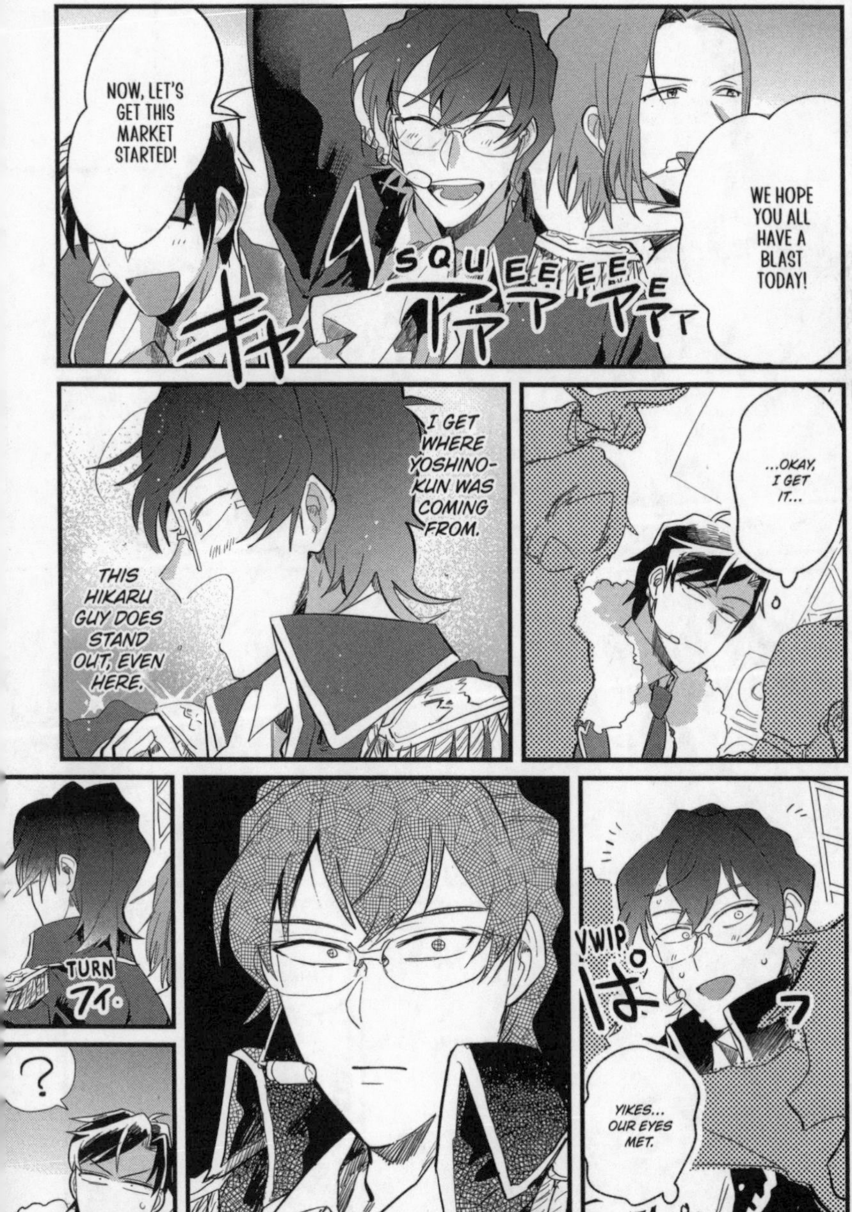
WE HOPE YOU ALL HAVE A BLAST TODAY!
NOW, LET'S GET THIS MARKET STARTED!
SQUEEEEEEE
キャアアアアアア
...OKAY, I GET IT...
I GET WHERE YOSHINO-KUN WAS COMING FROM.
THIS HIKARU GUY DOES STAND OUT, EVEN HERE.
VWIP
ぱっ
YIKES... OUR EYES MET.
TURN
フイ。
?

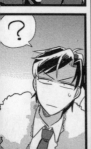

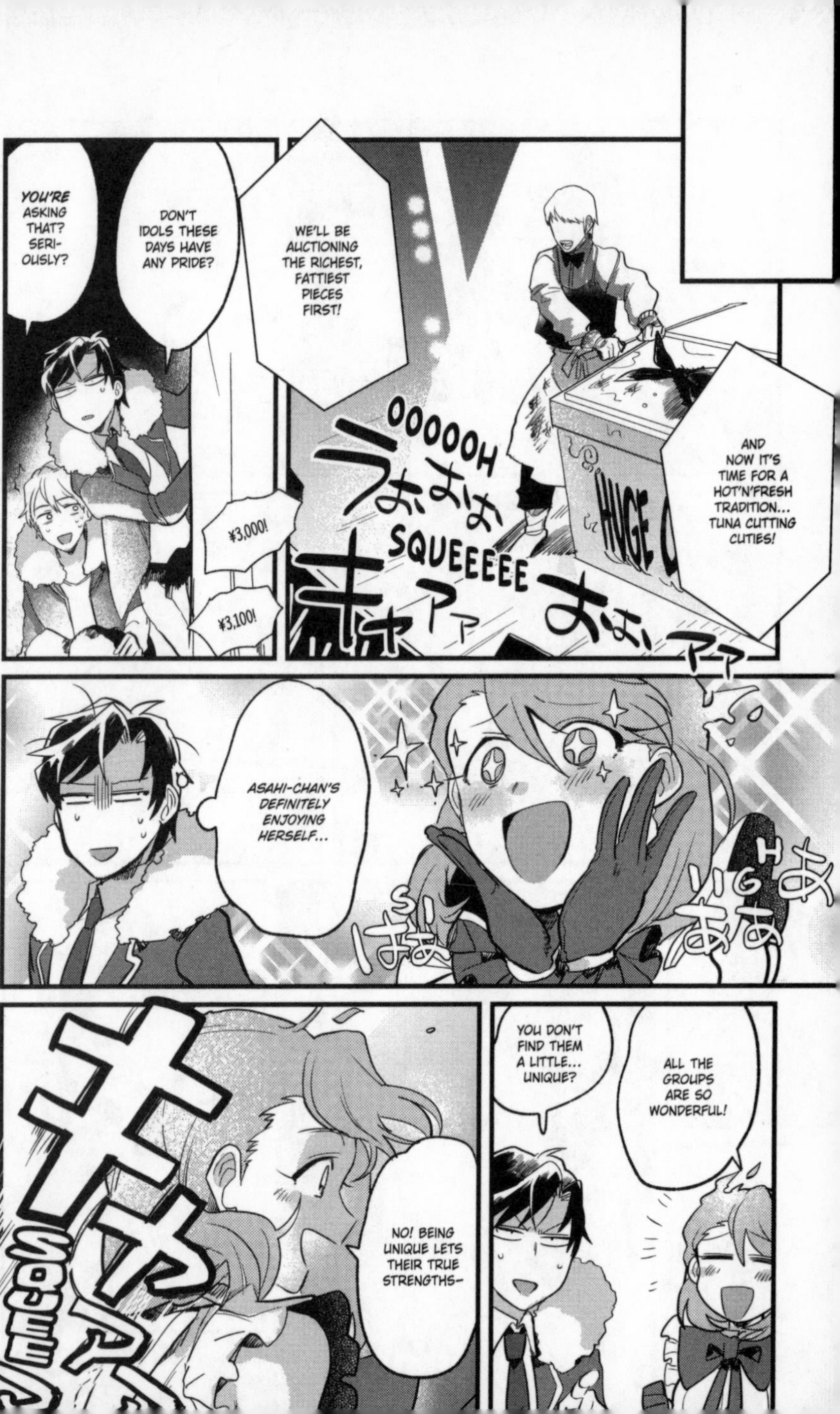
AND NOW IT'S TIME FOR A HOT'N'FRESH TRADITION... TUNA CUTTING CUTIES!
WE'LL BE AUCTIONING THE RICHEST, FATTIEST PIECES FIRST!
OOOOOH
SQUEEEEE
HUGE C
DON'T IDOLS THESE DAYS HAVE ANY PRIDE?
YOU'RE ASKING THAT? SERIOUSLY?
¥3,000!
¥3,100!
ASAHI-CHAN'S DEFINITELY ENJOYING HERSELF...
ALL THE GROUPS ARE SO WONDERFUL!
YOU DON'T FIND THEM A LITTLE... UNIQUE?
NO! BEING UNIQUE LETS THEIR TRUE STRENGTHS-

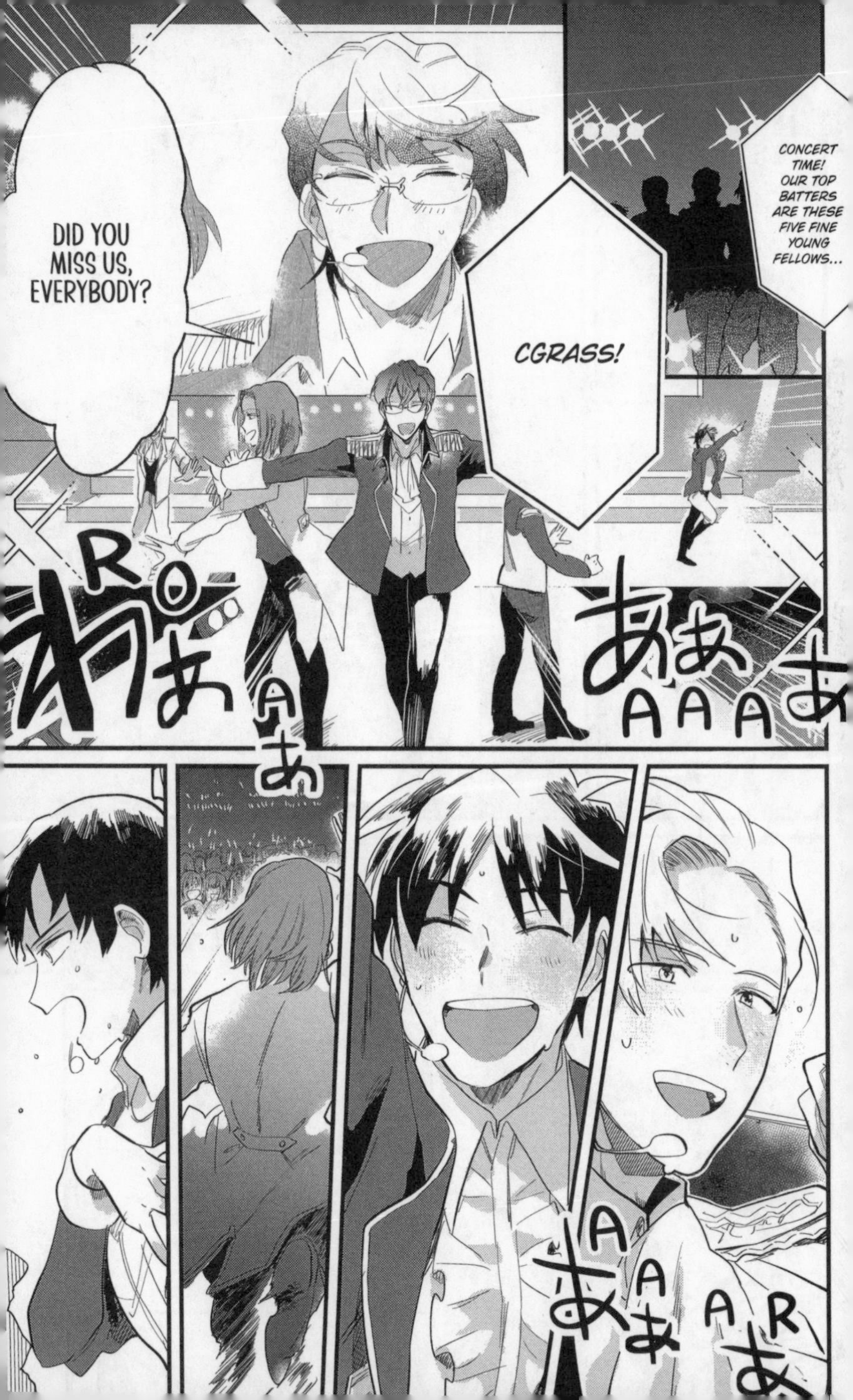

CONCERT TIME! OUR TOP BATTERS ARE THESE FIVE FINE YOUNG FELLOWS...
CGRASS!
DID YOU MISS US, EVERYBODY?

WAAAAA
わぁ あぁ あぁ

EEEK! SETO-UCHI-KUN!

YOU'RE NEXT IN LINE TO INHERIT MY SOUL!

?

I CAN'T BELIEVE WE'RE SEEING CGRASS WITHOUT EVEN BUYING TICKETS...

SWOOON

WAIT!

HOW LONG AM I GONNA STAND HERE LIKE AN AUDIENCE MEMBER?!

I'VE GOT TO GET IT TOGETHER.

SHAKE

SHAKE

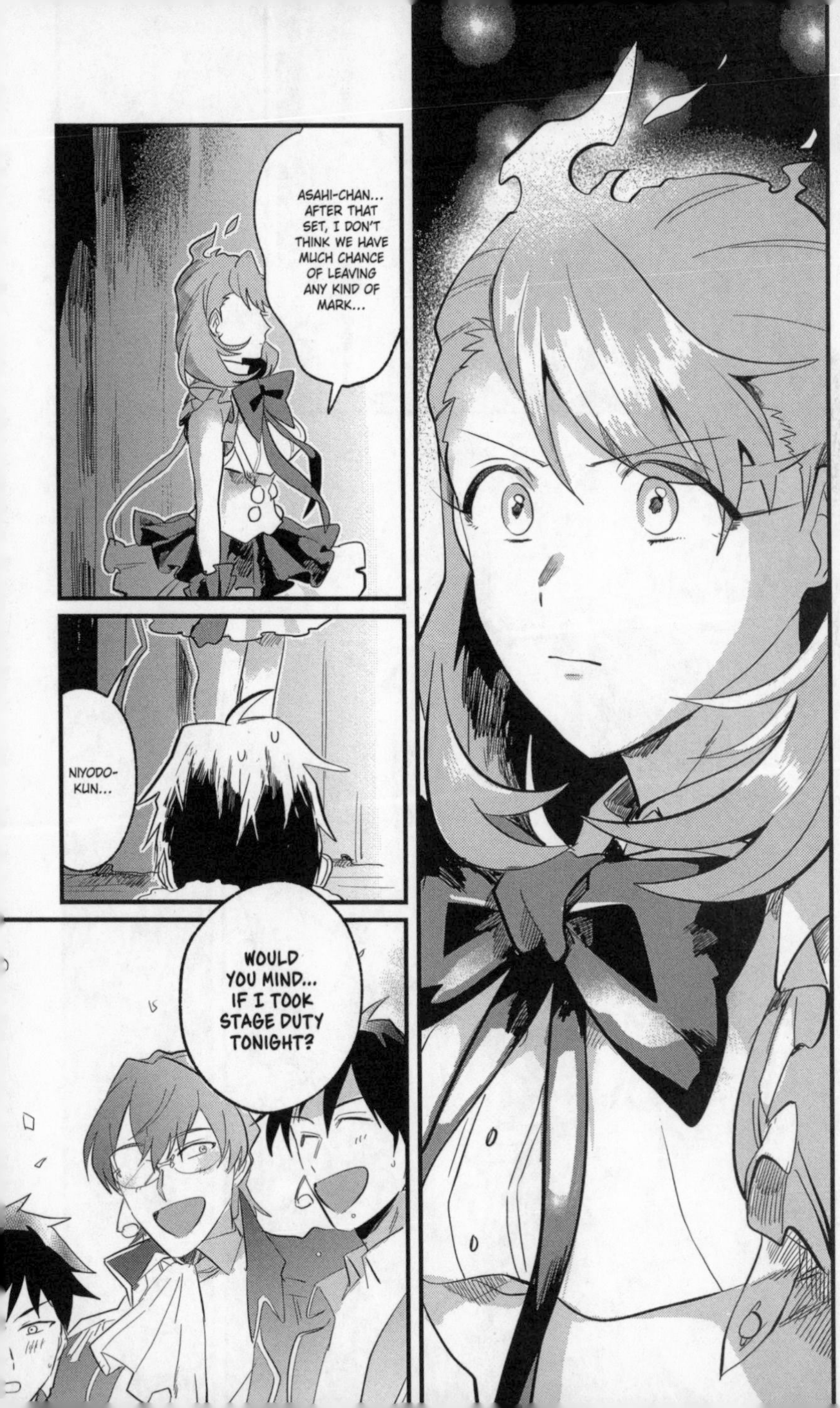
ASAHI-CHAN... AFTER THAT SET, I DON'T THINK WE HAVE MUCH CHANCE OF LEAVING ANY KIND OF MARK...
NIYODO-KUN...
WOULD YOU MIND... IF I TOOK STAGE DUTY TONIGHT?

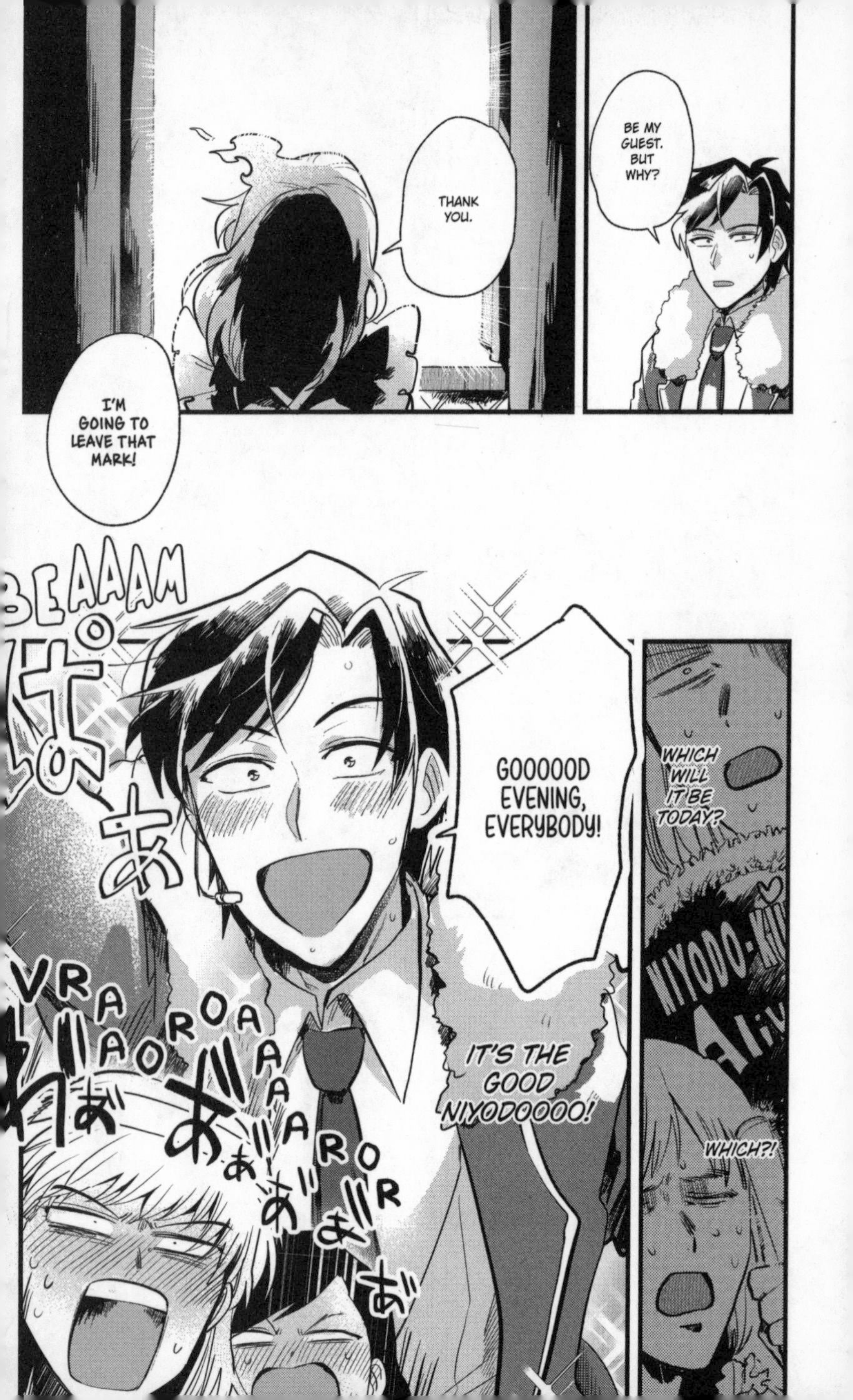
BE MY GUEST. BUT WHY?
THANK YOU.
I'M GOING TO LEAVE THAT MARK!
WHICH WILL IT BE TODAY?
WHICH?!
BEAAAM
GOOOOOD EVENING, EVERYBODY!
IT'S THE GOOD NIYODOOOOO!

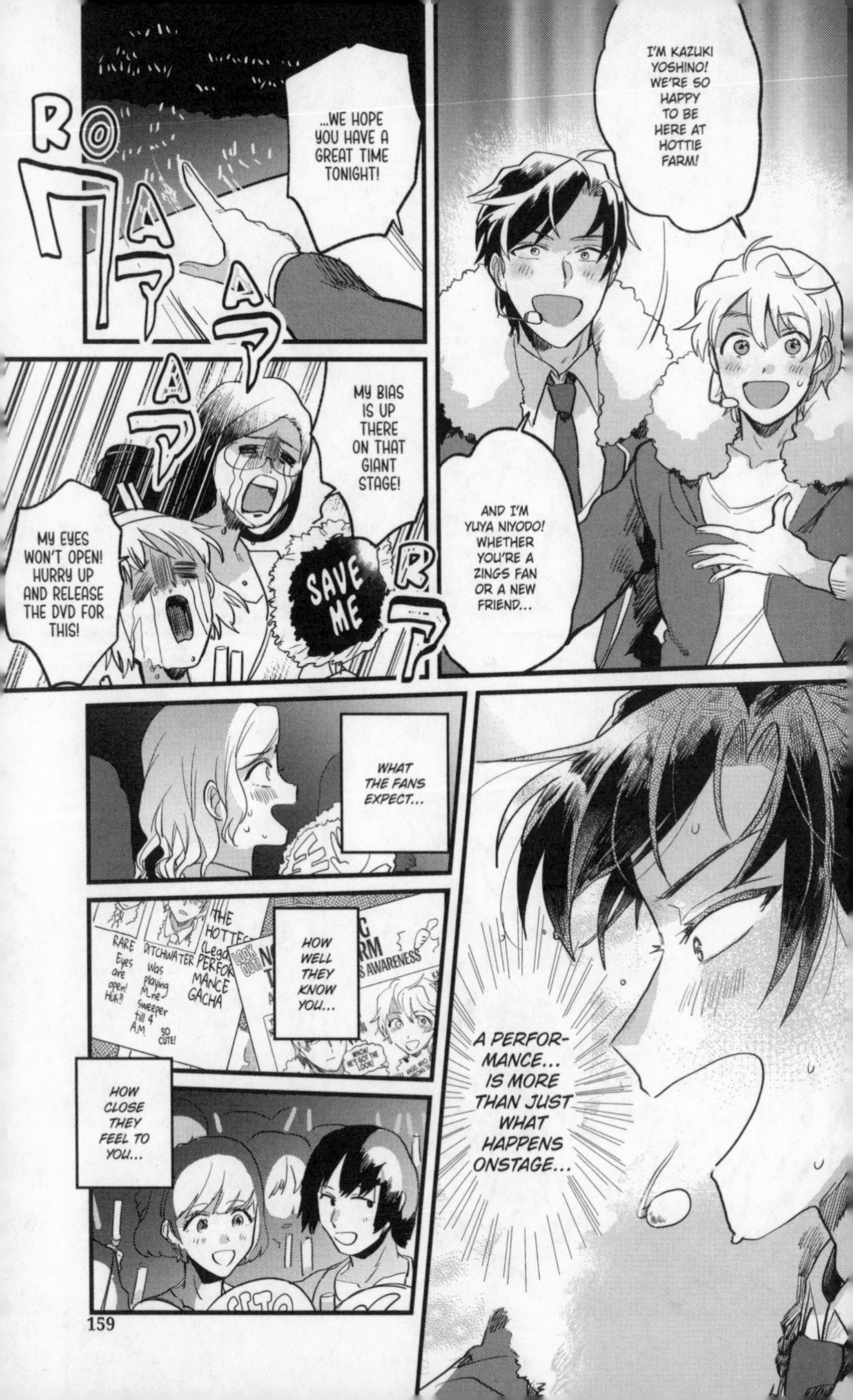
I'M KAZUKI YOSHINO! WE'RE SO HAPPY TO BE HERE AT HOTTIE FARM!
AND I'M YUYA NIYODO! WHETHER YOU'RE A ZINGS FAN OR A NEW FRIEND...
...WE HOPE YOU HAVE A GREAT TIME TONIGHT!
ROAAAR
MY BIAS IS UP THERE ON THAT GIANT STAGE!
SAVE ME
MY EYES WON'T OPEN! HURRY UP AND RELEASE THE DVD FOR THIS!
A PERFORMANCE... IS MORE THAN JUST WHAT HAPPENS ONSTAGE...
WHAT THE FANS EXPECT...
HOW WELL THEY KNOW YOU...
THE HOTTEST (Legal) PERFORMANCE GACHA
RARE
Eyes are open! Huh?!
DITCHWATER
Was playing M_ne sweeper till 4 A.M.
SO CUTE!
LOOK OUT
WHOA! HE'S GOT THE LOOK!
HOW CLOSE THEY FEEL TO YOU...

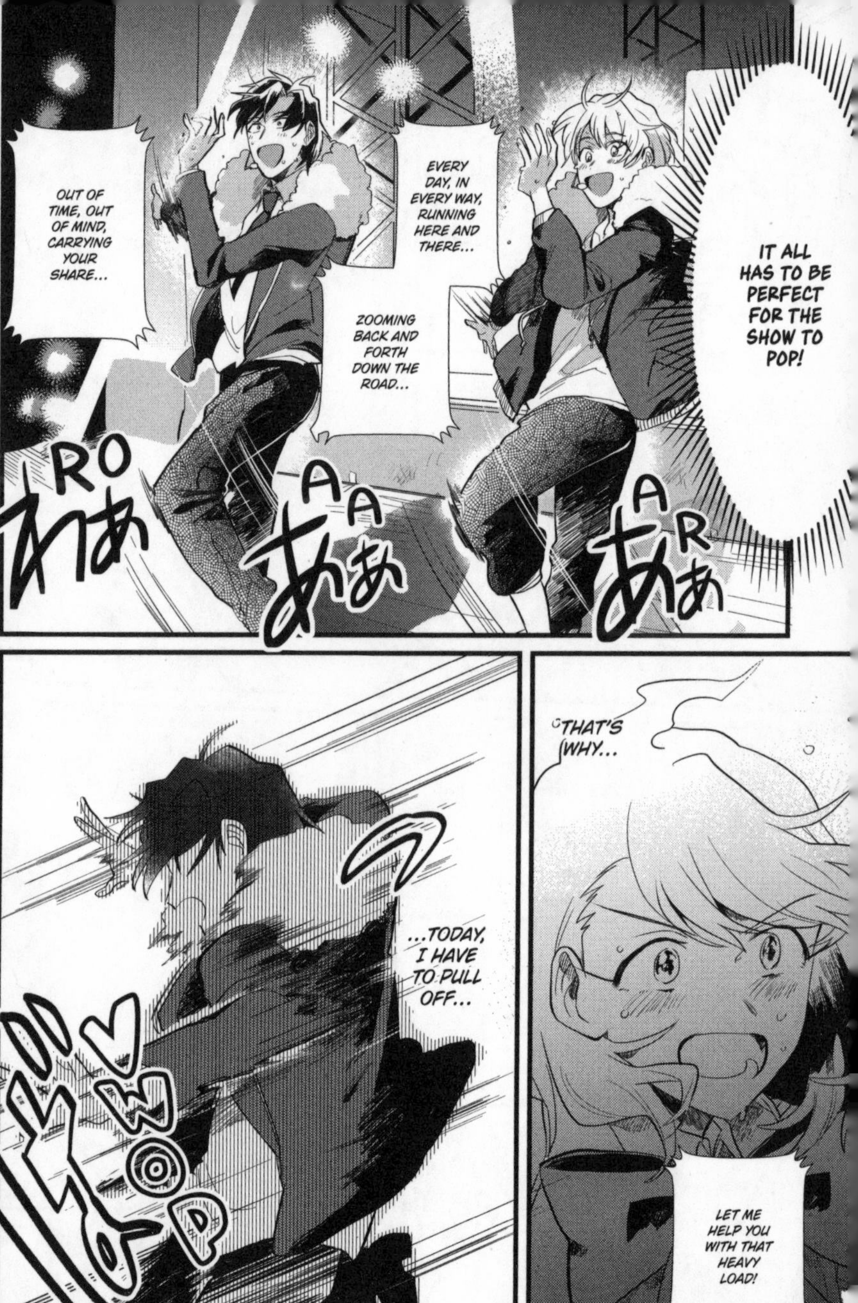
IT ALL HAS TO BE PERFECT FOR THE SHOW TO POP!
EVERY DAY, IN EVERY WAY, RUNNING HERE AND THERE...
ZOOMING BACK AND FORTH DOWN THE ROAD...
OUT OF TIME, OUT OF MIND, CARRYING YOUR SHARE...
ROAAAAR
THAT'S WHY...
LET ME HELP YOU WITH THAT HEAVY LOAD!
...TODAY, I HAVE TO PULL OFF...
WOOP

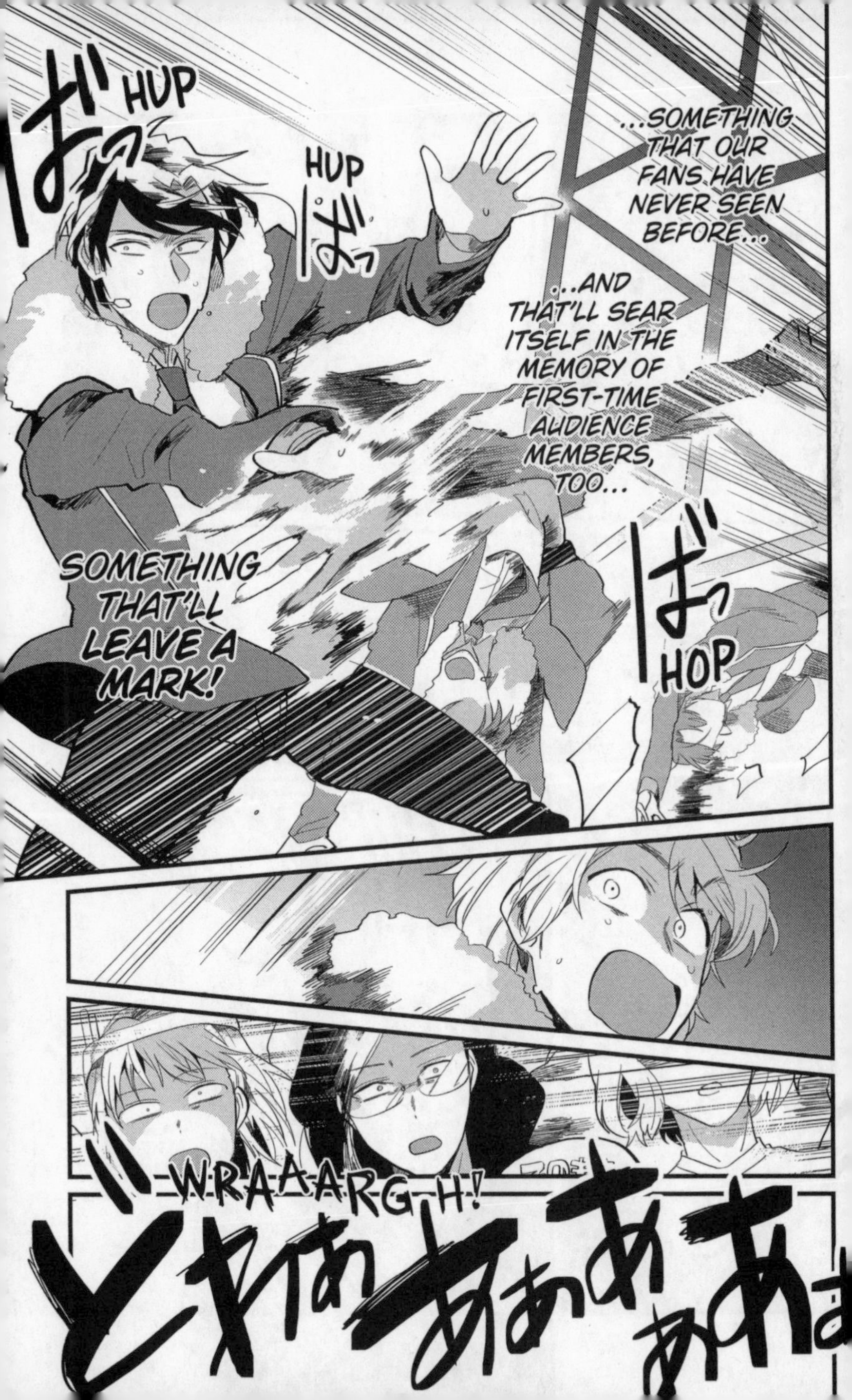

...SOMETHING THAT OUR FANS HAVE NEVER SEEN BEFORE...
...AND THAT'LL SEAR ITSELF IN THE MEMORY OF FIRST-TIME AUDIENCE MEMBERS, TOO...
ぱっ HUP
おっ HUP
ばっ HOP
SOMETHING THAT'LL LEAVE A MARK!
どわあああああ
WRAAARGH!

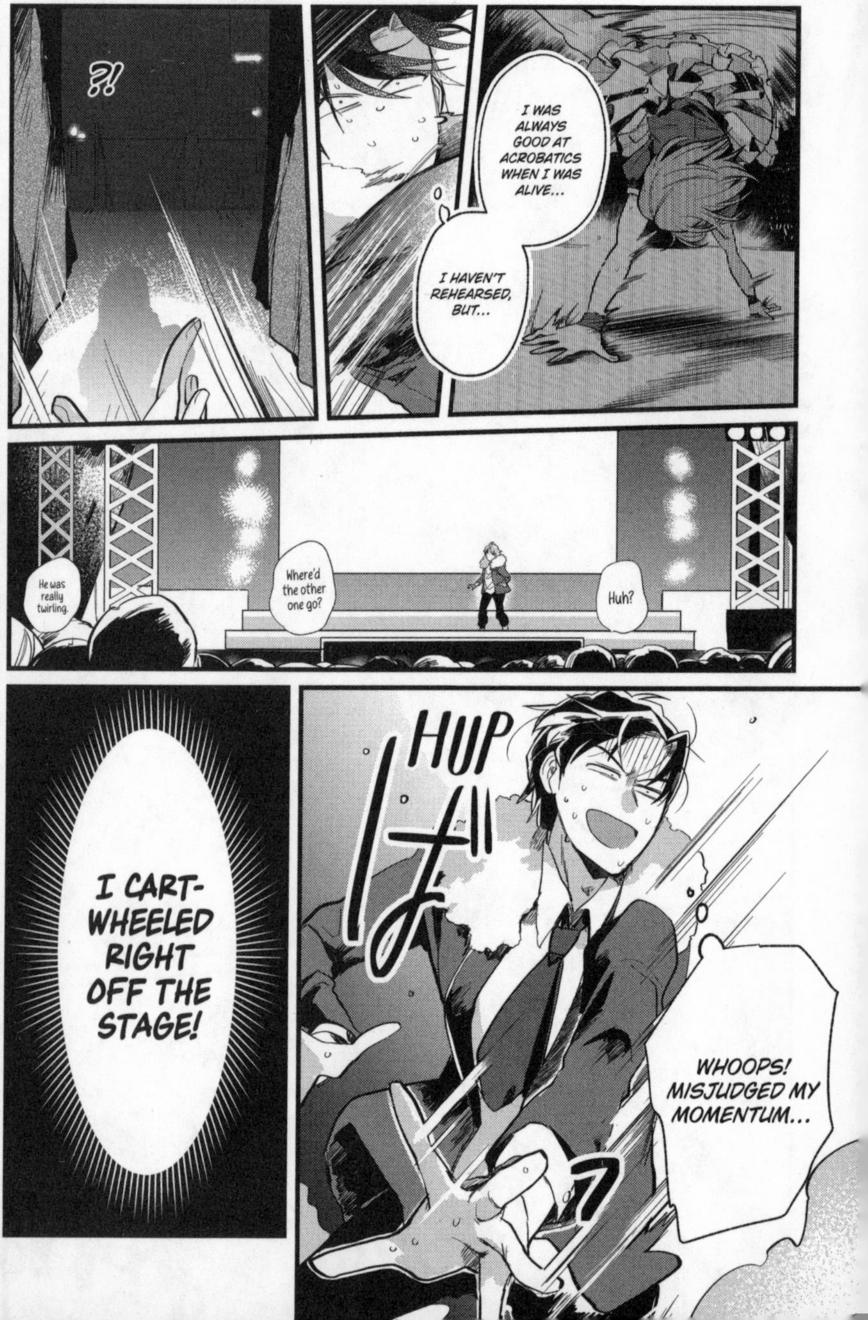

I WAS ALWAYS GOOD AT ACROBATICS WHEN I WAS ALIVE...
I HAVEN'T REHEARSED, BUT...
?!
Huh?
Where'd the other one go?
He was really twirling.
HUP
WHOOPS! MISJUDGED MY MOMENTUM...
I CART-WHEELED RIGHT OFF THE STAGE!

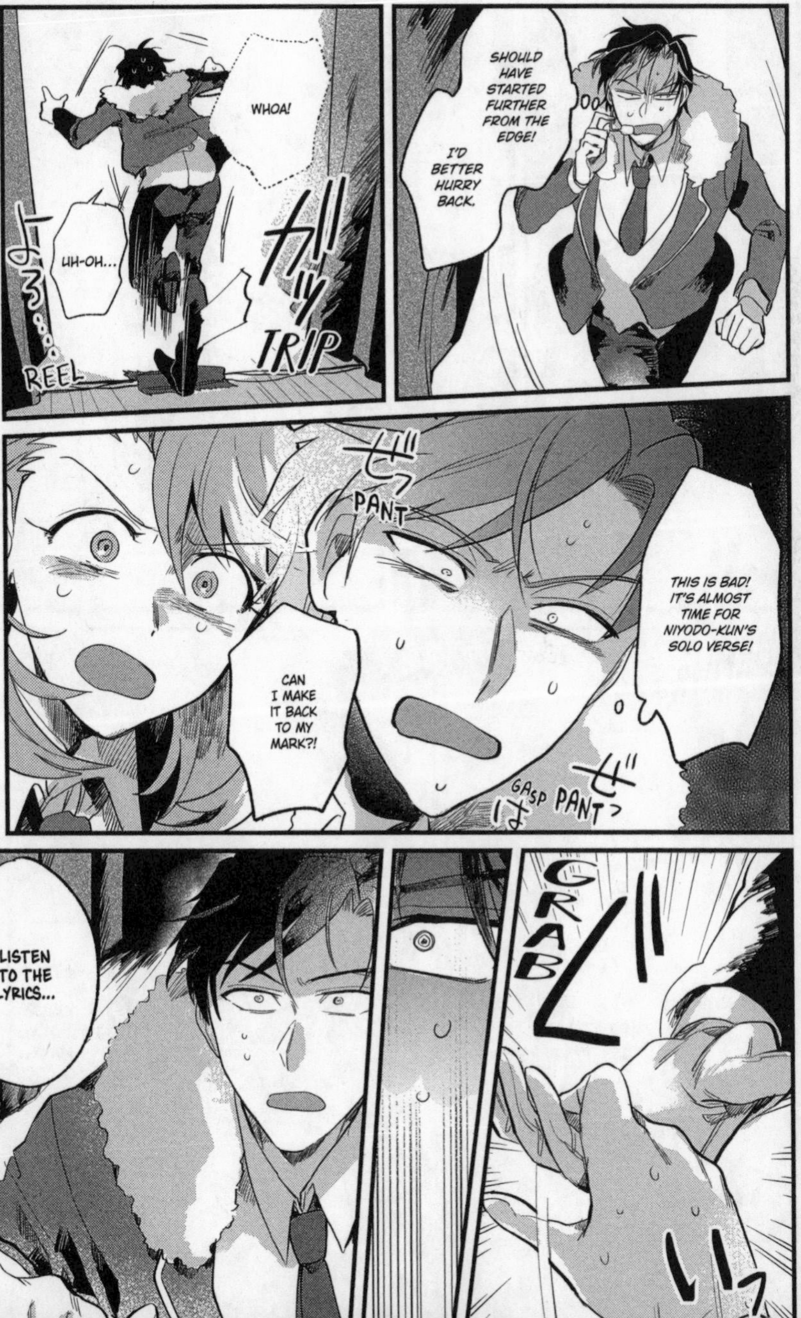
SHOULD HAVE STARTED FURTHER FROM THE EDGE!
I'D BETTER HURRY BACK.
WHOA!
ガッ
TRIP
UH-OH...
よろ...
REEL
ぜっ
PANT
THIS IS BAD! IT'S ALMOST TIME FOR NIYODO-KUN'S SOLO VERSE!
CAN I MAKE IT BACK TO MY MARK?!
ぜっ
PANT
は
GASP
ぐ
GRAB
いっ
LISTEN TO THE LYRICS...

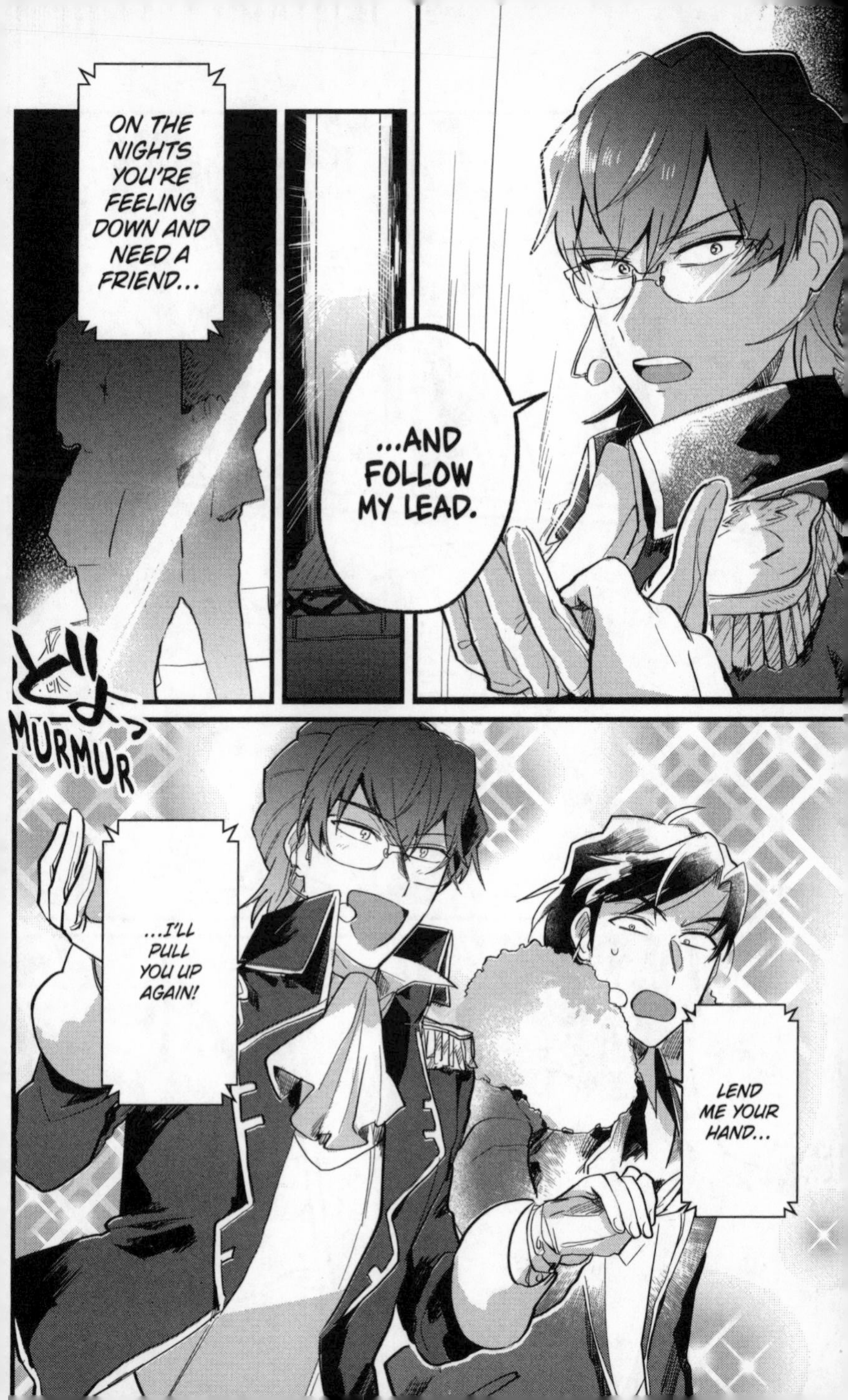
...AND FOLLOW MY LEAD.
ON THE NIGHTS YOU'RE FEELING DOWN AND NEED A FRIEND...
MURMUR
LEND ME YOUR HAND...
...I'LL PULL YOU UP AGAIN!

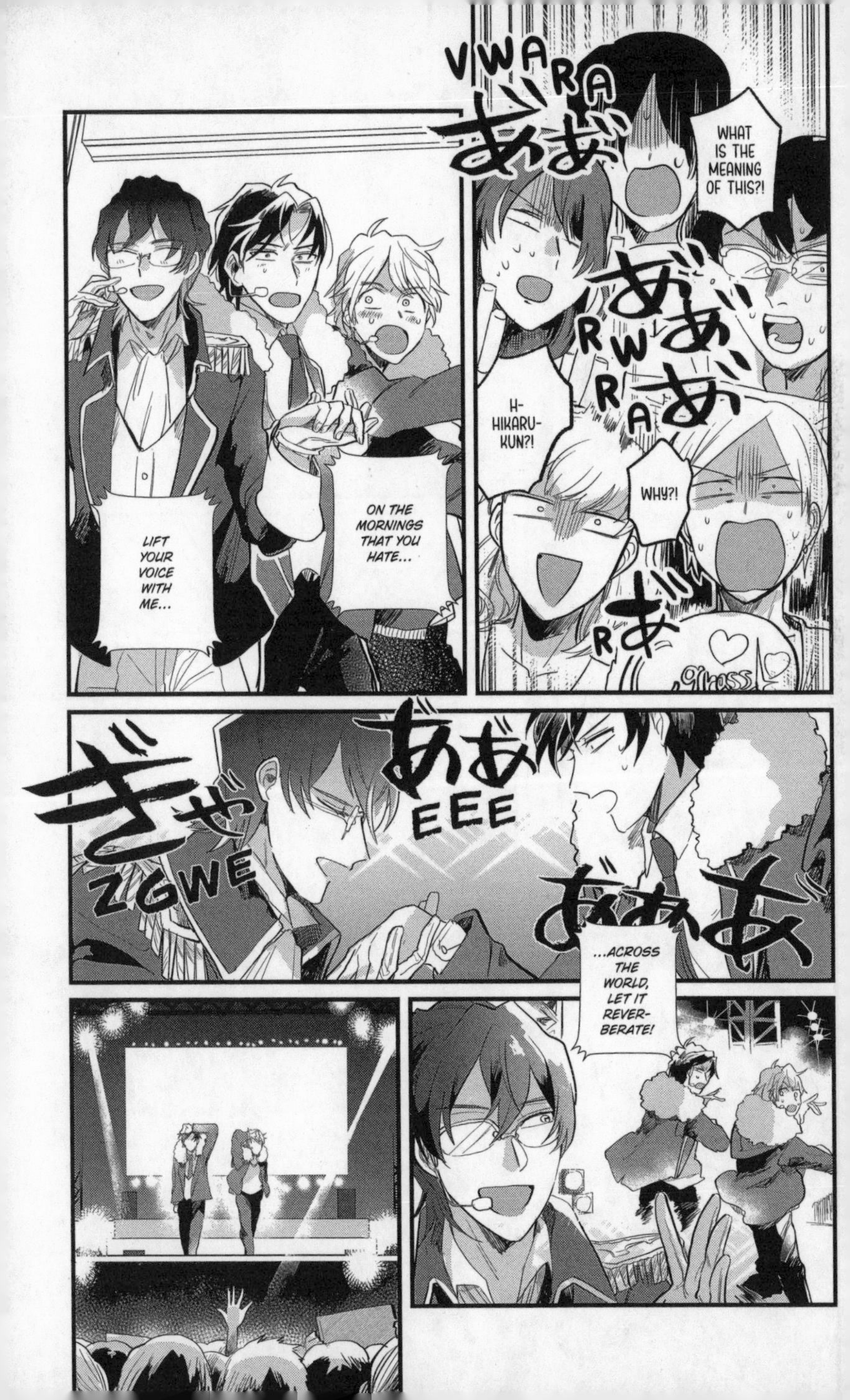
VWARA
WHAT IS THE MEANING OF THIS?!
RWRA
H-HIKARU-KUN?!
WHY?!
R
ON THE MORNINGS THAT YOU HATE...
LIFT YOUR VOICE WITH ME...
EEE
ZGWE
...ACROSS THE WORLD, LET IT REVERBERATE!

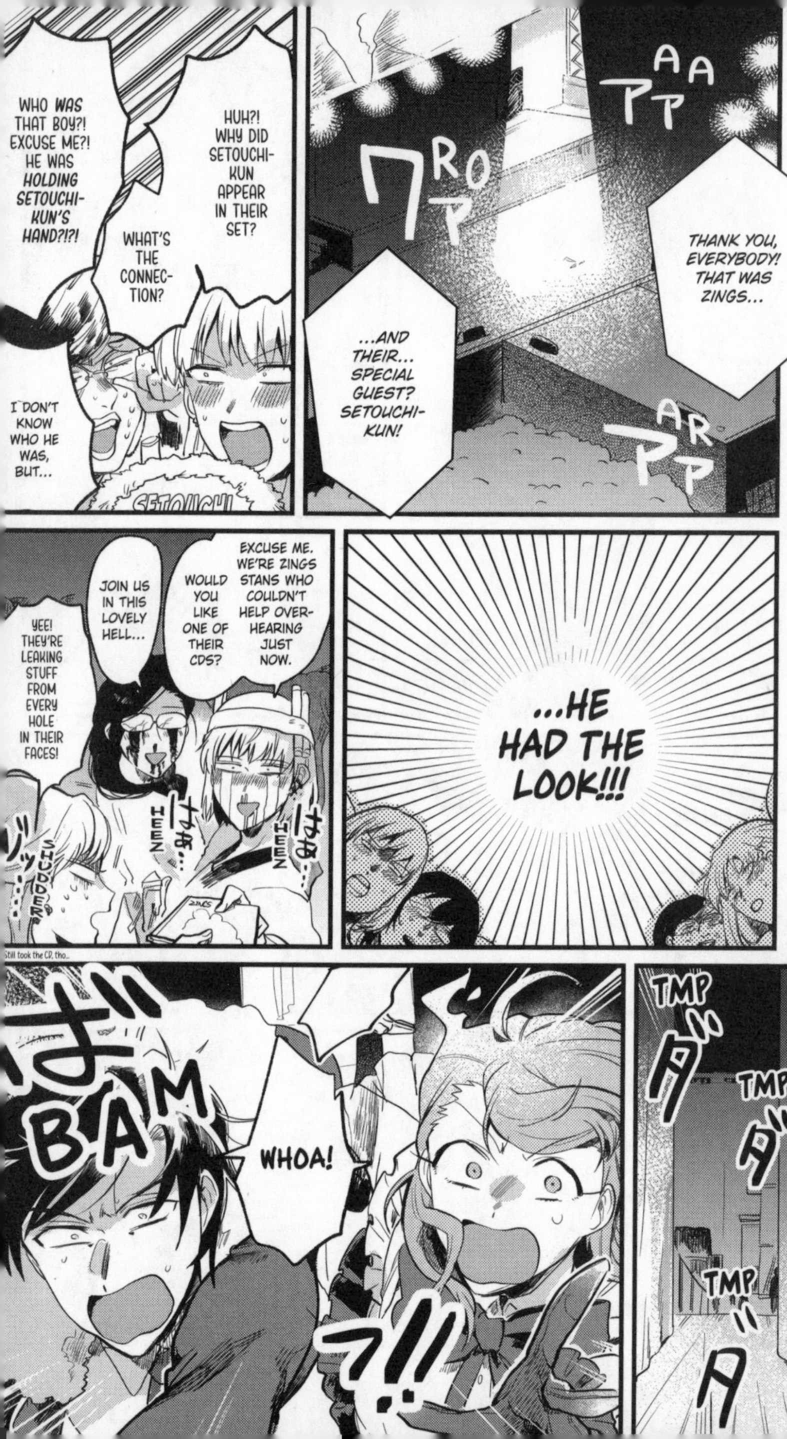
AAAA
THANK YOU, EVERYBODY! THAT WAS ZINGS...
ROAR
...AND THEIR... SPECIAL GUEST? SETOUCHI-KUN!
ARRR
HUH?! WHY DID SETOUCHI-KUN APPEAR IN THEIR SET?
WHO WAS THAT BOY?! EXCUSE ME?! HE WAS HOLDING SETOUCHI-KUN'S HAND?!?!
WHAT'S THE CONNECTION?
I DON'T KNOW WHO HE WAS, BUT...
...HE HAD THE LOOK!!!
EXCUSE ME. WE'RE ZINGS STANS WHO COULDN'T HELP OVER-HEARING JUST NOW.
WOULD YOU LIKE ONE OF THEIR CDS?
JOIN US IN THIS LOVELY HELL...
YEE! THEY'RE LEAKING STUFF FROM EVERY HOLE IN THEIR FACES!
HEEZ
HEEZ
SHUDDER
Still took the CD, tho...
TMP
TMP
TMP
TMP
WHOA!
BAM
?!!

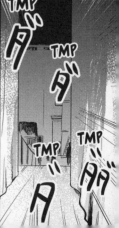

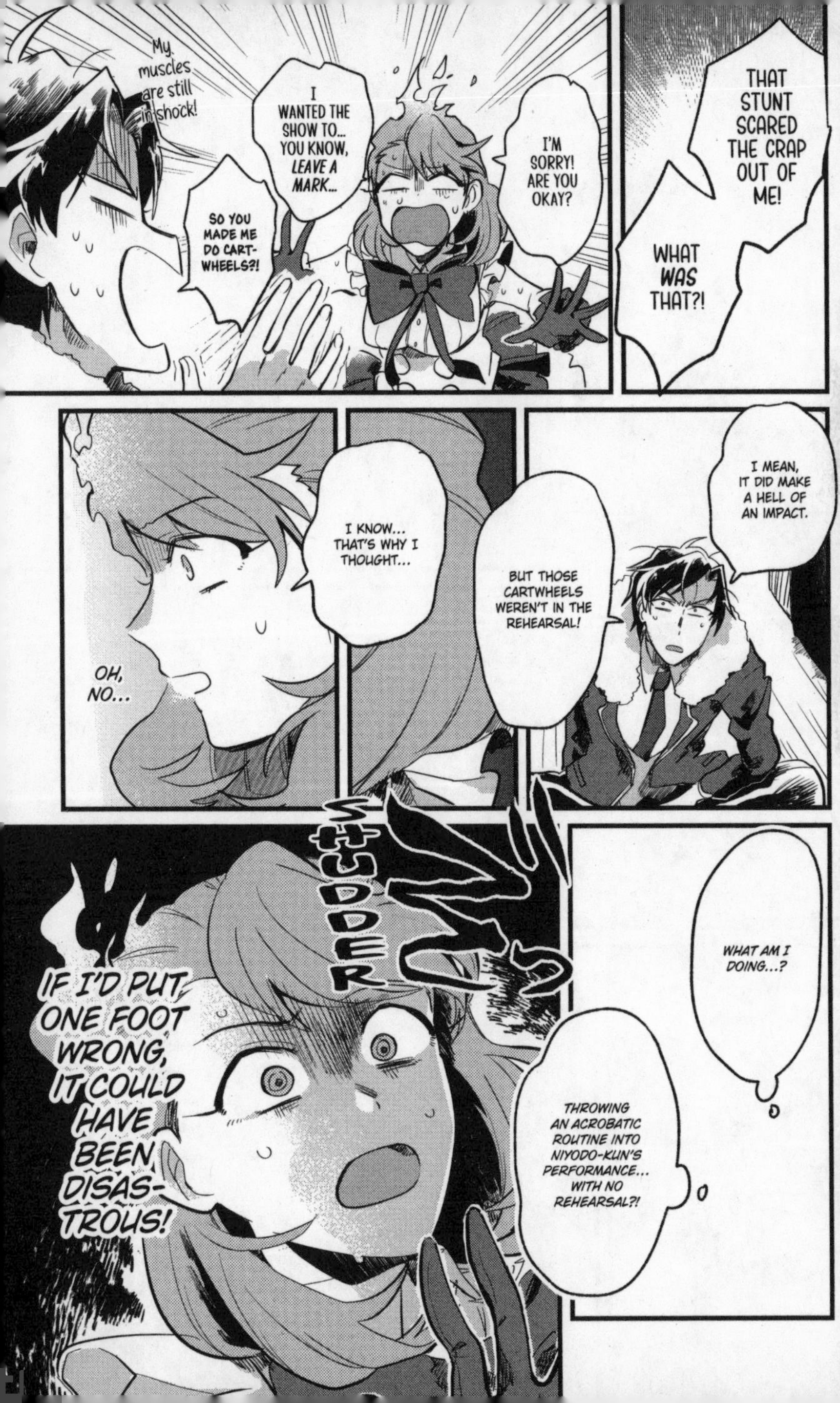
THAT STUNT SCARED THE CRAP OUT OF ME!
WHAT WAS THAT?!
I'M SORRY! ARE YOU OKAY?
I WANTED THE SHOW TO... YOU KNOW, LEAVE A MARK...
My muscles are still in shock!
SO YOU MADE ME DO CART-WHEELS?!
I MEAN, IT DID MAKE A HELL OF AN IMPACT.
BUT THOSE CARTWHEELS WEREN'T IN THE REHEARSAL!
I KNOW... THAT'S WHY I THOUGHT...
OH, NO...
WHAT AM I DOING...?
THROWING AN ACROBATIC ROUTINE INTO NIYODO-KUN'S PERFORMANCE... WITH NO REHEARSAL?!
SHUDDER
IF I'D PUT ONE FOOT WRONG, IT COULD HAVE BEEN DISAS-TROUS!

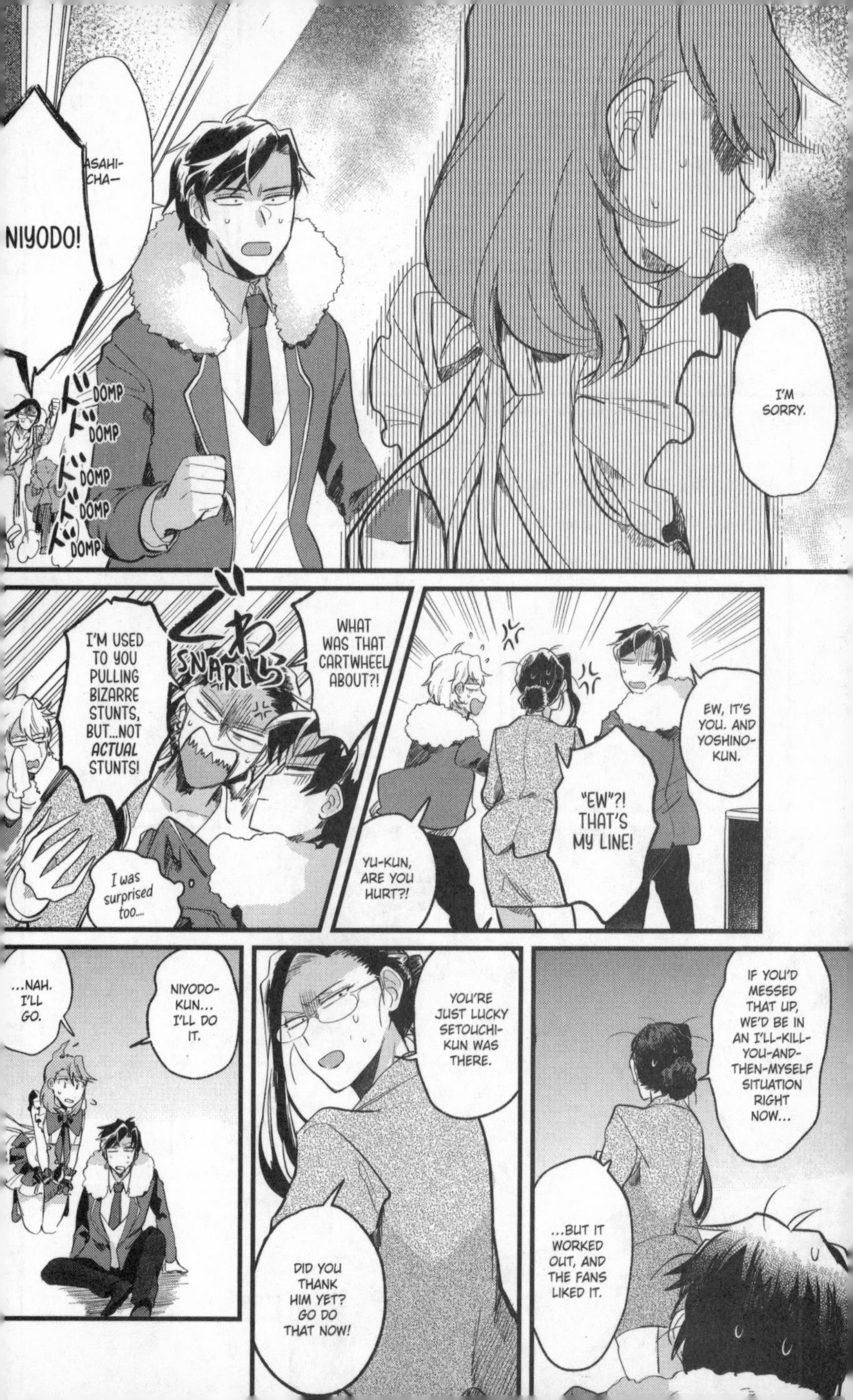
I'M SORRY.
ASAHI-CHA—
NIYODO!
DOMP
DOMP
DOMP
DOMP
DOMP
EW, IT'S YOU. AND YOSHINO-KUN.
"EW"?! THAT'S MY LINE!
YU-KUN, ARE YOU HURT?!
WHAT WAS THAT CARTWHEEL ABOUT?!
SNARL
I'M USED TO YOU PULLING BIZARRE STUNTS, BUT...NOT *ACTUAL* STUNTS!
I was surprised too...
IF YOU'D MESSED THAT UP, WE'D BE IN AN I'LL-KILL-YOU-AND-THEN-MYSELF SITUATION RIGHT NOW...
...BUT IT WORKED OUT, AND THE FANS LIKED IT.
YOU'RE JUST LUCKY SETOUCHI-KUN WAS THERE.
DID YOU THANK HIM YET? GO DO THAT NOW!
NIYODO-KUN... I'LL DO IT.
...NAH. I'LL GO.

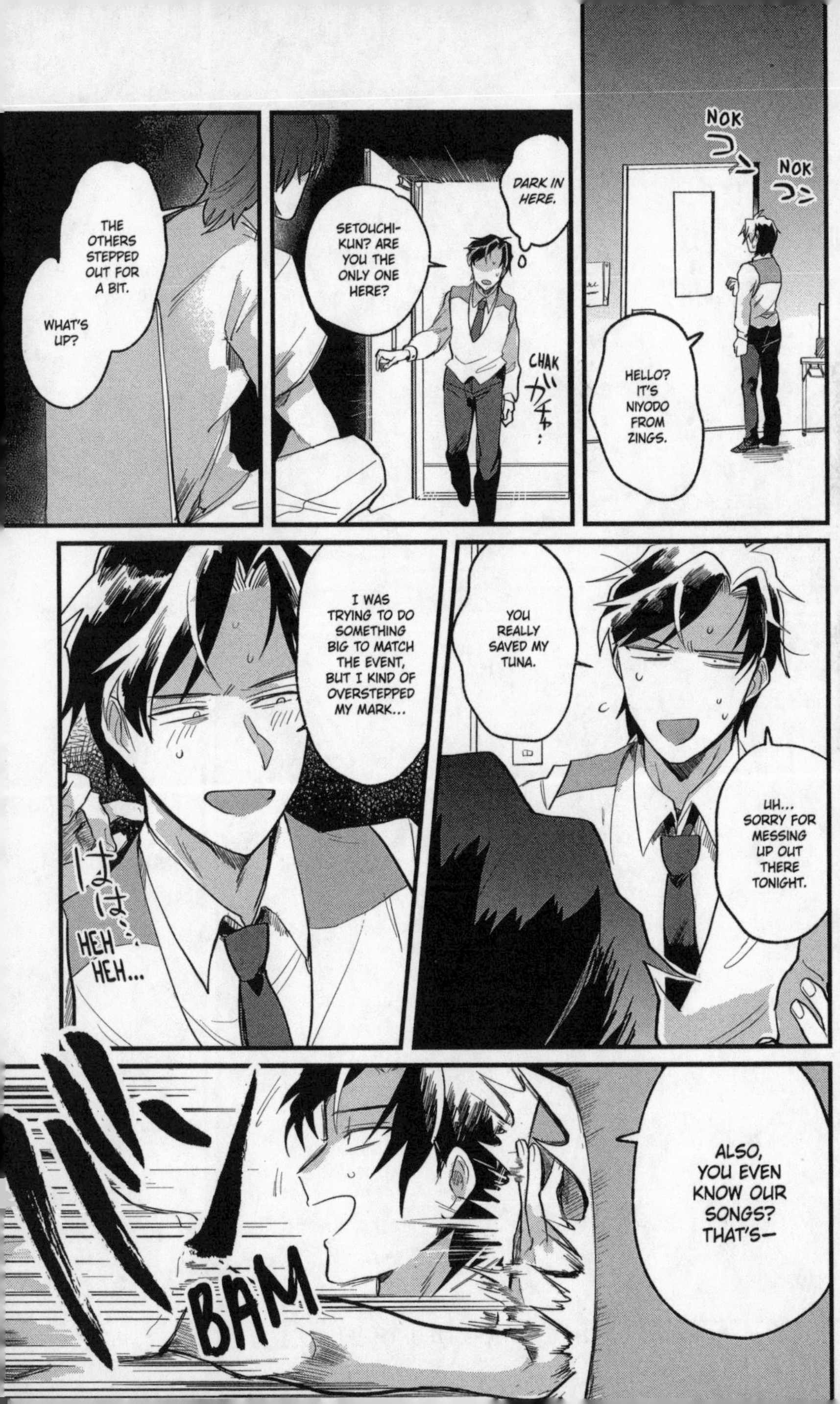
NOK
NOK
HELLO? IT'S NIYODO FROM ZINGS.
DARK IN HERE.
SETOUCHI-KUN? ARE YOU THE ONLY ONE HERE?
CHAK
THE OTHERS STEPPED OUT FOR A BIT.
WHAT'S UP?
UH... SORRY FOR MESSING UP OUT THERE TONIGHT.
YOU REALLY SAVED MY TUNA.
I WAS TRYING TO DO SOMETHING BIG TO MATCH THE EVENT, BUT I KIND OF OVERSTEPPED MY MARK...
HEH HEH...
ALSO, YOU EVEN KNOW OUR SONGS? THAT'S—
BAM

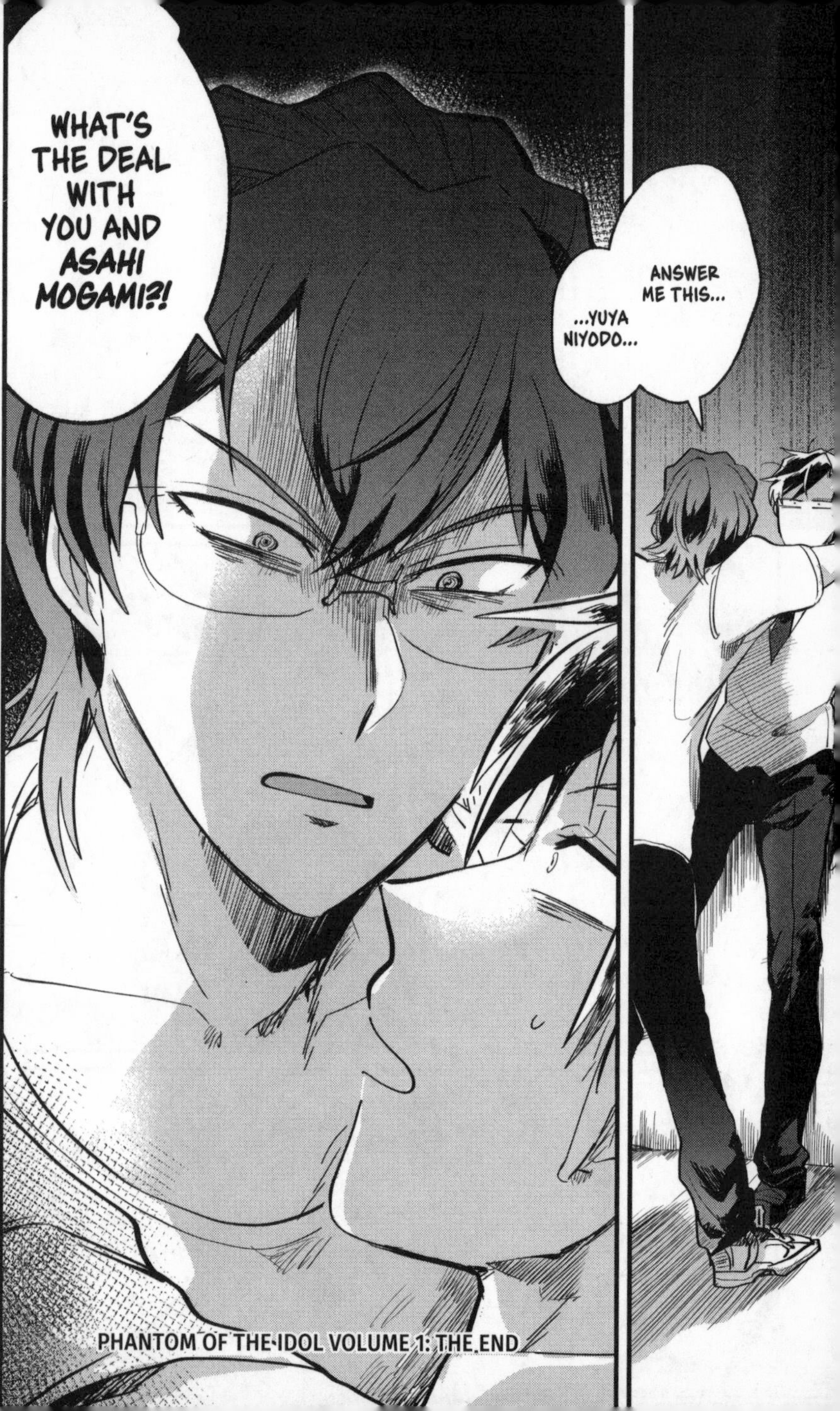
ANSWER ME THIS...
...YUYA NIYODO...
WHAT'S THE DEAL WITH YOU AND ASAHI MOGAMI?!
PHANTOM OF THE IDOL VOLUME 1: THE END

First published in Monthly Comic Zero Sum, July 2017 and February–June 2018

SPECIAL EXCLUSIVE!

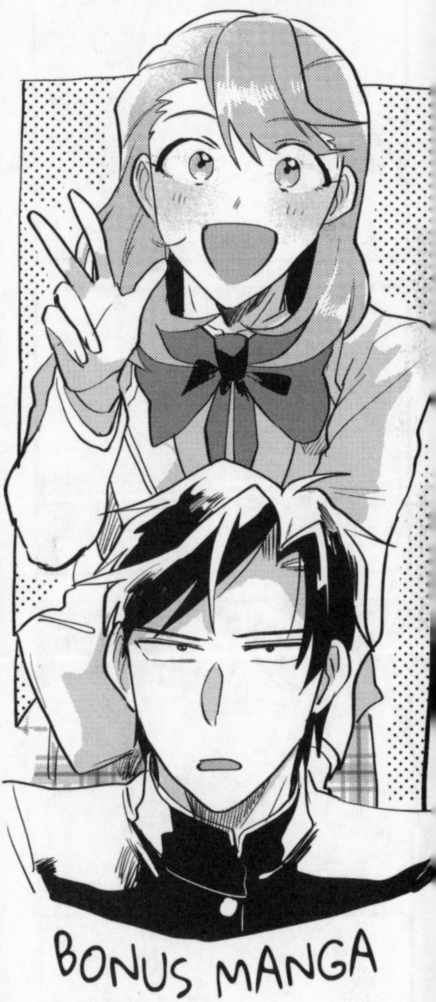

BONUS MANGA

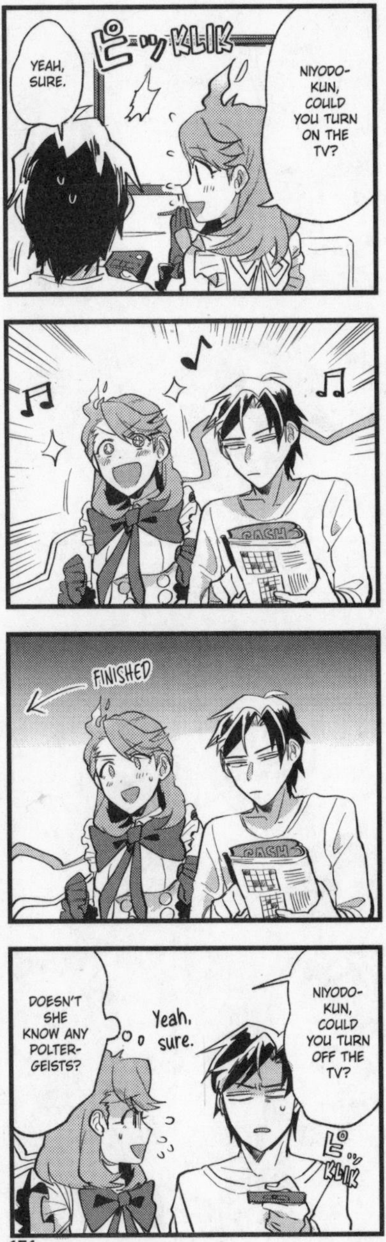
NIYODO-KUN, COULD YOU TURN ON THE TV?
ピッ KLIK
YEAH, SURE.
FINISHED
NIYODO-KUN, COULD YOU TURN OFF THE TV?
Yeah, sure.
DOESN'T SHE KNOW ANY POLTER-GEISTS?
ピッ KLIK

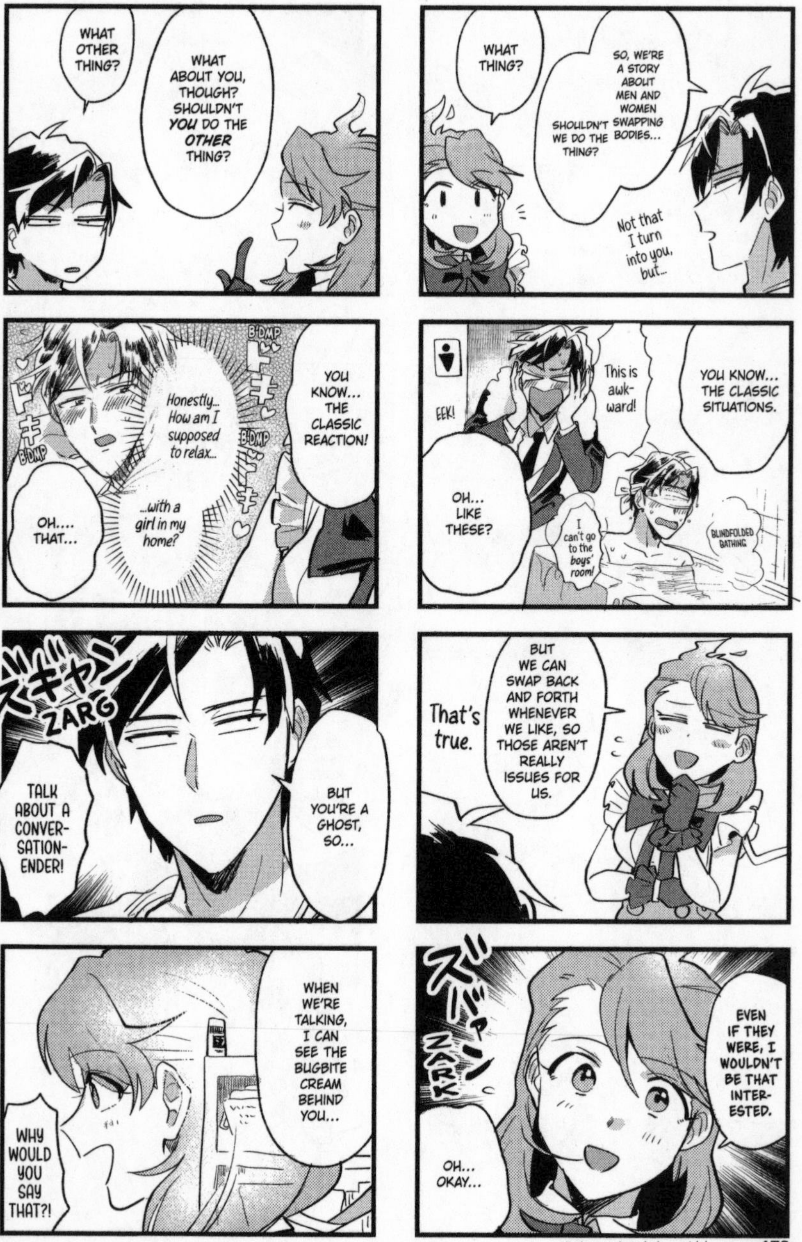
SO, WE'RE A STORY ABOUT MEN AND WOMEN SWAPPING BODIES...
SHOULDN'T WE DO THE THING?
WHAT THING?
Not that I turn into you, but...
WHAT ABOUT YOU, THOUGH? SHOULDN'T *YOU* DO THE *OTHER* THING?
WHAT OTHER THING?
YOU KNOW... THE CLASSIC SITUATIONS.
This is awk-ward!
EEK!
OH... LIKE THESE?
I can't go to the boys' room!
BLINDFOLDED BATHING
B'DMP
YOU KNOW... THE CLASSIC REACTION!
Honestly... How am I supposed to relax...
B'DMP
...with a girl in my home?
B'DMP
OH.... THAT...
BUT WE CAN SWAP BACK AND FORTH WHENEVER WE LIKE, SO THOSE AREN'T REALLY ISSUES FOR US.
That's true.
BUT YOU'RE A GHOST, SO...
ZARG
TALK ABOUT A CONVERSATION-ENDER!
EVEN IF THEY WERE, I WOULDN'T BE THAT INTERESTED.
ZARK
OH... OKAY...
WHEN WE'RE TALKING, I CAN SEE THE BUGBITE CREAM BEHIND YOU...
WHY WOULD YOU SAY THAT?!

All she wants is to be an idol.

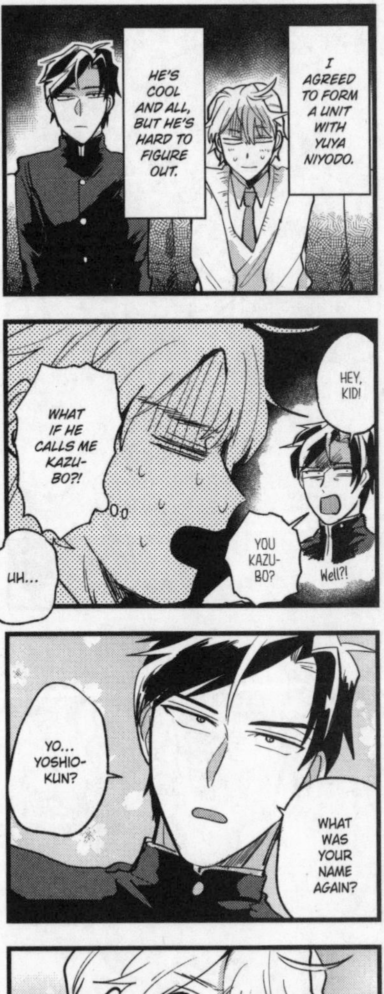

I AGREED TO FORM A UNIT WITH YUYA NIYODO.
HE'S COOL AND ALL, BUT HE'S HARD TO FIGURE OUT.
HEY, KID!
WHAT IF HE CALLS ME KAZU-BO?!
YOU KAZU-BO?
Well?!
UH...
WHAT WAS YOUR NAME AGAIN?
YO... YOSHIO-KUN?
MY SURNAME AND "KUN"?!
HE'S A GOOD GUY!
MOVED

He got it wrong, though.

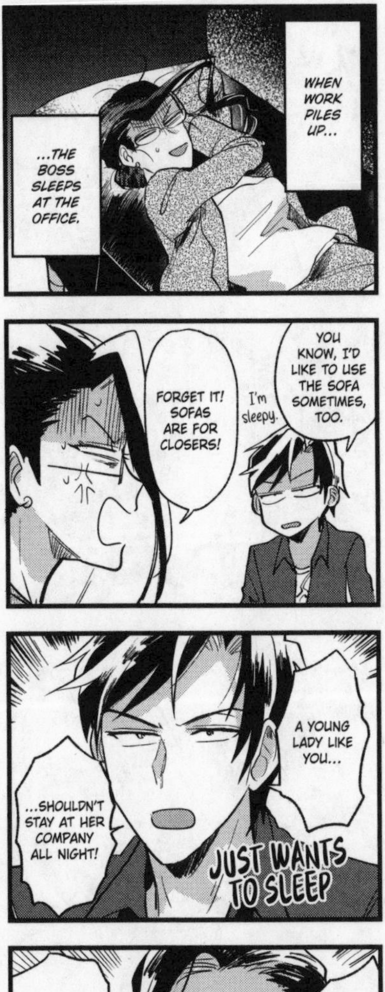

WHEN WORK PILES UP...
...THE BOSS SLEEPS AT THE OFFICE.
YOU KNOW, I'D LIKE TO USE THE SOFA SOMETIMES, TOO.
I'm sleepy.
FORGET IT! SOFAS ARE FOR CLOSERS!
A YOUNG LADY LIKE YOU...
...SHOULDN'T STAY AT HER COMPANY ALL NIGHT!
JUST WANTS TO SLEEP
WH-WHAT DO YOU MEAN, YOUNG LADY? DON'T BE SO OLD-FASHIONED!
ALSO, DO YOU WANT A MANJU?!?!
FINE SWEETS
SCARLET GLOW MANJU

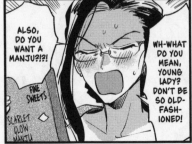

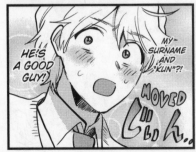

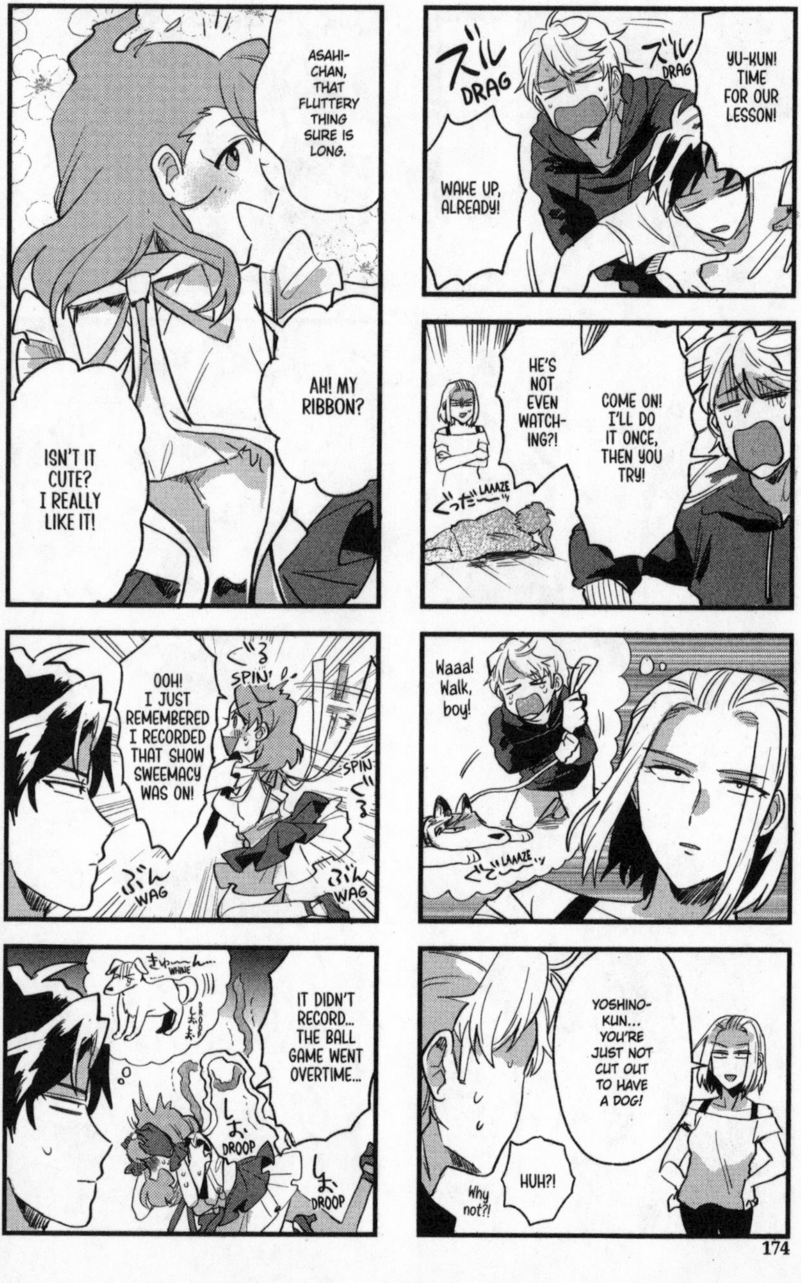
ズル
DRAG
ズル
DRAG
YU-KUN! TIME FOR OUR LESSON!
WAKE UP, ALREADY!
COME ON! I'LL DO IT ONCE, THEN YOU TRY!
HE'S NOT EVEN WATCHING?!
ぐっだ〜〜
LAAAZE
Waaa! Walk, boy!
ぐで〜〜
LAAAZE
YOSHINO-KUN... YOU'RE JUST NOT CUT OUT TO HAVE A DOG!
HUH?!
Why not?!
ASAHI-CHAN, THAT FLUTTERY THING SURE IS LONG.
AH! MY RIBBON?
ISN'T IT CUTE? I REALLY LIKE IT!
ぐる
SPIN
OOH! I JUST REMEMBERED I RECORDED THAT SHOW SWEEMACY WAS ON!
SPIN
ぐる
ぶん
WAG
ぶん
WAG
IT DIDN'T RECORD... THE BALL GAME WENT OVERTIME...
きゅ〜〜ん...
WHINE
しお
DROOP
しお
DROOP
しお
DROOP

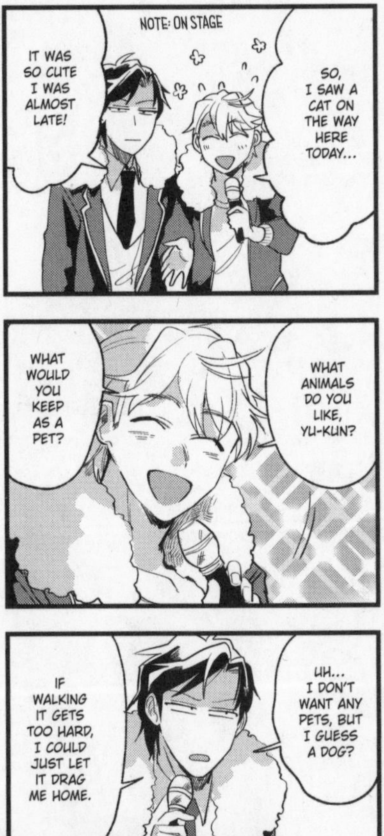
NOTE: ON STAGE
SO, I SAW A CAT ON THE WAY HERE TODAY...
IT WAS SO CUTE I WAS ALMOST LATE!
WHAT ANIMALS DO YOU LIKE, YU-KUN?
WHAT WOULD YOU KEEP AS A PET?
UH... I DON'T WANT ANY PETS, BUT I GUESS A DOG?
IF WALKING IT GETS TOO HARD, I COULD JUST LET IT DRAG ME HOME.
WHAT?! THAT POOR DOG!
Yu-kuuun!
キュー WHINE
キュー WHINE
ズルズル DRAAAAAGGG
ズル DRAG
YOSHINO THE DOG

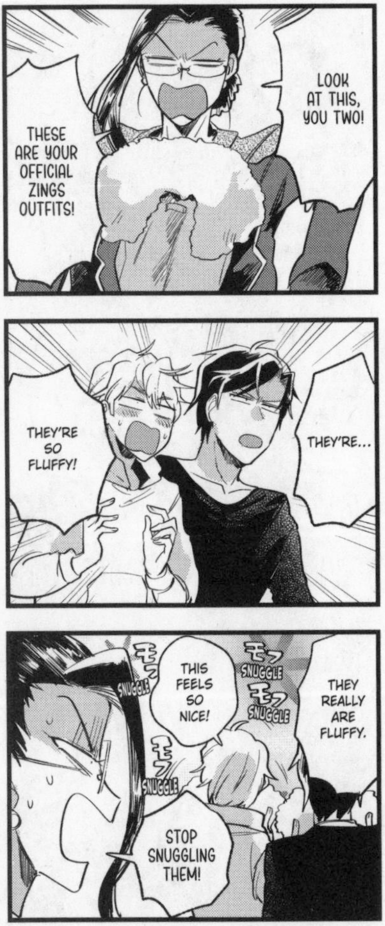
LOOK AT THIS, YOU TWO!
THESE ARE YOUR OFFICIAL ZINGS OUTFITS!
THEY'RE...
THEY'RE SO FLUFFY!
THEY REALLY ARE FLUFFY.
モフ SNUGGLE
モフ SNUGGLE
THIS FEELS SO NICE!
モフ SNUGGLE
モフ SNUGGLE
STOP SNUGGLING THEM!
YOU ONLY GET ONE SUIT EACH, SO TAKE CARE OF IT!
モフ SNUGGLE
モフ SNUGGLE
YOU'RE SNUGGLING THEM, TOO!
モフ SNUGGLE
モフ SNUGGLE

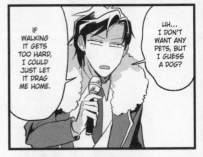

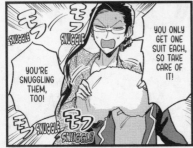

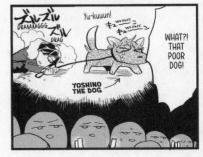

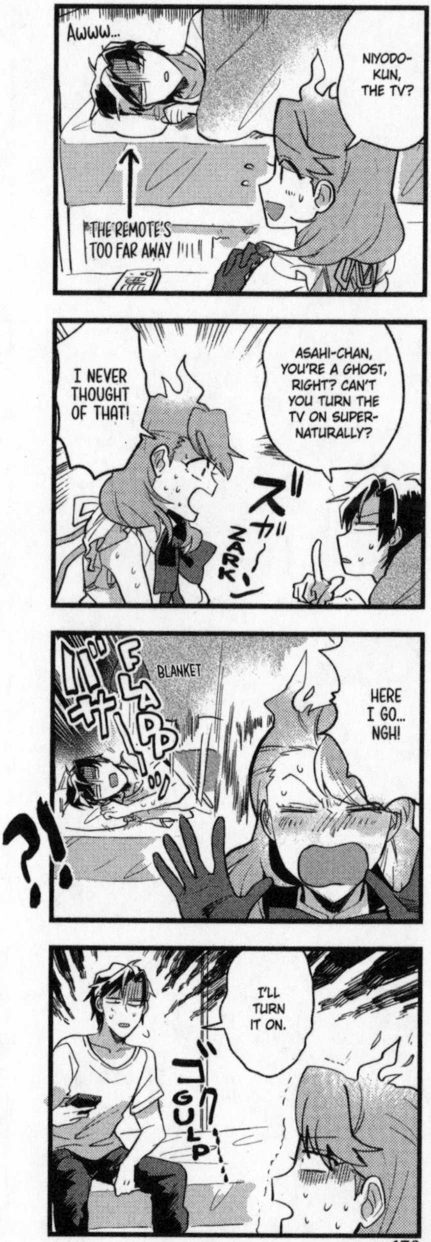
NIYODO-KUN, THE TV?
Awww...
THE REMOTE'S TOO FAR AWAY
ASAHI-CHAN, YOU'RE A GHOST, RIGHT? CAN'T YOU TURN THE TV ON SUPER-NATURALLY?
ズガ〜ン
ZARK
I NEVER THOUGHT OF THAT!
HERE I GO... NGH!
BLANKET
FLAPP
バサ
?!
I'LL TURN IT ON.
ゴクッ
GULP

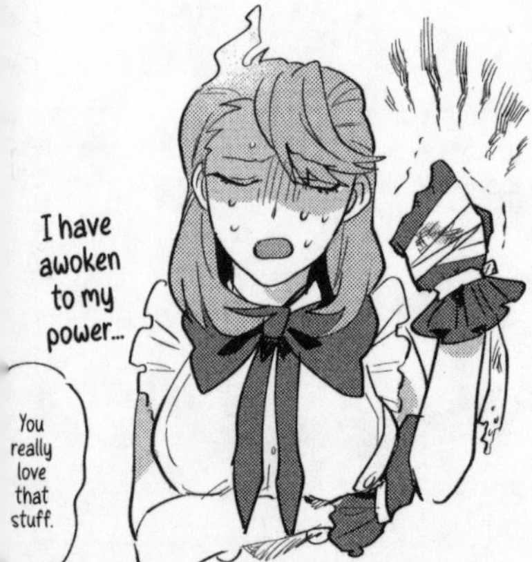
I have awoken to my power...
You really love that stuff.

AFTERFLAVONE

Hello. This is the artist, Hijiki Isoflavone (what's with this name...?).
Isoflavone's the surname, Hijiki's the given name...is how it works.
Thank you for reading *Phantom of the Idol*, volume 1!
Who knew I'd draw a manga that would be published as a book one day?
You can never tell what life will bring.

I love people who have something to cheer on.
That could be an idol who supports other idols, or an idol who supports their fans' everyday lives—I like the whole world surrounding idols.
Being able to draw a manga about that makes me happiest of all.

I hope to continue cheerfully drawing smiling women with big mouths and vertical lines on their faces and also glasses!
Please come along for the ride!

Special Thanks
Everyone who supports me

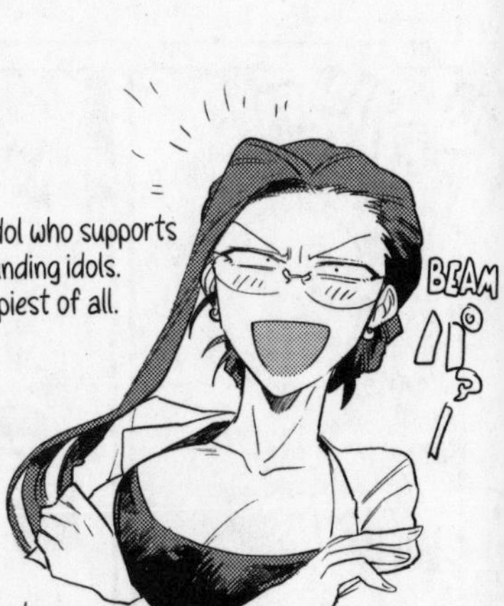
BEAM

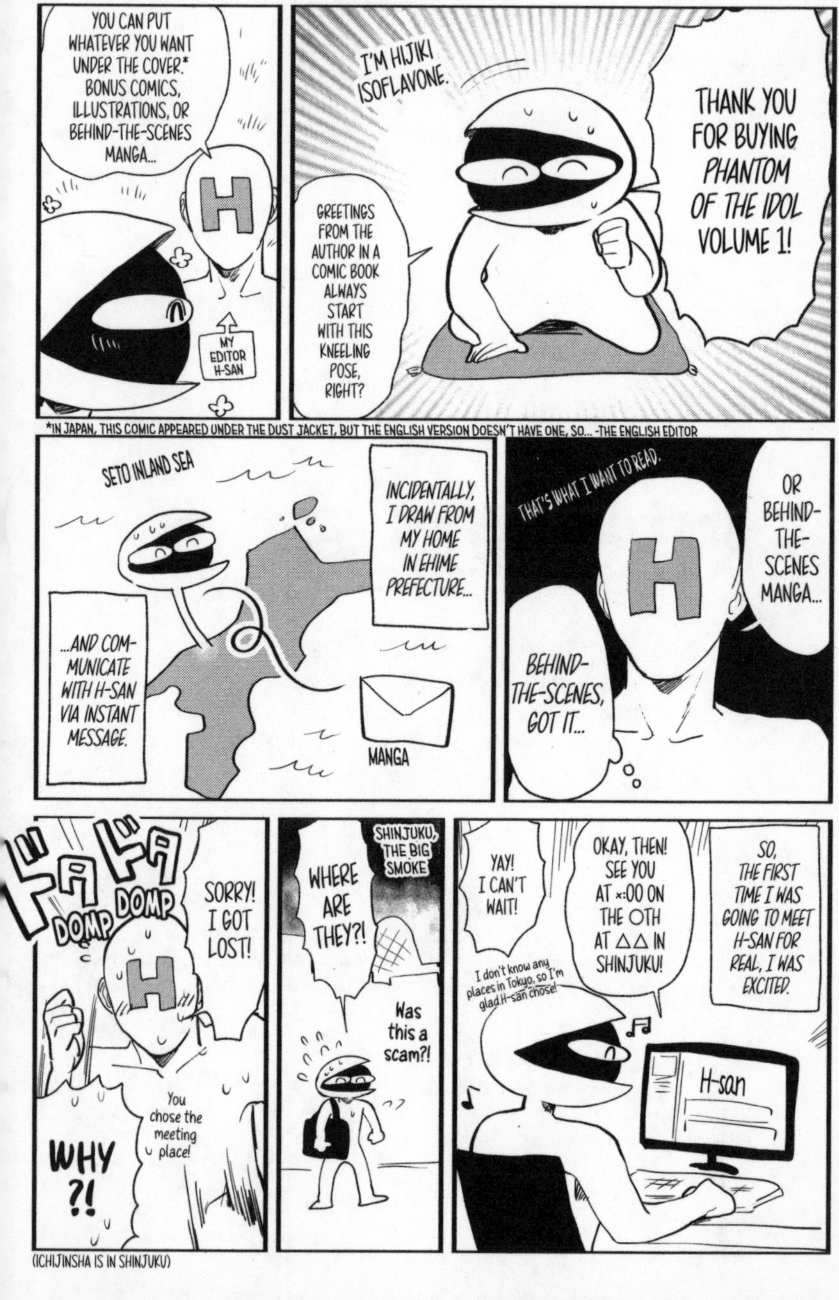
THANK YOU FOR BUYING PHANTOM OF THE IDOL VOLUME 1!
I'M HIJIKI ISOFLAVONE.
GREETINGS FROM THE AUTHOR IN A COMIC BOOK ALWAYS START WITH THIS KNEELING POSE, RIGHT?
YOU CAN PUT WHATEVER YOU WANT UNDER THE COVER.* BONUS COMICS, ILLUSTRATIONS, OR BEHIND-THE-SCENES MANGA...
MY EDITOR H-SAN
*IN JAPAN, THIS COMIC APPEARED UNDER THE DUST JACKET, BUT THE ENGLISH VERSION DOESN'T HAVE ONE, SO... -THE ENGLISH EDITOR
OR BEHIND-THE-SCENES MANGA...
THAT'S WHAT I WANT TO READ.
BEHIND-THE-SCENES, GOT IT...
INCIDENTALLY, I DRAW FROM MY HOME IN EHIME PREFECTURE...
SETO INLAND SEA
...AND COM-MUNICATE WITH H-SAN VIA INSTANT MESSAGE.
MANGA
SO, THE FIRST TIME I WAS GOING TO MEET H-SAN FOR REAL, I WAS EXCITED.
OKAY, THEN! SEE YOU AT ×:00 ON THE ○TH AT △△ IN SHINJUKU!
YAY! I CAN'T WAIT!
I don't know any places in Tokyo, so I'm glad H-san chose!
H-san
SHINJUKU, THE BIG SMOKE
WHERE ARE THEY?!
Was this a scam?!
ドタドタ
DOMP DOMP
SORRY! I GOT LOST!
You chose the meeting place!
WHY ?!
(ICHIJINSHA IS IN SHINJUKU)

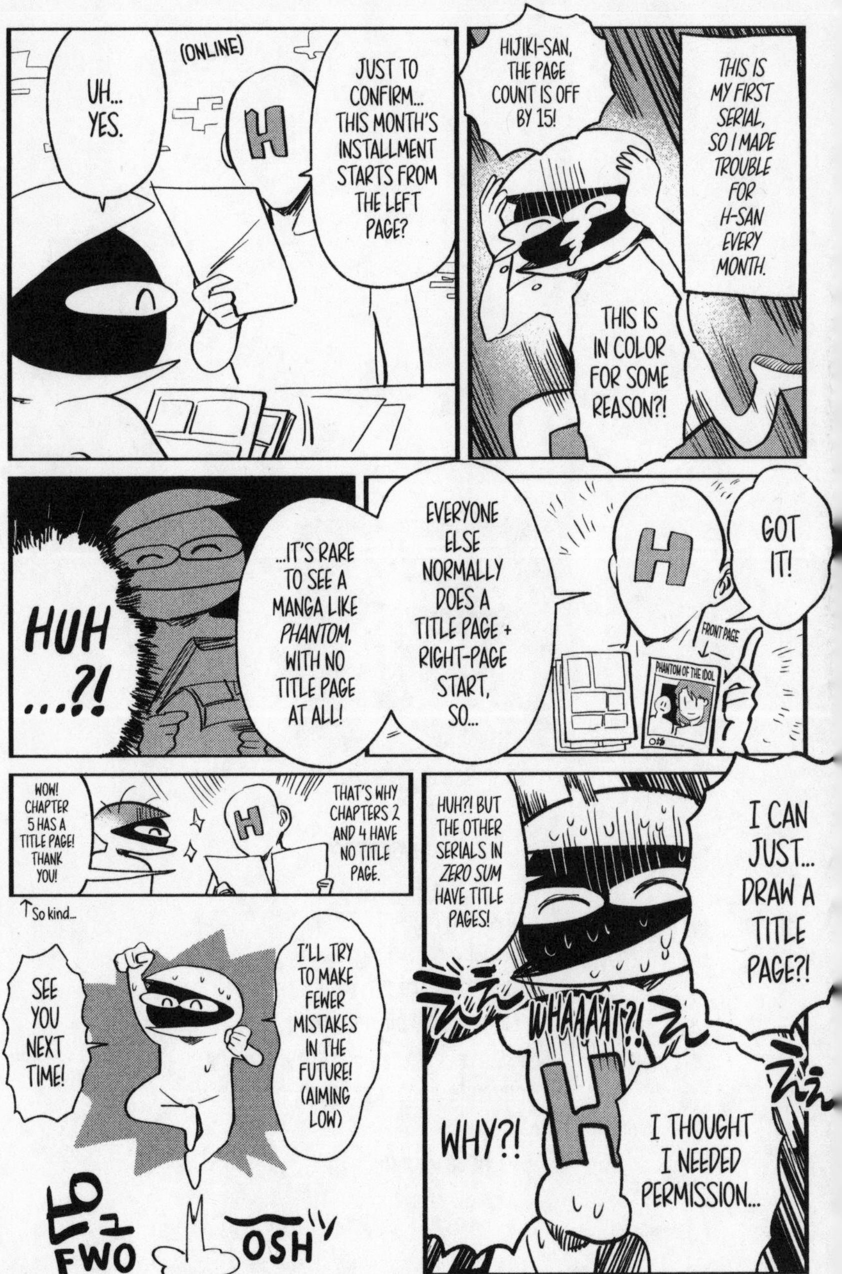
THIS IS MY FIRST SERIAL, SO I MADE TROUBLE FOR H-SAN EVERY MONTH.
HIJIKI-SAN, THE PAGE COUNT IS OFF BY 15!
THIS IS IN COLOR FOR SOME REASON?!
JUST TO CONFIRM... THIS MONTH'S INSTALLMENT STARTS FROM THE LEFT PAGE?
(ONLINE)
UH... YES.
GOT IT!
FRONT PAGE
PHANTOM OF THE IDOL
EVERYONE ELSE NORMALLY DOES A TITLE PAGE + RIGHT-PAGE START, SO...
...IT'S RARE TO SEE A MANGA LIKE *PHANTOM*, WITH NO TITLE PAGE AT ALL!
HUH ...?!
I CAN JUST... DRAW A TITLE PAGE?!
HUH?! BUT THE OTHER SERIALS IN *ZERO SUM* HAVE TITLE PAGES!
WHAAAAT?!
I THOUGHT I NEEDED PERMISSION...
WHY?!
THAT'S WHY CHAPTERS 2 AND 4 HAVE NO TITLE PAGE.
WOW! CHAPTER 5 HAS A TITLE PAGE! THANK YOU!
↑So kind...
I'LL TRY TO MAKE FEWER MISTAKES IN THE FUTURE! (AIMING LOW)
SEE YOU NEXT TIME!
FWOOSH

Hijiki Isoflavone here.

Starting my first serial was nerve-wracking, but I strove to be true to my love of women with big-mouthed smiles, vertical lines on faces, and white-eyed gag faces.

I hope you enjoy it!

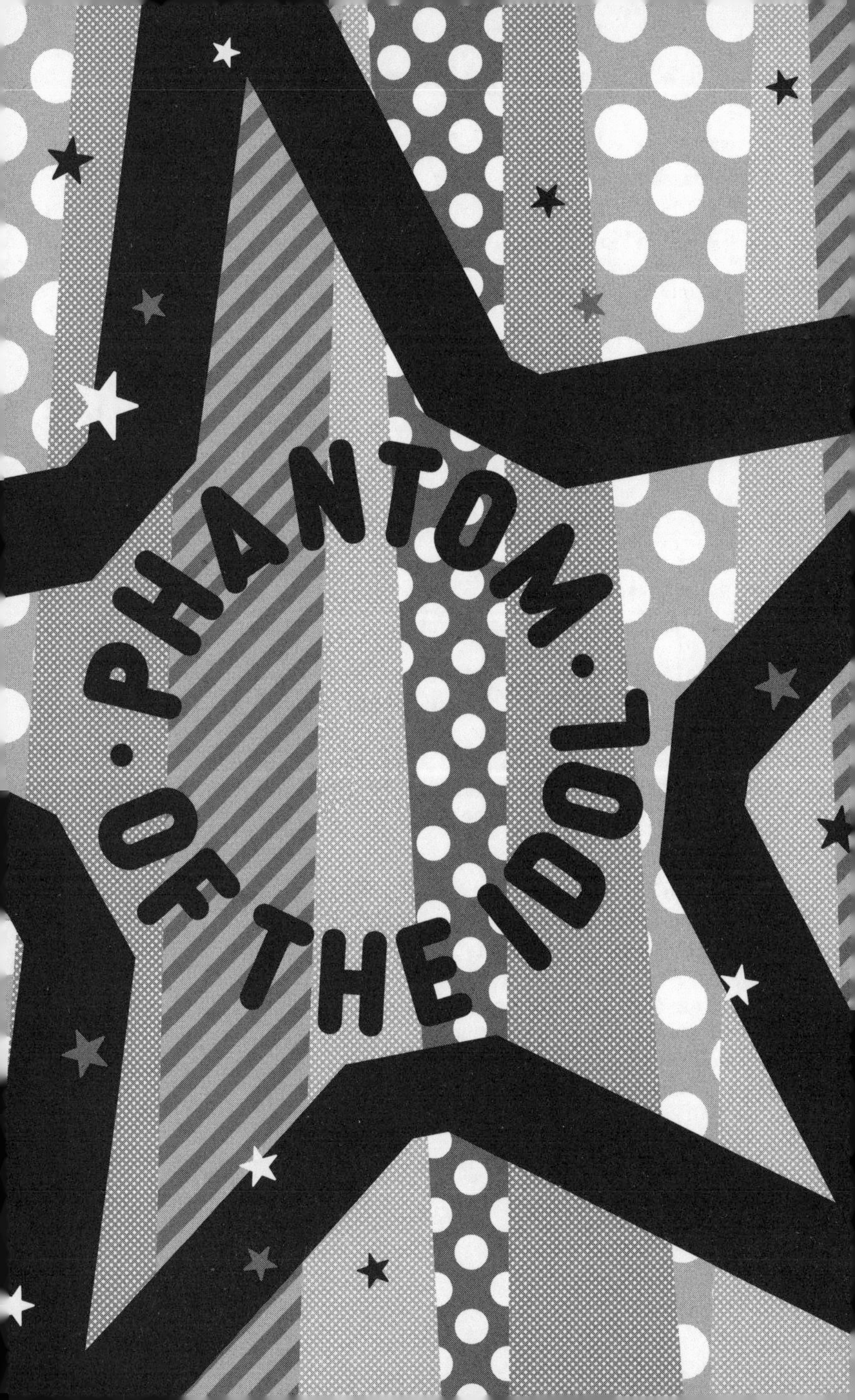
PHANTOM OF THE IDOL

Translation Notes

Signed oversized photo, page 1
In Japanese these are called “bromides” (*buromaido*), after the bromide paper originally used to make them. They’ve been a staple of Japanese celebrity culture for a century now.

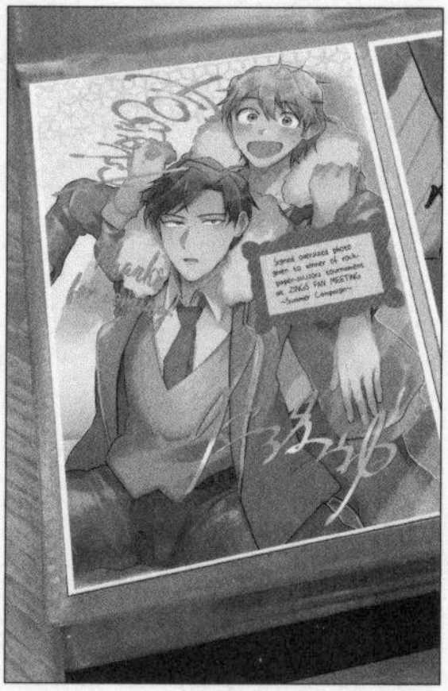
Signed oversized photo given to winner of rock-paper-scissors tournament at ZINGS FAN MEETING ~Summer Campaign~

Bias, page 2
“Bias” as a term for “favorite member of a group” entered English from K-pop fandom. The Japanese equivalent is *oshi* (push), roughly meaning the group member one “promotes” or “pushes.”

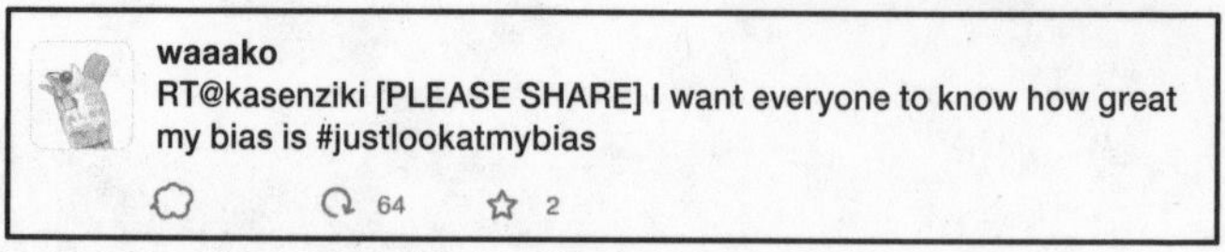
waaako
RT@kasenziki [PLEASE SHARE] I want everyone to know how great my bias is #justlookatmybias
64
2

Live house, page 7
A “live house” is an establishment specifically for playing music. Although drinks and refreshments may be available, it is unlike a club or pub in that the music is the focus. It is rented by the performers, who then have to sell tickets to recoup their investment. Often several groups with some connection will rent a live house for the evening together.

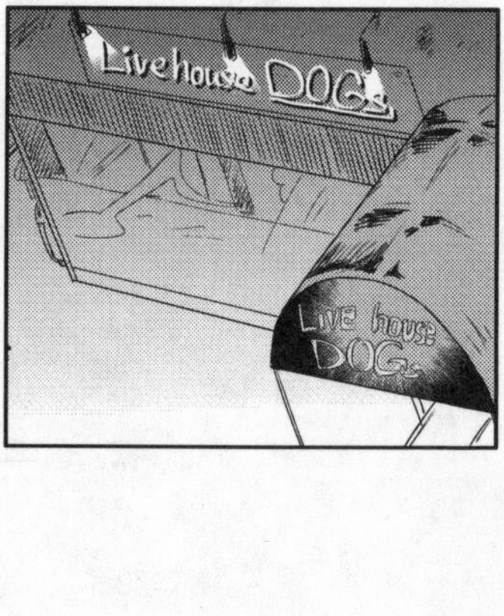
Live house DOGs
Live house DOGs

Center, page 19
The "center" of an idol group is the member who appears at the literal center in promotional photos and often becomes the "ambassador" of the group to the general public. This position typically goes to the group's best all-around performer. Other positions include "leader" (who speaks for the group and makes official decisions), "visual" (the member considered most attractive), and role-based positions like "vocalist," "dancer," and "rapper."

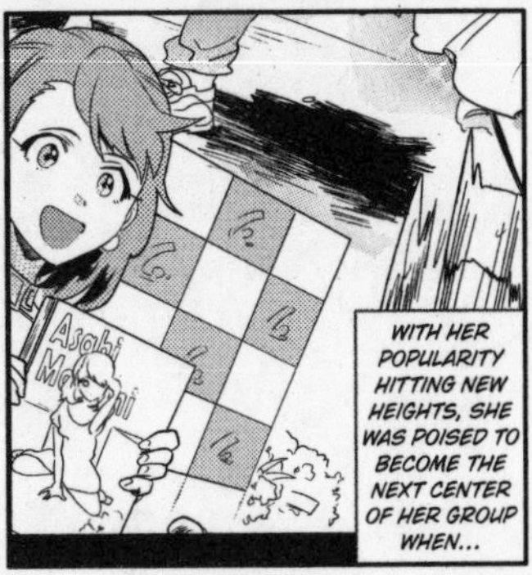
WITH HER POPULARITY HITTING NEW HEIGHTS, SHE WAS POISED TO BECOME THE NEXT CENTER OF HER GROUP WHEN...

Skewer of Love, page 28
The "skewer" referred to here is *dengaku-zashi*, a strategy used in the game of shogi, a variant of chess.

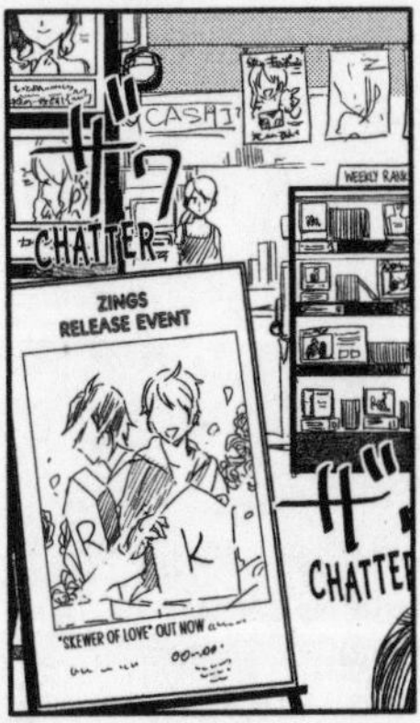
CHATTER
CHATTER
ZINGS RELEASE EVENT
"SKEWER OF LOVE" OUT NOW

Niyodo *responded?!*, page 30
A "response" from an idol is a specific acknowledgment of an individual fan. It can be as subtle as a wink, as long as the message is received. Fans sometimes write requests on handheld fans in the hope that their bias will see it from the stage and "respond."

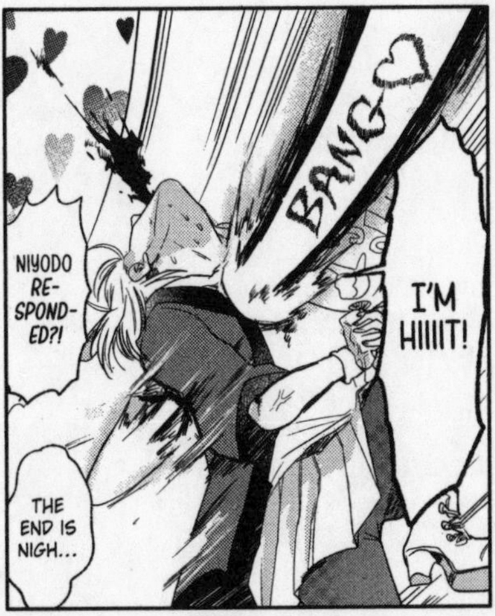
BANG♡
I'M HIIIIT!
NIYODO RE-SPOND-ED?!
THE END IS NIGH...

Handshake event, page 32
A handshake event is what it sounds like: an event where fans can go and shake hands with their favorite idol. Tickets to handshake events are often linked to purchases of CDs or other products.

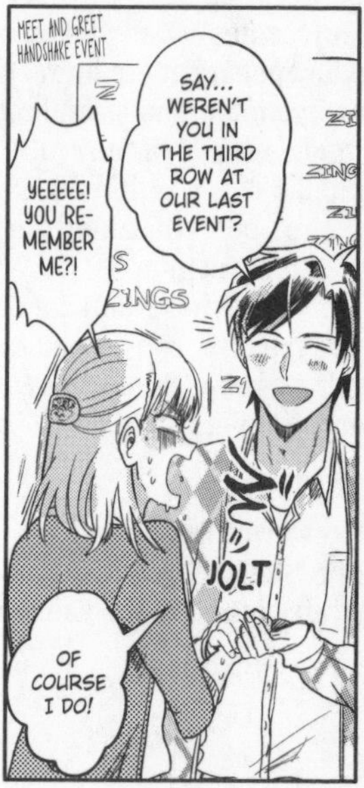
MEET AND GREET HANDSHAKE EVENT
SAY... WEREN'T YOU IN THE THIRD ROW AT OUR LAST EVENT?
ZING
YEEEEE! YOU RE-MEMBER ME?!
ZINGS
JOLT
OF COURSE I DO!

Release event, page 51
A release event is an event held to officially release a new single, album, book, or other product. It often turns out to be half mini-concert, half press conference.

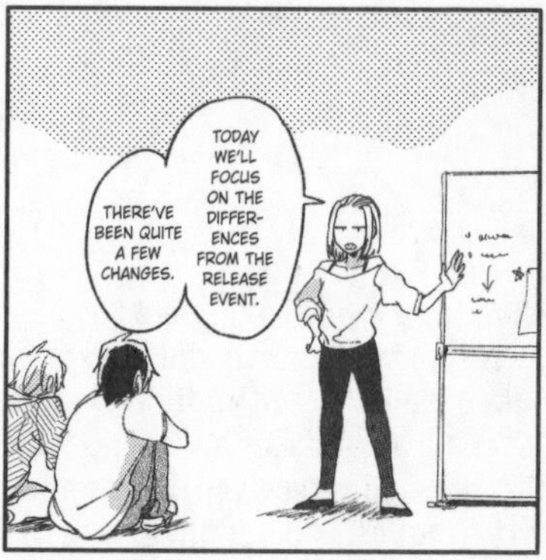
TODAY WE'LL FOCUS ON THE DIFFER-ENCES FROM THE RELEASE EVENT.
THERE'VE BEEN QUITE A FEW CHANGES.

Those Buddhist mummies, page 62
Also known as *sokushinbotsu,* which means "a buddha in this very body," these are the remains of Buddhist priests who intentionally mummified themselves through extreme asceticism.

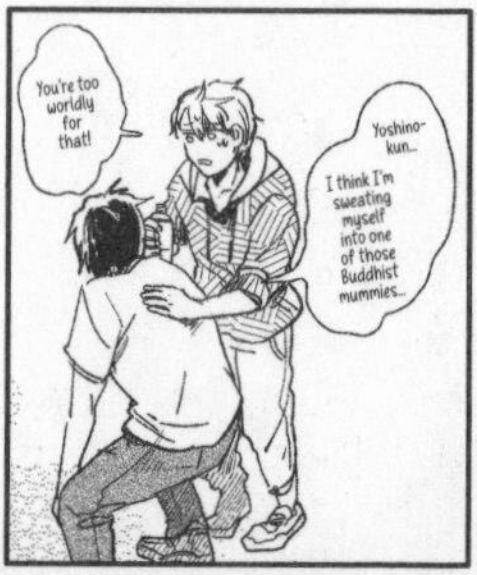
Yoshino-kun...
I think I'm sweating myself into one of those Buddhist mummies...
You're too worldly for that!

Kusaya, page 78
A salted, dried, fermented fish. Notoriously strong-smelling and something of an acquired taste.

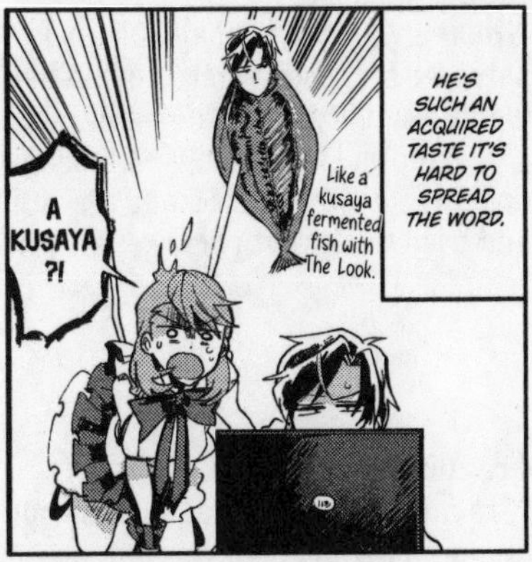
HE'S SUCH AN ACQUIRED TASTE IT'S HARD TO SPREAD THE WORD.
Like a kusaya fermented fish with The Look.
A KUSAYA ?!

Slam book, page 79
A book with room to write answers to questions about your likes, dislikes, personality, and so on. Often used to get to know friends better.

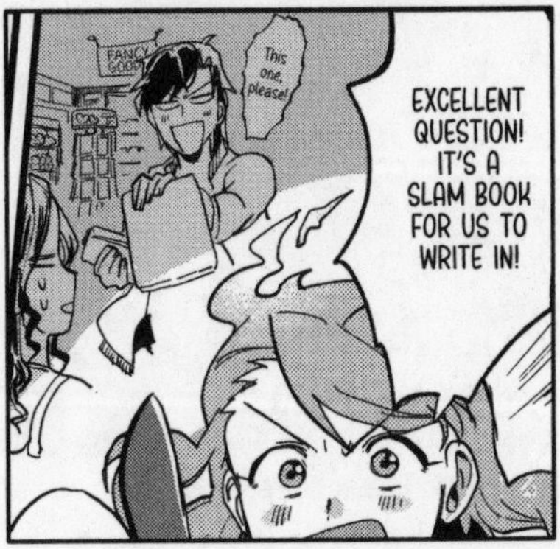
EXCELLENT QUESTION! IT'S A SLAM BOOK FOR US TO WRITE IN!
This one, please!

Ichiyo Higuchi, page 81
A late-nineteenth-century author currently on the ¥5,000 note.

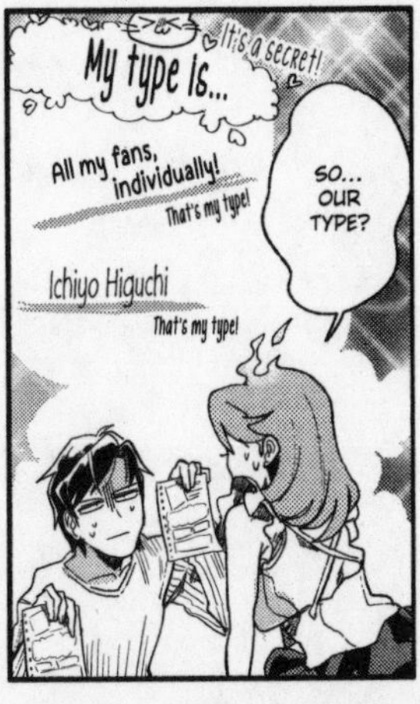
It's a secret!
My type is...
SO... OUR TYPE?
All my fans, individually!
That's my type!
Ichiyo Higuchi
That's my type!

Hanko, page 86
A *hanko,* or more formally *inkan,* is a personal seal used where people in the US would usually sign. Some hanko are big and elaborate for the most important documents. Others are small and simple and used to sign for packages and so on.

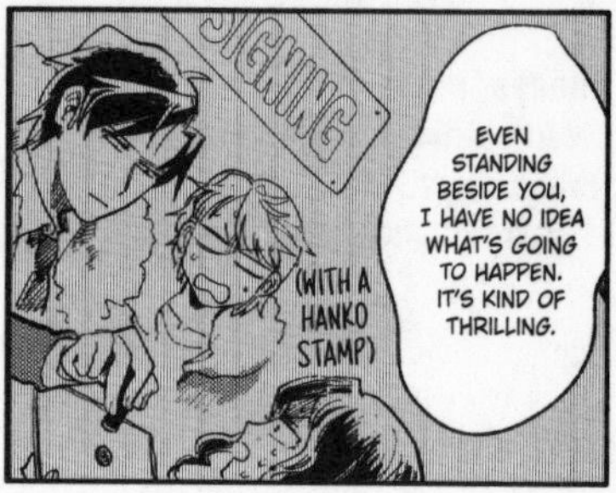
EVEN STANDING BESIDE YOU, I HAVE NO IDEA WHAT'S GOING TO HAPPEN. IT'S KIND OF THRILLING.
(WITH A HANKO STAMP)
SIGNING

Gravure, page 96
"Gravure" is the catchall term for pinup-style photography in Japan.

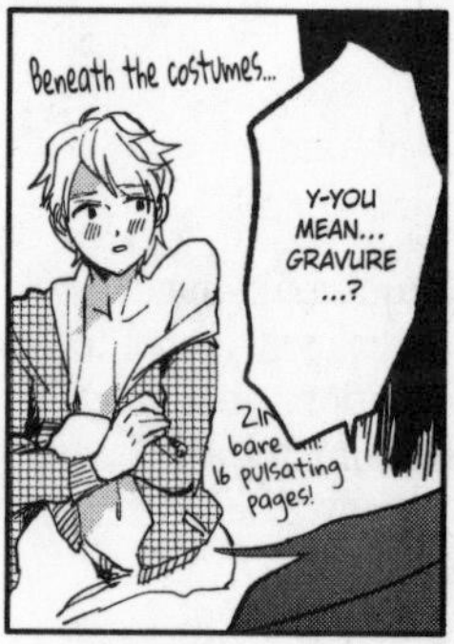
Y-YOU MEAN... GRAVURE ...?
Beneath the costumes...
bare
16 pulsating pages!

Seto Groom, page 122
A reference to the classic song "Seto Bride" (*Seto no hanayome*), recorded by Rumiko Koyanagi and many other singers.

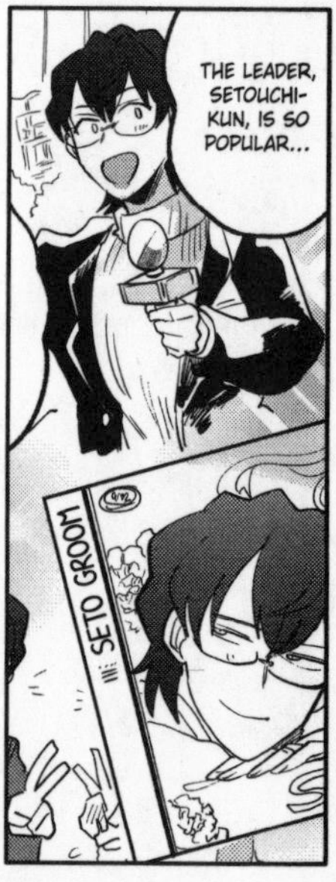
THE LEADER, SETOUCHI-KUN, IS SO POPULAR...
SETO GROOM

Niyodoid names, page 125
The three Niyodoids have slightly evocative names.
Tsugiko: *Tsugu* or *Tsugikomu* means to pour something in—like money.
Shigutaro: Adding -taro to a name adds a bit of anonymity and Taro is commonly used as a "John Doe."
Kasenjiki: Literally means "Riverbank."

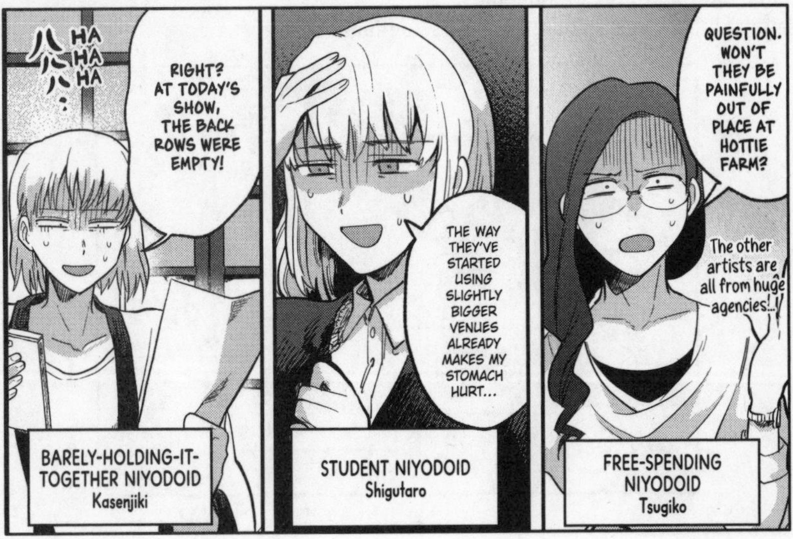
QUESTION. WON'T THEY BE PAINFULLY OUT OF PLACE AT HOTTIE FARM?
The other artists are all from huge agencies!
FREE-SPENDING NIYODOID
Tsugiko
THE WAY THEY'VE STARTED USING SLIGHTLY BIGGER VENUES ALREADY MAKES MY STOMACH HURT...
STUDENT NIYODOID
Shigutaro
RIGHT? AT TODAY'S SHOW, THE BACK ROWS WERE EMPTY!
ハハハ
HA HA HA
BARELY-HOLDING-IT-TOGETHER NIYODOID
Kasenjiki

Gathering the hearts/Of fans in the morning sun/River Mogami, page 147

A reference to the famous haiku by Basho about the Mogami River in Yamagata Prefecture:

samidare o	Gathering the rains
atsumete hayashi	of early summer—rushing
Mogami-gawa	River Mogami

("Morning sun" is the literal meaning of "Asahi")

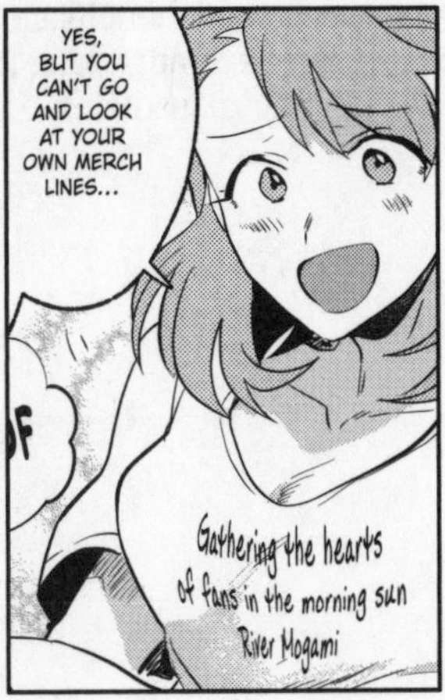
YES, BUT YOU CAN'T GO AND LOOK AT YOUR OWN MERCH LINES...
Gathering the hearts of fans in the morning sun River Mogami

Cgrass names, page 148
The Cgrass members are all named after the Seto Inland Sea and nearby areas.
Hakata: One of the islands in the inland sea, known for shipbuilding and salt.
Uchihama: Literally means “inshore.”
Misaki: Literally a “peninsula” or “cape,” such as Sadamisaki.
Nada: Literally means “strait” and used for many parts of the sea such as Iyo Nada, Aki Nada, and Shimonada.
Setouchi: The “Seto Inland” part of “Seto Inland Sea.”

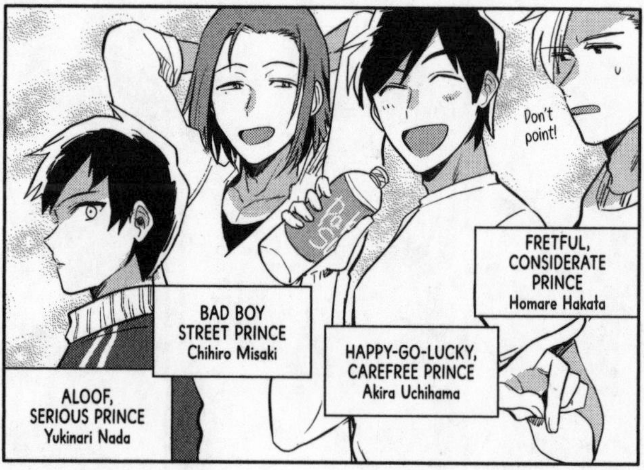
Don't point!
FRETFUL, CONSIDERATE PRINCE Homare Hakata
HAPPY-GO-LUCKY, CAREFREE PRINCE Akira Uchihama
BAD BOY STREET PRINCE Chihiro Misaki
ALOOF, SERIOUS PRINCE Yukinari Nada

Uiro patter, page 152
A famous kabuki monologue consisting of extended sales patter by a vendor of *uiro* medicine.

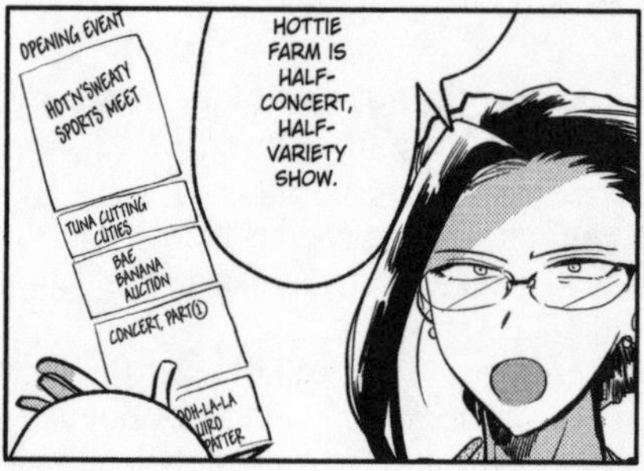
HOTTIE FARM IS HALF-CONCERT, HALF-VARIETY SHOW.
OPENING EVENT
HOT'N'SWEATY SPORTS MEET
TUNA CUTTING CUTIES
BAE BANANA AUCTION
CONCERT, PART①
OOH-LA-LA UIRO PATTER

SAVE ME, page 159

In the original Japanese, it says "*Inochi daiji ni,*" which can directly translate to "Take care of your life!" In online communities such as Nico Nico, it's used during "killing point" scenes, when you feel you might die. So if an idol does a wink or dances crazily (or just stands there), a fan may comment warning other fans about that specific scene.

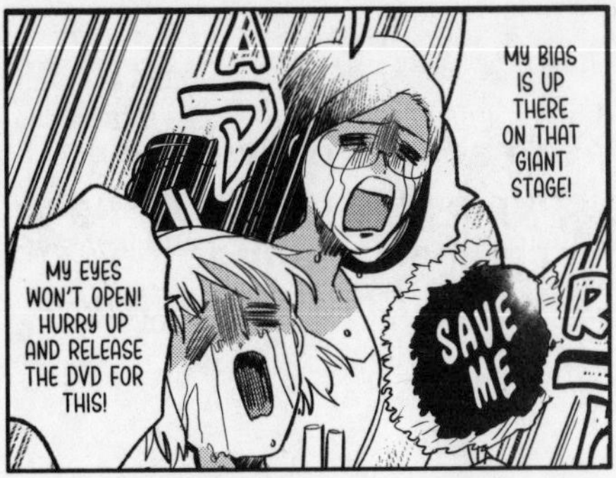
MY BIAS IS UP THERE ON THAT GIANT STAGE!
MY EYES WON'T OPEN! HURRY UP AND RELEASE THE DVD FOR THIS!
SAVE ME

The adorable new odd-couple cat comedy manga from the creator of the beloved *Chi's Sweet Home*, in full color!

Praise for Chi's Sweet Home

"Nearly impossible to turn away... a true all-ages title that anyone, young or old, cat lover or not, will enjoy. The stories will bring a smile to your face and warm your heart."

~School Library Journal

Sue & Tai-chan
Konami Kanata

Sue is an aging housecat who's looking forward to living out her life in peace... but her plans change when the mischievous black tomcat Tai-chan enters the picture! Hey! Sue never signed up to be a catsitter! *Sue & Tai-chan* is the latest from the reigning meow-narch of cute kitty comics, Konami Kanata.

SAINT ☆ YOUNG MEN

A LONG AWAITED ARRIVAL IN PREMIUM 2-IN-1 HARDCOVER

After centuries of hard work, Jesus and Buddha take a break from their heavenly duties to relax among the people of Japan, and their adventures in this lighthearted buddy comedy are sure to bring mirth and merriment to all!

"Brilliant...the physical comedy and facial expressions will make you literally LOL."

—Sam Humphries
(host of *DC Daily*; writer, *Green Lanterns*, *Legendary Star-Lord*)

Young characters and steampunk setting, like *Howl's Moving Castle* and *Battle Angel Alita*

Beyond the Clouds © 2018 Nicke / Ki-oon

A boy with a talent for machines and a mysterious girl whose wings he's fixed will take you beyond the clouds! In the tradition of the high-flying, resonant adventure stories of Studio Ghibli comes a gorgeous tale about the longing of young hearts for adventure and friendship!

Phantom of the Idol 1 is a work of fiction. Names, characters, places, and incidents are the products of the author's imagination or are used fictitiously. Any resemblance to actual events, locales, or persons, living or dead, is entirely coincidental.

A Kodansha Trade Paperback Original

Published in the United States by
Kodansha USA Publishing, LLC, New York.

Publication rights for this English edition arranged through
Kodansha Ltd., Tokyo.

First published in Japan in 2018 by Ichijinsha Inc., Tokyo
as *Kami Kuzu Aidoru*, volume 1.

ISBN 978-1-64651-465-6

Printed in the United States of America.

9 8 7 6 5 4 3 2 1

Translation: Max Greenway
Lettering: Michael Martin
Editing: Maggie Le
Kodansha USA Publishing edition cover design by Matthew Akuginow

Publisher: Kiichiro Sugawara

Director of Publishing Services: Ben Applegate
Associate Director of Publishing Operations: Stephen Pakula
Publishing Services Managing Editors: Alanna Ruse, Madison Salters
Production Managers: Emi Lotto, Angela Zurlo

KODANSHA.US

KODANSHA

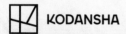